What people are saying about
Building Community . . .

"This important book has come at just the 1
the chaos and confusion that currently s
workplace. THIS IS ONE OF THE MOST W~~ELL WRITTEN~~
AND MOVING BOOKS ON LEADERSHIP AND
ORGANIZATIONAL CHANGE I HAVE EVER READ."

—*Dr. Jerry Eppler*
Principal of Personal Peak Performance, Inc.

"*BUILDING COMMUNITY* PROVIDES POWERFUL AND
PRACTICAL TOOLS THAT ENABLE US TO CRAFT A
FUTURE WHERE COMMUNITY IS A MANIFESTATION OF
THE HUMAN SPIRIT."

—*Debra A. Dinnocenzo*
Organizational Development/Marketing Consultant

"This book corrects a serious imbalance in changing
organizations today. All the emphasis on structure and
business processes has neglected the critical human
component. It takes people working together to make
organizations effective. FOLLOWING THE GUIDELINES IN
THIS BOOK CAN GENERATE EXCITEMENT AND FOCUS,
ALONG WITH A SENSE OF SECURITY IN TODAY'S
TURBULENT BUSINESS ENVIRONMENT."

—*Dr. John E. Jones*
Co-Founder of University Associates
President of Organizational Universe Systems

"In their push for higher and higher short-term performance, many organizations have shattered their people's connection and long-term commitment. *BUILDING COMMUNITY* SEEKS TO HELP AVOID THE HORRENDOUS COSTS SUCH INATTENTION TO THE 'HUMAN SIDE' CAN FORCE THE ORGANIZATION TO PAY. Well worth the effort."

—Ed Musselwhite
President and CEO of Zenger Miller, Inc.

"A FRESH APPROACH TO BUILDING (LEARNING) COMMUNITIES AT WORK AT A TIME WHEN THERE ARE MANY FORCES THAT DIVIDE US. Full of practical ideas that can help individuals and organizations become more productive, this book can result in a deeper understanding of yourself and others—and helps you see how to develop your full potential not in isolation, but in a community built on shared values."

—Dr. Michael O'Brien
Author of Profit From Experience

"Comprehensive and inspiring—looks at successful organizations and how they get to be that way. A GREAT TOOL FOR BUILDING ORGANIZATIONAL SUCCESS WITHIN BUSINESS, SCHOOL, CIVIL ORGANIZATIONS, AND FAMILIES!"

—Jim Merrell
Vice President/Human Resources of Gulf States Paper Corporation

BUILDING

The Human Side of Work

COMMUNITY

George Manning
Kent Curtis
Steve McMillen

THOMSON EXECUTIVE PRESS
A Division of South-Western College Publishing

Sponsoring Editor: Jim Sitlington
Production Editor: Holly Terry
Production House: Shepherd, Inc.
Internal Design: Russell Schneck Design
Cover Design: Joseph M. Devine
Marketing Manager: Stephen E. Momper

I(T)P
International Thomson Publishing
Thomson Executive Press (a Division of South-Western College Publishing) is an ITP Company. The
ITP trademark is used under license.

1 2 3 4 5 MA 9 8 7 6 5

Printed in the United States of America

Library of Congress Cataloging-in-Publication Data:

Building community: the human side of work / George Manning, Kent Curtis, Steve McMillen.
    p.   cm.
Includes bibliographical references and index.
1. Work groups. 2. Diversity in the workplace. 3. Interpersonal communication. 4. Employee
empowerment. 5. Employee motivation. 6. Quality of work life.   I. Manning, George. II. Curtis,
Kent. III. McMillen, Steve.
HD66.B83   1996
658.3'14--dc20   95-7812
                                                                                             CIP

ISBN No. 0-538-83586-9

Dedication

We dedicate this book to our families.

ACKNOWLEDGMENTS

Theorists, practitioners, and authors per chapter:

Chapter One Vision and Community	Joel Barker Stephen Covey Peter Drucker Brendan Reddy Martin Seligman Peter Senge Marvin Weisbord
Chapter Two Character and Community	Amitai Etzioni John Gardner Rollo May Joseph Petrick Leon Wieseltier
Chapter Three Sustaining Community	Jay Conger Robert Greenleaf Edward Lawler Rensis Likert Harry Levinson Ren McPherson Thomas Peters Robert Waterman
Chapter Four Effective Human Relations	Chris Argyris Stephen Covey Karen Horney Harry Ingram Joseph Luft Scott Peck Carl Rogers

Chapter Five
The Miracle of Dialogue

Stephen Boyd
Helen Keller
Gordon Lippitt
Ralph Nichols
Malcolm X

Chapter Six
Interpersonal Styles

Thomas Bier

Chapter Seven
Understanding People

Gordon Allport
Erik Erikson
Sigmund Freud
Soren Kierkegaard
Jean-Paul Sartre

Chapter Eight
Culture and Values

Ruth Benedict
Stephen Covey
Morris Massey
Margaret Mead
Robert Reich

Chapter Nine
Social Tolerance

Gordon Allport
Rosabeth Moss Kanter
Scott Peck
Alvin Poussaint

Chapter Ten
Valuing Diversity

Lennie Copeland
Jane Elliot
Carl Jung
Scott Peck
Deborah Tannen

Chapter Eleven
Group Dynamics

Warren Bennis
Peter Drucker
Irving Janis
Harry Levinson
Kurt Lewin
Douglas McGregor
Carl Moore
Scott Peck
Brendan Reddy
Marvin Weisbord

Chapter Twelve Communication at Work	Gordon Lippitt Thomas Peters Robert Waterman Alan Zimmerman
Chapter Thirteen The Quality Movement	Warren Bennis Robert Cole W. Edwards Deming Kaoru Ishikawa Joseph Jablonski William Lindsay

Review, advice, and research:

Ray Benedict
Terri Bonar-Stewart
Richard Boyle
Christopher Brill
Mike Campbell
Robert Caplon
Ron Carmack
David Davis
Jack Eversole
Dan Gibbons
Andrea Grayson
Ronald Heineman
Rhonda Hembree
Ray Henschen
Larry Hitch
Angela Lipsitz
Nan Littleton
Walter Lovenberg
Deborah Lubbie

Judith Marksberry
Steven Martin
Barbara Mathews
Pam Person
Pamela Pfaff
Mary Pommert
Paul Quealy
Ann Royalty
Robert Runk
Miriam Sekhon
John Shephard
Penny Skirvin
Sam Vinci
Earl Walz
Steve Weatherly
Susan Wehrspann
Angela Woodward
Paul Young

BUILDING COMMUNITY
THE HUMAN SIDE OF WORK

TABLE OF CONTENTS

CHAPTER THREE: SUSTAINING COMMUNITY 66

CHAPTER FOUR: EFFECTIVE HUMAN RELATIONS 97

CHAPTER FIVE: THE MIRACLE OF DIALOGUE 127

CHAPTER SIX: INTERPERSONAL STYLES 155

COMMUNITY-BUILDING TOOLS

BUILDING COMMUNITY
THE HUMAN SIDE OF WORK

BUILD, v., building, n.-v.t. 1. To establish or strengthen, as to build a nation. 2. To form or create, as to build swords into plough shares. 3. To construct a plan or system of thought, as to build on the philosophies of the past. 4. To increase or develop toward a maximum, as of intensity, tempo, magnitude.

COMMUNITY, n. 1. A group of any size whose members have a common cultural and historical heritage, as in the church or tribe. 2. A group sharing common characteristics or interests as in the business community; the community of scholars; the family of origin. 3. A group of people with common purpose, shared values, and agreement on goals, as in the work group or organization. 4. The public or society at large, as in the American people.

INTRODUCTION

Each of us, individually, walks with the tread of a fox, but collectively we fly as the geese!

Solon, Ancient Greece

Thomas Carlisle, the Scottish philosopher, thought that each person wanted to be treated as a unique and valuable individual. He also believed we each have a simultaneous need to belong to something greater than self, something more than one alone can do or be. For many people, feelings of self-worth and transcendence to something greater than self occur in the experience of community.

Building Community: The Human Side of Work teaches the importance of community and what can be done to achieve it. In *Productive Workplaces*, Marvin Weisbord writes that we hunger for community and are a great deal more productive when we find it. If we feed this hunger in ways that preserve individual dignity, opportunity for all, and mutual support, we will harness energy and productivity beyond imagining.[1]

The tension between individual freedom and collective responsibility is a dominant characteristic of the American experience. We are a country that celebrates individualism—individual effort, equal opportunity, freedom from tyranny—but we are also a people who, as Alexis de Tocqueville observed in the 1830s, are remarkable for our variety of organizations and associations, that is, for our outstanding array of community activities.[2]

Robert Bellah's book *Habits of the Heart* has had widespread influence because its essential premise rings true. Americans value the individual first and foremost, but we have learned paradoxically that it is only through community—the meaningful interaction with others—that we can make sense of our own lives.[3]

The benefits of interrelationship can be found everywhere in nature. If a gardener places two plants close together, the roots commingle and improve the quality of the soil, thus helping both plants grow better than if they were separated. If a carpenter joins two boards together, they will hold much more weight than the total held by each alone.

In the human sphere, our challenge is to apply the creative cooperation we learn from nature in dealing with those around us. The essence of this is to value differences, build on each other's strengths, transcend individual limitations, and achieve the full potential of community.

Writer and educator John Gardner states, "We are a community-building species." He goes on to describe the conditions necessary to experience true community.[4]

- *Shared vision.* A healthy community has a sense of where it should go, and what it might become. A positive and future-focused role image provides direction and motivation for its members.

- *Wholeness incorporating diversity.* A group is less of a community if fragmentation or devisiveness exists—and if the rifts are deep, it is no community at all. We expect and value diversity, and there is dissent in the best of groups. But true community requires facing and resolving differences.

■ *Shared culture.* Success is enhanced when people have a shared culture, that is, shared norms of behavior and core values to live by. If a community is lucky, it has shared history and traditions as well. This is why developing communities must form symbols of group identity and generate stories to pass on core values, customs, and central purpose.

■ *Internal communications.* Members of a well-functioning community communicate freely with one another. There are regular occasions when people gather and share information. There are opportunities and means for people to get to know and understand what others need and want. Communication is uncensored and flows in all directions within the community.

■ *Consideration and trust.* A healthy community cares about its members and fosters an atmosphere of trust. People deal with one another humanely; they respect each other and value the integrity of each person.

■ *Maintenance and government.* A fully functioning community has provision for maintenance and governance. Roles, responsibilities, and decision-making processes are conducive to achieving tasks while maintaining a supportive group climate.

■ *Participation and shared leadership.* The healthy community encourages the involvement of all individuals in the pursuit of shared goals. All members have the opportunity to influence events and outcomes. The good community finds a productive balance between individual interests and group responsibilities as community tasks are accomplished.

■ *Development of younger members.* Opportunities for growth are numerous and varied for all members. Mature members ensure that younger members develop knowledge, skills, and attitudes that support continuation of the community's purpose and values.

■ *Affirmation.* A healthy community reaffirms itself continuously. It celebrates its beginnings, rewards its achievements, and takes pride in its challenges. In this way, community morale and confidence is developed.

■ *Links with outside groups.* There is a certain tension between the community's need to draw boundaries to accomplish its tasks and its need to have fruitful alliances with external groups and the larger community of which it is a part. A successful community masters both ends of this spectrum.

Building Community is an applied book filled with concepts and tools for *building community in the workplace.* It has a broad range of uses, from courses in human relations and organization behavior, to teambuilding applications for virtually any group or organizational setting. Each part of the book features an important theme in the community building process: The Power of Vision; Interpersonal Skills Development; Valuing Human Diversity; The Empowerment of People.

The material is presented in a usable and easily accessible way, so the reader can tailor the book to specific interests and needs. Although each chapter stands alone and can be used individually, the sequence of chapters and subjects is appropriate for most community-building applications. The following model shows each chapter as a block in the community-building process.

MODEL FOR BUILDING COMMUNITY IN THE WORKPLACE

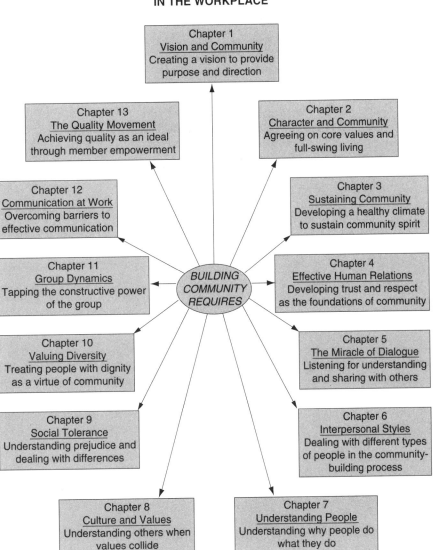

Chapter 1
Vision and Community
Creating a vision to provide purpose and direction

Chapter 13
The Quality Movement
Achieving quality as an ideal through member empowerment

Chapter 2
Character and Community
Agreeing on core values and full-swing living

Chapter 12
Communication at Work
Overcoming barriers to effective communication

Chapter 3
Sustaining Community
Developing a healthy climate to sustain community spirit

Chapter 11
Group Dynamics
Tapping the constructive power of the group

BUILDING COMMUNITY REQUIRES

Chapter 4
Effective Human Relations
Developing trust and respect as the foundations of community

Chapter 10
Valuing Diversity
Treating people with dignity as a virtue of community

Chapter 5
The Miracle of Dialogue
Listening for understanding and sharing with others

Chapter 9
Social Tolerance
Understanding prejudice and dealing with differences

Chapter 6
Interpersonal Styles
Dealing with different types of people in the community-building process

Chapter 8
Culture and Values
Understanding others when values collide

Chapter 7
Understanding People
Understanding why people do what they do

Every book has a premise—explicit or implied. The following are the foundations for *Building Community:*

PREMISES OF THE BOOK

- The group exists for the individual, not the other way around.
- Individuals achieve their fullest potential in relationship to people and values beyond themselves.

PREMISES OF PART ONE: THE POWER OF VISION

- Everyone needs a purpose or meaning in life, something important yet to be done.
- Because beliefs can create reality, a positive vision of the future is important for individual and community success.
- A community is defined by the values it holds and its strength of commitment to these ideals.

PREMISES OF PART TWO: INTERPERSONAL SKILLS DEVELOPMENT

- The best human relationships are based on trust and respect.
- Understanding people is a core competency for building and sustaining community.
- Each person is a unique individual deserving of respect and appreciation.

PREMISES OF PART THREE: VALUING HUMAN DIVERSITY

- Understanding people requires understanding culture and how values are formed.
- Social tolerance and valuing diversity enrich a community.

PREMISES OF PART FOUR: THE EMPOWERMENT OF PEOPLE

- Communication is the essential ingredient and the best benefit of community.
- By working together, everyone can accomplish more.
- Quality is a team effort requiring participative leadership.

Building Community: The Human Side of Work explains what community is, why it is needed by people today, and, importantly, it provides tools and techniques that show how to build community. The best way to use the book is to *interact* with the material. Read the narrative, complete the questionnaires and exercises, examine the interpretations, and review the principles and techniques. Ask, "How does this apply to me? How can I use this concept or process to improve?" Then take *action*.

To increase interest and improve overall learning, try the following:

- Discuss the results of questionnaires and exercises with others. In this way, you can make tangible use of what is learned and may even help others.

- Write in the book. Use the margins; underline; write ideas and observations; personalize the material.

In summary, what does this book do? It raises consciousness, teaches skills, strengthens relationships, and provides a means for building community in the workplace. It is written for the work setting, but it applies to any setting where communication, teamwork, and valuing diversity are important. For whom is the book written? It is written for anyone interested in the human side of work, anyone who is concerned with the experience of community in all of its forms—productive partnerships, high performance teams, organizational excellence, and a healthy society.

The authors celebrate the individual as valuing and most valuable, but also believe that together everyone *can* accomplish more. *Building Community* is intended to help achieve this goal. The following reflects both the spirit and message of the book.

Lessons from the Geese

As each goose flaps its wings, it creates an "uplift" for the bird following. By flying in a "V" formation, the whole flock adds 71 percent more flying range than if each bird flew alone.

Lesson: People who share a common direction and sense of community can get where they are going quicker and easier because they are traveling on the thrust of one another.

Whenever a goose falls out of formation, it suddenly feels the drag and resistance of trying to fly alone and quickly gets back into formation to take advantage of the lifting power of the birds immediately in front.

Lesson: If we have as much sense as a goose, we will join in formations with those who are headed where we want to go.

When the lead goose gets tired or disoriented, it rotates back into the formation and another goose flies at the point position.

Lesson: It pays to take turns doing the hard tasks and sharing leadership—with people, as with geese, interdependent with one another.

The geese in formation honk from behind to encourage those up front to keep up their speed.

Lesson: We need to make sure our honking from behind is encouraging, not something less helpful.

When a goose gets sick or wounded or shot down, two geese drop out of formation and follow their fellow member down to help and provide protection. They stay with this member of the flock until he or she either is able to fly again or dies. Then they launch out on their own, with another formation, or to catch up with their own flock.

Lesson: If we have as much sense as the geese, we'll stand by one another like they do.[5]

REFERENCES

1. Marvin R. Weisbord, *Productive Workplaces* (San Francisco: Jossey-Bass, 1990).

2. Alexis de Tocqueville (1805–1859), *Democracy in America* (New York: Vintage Books, 1990), the Henry Reeve text as revised by Francis Bowen. Originally published by Knopf, 1945.

3. Robert N. Bellah, Richard Madsen, William M. Sullivan, Ann Swidler, and Steven M. Tipton *Habits of the Heart: Individualism and Commitment in American Life* (New York: Harper and Row, 1985).

4. John W. Gardner, "Building Community"—prepared for the Leadership Studies Program of Independent Sector (Washington, DC: American Institutes for Research, 1991).

5. "Lessons from the Geese" by Merle W. Boos from Issue 97 of *Agricultural Notes*, copyright © Evangelical Lutheran Church in America. Used by permission of Augsburg Fortress.

PART 1

The Power of Vision

Vision and Community

It was the best of times, it was the worst of times, it was the age of wisdom, it was the age of foolishness, it was the epoch of belief, it was the epoch of incredulity, it was the season of light, it was the season of darkness, it was the spring of hope, it was the winter of despair, we had everything before us, we had nothing before us . . . in short, the period was . . . like the present period.

Charles Dickens

A community has the power to motivate its members to exceptional performance. It can set standards of expectation for the individual and provide the climate in which great things happen. The achievements of Greece in the fifth century B.C. were not the performances of isolated persons but of individuals acting in a moment of shared excellence. The community can tap levels of emotion and energy that otherwise remain dormant.[1]

Communities are always in a state of change. The direction may be toward decay and death; or it may be toward growth and life; or change may be a transformation from one personality or culture to another that is of equal, but different, quality. The primary mechanism that determines the path and fate of a community is its image of itself—its image of its past, present, and future.

This chapter features the power of vision in the creation of community. It presents a framework or model for developing a vision that is leader initiated, member supported, comprehensive and detailed, and above all, worth doing. Points to remember are:

- people are shaped by assumptions and expectations they hold about themselves and their futures—beliefs create reality;

- as with individuals, every community needs a vision of something important yet to be done;

- leadership is critical in creating a vision, mobilizing people, and sustaining community; and

- in the final analysis, it is the responsibility of each person to get involved and choose to make a difference.

A community's vision includes five key elements: *purpose* or reason for existence; *goals* or enduring intentions to act; *core values* or principles to measure the rightness and wrongness of behavior; *stakeholders* or those who care about the community, including what it will mean to them when the vision is achieved; and *initiatives*—immediate, short-term, and long-range—that guide and energize members of the community.

BELIEFS CREATE REALITY

Martin Seligman, author of *Learned Optimism*, describes the importance of a positive attitude, the expectation that one will succeed. It is the attitude of optimism that is so helpful in energizing and focusing behavior. When energy and focus are added to ability and desire, one's greatest potential can be achieved.[2]

The same phenomenon can be seen with people in community. There may be a great deal of ability and desire within a group or organization, but it is only when there is a shared positive image of the group's future state that the individuals in the group generate the energy, focus, and commitment that are needed to achieve that state. The role of beliefs in creating reality through the mechanism of expectation has been known since antiquity and has been well documented in modern times.[3]

Perhaps the clearest description of this process comes from the German writer, Johann Goethe, who said, "If we take a person as he is, he will be less than he can be. But if we expect more and view a person as he should be, we help him achieve his full potential. We help him become the full self of which he is capable."

THE IMPORTANCE OF VISION

The philosopher Julian Huxley believed that human life is a struggle—against frustration, ignorance, suffering, evil, the maddening inertia of things in general—but he also believed it is a struggle for something, the attainment of something worthwhile. He wrote, "Fulfillment seems to describe better than any other word the positive side of human development and human evolution—the realization of inherent capacities by the individual and of new possibilities by the race."[4]

This is what is meant by living a big life. Fulfilled lives entail bold and realistic dreams, not settling for minor accomplishments when major ones are possible. Individuals and groups too often fill their minds and hours with trifling matters and pursue insignificant tasks, when fully in their capabilities is the accomplishment of something great, something meaningful. The key is **vision**; the answer is to focus on possibilities and potentialities. Thomas Carlisle, the Scottish philosopher, believed that people do not fear extinction. We know we have to die. What we fear is death without meaning. We want to leave our mark and make a difference. This begins with vision.

Organizational theorist Peter Senge sees vision as the cornerstone of personal mastery and one of the five disciplines necessary for community success. He writes, "One is hard-pressed to think of any organization that has sustained some measure of greatness in the absence of missions, values, and goals that become deeply shared throughout the organization. Though radically different in content and kind, all of these organizations managed to bind people together around a common identity and a sense of destiny."[5]

Occupying center stage in explaining the importance of vision is author and educator, Joel Barker. Barker's books and films are truly excellent resources in the community-building process.[6] Barker's ideas on vision are drawn primarily from three individuals—Frederick Polak, Benjamin Singer, and Viktor Frankl.

Historian Frederick Polak asked the question: "Is a nation's positive image of its future the consequence of its success, or is a nation's success the consequence of its positive image of the future?" He concluded that the fates of nations and civilizations have depended primarily on their visions for the future. He cites examples in history of ancient Greece, Rome, Spain, England, and America to support this thought. Polak makes three main points: 1) significant vision precedes significant success; 2) a compelling image of the future is shared by leaders with their followers, and together they strive to make this vision a reality; and 3) a nation with vision is enabled, and a nation without vision is at risk.[7]

Psychologist Benjamin Singer, building on the ideas of personality theorist Gordon Allport, showed how children's lives are similarly shaped by positive self-concepts and expectations for the future. Children without vision become powerless, feeling no control over their own futures. Children with vision are focused and energized, and these are strong and positive agents in a self-fulfilling prophecy. Adults should always take seriously a child's dreams of what he or she wants to be. The interest and support shown communicates the message that the child is worthy and his or her future is important.[8] Consider the power of vision for one child, somehow conveyed by her father:

> I was fourteen years old the night my daddy died. He had holes in his shoes but two children out of college, one in college, another in divinity school, and a vision he was able to convey to me as he lay dying in an ambulance that I, a young Black girl, could be and do anything; that race and gender are shadows; and that character, self-discipline, determination, attitude, and service are the substance of life.[9]

The third individual who influenced Barker was Viktor Frankl, author of *Man's Search for Meaning*, based on his experiences in the Nazi death camps of World War II. Frankl identifies a trilogy of powerful forces that act as the primary determinants of our existence. When these are distorted or untapped, people become less than they could be, less than their full potential as human beings. These forces are free will, will to meaning, and meaning of life. Meaning in life can be *experiential*—how one is living; *creative*—what one is achieving; or *attitudinal*—one's inner thoughts and feelings in the face of unavoidable suffering.[10]

Citing the philosopher Friedrich Nietzsche, Frankl states that we can endure any *what* in our lives if we just know *why*. He explains that it is a requirement of the human spirit, that every person needs something important yet to be done. Frankl writes: "Man's concern about the meaning of life is the truest expression of the state of being human."[11]

Frankl's ideas are relevant for the community-building process. Everyone needs a unifying purpose or meaning in life, and often this can be attained in the experience and achievements of community. Indeed, in Frankl's view, meaning that transcends the self and extends to people and ideals beyond the individual is meaning on its highest and most human plane. Just as an airplane is most like an airplane when it rises from the runway and flies, so are we most human when we exercise free will, seek meaning in our lives, and commit to a purpose or mission that transcends the self.[12]

There is no deeper or more powerful human need than to live a life that is meaningful according to one's beliefs and value system. This is the role of vision. The more our activities and relationships have meaning, the more alive we feel. We have inner joy, peace of mind, and a sense of being in the right place at the right time.

VISION AS AN IDEAL

The word *vision* evokes pictures in the mind. It suggests a future orientation, implies a standard of excellence or virtuous condition, and has the quality of uniqueness. Vision is an ideal image of what could and should be. These are the elements that give strength to vision. Read and feel the power of the words of Martin Luther King, Jr., as he delivered his vision of civil rights before the Lincoln Memorial on August 28, 1963.[13]

I Have a Dream

So I say to you, my friends, that even though we must face the difficulties of today and tomorrow, I still have a dream. It is a dream deeply rooted in the American dream that one day this nation will rise up and live out the true meaning of its creed—we hold these truths to be self-evident, that all men are created equal.

I have a dream that one day on the red hills of Georgia, sons of former slaves and sons of former slaveowners will be able to sit down together at the table of brotherhood.

I have a dream that one day, even the state of Mississippi, a state sweltering with the heat of injustice, sweltering with the heat of oppression, will be transformed into an oasis of freedom and justice.

I have a dream my four little children will one day live in a nation where they will not be judged by the color of their skin, but by content of their character. I have a dream today!

I have a dream that one day, down in Alabama, with its vicious racists, with its governor having his lips dripping with the words of interposition and nullification, that one day, right there in Alabama, little black boys and little black girls will be able to join hands with little white boys and little white girls as sisters and brothers. I have a dream today!

I have a dream that one day every valley shall be exalted, every hill and mountain shall be made low, the rough places shall be made plain, and the crooked places shall be made straight and the glory of the Lord will be revealed and all flesh shall see it together. . . .

So let freedom ring from the prodigious hilltops of New Hampshire.

Let freedom ring from the mighty mountains of New York.

Let freedom ring from the heightening Alleghenies of Pennsylvania.

Let freedom ring from the snow-capped Rockies of Colorado.

Let freedom ring from the curvaceous slopes of California.

But not only that.

Let freedom ring from Stone Mountain of Georgia.

Let freedom ring from Lookout Mountain of Tennessee.

Let freedom ring from every hill and molehill of Mississippi, from every mountainside, let freedom ring.

And when we allow freedom to ring, when we let it ring from every village and hamlet, from every state and city, we will be able to speed up that day when all of God's children—black men and white men, Jews and Gentiles, Catholics and Protestants—will be able to join hands and to sing in the words of the old Negro spiritual, "Free at last, free at last; thank God Almighty, we are free at last."

REQUIREMENTS FOR AN EFFECTIVE VISION

The requirements for an effective vision are as follows.[14]

First, *vision must be developed by leaders, those individuals with strength and influence to establish direction and mobilize the community.* Leadership is dreaming a dream and then making it come true. Leaders create clear and worthy images that motivate the community, and then create a climate so that ideas are transformed into deeds. Leadership is commitment to purpose along with persistence to see it through. The leader's vision should appeal to a common good and be believed passionately. Of six characteristics common to peak performers, management author Charles Garfield describes as the most important, commitment to a mission that motivates.[15]

Second, *a vision must be communicated to followers and be supported by them.* Leaders have to let others see, hear, taste, touch, and feel their vision. A picture in the mind of the general is merely that until it is understood in the minds and adopted in the hearts of the soldiers. Only then will hands and feet be activated and the vision be implemented in fact. It may take leadership to articulate and give legitimacy to a vision, but it takes the strength of an empowered people to get things done. In this regard, the vision of leaders must be in harmony with the nature and needs of the people.[16]

Third, *a vision must be comprehensive and detailed, so that every member of the community can understand his or her part in the whole.* Roles and responsibilities must be well understood if the vision is to be fulfilled. Each person must know what is expected and the rewards that will accrue when the vision is achieved. Put yourself in the shoes of the soldier, who, upon hearing the vision and seeing the battle plan of the general, can't help but wonder, "Yes, but what about me?" A clear line of sight between personal effort and personal reward is a major determinant of the ultimate fulfillment of the vision.[17]

Fourth, *and critically, a vision must be uplifting and inspiring.* It must be worth the effort; it must be big enough. Relating to Frankl's message that every person needs meaning in life and something important yet to be done, the community's vision must be meaningful and important for the members to do.[18] Psychologist Abraham Maslow once remarked, "If you purposefully choose to be less than you can be, then you are surely doomed to be unhappy."[19] The same is true for communities; the members of a community must seek to achieve the community's fullest potential.

A PERSONAL CHALLENGE

Barker's discussion of vision includes a challenge to every person. He tells a story about Loren Eiseley, the poet and scientist, who was walking on a beach when he came upon a young man throwing starfish into the ocean. When asked why, the young man said the tide had gone out and the sun had come up. If he didn't do it, the starfish would die.

Eiseley reminded the young man that there were literally thousands of starfish on the beach, and he was just one person—what possible difference could he make? To this, the young man picked up another starfish, went to the water's edge, and threw the starfish into the sea, saying, "It made a difference for that one."

Stunned, Eiseley could not stop thinking about the meaning of the young man's action. Moved in this way, his response was to join him; and he spent the day . . . throwing starfish into the ocean.[20]

The message is that each person faces the same dilemma in life—the choice to be a bystander in the universe and watch it go by, or the choice to be an active participant, get involved, and make a difference, however small.

We live in a world where every person can make a difference. When we are aware of this and are willing to act upon it, we can use this power to change relationships, communities, and even nations by the way we choose to live our lives. This is what Erich Fromm meant when he wrote, "We have a unique capacity that differentiates us from all other living beings: the capacity to be aware of ourselves and our circumstances, and hence to plan and act according to this awareness. Our main task in life is to give birth to ourselves, to become what we potentially can be."[21]

According to this view, the never-lost kernel of human existence is the power to take a stand. In taking a stand, we express our freedom and our responsibility. It is the defining moment of truth in which each person becomes as authentic or truly human as she or he has the courage to be. Adding weight to this view is Frankl's admonition that our actions are recorded in history and, in this sense, are irretrievable.

Barker's powerful metaphor about personal freedom, responsibility, and commitment is at the root of what it means to be human. The prescription is for each person and each community to discover their own starfish, their purpose for being, and then to act upon it. The challenge is to remember:

Vision without action is a dream;
Action without vision merely passes the time;
Vision with action is the hope of the world.[22]

WHERE AND WHEN DO YOU BEGIN?

Every individual and community can benefit from a positive image of the future, and it is not necessary to wait for the creation of a vision at higher levels of influence or in larger sizes of groups. Begin where you are now, knowing that the power of vision impacts in all directions and in many ways. See figure 1–1 on the following page.

There are many cases of individuals and groups at lower levels of the social strata creating a vision that influences events upward and outward. Some of the best examples are the stories of Mohammed, Jesus, Buddha, Confucius, and their followers, and the impact of their ideas on the course of history.

A powerful vision sets many forces in motion, not all of which can be predicted. Some of these forces may expand the vision in ways that could not have been foreseen. For example, you may start with a vision of helping the children in your community. As your work proceeds, you may find that the energy and support you have sparked on children's issues can be used to tackle other important social problems.

So if you are the governor, don't say, "We can't create a vision for our state until the federal government gets things straight." And if you are the mayor, don't say, "We can't create a vision for our city until the state gets things straight." And if you are the manager, don't say, "We can't create a vision for our department or site until the company gets things straight." And if you are the parent, don't say, "We can't create a vision for our family until society gets things straight." As an individual, or as a community, begin now to achieve what you believe should and could be done through the power of vision.

WHY CREATE A VISION?

A vision keeps the community on track. As an old saying goes, "If you don't know where you are going, any road will take you there." Creating a vision lets people know where they are going and provides milestones to track progress. The time taken to develop a vision will pay off by lessening the time spent trying to decide policy, make decisions, and resolve disputes. At any crossroad and in any conflict, members of the community need only ask, what will help us accomplish our mission and goals, what will fit our value system, and what will best serve our stakeholders?[23]

Management author Peter Drucker explains:

Because the modern organization is composed of specialists, each with his or her own narrow area of expertise, its purpose must be crystal clear. The organization must be single-minded, or its members will become confused. They will follow their own specialty rather than apply it to the common task. They will each define 'results'

FIGURE 1–1   Vision Impacts in All Directions

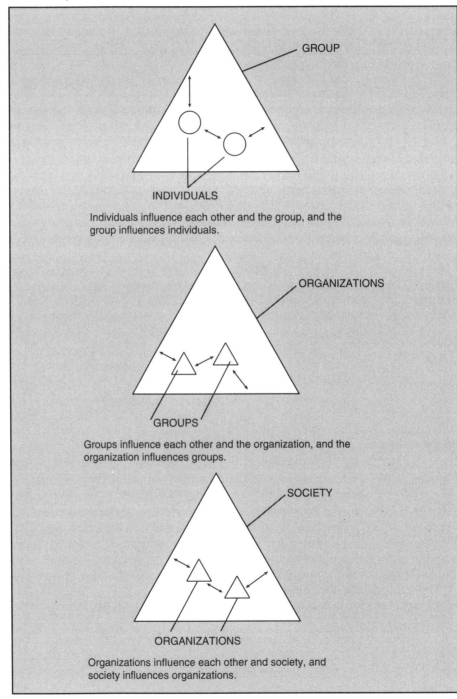

in terms of their own specialty and impose its values on the organization. Only a focused and shared vision will hold an organization together and enable it to produce. Without agreement on purpose and values, the organization will soon lose credibility and, with it, its ability to attract the very people it needs to perform.[24]

Management authors James Collins and Jerry Porras report on the business benefits of having a vision. They asked a sample of CEOs from Fortune 500 and Inc 100 companies to identify "visionary" organizations. For the twenty companies most frequently selected they "invested" one dollar in stock in 1926 or whenever the firm was first listed. They found that, as a group, these "visionary" companies performed fifty-five times better than the general market. They also compared visionary companies to nonvisionary counterparts—companies that started at the same time—such as Motorola and Zenith, and Disney and Columbia. Again, vision-driven companies proved more successful, performing eight times better than their competitors.[25]

The specific benefits of having a vision are: 1) decreased frustration of community members because there is clarity of purpose and agreement on values; 2) improved performance of the community because there is agreement on goals and initiatives; 3) better use of resources to meet the community's expressed needs; and 4) meaning for individuals by contributing to people and ideals beyond themselves.[26]

EXAMPLES OF POWERFUL VISIONS

Consider the moving vision of Collis Huntington, founder of Newport News Shipbuilding and Dry Dock Company in 1886.

> We shall build good ships here.
> At a profit—if we can.
> At a loss—if we must.
> But always good ships.

Consider the strong and all-embracing vision of Johnson & Johnson that has helped thousands of employees throughout the world understand that their first obligation is to the customer.

> We believe our first obligation is to the doctors,
> nurses, and patients; to mothers and all others
> who use our products and services.[27]

Finally, consider the mission, values, and guiding principles of one of the world's largest and most respected companies. See table 1–1.

TABLE 1–1   Ford Motor Company Mission, Values, and Guiding Principles

Mission
Ford Motor Company is a worldwide leader in automotive and automotive related products and services as well as in newer industries such as aerospace, communications, and financial services. Our mission is to improve continually our products and services to meet our customers' needs, allowing us to prosper as a business and to provide a reasonable return for our stockholders, the owners of our business.

Values
How we accomplish our mission is as important as the mission itself. Fundamental to success for the Company are these basic values. **People**—Our people are the source of our strength. They provide our corporate intelligence and determine our reputation and vitality. Involvement and teamwork are our core human values. **Products**—Our products are the end result of our efforts, and they should be the best in serving customers worldwide. As our products are viewed, so are we viewed. **Profits**—Profits are the ultimate measure of how efficiently we provide customers with the best products for their needs. Profits are required to survive and grow. **Quality comes first**—To achieve customer satisfaction, the quality of our products and services must be our number-one priority. **Customers are the focus of everything we do**—Our work must be done with our customers in mind, providing better products and services than our competition. **Continuous improvement is essential to our success**—We must strive for excellence in everything we do: in our products, in their safety and value—and in our services, our human relations, our competitiveness, and our profitability. **Employee involvement is our way of life**—We are a team. We must treat each other with trust and respect. Dealers and suppliers are our partners. The Company must maintain mutually beneficial relationships with dealers, suppliers, and other business associates. **Integrity is never compromised**—The conduct of our company worldwide must be pursued in a manner that is socially responsible and commands respect for its integrity and for its positive contributions to society. Our doors are open to men and women alike without discrimination and without regard to ethnic origin or personal beliefs.

VISION AND CHANGE

What is the role of *vision* in helping communities through periods of change? As figure 1–2 shows, successful change begins with a clear compelling vision, a picture in the minds of the members of the community of how things should and could be. Without vision there is confusion. Also required for successful change are other important ingredients: skills, incentives, resources, and an action plan.

DEVELOPING A VISION

Management author Stephen Covey sees *vision* as the single most important influence on the success of an organization. He states, "It is the written expression of the organization's very identity. It becomes the organization's governing constitution, its supreme law, the standard by which all behavior is judged. It is the source of purpose and values that guide the development and implementation of strategy, tactics, systems, policy, procedure, and decision making throughout the organization."[29]

Table 1–2 defines six *process* principles, five *content* principles, and five *application* principles for developing and maintaining a vision.

FIGURE 1–2   Managing Complex Change[28]

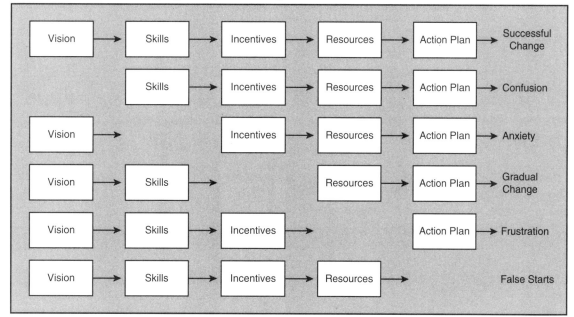

TABLE 1–2   Principles for Developing and Maintaining a Vision[30]

Visioning Process Principles
1. *Initiation and constant vigilance by leaders.* It is the proper role of leadership to begin the process, to discuss and articulate the basis for developing a community vision, and to start drafting a document. This begins the *top down* portion of the visioning process. 2. *Significant early involvement by other members of the community.* This includes discussion, writing, and wordsmithing. In this *joint effort* phase, senior leaders in effect say, "We've begun—but we need your input. Your involvement is essential." 3. *Widespread review and comment.* Involvement fosters commitment. Include as many people in the organization as possible. This *bottom up* period of mass review invites critical analysis. Here, leaders are saying, "We've worked hard on this and like it—but what do you think? Give us your ideas. We want this to belong to everyone." Be open and show appreciation for suggestions. Incorporate modifications and the best thinking of all members of the community. 4. *Keep communications flowing.* Don't assume everyone knows what is going on. Report on progress for developing the vision. Give acknowledgement and appreciation, and report on the adoption of elements of the vision—agreement on purpose, broad goals, core values, stakeholders, strategic initiatives, etc. 5. *Allow time for the process to work.* People need time to think, feel, and adjust to change, even positive change. The development of a vision may take longer than people expect. Top leaders may spend weeks on the original draft, months on the involvement and feedback process, and could spend a year or more to finished product. 6. *Commitment, follow-through, and concurrent action by leaders.* Leaders must make reality match rhetoric. Any sincere effort to put words into action will lend credibility and will reinforce the actual attainment of the vision.
Visioning Content Principles
1. *Identify the mission and goals.* This is the overall direction the organization should take. 2. *Agree on core values or principles.* These are basic guidelines on how to fulfill the mission. 3. *Meet the needs of stakeholders.* A vision should address more than just financial needs. Consider the needs of customers, employees, suppliers, owners, and the larger community. What will it mean to them when the organization is successful? 4. *Be challenging, yet realistic.* Set the mark high, but stay in touch with reality. A vision should stretch the community, but not destroy its members. 5. *Maintain harmony of sub-units.* The content of the vision statements for sub-units (divisions, plants, departments, work teams, etc.) should be in harmony with the overall vision of the organization.

TABLE 1–2   Principles for Developing and Maintaining a Vision (continued)

Visioning Application Principles
1. *Honor and live the vision as the organization's constitution.* The values and principles of the vision, not the personal style of individuals, should govern organizational culture and behavior. 2. *Encourage new member understanding and commitment through early introduction.* Those not involved in the development process can identify with the vision from the first association: "This is what we are all about; if you can embrace this mission and these values as your own, then we may join together." The vision should be the centerpiece of the orientation program for all new members. 3. *Make it constantly visible.* Express constancy of purpose through a written statement. The vision should be publicized to customers, employees, suppliers, owners—everyone. 4. *Create integrity through alignment and congruency.* Use the vision as a leadership tool and decision-making guide, as a checkpoint to test alignment of strategy, structures, systems, and member behavior, and to track progress. 5. *Review the vision periodically, revising as appropriate to reflect changing conditions.* Even the U.S. Constitution has ben amended over the long term. View the vision as a program with people as the programmers.

THE VISIONING PROCESS—YESTERDAY, TODAY, AND TOMORROW

What steps should be taken to achieve the power of vision in building community? The following process can be adapted to meet the needs of all sizes and types of groups—business, industry, and government. It is appropriate for new communities just getting started and for mature communities interested in self-assessment and development to a higher level. It is based on the work of a long line of theorists and practitioners in organization development.[31]

This process uses a model of *yesterday, today,* and *tomorrow.* It is ideal for off-site gatherings free of interruptions in settings conducive to open exchange of ideas. The format varies, but it follows the philosophy of inclusion versus exclusion and the principle of patience, as sufficient time is taken to gather information, discuss ideas, and agree on an ideal vision for the future of the community.[32]

The process of creating a vision can be as important as the statement itself. If a vision is not "owned" by the members of the community, it will be empty platitudes on a plaque and a meaningless document in a desk, never realizing the full potential of uplifting, guiding, and energizing. The following is an outline of steps and activities to create a vision and build community.

Yesterday

To plan for the future, it helps to review the past. It helps to know the forces and impactors that have brought a community to its present state. There are at least three good ways to consider the past—the historian's perspective, the snake on the wall, and the color-coded timeline.

With the *historian's perspective*, respected individuals recall significant people and events that have helped shape the community, past to present. Typically featured in this review are heroes and villains, quests and key crises, and other defining elements and moments in the life of the community.

The *snake on the wall* is a more participative method for reviewing the past. Paper is placed on the wall, and a line is drawn from the date of the community's founding to the present. The line is divided into parts such as weeks, months, or years. People are asked to identify their own arrival dates, and to indicate with words or symbols the people and events that have influenced the community since that time. Forces considered to be positive are placed *above* the line; forces considered to be negative are placed *below* the line; and mixed or questionable forces are placed *upon* the line.[33]

The *color coded* timeline is a similar participative approach for considering the past. People are asked to write on flip charts or paper with green, red, and orange markers, indicating the positive, negative and mixed or questionable forces that have influenced them as *individuals*, the *community* as a group, and the *industry*, *profession*, or *society* at large during the pre-1970s, 1970s, 1980s, and from 1990 to the present. These forces and impactors are then discussed to gain a sense of history.[34] See table 1–3 in the appendix to this chapter.

Today

Having looked at the past, the community is now ready to consider the present. The focus of this evaluation is the community itself. A good way to do this in a nonthreatening way is to list *prouds* and *sorries*—people, products, policies, processes, practices, etc.—that are viewed as assets on the one hand, and those that are seen as areas for improvement on the other. An effective approach is to have people list these as individuals first, and then share and discuss them in group format. It is not unusual for a group to generate as many as twenty to forty prouds and sorries. Narrowing lists to the Top Five Prouds and Top Five Sorries is a good way to focus the community on current strengths and areas for improvement. See table 1–4 in the appendix to this chapter.

Tomorrow

Having considered the people and events that have brought the community to its present state, and having identified factors in the present—prouds and sorries—that describe the community's current condition, members are now ready to create a vision for the future. This entails agreement on a preferred tomorrow and commitment to achieving that vision.

Table 1–5 in the appendix to this chapter presents a planning guide for use in the visioning process. Completed individually and discussed in group format, a spirit of community can be achieved as members agree on key elements of an overall vision, strategic plan, and tactical actions. These elements are:

1. *Central purpose or mission (reason for existence).* This is a clear, compelling statement of purpose that provides focus and direction for the community. It is the organization's answer to the question, "Why do we exist?"

2. *Broad goals to achieve the mission (enduring intentions to act).* These are process or functional accomplishments that must be met to achieve the mission.

3. *Core values to measure the rightness and wrongness of behavior (hills worth dying on).* Sometimes called operating principles, these values define the moral tone or character of the community.

4. *Stakeholders and what the attainment of the vision will mean to them (the human element).* These are the people who will be affected by what the community does or does not do.

5. *Analysis of community **s**trengths, **w**eaknesses, **o**pportunities, and **t**hreats (environmental scan).* This is a **swot** assessment of current conditions.

6. *Strategic initiatives* (sometimes called critical success factors). These are short-term, intermediate, and long-term objectives necessary to achieve the goals and mission. They may be person- or group-specific, or may involve all members of the community. They are **s**trategic, **m**easurable, **a**ction-oriented, **r**ealistic, and **t**imely with dates or numbers to measure accomplishment.

7. *People involved.* Players include individuals and groups who could be potential adversaries or allies as the community strives to achieve its vision.

8. *Unit or person-specific assignments (projects and activities) to support strategic initiatives, broad goals, and the attainment of the mission.* These projects and activities guide in performance planning for units and members of the community, and constitute the plan of work.

The first four elements of the planning guide—central purpose through stakeholders and benefits—constitute a vision. This vision provides general direction for the community. Adding elements five through seven constitutes strategic planning. This gives definition to the vision and focuses the people and resources of the community on specific objectives that can be measured.

The word *strategy* comes from the Greek word *stratego* and has its roots in military parlance. Literally, it means "the art of the general." The term was originally used to describe the grand plan behind a war or battle. Communities adopt the term "strategic" to describe the planning process and the management of resources needed to achieve their vision. Decisions that impact on the vision are also described as strategic.

The last element of the guide, tactical planning, refers to projects and activities designed to implement strategy, the plays that drive the game to success. Tactical planning results in group- and person-specific assignments and concrete actions.

Round-Robin Cameos for Tactical Planning

A highly effective way to move from vision and strategic planning to tactical planning and concrete action is the *round-robin cameo*. The constructive power of the group is tapped, as members help each other in recommending projects and activities that should be continued, started, and stopped if the overall vision of the community is to be achieved.

Example applications include:

- Research scientists who make suggestions across labs to facilitate an overall mission, "the discovery of drugs to benefit mankind."[35]

- Government officials who make recommendations across departments to provide the best services possible for their communities.[36]

- Physician partners who share ideas with each other to improve medical care for the patients in their practice.[37]

- Company managers who work with each other to improve product quality, meet customer needs, and succeed as a business.[38]

The process is as follows:

1. Person (or unit) A highlights past accomplishments and future challenges for his or her area of responsibility (three to five minutes).

2. Members of the community are given a few minutes to make notes on 5" × 7" cards on projects and activities they think A should *continue doing, start doing, or stop doing* in order to achieve the broad goals and overall mission of the community. These ideas should be given in the spirit of helpfulness, and not self-censored for feasibility. Person A will be able to consider the suggestions and make final judgement. What is needed is uninhibited and creative ideas from other members of the community.

3. Person (or unit) A then solicits ideas clockwise, counterclockwise, or in shotgun manner until all suggestions are written on a flip chart or note paper. It is important for A to personally and physically write these down. At this point, communication is one-way and A is not supposed to respond to suggestions, such as to say, "Well, you know I am doing that." All A can

do is record the suggestions. This will usually take fifteen to twenty minutes for each individual or unit.

4. When finished, A selects the next person or group to be the subject of the round-robin cameo. Person (or unit) B follows the same procedure.

5. After all members have completed round-robin cameos, and after a break to think about these suggestions, reverse round-robin cameos are conducted. In the reverse round-robin, person (or unit) A has open discussion to clarify points and communicate what will be needed from other members of the community in order to follow through on suggestions. A is followed by B, C, etc., in the reverse round-robin cameos.

6. The ideas gathered in the round-robin exercise can be shared by persons A, B, C, etc., in subsequent meetings with others in their specific function or area of responsibility. With these ideas as backdrop, a work plan of projects and activities can be developed. This represents tactical or operational planning to support strategic planning and the ultimate accomplishment of the community's vision.

VISIONING GUIDELINES

Although the "yesterday, today, and tomorrow" format is versatile and can be tailored to fit the nature and needs of each community, there are six points that should be remembered.

Be Real. The creation of a vision is important and should not be viewed as an idle exercise. Because it matters, show that it matters by giving *real time* and *real energy* to the effort.

Be Honest. Honesty is the best policy in the visioning process. If a product or practice is a weakness, say so; with tact, but say so. If a value discussed is not a core value, a "hill worth dying on," say so. If an initiative or proposed project does not support the vision, say so; again, with sensitivity to the views of others. If a vision is not built on such honesty, it will be a house of cards that will not withstand the test of time.

Listen to Feelings. Visions are created in the heart as well as the head; they do not conform to a formula. Sometimes it helps to brainstorm an emerging vision by coming up with spontaneous ideas and pictures of how things could be. To create a vision, people have to get beyond their current inhibitions, they have to *dream*.

Give It Time. It takes time to make a good stew, and it takes time and patience for a community to consider and ultimately agree upon all of the elements of a great vision. A series of meetings and discussions over a period of time is the norm.

Involve the People. Only by tapping the knowledge, enthusiasm, and energy of all of its members can a community achieve its full potential. This means opening up the visioning process. Leaders must be open to information, ideas, and suggestions from all members of the community as the vision is developed and refined. Then, the vision must be communicated in a way that is understood and supported by those who must implement it. By engaging the minds and hearts of the people, the hands and feet will follow and a powerful vision can be achieved. Writing in *Leadership and the New Science*, Margaret Wheatley explains the importance of involving people.

> In a field view of organizations, clarity about values or vision is important, but it's only half the task. Creating the field through the dissemination of those ideas is essential. The field must reach all corners of the organization, involve everyone, and be available everywhere. Vision statements move off the walls and into the corridors, seeking out every employee, every recess of the organization. In the past, we may have thought of ourselves as skilled crafters of organizations, assembling the pieces of an organization, exerting our energy on the painstaking creation of links between all those parts. Now, we need to imagine ourselves as broadcasters, tall radio beacons of information, pulsing out messages everywhere. We need all of us out there, stating, clarifying, discussing, modeling, filling all of space with the messages we care about. If we do that, fields develop—and with them, their wondrous capacity to bring energy into form.[39]

Put First Things First. A community should strive to reach the point where vision precedes and guides strategic planning, and strategic planning precedes and guides tactical planning, and tactical planning precedes and guides budget allocation. Too often, the sequence is just the opposite and the tail wags the dog as past history and well-entrenched budgetary practices dictate the course of a community. Again, the flow should be vision to budget, not the other way around. See table 1–6.

VISIONING IN BRIEF

A community's vision fulfills four powerful functions—its *mission* justifies existence; its *goals* provide direction; its *values* define acceptable behavior and hold everyone together; its *benefits* to stakeholders energize the work. When John Kennedy announced a vision to send a man to the moon and bring him back

TABLE 1–6   Elements and Sequence for Visioning, Strategic Planning, Tactical Planning, and Budget Allocation

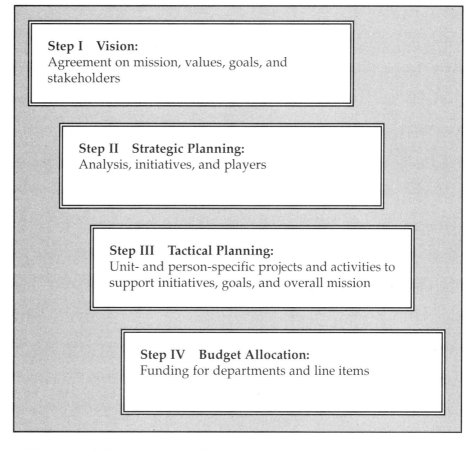

Step I   Vision:
Agreement on mission, values, goals, and stakeholders

Step II   Strategic Planning:
Analysis, initiatives, and players

Step III   Tactical Planning:
Unit- and person-specific projects and activities to support initiatives, goals, and overall mission

Step IV   Budget Allocation:
Funding for departments and line items

safely, none of the resources needed to do the job were in place. By creating a vision for the American people, Kennedy motivated the technical and scientific community who ultimately accomplished the feat. On another level, but equally visionary, is a manager's goal of fostering cooperation and efficiency in the department, or a coach's dream of building character and team spirit that goes beyond the winning of a single game.

Here is a short review of the visioning process, using a who, what, and why format:

What Is a Vision? A vision is a picture of the ideal future state of the community. It is a force in people's hearts and minds, a force of tremendous power. Using words and symbols, a vision is comprehensive and detailed and includes purpose, goals, values, and benefits to stakeholders.

Why Create a Vision? Beliefs can influence reality. A person or group with a negative self-image tends to live *down* to this image, acting out what they think they are. On the other hand, people who have a positive image of themselves and their future tend to live *up* to this ideal and become or fulfill it. A positive vision energizes and focuses behavior. With energy and focus, people are empowered to achieve their full potential.

Who Creates a Vision? Leaders must initiate the effort and involve their followers in creating and sustaining a powerful vision for the community. Followers must understand and support the vision, or it will never be achieved.

How Can a Vision Be Developed? The yesterday, today, and tomorrow format is a highly effective way to look at the past and learn from it, evaluate the present and build on it, imagine the future and create it. In doing this, there are general principles to guide—be real, be honest, listen to feelings, take time, put first things first, and involve the people.

When Should a Vision Be Formed? The power of vision can be tapped when people first come together to form a group or an organization, and it can be developed at later stages when there is need for self-evaluation, renewal, and growth.

Where Should a Vision Be Created? An atmosphere conducive to open communication is important so that all ideas can be expressed and considered in the creation of a shared vision.

An example of a company that is striving to create a vision and experience community is Kentucky Power, a fully owned subsidiary of American Electric Power. In reading the Company Mission and Goals, Management Plan, and Quality Handbook, one senses just the right blend between rationality, logic, and coherence on the one hand, along with leadership, service, and values on the other. The result is reminiscent of Robert Pirsig's philosophical work, *Zen and the Art of Motorcycle Maintenance*, a marriage of eastern world emotion and feeling with western world logic and reason.[40]

In the spirit of fifth century Greece and the Age of Pericles, this modern-day company is working to develop a culture based on customer service, participative leadership, member empowerment, and a "we care" attitude. Manager of education Michael Campbell explains, "Our vision is the guiding force in all of our endeavors. Over three thousand years ago, it was written, 'where there is no vision, the people perish.' This is true in the workplace as well. It is through a shared vision of what we can and should be that our company *community* will blossom and we will endure."

THE IMPORTANCE OF LEADERSHIP IN THE VISIONING PROCESS

The most important function of a leader is to develop a clear and compelling vision for the community and to secure commitment to that vision. Consider the words of Henry Ford as he communicated his vision to make a car for the masses:

> We will build a motor car for the great multitude. It will be so low in price that no man making a good wage will be unable to own one—and enjoy with his family the blessing of hours of pleasure in God's great open spaces.[41]

In addition to vision, the successful leader must have competence and intensity and stamina to see it through. As CEO at Johnson & Johnson, James Burke estimated that he spent 40 percent of his time communicating the company's credo, its core values and beliefs.[42]

Some leaders protest that vision and community are too abstract—too metaphysical—and are of little consequence compared with the importance of achieving results and hitting the bottom line. Others point out that it is only through *vision* and *community* that the bottom line is known and that meaningful results can be achieved.

Representing the second camp, Peter Drucker writes, "The leaders of a community must believe deeply in its purpose and task, and be committed to its welfare and future. If they do not, the community will lose faith in itself, self-confidence, pride, and the ability to perform."[43]

In his wonderful book *Leadership is an Art*, Max DePree describes the role of the leader and the importance of having a vision:

> The first responsibility of a leader is to define what can be. The last is to say thank you. In between the two, the leader must become a servant and a debtor. This, to me, is the role of the leader.
>
> Momentum comes from having a clear vision of what the organization ought to be, from a well-thought-out strategy to achieve that vision, and from carefully conceived and communicated directions and plans that let everyone participate and be accountable in achieving these plans.[44]

There is a clear connection between leadership and vision. Each is necessary for a community to realize its full potential and become all that it can be.

REFERENCES

1. John W. Gardner, "Building Community,"—prepared for the Leadership Studies Program of Independent Sector, (Washington, DC: American Institutes for Research, 1991).

2. Martin E. P. Seligman, *Learned Optimism* (New York: Knopf, 1991).

3. Robert Rosenthal and Lenore Jacobson, *Pygmalion in the Classroom* (New York: Holt, Rinehart and Winston, 1968); and George Bernard Shaw, "My Fair Lady."

4. Julian Huxley in Raymond F. Gale, *Developmental Behavior* (New York: Macmillan, 1969), 79.

5. Peter M. Senge, *The Fifth Discipline* (New York: Doubleday, 1990).

6. Joel Barker, *Future Edge: Discovering the New Paradigms of Success* (New York: Morrow, 1992); and Joel Barker, "The Power of Vision" and "The Business of Paradigms" videos from "Discovering the Future" series from ChartHouse Learning Corp.

7. Fred Polak, *The Image of the Future*, trans. from the Dutch and abridged by Elise Boulding (Amsterdam: Elsevier Scientific Publishing, 1973); and Barker, "The Power of Vision."

8. Benjamin Singer, *The Future Focused Role Image* in *Learning for Tomorrow*, Alvin Toffler, ed. (New York: Random House, 1974); Barker, *Future Edge*; and Barker, "The Power of Vision."

9. Marian Wright Edleman, *The Measure of Our Success: A Letter to My Children and Yours* (Boston: Beacon Press, 1992).

10. Viktor Frankl, *Man's Search for Meaning* (New York: Pocket Books, 1985).

11. Frankl, *Man's Search for Meaning*.

12. "Viktor Frankl and The Search for Meaning," *Notable Contributors to the Psychology of Personality Series*. The University of Pennsylvania Audio-Visual Department, 1986.

13. Excerpted from Martin Luther King, Jr's. speech at the Lincoln Memorial, Washington, D.C., August 28, 1963.

14. Barker, *Future Edge*; and Barker, "Discovering the Future: The Power of Vision."

15. Charles A. Garfield, *Peak Performers: The New Heroes of American Business* (New York: Morrow, 1986).

16. Barker, *Future Edge*; and Barker, "Discovering the Future: The Power of Vision."

17. Barker, *Future Edge*; and Barker, "Discovering the Future: The Power of Vision."

18. Barker, *Future Edge*; and Barker, "Discovering the Future: The Power of Vision."

19. Duane Schultz, *Theories of Personality*, 2nd ed., (Monterey, CA: Brooks/Cole, 1981).

20. Loren Eiseley, "The Star Thrower," *The Unexpected Universe* (New York: Harcourt, Brace and World, 1969), 67–92; and Barker, "Discovering the Future: The Power of Vision,"—video.

21. Eric Fromm, *Man for Himself* (New York: Holt, Rinehart and Winston, 1941).

22. Barker, "Discovering the Future: The Power of Vision."

23. Jane Firth, "A Proactive Approach to Conflict Resolution," *Supervisory Management*, 36 (November 1991): 3–4.

24. Adapted from Peter Drucker, "The New Society of Organizations," *Harvard Business Review* (September/October, 1992): 95–104.

25. Chris Lee, "The Vision Thing," *Training* (February 1993): 27.

26. Lee, "The Vision Thing."

27. General Johnson, *Johnson & Johnson Mission Statement*, 1945.

28. William Stavropolus, Marion Merrell Dow Chemical Co., 1993.

29. Stephen R. Covey and Keith Gulledge, "Principled Centered Leadership" *Journal for Quality and Participation* (July/August 1992): 70–78.

30. Covey and Gulledge, "Principled Centered Leadership."

31. Based on the work of Kurt Lewin, Gordon Lippitt, Marvin R. Weisbord, Brendan Reddy, Angela Woodward, and others.

32. Weisbord, *Productive Workplaces*, 284–292.

33. Angela Woodward, "Leadership Kentucky," 1993.

34. Brendan Reddy, Institute for Organizational Development, University of Cincinnati.

35. From the authors' files, Marion Merrell Dow Company.

36. From the authors' files, Hamilton County (OH) Commissioners.

37. From the authors' files, Monnig, Elicker, Creevy, Schwartz, and Frey, Urology Associates.

38. From the authors' files, Kentucky Power Company.

39. Margaret Wheatley, "Leadership and the New Science: Learning About Organizations from an Orderly Universe," *Management Journal* (November 1992).

40. Robert Pirsig, *Zen and the Art of Motorcycle Maintenance* (New York: Morrow, 1974).

41. James C. Collins and William C. Lazier, *Beyond Entrepreneurship* (Englewood Cliffs, NJ: Prentice-Hall, 1992), 4.

42. Collins and Lazier, *Beyond Entrepreneurship*, 91.

43. Drucker, "The New Society of Organizations," 103.

44. Max DePree, *Leadership is an Art* (New York: Doubleday, 1989).

Appendix

TABLE 1–3   Yesterday—Individual, Community, and Societal Influences

Pre-1970 Forces and Impactors—People and Events		
Individual	Company/Organization/ Community	Industry/Profession/ Society
_____	_____	_____
_____	_____	_____
_____	_____	_____
_____	_____	_____
_____	_____	_____
_____	_____	_____
_____	_____	_____
_____	_____	_____
_____	_____	_____
_____	_____	_____

1970s Forces and Impactors—People and Events		
Individual	Company/Organization/ Community	Industry/Profession/ Society
_____	_____	_____
_____	_____	_____
_____	_____	_____
_____	_____	_____
_____	_____	_____
_____	_____	_____
_____	_____	_____
_____	_____	_____
_____	_____	_____
_____	_____	_____

TABLE 1–3   Yesterday—Individual, Community, and Societal Influences (continued)

1980s Forces and Impactors—People and Events		
Individual	Company/Organization/ Community	Industry/Profession/ Society
_____	_____	_____
_____	_____	_____
_____	_____	_____
_____	_____	_____
_____	_____	_____
_____	_____	_____
_____	_____	_____
_____	_____	_____
_____	_____	_____
_____	_____	_____

1990 to Present Forces and Impactors—People and Events		
Individual	Company/Organization/ Community	Industry/Profession/ Society
_____	_____	_____
_____	_____	_____
_____	_____	_____
_____	_____	_____
_____	_____	_____
_____	_____	_____
_____	_____	_____
_____	_____	_____
_____	_____	_____
_____	_____	_____

TABLE 1–4   Prouds and Sorries

Today Community/Company/Organization		
Organizational Elements	Prouds	Sorries
People	_____	_____
	_____	_____
	_____	_____
	_____	_____
Products	_____	_____
	_____	_____
	_____	_____
	_____	_____
Policies	_____	_____
	_____	_____
	_____	_____
	_____	_____
Processes	_____	_____
	_____	_____
	_____	_____
	_____	_____
Practices	_____	_____
	_____	_____
	_____	_____
	_____	_____
etc.	_____	_____
	_____	_____
	_____	_____
	_____	_____

TABLE 1–5   Planning Guide

> A vision without a task is a dream,
> A task without a vision is a drudgery,
> A vision with a task is the hope of the world.
>
> Church window in Sussex, England, c. 1730

Central Purpose or Mission
(Reason for Existence)

_____

_____

_____

_____

_____

_____

_____

_____

_____

_____

_____

_____

_____

_____

_____

_____

_____

_____

A vision is: — Leader initiated
                    — Shared and supported by members
                    — Comprehensive and detailed
                    — Positive and inspiring

— Vision —

1

TABLE 1–5   Planning Guide (continued)

Broad Goals to Achieve the Mission (Enduring Intentions to Act)
1. _____
2. _____
3. _____
4. _____
5. _____
— Vision —
2

TABLE 1–5   Planning Guide (continued)

Core Values (To Measure the Rightness and Wrongness of Policies and Actions)
• _____ _____ _____ _____ _____ _____ _____ _____ _____ _____ • _____ _____ _____ _____ _____ _____ _____ _____ _____ _____ • _____ _____ _____ _____ _____ _____ _____ _____ _____   — Vision — 3

TABLE 1–5   Planning Guide (continued)

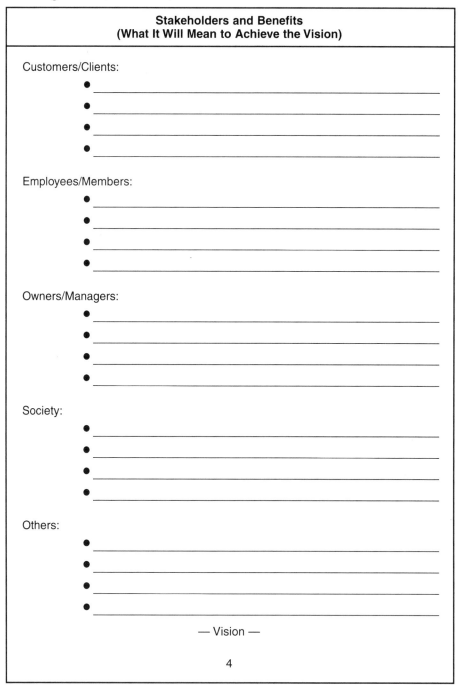

Stakeholders and Benefits **(What It Will Mean to Achieve the Vision)**
Customers/Clients: ● _____ ● _____ ● _____ ● _____
Employees/Members: ● _____ ● _____ ● _____ ● _____
Owners/Managers: ● _____ ● _____ ● _____ ● _____
Society: ● _____ ● _____ ● _____ ● _____
Others: ● _____ ● _____ ● _____ ● _____
— Vision —
4

TABLE 1–5   Planning Guide (continued)

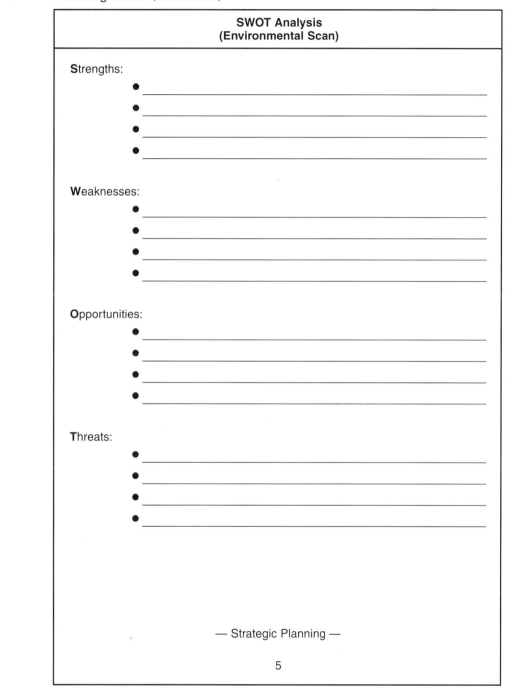

**SWOT Analysis
(Environmental Scan)**

Strengths:

- _____
- _____
- _____
- _____

Weaknesses:

- _____
- _____
- _____
- _____

Opportunities:

- _____
- _____
- _____
- _____

Threats:

- _____
- _____
- _____
- _____

— Strategic Planning —

5

TABLE 1–5   Planning Guide (continued)

Strategic Initiatives
(**S**trategic, **M**easurable, **A**ction-Oriented, **R**ealistic, **T**imely Objectives)

Short-term

- _____

- _____

- _____

- _____

Intermediate

- _____

- _____

- _____

Long-term

- _____

- _____

- _____

- _____

— Strategic Planning —

6

TABLE 1–5   Planning Guide (continued)

Players	
Adversaries	Allies
• _____	• _____
• _____	• _____
• _____	• _____
• _____	• _____
• _____	• _____
• _____	• _____
• _____	• _____
• _____	• _____
• _____	• _____
• _____	• _____
• _____	• _____
• _____	• _____

— Strategic Planning —

7

TABLE 1–5   Planning Guide (continued)

Specific Assignments (Projects and Activities)		
Individual or Unit A	Current	New
_____	_____	_____
_____	_____	_____
_____	_____	_____
Individual or Unit B	Current	New
_____	_____	_____
_____	_____	_____
_____	_____	_____
Individual or Unit C	Current	New
_____	_____	_____
_____	_____	_____
_____	_____	_____
Individual or Unit D	Current	New
_____	_____	_____
_____	_____	_____
_____	_____	_____
Individual or Unit E	Current	New
_____	_____	_____
_____	_____	_____
_____	_____	_____
Individual or Unit F	Current	New
_____	_____	_____
_____	_____	_____
_____	_____	_____

— Tactical Planning —

8

Character and Community

Always do what is right. It will please most of the people, and it will astound the rest.

Mark Twain

T o require that a community agree on everything would be unrealistic and would reduce the richness that comes from diversity. But a community must agree on something. There has to be a core of shared values. Of all the ingredients of community, this is the most important.[1]

Values define the character of a community. What people say is important, what they do is more important, but what they value is most important. These are the layers of identity and character formation for individuals and groups. In its highest form, character is based on a value system that is known, cherished, stated, lived, and lived habitually.

This chapter discusses the importance of character in defining an individual life and a community of people. Topics include:

- the role of character in building community;

- traditional and contemporary definitions of good; and

- the importance of courage.

CHARACTER AND HUMANKIND

Character is concerned with moral judgments and right and wrong conduct. Some human judgments are factual (the earth is round), others are aesthetic (she is beautiful), and still others deal with character (one should be honest and should not steal). Character is a concern unique to humankind. People are the only creatures who combine emotion (feelings) with knowledge (information) and through abstract reasoning (thought) produce a moral conscience, or a sense of what should be.

Some ideas about right and wrong are of prehuman origin. Indeed, such social virtues as self-sacrifice, sympathy, and cooperation can be seen among many other species, such as elephants, porpoises, and lions. However, more than forty-thousand years ago, the human race developed into beings who could distinguish between what is and what ought to be, and it is this attribute that separates people from all other animals.[2]

English essayist William Hazlitt writes, "Man is the only animal that laughs and weeps; for he is the only animal struck by the difference between how things are and how they might have been."[3] In *The Origin of Species*, biologist and social philosopher Charles Darwin concludes of character and humankind:

> Of all the differences between man and the lower animals, the moral sense of conscience is by far the most important . . . it is summed up by that short but impervious word, *ought*, so full of high significance. It is the most noble of all attributes of man, leading him without a moment's hesitation to risk his life for the life of a fellow creature, or after due deliberation, impelled simply by the deep feeling of right or duty, to sacrifice it for some great cause.[4]

The Greek philosopher Aristotle believed that the highest good or purpose of life is happiness, but to be happy requires the development of character in community (the *polis* or city-state). Such character consists of wisdom, understanding, and knowledge, as well as justice, courage, moderation, and prudence. More than health, wealth, or luck, virtuous character leads to happiness in the long run.

CHARACTER IN THE WORKPLACE

John Gardner writes that communities are the ground-level generators and preservers of character. Further, character is not established by edict from kings and parliaments. Rather, it is developed chiefly in the family, school, church, and other intimate settings in which people deal with one another face to face. Important among these settings is the workplace.[5]

History has witnessed many examples of people who were profoundly concerned with the character of their professions and work communities. Hippocrates, the Greek physician known as the father of medicine, who lived during the fifth and fourth centuries B.C., laid down one of the first professional codes of conduct, the Hippocratic Oath, which embodies the ideals of the medical profession even today. Similarly, stonecutters and masons established codes and standards for their trades before the time of Christ.

In 1727 Benjamin Franklin formed the Junto, a forerunner of modern-day civic clubs. It was dominated by businessmen having goals of community fellowship and service. Character was a significant concern of that organization.[6] Franklin's own character ideals included temperance, order, resoluteness, industry, sincerity, justice, moderation, cleanliness, and humility. Clearly these are poles apart from current day words and expressions like "one-upmanship," "looking out for number one," and "assertiveness" that have captured considerable public following.[7]

Franklin believed strongly in the importance of habits for character formation. He believed the path to individual and community development centered on the formation of good habits. This idea is reflected in the philosopher William James's famous saying, "Sow an action and reap a habit; sow a habit and reap a character; sow a character and reap a destiny."[8]

THE ROLE OF VALUES IN DEFINING CHARACTER

Management author Peter Drucker states, "Each organization has a value system that is influenced by its task. In every hospital in the world, health is the ultimate good. In every school in the world, learning is the ultimate good. In every business in the world, production of goods and services that please the customer is the ultimate good. For an organization to perform at its highest level, its members must believe that what it is doing is, in the last analysis, an important contribution to people and society, one which is needed or adds some value."[9]

Some organizations view values as a fundamental requirement for success. James Burke, former chairman of Johnson & Johnson, states that J & J's *credo*, first articulated in 1945, was responsible for the company's rapid action in taking Tylenol off the market after poisoning incidents in which seven people died. To support the importance of values, he cites a study of the financial performance of U.S. companies that have had written value statements for at least a generation. The net income of those companies increased by a factor of 23 during a period when the gross national product grew by a factor of 2.5.[10]

For many organizations, values are a social glue. Global enterprises requiring long distance management may use values to provide structure and stability for people of diverse backgrounds in far-flung locations. Jack Welch, CEO of General Electric, sees "management values" as a primary source of corporate identity, adding to a sense of cohesion among GE's highly diverse business units. Also, values can provide guidance for members who function as independent decision makers—for example, the factory team with the power to stop production if a *core principle* is violated.[11]

In *A Business and Its Beliefs: The Ideas that Helped Build IBM*, Thomas Watson, Jr., explains the importance of corporate values: 1) In order to survive and achieve success, an organization must have a sound set of values on which it premises all policies and actions; 2) the single most important factor in corporate success is leaders' faithful adherence to these values; and 3) if an organization is to meet the challenges of a changing world, it must be prepared to change everything about itself except its core values.

Watson goes on to say that when IBM has been successful, it has been true to its three core values—*respect for the individual*, *giving the best customer service possible*, and *performing every job with excellence*. And when IBM has gone astray at different times in its history, it is because it lost sight of—or deviated from—these three basic business beliefs.

It should be noted that value statements can mask hypocrisy. If a company espouses "quality" in its written vision or promotional literature, but sacrifices it for short-term profits, cynicism will prevail among customers and employees. To be meaningful, values must enter into the daily practices of the community. Values must reflect enduring commitments, not vague notions and empty platitudes. Thus, leaders who seek to manage through values must examine their own value systems, and put good intentions into concrete actions that others can witness.

A community can have an abundance of values but lack clarity and reinforcement of those that are the most important. There may be a lack of agreement on core values that all members will live by and thus will define the character and strength of the community. Author Leon Wieseltier writes, "The contemporary problem in American society is not that people believe in too little, it is that they believe in too much. Too much of what too many people believe is too easily acquired and too thoughtlessly held." Wieseltier believes Americans are choking on identities. Not the lack of meaning, but the glibness of meaning is the trouble.[12]

How can an organization know if it needs to clarify or reinforce its values? What are the signs of a culture or community in trouble? Red flags are:

- Members lack clear understanding about how they should behave as they attempt to meet organizational goals;

- Different individuals and groups have fundamentally different value systems;

- Top leaders send mixed messages about what is important;

- Day-to-day life is disorganized with people doing their own things for their own reasons, the left hand and the right hand often working at cross-purposes;

- Like the person who has ears, but hears not, the organization has values, but does not practice them.

VALUES CLARIFICATION

Every individual and community should have a code of conduct or value system that serves as a compass to guide and judge behavior. By having such a code, the question can be asked of any act, "Is it right and to what extent?"

People will forgive the individual who fails to manage by objectives, or is inefficient in the use of time, or fails to have smooth human relations, but they will not forgive the person who does not live by values. Such a person lacks character and will not be trusted or respected.

Concern over ethical questions is a mark of maturity and strong leadership. Because of the ability to influence moral behavior, leaders especially should address two questions: (1) What values do I want to promote? (2) Are my actions helping to accomplish this?

The following group exercise can be used as a prelude for clarifying core individual and community values.[13]

APPLICATION: VALUES AUCTION

Introduction

We are not born with values, but we are born into cultures and societies that promote, teach, and impart their values to us. The process of acquiring values begins at birth. But it is not a static process. Our values change continually throughout our

lives. For example, as children, our highest value might have been play; as adoles-
cents, perhaps it was peer relationships; as young adults, our highest value may be
raising children or the work we do. For many older people, service to others is the
highest value. We are formed largely by the experiences we have, and our values
form, grow, and change accordingly.

Maury Smith

Because values are important in an individual's personal, social, and occupational affairs, it is important to understand basic value patterns. The purpose
of this exercise is to:

- determine those life values that are of greatest importance to you;

- explore the degree of trust you have in the group;

- examine how well you compete and cooperate; and

- invite consideration of how your values affect your decisions concerning
  personal and professional life goals.

Auction Rules

During this values auction, you will have the opportunity to buy, and thus
own, any of the values listed—if your bid is highest. Owning a value means
you have full rights and privileges to do with the value whatever you choose
at the conclusion of the exercise. Keep in mind the following rules:

1. Gather in a group for the purpose of having an auction for the twenty values listed on the Values Auction Sheet.

2. Choose one person to be the auctioneer.

3. Each person should receive ten tokens valued at $100 each to be used for bid-
   ding. Only these tokens will be accepted as payment for any value purchased.

4. You may elect to pool your resources with other group members in order
   to purchase a particularly high-priced value. This means that two, three,
   four, or more people may extend a bid for any one value. You are allowed
   to participate, and win, in such a pool *one time only*. If you pool, but lose,
   you are allowed to pool again.

5. The auctioneer's task is to collect the highest number of tokens possible in
   the course of the auction. After the auction has begun, no further questions
   will be answered by the auctioneer.

6. Allow five to ten minutes for participants to budget desired amounts for
   preferred values. Notice that these amounts may change during the course
   of the auction. Use the values auction sheet to record budgeted amounts
   and to keep a record of winning bids.

7. Begin the auction.

Values Auction Sheet

	Amount I Budgeted	Highest Amount I Bid	Top Bid
1. All the food and drink you want without ever getting fat	_____	_____	_____
2. Freedom to be and do what you want in life	_____	_____	_____
3. A chance to direct the destiny of a nation	_____	_____	_____
4. The love and admiration of good friends	_____	_____	_____
5. Travel and tickets to any cultural or athletic event as often as you wish	_____	_____	_____
6. Complete self-confidence with a positive outlook on life	_____	_____	_____
7. A happy, healthy family	_____	_____	_____
8. Recognition as the most desirable person in the world	_____	_____	_____
9. A long life free of illness	_____	_____	_____
10. A complete library with all the time you need to enjoy it	_____	_____	_____
11. A deep and satisfying religious faith	_____	_____	_____
12. A lifetime of financial security and material wealth	_____	_____	_____
13. A lovely home in a beautiful setting	_____	_____	_____
14. A world without prejudice and cruelty	_____	_____	_____
15. A world without sickness and poverty	_____	_____	_____
16. International fame and renown for your achievements	_____	_____	_____

	Amount I Budgeted	Highest Amount I Bid	Top Bid
17. An understanding of the meaning of life	_____	_____	_____
18. As much sexual pleasure as you want with anyone, anytime— without getting sick	_____	_____	_____
19. The highest success in your chosen profession	_____	_____	_____
20. A deep and satisfying love with someone	_____	_____	_____

Discussion

At the conclusion of the values auction, consider the following questions:

a. What values did you win that are truly important to you? What values did you miss?

b. How competitive and cooperative were you during the values auction? Does this suggest a need to be more aggressive if you are going to achieve what is important to you? Does this indicate a need to be more cooperative and open to strategic alliances?

c. Are you living your life in line with your values? Do your work, community, and personal life support your value system?

After completing the values auction, people should discuss and agree upon core values for the community, usually three. These values should be the stars that guide members of the community in all moral dilemmas. They should be the "hills worth dying on," or the principles worth losing one's position or community membership to uphold.

Core values are more important than any other factor in defining the character of individuals and groups. Norms of behavior and questions of style are important, but these cannot approximate the high level of influence of core values.

The question may be asked, "Why *three* core values? Why not more?" The answer is that people rarely remember more than three things in a crisis or under stress. The Ten Commandments or a procedures manual may be important, but three core values will be *remembered* by the members of the community.

Also, the questions may be asked, "What if people have countervailing values? What if two parties are committed to different value systems?" One imagines the pope and the ayatollah; or one imagines a husband and wife, each acting habitually according to strongly held but different values. Here, people may have to agree to disagree and walk separate paths.

FIGURE 2–1   Core Values Are Points of Common Interest

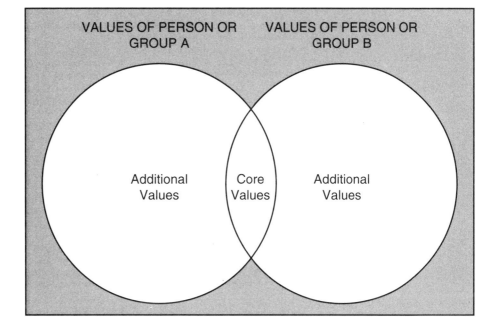

Disputes can often be avoided if people will discuss their value systems and find points of common interest and agreement. This is pictured in figure 2–1.

Through discussion, shared values can become emphasized that define the basic character of the group, tribe, or family. For example, shared values may represent the Catholic church, the Cherokee tribe, the Smith family, or a particular business organization. Additional individual values at the fourth, fifth, and sixth levels can serve to enrich a community, especially if there is tolerance and appreciation of diversity.

A healthy community is comprised of individuals who feel free to express their differences and who have learned, through communication and cooperation, to develop and sustain shared values, while at the same time maintaining respect for others.[14]

MOST-MENTIONED VALUES

In building community, certain values are mentioned most often:

■ *Honesty* in all dealings . . . as a foundation for all other values.

■ *Respect for others* . . . as shown by consideration for their beliefs and needs.

- *Service to others* . . . guided by the principle of doing for others as you would have them do for you.

- *Integrity* . . . courage to act and live by convictions.

In *The Spirit of Community*, Amitai Etzioni explains the importance of character in the formation of community, and the role of values in defining a community's character. His prescription for a healthy balance between *individual rights* and *social responsibility* strikes a chord of reason.

> When the term *community* is used, the notion that typically comes to mind is a place in which people know and care for one another—the kind of place in which people do not merely ask "How are you?" as a formality, but care about the answer. This we-ness is indeed part of its essence. Our focus also must be on another element of community: *Communities must speak in moral voices. They must lay claims on their members.* Indeed, they are the most important sustaining source of moral behavior, other than the inner self.
>
> Our society is suffering from deficient we-ness and the values only communities can uphold. What is needed are shared core values, especially commitment to democracy, the Bill of Rights, and mutual respect among subgroups. Constituent communities can follow their own subsets of values without endangering the body society, as long as they accept these shared values. They provide the frame of unity to contain the "plurals" from falling out.[15]

In *Managing Workforce 2000*, David Jamieson and Julie O'Mara identify values that are important in the contemporary American workplace. Nine values stand out:

1. *Recognition for competence and accomplishments.* People want to be recognized, both as individuals and teams, for their skills and accomplishments. They want to know that their contributions are appreciated.

2. *Respect and dignity.* This value focuses on how people are treated—through the jobs they hold, in response to their ideas, or by virtue of their background. The strong support for this value indicates that people want to be respected for who they are.

3. *Personal choice and freedom.* People want to be as free as possible from constraints and decisions made for and about them. They want to be autonomous and able to rely on their own judgment. They want personal choice in what affects their lives.

4. *Involvement at work.* Members of the workforce want to be kept informed and involved in important decisions at work, particularly as these decisions affect their quality of work and quality of work life.

5. *Pride in one's work.* People want to do a good job and feel a sense of accomplishment. Fulfillment and pride come through quality workmanship.

6. *Quality of lifestyle.* People pursue many different lifestyles and each person wants his or hers to be of high quality. Work policies and practices have great impact on lifestyle pursuits. The desire for time with family and time for leisure are strongly emphasized.

7. *Financial security.* People want security from economic cycles and devastating financial situations. This appears to be a new variation on the desire for money—not continual pursuit of money, but enough to feel secure in today's world, enjoy a comfortable lifestyle, and ride out bad times.

8. *Self-development.* The focus here is on the desire to continually improve, to do more with one's life, to reach one's potential, to learn and grow. There is a strong desire by individuals to have opportunities for self-improvement.

9. *Health and wellness.* This value reflects a maturing work force and increased information on wellness. People want to organize life and work in ways that are healthy and contribute to long-term wellness.[16]

VALUES COMPATIBILITY

The following exercise allows you to compare your values with those of another person. It is particularly helpful in developing understanding and appreciation between individuals and groups.[17]

APPLICATION: DO WE THINK ALIKE?

Directions

The personal matrix on page 49, and the partner matrix on page 50, evaluate twenty-one values, one against another. You will be comparing the numbered values down the left side with the lettered values across the top. Start with the top row on the far left (Row 1) and move across the page from left to right, placing an X under each lettered column in which the value in the numbered row is currently more important to you than the one in the lettered column. For example, if aesthetic values are more important than achievement, place an X in the box where Row 1 and Column B intersect; if achievement is more important, leave that box blank. Also leave the box blank if the value named in the row matches the value named in the column (for example, "power" and "power," "love" and "love," and so on). Read the "Value Descriptions" section that follows, and then complete this process for each of the twenty-one rows. Note that each person should complete the matrix independently.

Value Descriptions[18]

Aesthetic Values pertaining to the appreciation of beauty and the beautiful.

Achievement gains accomplished or fulfilled by work or effort.

Helpfulness the desire to aid another; making it easier for a person to do something.

Human Relationships the state of being mutually interested or involved with other people.

Independence a state of freedom; not relying on someone else; not easily influenced.

Leadership the ability to guide or direct an operation, activity, or performance in a specified manner or direction; to guide or direct others.

Leisure freedom from work or duties; relaxation; free time to do what one chooses to do.

Love strong affection; feelings of passion, devotion, or tenderness for another.

Material Wealth large amount of possessions or resources having economic value.

Naturalness having to do with nature, innocence, and basic simplicity.

Order the desire for every part or unit to be in its right place in a normal or efficient state.

Physical Health a state of physical well-being and freedom from illness; functioning well.

Physical Pleasure a state of physical gratification; bodily enjoyment or satisfaction.

Power the ability to act or produce an effect; to have control or authority over others.

Privacy the quality or state of being content when alone; enjoying seclusion.

Recognition gaining special notice or attention; receiving social respect, honor, or reward.

Religious Faith beliefs related to divinity and spiritual experience.

Responsibility the ability to answer for one's acts or decisions; the ability to fulfill one's obligations; meeting one's duties.

Security   freedom from worry, especially in matters dealing with physical and economic needs.

Self-expression   the ability to make known, show, or state one's personal feelings, ideas, or beliefs.

Truth   honesty; the real state of things; actuality; the quality of being in accordance with facts.

TABLE 2–1   Personal Matrix

Personal Matrix	A. Aesthetic Values	B. Achievement	C. Helpfulness	D. Human Relationships	E. Independence	F. Leadership	G. Leisure	H. Love	I. Material Wealth	J. Naturalness	K. Order	L. Physical Health	M. Physical Pleasure	N. Power	O. Privacy	P. Recognition	Q. Religious Faith	R. Responsibility	S. Security	T. Self-expression	U. Truth
1. Aesthetic Values																					
2. Achievement																					
3. Helpfulness																					
4. Human Relationships																					
5. Independence																					
6. Leadership																					
7. Leisure																					
8. Love																					
9. Material Wealth																					
10. Naturalness																					
11. Order																					
12. Physical Health																					
13. Physical Pleasure																					
14. Power																					
15. Privacy																					
16. Recognition																					
17. Religious Faith																					
18. Responsibility																					
19. Security																					
20. Self-expression																					
21. Truth																					

TABLE 2–2   Partner Matrix

Partner Matrix	Aesthetic Values	Achievement	Helpfulness	Human Relationships	Independence	Leadership	Leisure	Love	Material Wealth	Naturalness	Order	Physical Health	Physical Pleasure	Power	Privacy	Recognition	Religious Faith	Responsibility	Security	Self-expression	Truth
	A.	B.	C.	D.	E.	F.	G.	H.	I.	J.	K.	L.	M.	N.	O.	P.	Q.	R.	S.	T.	U.
1. Aesthetic Values																					
2. Achievement																					
3. Helpfulness																					
4. Human Relationships																					
5. Independence																					
6. Leadership																					
7. Leisure																					
8. Love																					
9. Material Wealth																					
10. Naturalness																					
11. Order																					
12. Physical Health																					
13. Physical Pleasure																					
14. Power																					
15. Privacy																					
16. Recognition																					
17. Religious Faith																					
18. Responsibility																					
19. Security																					
20. Self-expression																					
21. Truth																					

Scoring

The numbered rows with the most Xs represent the values that are most important to you. In the following blank spaces, list these values, highest to lowest, for yourself and your partner.

VALUES IN ORDER OF IMPORTANCE TO YOU

High-Order Values	Middle-Order Values	Low-Order Values
1. _____	8. _____	15. _____
2. _____	9. _____	16. _____
3. _____	10. _____	17. _____
4. _____	11. _____	18. _____
5. _____	12. _____	19. _____
6. _____	13. _____	20. _____
7. _____	14. _____	21. _____

VALUES IN ORDER OF IMPORTANCE TO PARTNER

High-Order Values	Middle-Order Values	Low-Order Values
1. _____	8. _____	15. _____
2. _____	9. _____	16. _____
3. _____	10. _____	17. _____
4. _____	11. _____	18. _____
5. _____	12. _____	19. _____
6. _____	13. _____	20. _____
7. _____	14. _____	21. _____

Determine the values compatibility between you and your partner according to the following formula.

a. Count the number of high-order values you share (the exact ranking of the values may differ) and multiply this number by 3.

Total _____

b. Count the number of middle-order values you share (the exact ranking of the values may differ) and multiply this number by 2.

Total _____

FIGURE 2–2   Values Compatibility Index

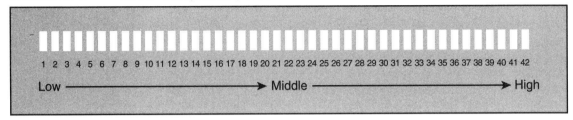

c. Count the number of low-order values you share (the exact ranking of values may differ) and multiply this number by 1.

Total _____

d. Add the three totals (a, b, and c), then indicate your compatibility level on the above index, figure 2–2.

e. The higher the score on the index (0–42), the greater the level of values compatibility between you and your partner, and the less conflict you would be expected to experience.

Discussion

Compare the order in which you and your partner have placed the values and discuss the level of your compatibility index. Discuss how differences and similarities affect the relationship. Consider whether each person allows the full expression of the values most important to the other, and how points of agreement can be used to improve the relationship. Be tolerant in this discussion.

Remember, this matrix does not measure other important factors of compatibility, such as personal interests, individual temperament, and levels of morality. Remember also that different people may have different meanings for the words on the matrix. One person may define responsibility one way, and another may interpret the word differently. Finally, remember that the matrix does not measure negative values, and that differing positive values may in fact enrich a relationship and a community of people.

When people honor their differences, they tend to build their effectiveness as a team and cancel out deficiencies as individuals. One person may be a saver, storing for a rainy day, while another may prefer to heighten the here-and-now enjoyment of life. Why not give expression to both values?

Through communication and cooperation, different values can help all parties find optimum balance and wisdom. With this is mind, use the following thought as a guide: "Our errors and our controversies in the sphere of human relations often arise from looking on people as though they are altogether bad, or altogether good, when neither state is fully possible."[19]

TRADITIONAL AND CONTEMPORARY DEFINITIONS OF GOOD

The English philosopher Alfred North Whitehead wrote, "We are in the world, not the world in us."[20] He explains that while a concern for right and wrong may be universal to all people, what is considered right and wrong in human relationships depends on the universe and a person's place in it. We are evolving creatures in an evolving world, and human ethics are changing as well.

In the history of Western civilization, what ought to be has had different meaning in different times and circumstances. Generally, the cultures of the Western world condemn such practices as slavery, witchcraft, and dueling today, even though these were once considered to be acceptable.

There have been many definitions of the ethical person in Western culture. *Good* and *right* have been defined in terms of power, personal integrity, natural simplicity, will of God, pleasure, greatest good for the greatest number, and duty and right action. As you read the following, evaluate your own ideas on these central concepts of good.

Power

If life is a struggle for survival and human beings are fundamentally selfish and greedy, then the best individuals are those who adapt to these market forces and become masters of manipulative relations. So believed Niccolo Machiavelli (1469–1527), an Italian diplomat and political writer. Machiavelli argued for winning and retaining power in a world containing extensive political factionalism and lust for dominion. He maintained that flattery, deceit, and even murder may be necessary if a person is to win and retain power. He stated that a person should never cultivate private virtues that in public life can prove politically suicidal; instead, one should develop vices if these will help perpetuate one's rule. Machiavelli believed that ends justify means and taught that might makes right.[21]

Personal Integrity

The German philosopher Friedrich Nietzsche (1844–1900) believed that human resoluteness, born of independent judgment, was the highest good. Nietzsche was a champion of individualism and encouraged the individual to be independent in thought and strong in conviction, even in the face of group pressure and government authority. Nietzsche believed that nature is filled with conflict spilling over into society, and the best human beings are those who exhibit moral virtue—wisdom, justice, courage, and other ideals—regardless of personal loss or gain.[22]

In this vein, Martin Heidegger (1889–1976), the German existential philosopher, pointed to the Greek ideal of nobility and taught the importance of freely and resolutely adhering to personal principles rather than succumbing to social pressures to conform. Personal integrity, he believed, is inherently good regardless of the results. Practicing personal integrity, though, means that one may not comfortably coexist with everyone, so it is incumbent on each person to choose individual lifestyle and commitments carefully.[23]

Natural Simplicity

In the eighteenth century, the Frenchman Jean-Jacques Rousseau (1712–1778) wrote that nature in essence is good, and because humanity is part of nature, human beings too are naturally good. It follows that to achieve the highest good, one must strive to be most purely natural. Rousseau also held that corruption comes only with civilization, and that children should be raised in a state of simplicity.[24] Writer-philosopher Henry David Thoreau (1817–1862) wrote in a spirit of naturalness and simplicity in *Walden*, "Every morning was a cheerful invitation to make my life of equal simplicity, and I may say innocence, with Nature herself."[25] In this same spirit, many people today resist technological changes, complex lifestyles, and artificial creations.

The French writer Vauvenargues summarizes the importance of naturalness: "Naturalness gets a better hearing than accuracy. It speaks the language of feeling, which is better than that of logic and rationality, because it is beautiful and appeals to everyone."[26]

Will of God

Religious leaders announce visions and make moral judgments, drawing on the authority of a supreme being (or many gods). Saying, "It is the will of Allah," the prophet Muhammad (about 570–632) decreed the "five pillars" of Islamic faith: (1) the repetition of the belief, "There is no God but Allah, and Muhammad is the prophet of Allah," (2) prayer five times daily, (3) the thirty-day fast of Ramadan, (4) alms-giving, and (5) pilgrimage to Mecca. These religious and moral tenets are held most sacred by over 723 million Muslims today. Similarly, nearly three billion adherents of many other religions define the ethical good as the "will of God."[27]

No other body of thought has been embraced by so many people, nor has any been so influential in history, as has Christianity. At the core of Christian character formation are the life and teachings of Jesus of Nazareth. The ethic Jesus taught was to love God and to love humanity: "Thou shalt love the Lord thy God with all thy heart, and with all thy soul, and with all thy mind. This is the first and great commandment. And the second is like unto it, Thou shalt love thy neighbor as thyself. There is no other commandment greater than these."[28] Whether based on Christian teaching or not, a belief in love is the ethical ideal of millions of people.

Pleasure

The idea that pleasure, broadly interpreted as physical enjoyment and avoidance of pain, is the highest state of goodness dates back at least to Aristippus (about 435–366 B.C.). This pupil of the philosopher Socrates believed that experiencing pleasure and avoiding pain should be the goals of human existence, and that definite pleasure of the moment should not be postponed for uncertain pleasure of the future.[29] To understand the importance of this belief, consider the wars that have been fought because of passion between man and woman, the steps people take to avoid discomfort and pain, and the value people place on self-satisfaction in day-to-day affairs. In *Reflections and Maxims*, Vauvenargues wrote:

> The indifference we display toward moral truth is due to the fact that we determine to indulge our passions in any event, and that is why we do not hesitate when action becomes necessary, notwithstanding the uncertainty of our opinions, to satisfy desire. It is of little consequence, say men, to know where truth lies, if we know where pleasure lies.[30]

Greatest Good for the Greatest Number

Two of the principle architects of the belief that "what is best brings the greatest good for the greatest number" were the nineteenth-century political philosophers Jeremy Bentham (1748–1832) and John Stuart Mill (1806–1873).[31] Their moral philosophy, *utilitarianism*, reflects the official ethics of both American democracy and Marxist communism. Bentham wrote, "The greatest happiness of all those whose interest is in question is the right and proper, and the only right and proper and universally desirable, end of human action."[32] When we weigh the consequences of moral behavior by considering the best interests of everyone involved, we are being ethical according to utilitarian ideals.

Duty and Right Action

In *Criticism of Practical Reason* (1788) and *Fundamental Principles of the Metaphysics of Morals* (1785), the German philosopher Immanuel Kant (1724–1804) detailed a view of right and wrong that has had significant influence on the thinking of Western civilization. Kant believed that people must be their own lawgivers, freely choosing their obligations, and that these, in turn, become their duty. Because people are free to determine ethical beliefs and have free choice in moral dilemmas, all people must be responsible for their own actions.

Kant believed that a person with character will choose duty to conscience and will not succumb to base or expedient desires. Further, he believed that if an individual acts from a good motive and a sense of duty, the act is good regardless of the consequences. Thus, if a person seeks to help another, but because of unforeseen circumstances the result is a worsened condition for the other, the helper is nonetheless a good and ethical person. On the other hand, if a person seeks to harm another, but in doing so actually helps the other, this act is nonetheless immoral.[33] The role of Kant's call to duty can be seen in the following incident:

> A convoy of thirty-eight merchant ships was crossing the Atlantic during World War II. None of the ships were armed except the "Jervis Bay," which had only six six-inch guns and no armor plate. One night, an enemy ship suddenly appeared and began firing at the convoy with eleven-inch shells. Without a moment's hesitation, the "Jervis Bay" drove toward the enemy, laying down a smoke screen behind which the rest of the convoy could escape.
>
> The "Jervis Bay" fired at the German raider until the last active gun was submerged. Only when the bridge was destroyed and the ship could no longer fight did the wounded captain give the order to abandon ship. Only 68 out of the 250-man crew survived. The rest, along with the captain, went down with the "Jervis Bay." No one protested this act of duty; no one complained; no one suggested another action that should have been taken.[34]

The importance of personal conscience and duty can be seen in the words of Israeli stateswoman Golda Meir: "I can honestly say that I was never affected by the question of the success of an undertaking. If I felt it was the right thing to do, I was for it, regardless of the possible outcome."[35]

Values Today

In addition to these central concepts of good, Western society today is guided by seven commonly held values:

1. **Life should be preserved.** Physician-philosopher Albert Schweitzer said, "The fundamental idea of goodness is that it consists of preserving life, in favoring it, and wanting to bring it to its highest value, and evil consists in destroying life, doing it injury, hindering its development period."[36] Celebrating peace and life over war and death, psychologist Gordon Allport writes:

> Normal people everywhere reject the path of war and destruction. They want to live in peace and friendship with their neighbors. They prefer to love and be loved, rather than to hate and be hated.[37]

2. **It is important to have meaning in life.** In *The Apology*, the Greek philosopher Plato describes Socrates as saying, "The unexamined life is not worth living."[38] In this spirit, more than twenty-three centuries later, John Berrill wrote:

> I am a human being, whatever that may be. I speak for all of us who move and feel and whom time consumes. I speak as an individual unique in a universe

beyond my understanding, and I speak for man. I am hemmed in by limitations of sense and mind and body, of place and time and circumstance, some of which I know but most of which I do not. I am like a man journeying through a forest, aware of occasional glints of light overhead, with recollections of the long trail I have already traveled and conscious of wider space ahead. I want to see more clearly where I have been and where I am going, and above all I want to know why I am where I am and why I am traveling at all."[39]

People are faced with the necessity of self-direction. This responsibility requires that we determine the kind of creatures we are and the basic "roles" we should play as human beings. As psychologist Erich Fromm states, "Man is the only animal who finds his own existence a problem which he has to solve and from which he cannot escape."[40]

3. **The welfare of others should be the concern of each individual**. The Golden Rule exists in some form in at least eight major religions. The Hindus teach, "Do not to others which, if done to thee, would cause thee pain; this is the sum of duty." Confucius said, "What you would not want done to yourself, do not do unto others." And Jesus taught, "As ye would that men should do to you, do ye also to them likewise." When we make moral judgments in consideration of another person's welfare, we are using the Golden Rule.

4. **Happiness is a worthy goal that flows naturally**. The following story makes this point:

    A big cat saw a little cat chasing its tail and asked, "Why are you chasing your tail?" Said the kitten, "I have learned that the best thing for a cat is happiness and that happiness is in my tail. Therefore, I am chasing it. And when I catch it, I shall have happiness."
    Said the old cat, "My son, I too have paid attention to the problems of the universe. I too have judged that happiness is in my tail. But I have noticed that whenever I chase after it, it keeps running from me, and when I go about my business, it just seems to follow after me wherever I go."[41]

In the human sphere, think of the happiness represented in natural experiences: a child building sand castles, a craftsman whistling while working, a mother nursing her baby, a physician saving a life.

5. **Love is good**. In *The Art of Loving*, Erich Fromm writes:

    Beyond the element of giving, the active character of love becomes evident in the fact that it always implies certain basic elements. These are care, responsibility, respect, and knowledge. . . . Love is union with somebody or something outside oneself, under the condition of retaining the separateness or integrity of one's own self. It is an experience of sharing and communion that permits the full unfolding of one's inner activity. . . . Love is one aspect of what I have called the productive orientation: the active and creative relatedness of man to his fellow man, to himself, and to nature.[42]

6. **Knowledge is good**. Character is born both of the desire to be good and of the knowledge of what is good. One without the other is insufficient. In moral dilemmas, good intentions alone are not enough to guarantee good results. Also necessary is knowledge in its various forms: information, reason, imagination, wisdom, and truth. Knowledge must also be applied, as Rebecca McCann's poem "Inconsistency" implies:

> I'm sure I have a noble mind,
> And honesty and tact;
> And no one's more surprised than I,
> To see the way I act![43]

7. **Individual rights should be protected**. In 1776 a historic revolution was launched with the following declaration:

> We hold these truths to be self-evident, that all men are created Equal, that they are endowed by their Creator with certain inalienable Rights, that among these are Life, Liberty, and the Pursuit of Happiness—that to secure these rights, Governments are instituted among men, deriving their just powers from the consent of the Governed—that whenever any form of Government becomes destructive of these ends, it is the Right of the People to alter and abolish it and institute a new Government, laying its foundation and organizing its powers in such form, as to them should seem most likely to effect their safety and happiness.[44]

In 1789 the United States Constitution and the Bill of Rights elaborated on the rights of individuals in American society. Note, however, that as late as 1947 Harry Truman said, "I want our Bill of Rights implemented in fact. We have been trying to do this for 150 years." From this, you can see that moral goals do not ensure moral practices. Still, the idea is powerful and well entrenched in Western culture that the good of each individual, so long as it does not harm the good of other individuals, is the ethical ideal.

Character provides direction for people, indicating what should be done and how to do it. In the face of ethical questions, a person or a community with character tries to sort out right from wrong. In this effort, traditional and contemporary definitions of good have guided Western culture. Although not all beliefs are held to the same degree by all people, a sense of having done the right thing usually results when one behaves with strength, with personal conviction, in a state of naturalness, with religious authority, for personal satisfaction, for the welfare of all, out of personal conscience, to preserve life, to understand life, with love, with knowledge, and with respect for the individual.

As you consider the subject of character, what is your moral ideal? How are your values reflected in both your personal life and your public life? Individuals and groups must remember the truth of the saying, "People must stand for something; otherwise, they will fall for anything."

FULL-SWING LIVING—STRENGTH OF CHARACTER

In its highest form, character is based on a value system that is known, cherished, stated, lived, and lived habitually. These are the layers of character development. A concept that can be used to assess strength of character is called **full-swing living**.

An analogy can be made with baseball, in which a full swing is needed to hit a home run. An arrested swing results in less success—a triple, double, single, or a foul ball. The same is true for questions of right and wrong, good and bad: In moral dilemmas, a home run results only when one completes a full swing and does not suffer **values arrest**.

A full swing is comprised of five points, beginning through completion:[45]

Point 1 is to *know* one's values.

Point 2 is to *cherish* one's values.

Point 3 is to *declare* one's values.

Point 4 is to *act* on one's values.

Point 5 is to *act habitually* on one's values.

Arrested development occurs if a person or group fails to complete all five points in the character swing. Consider the case of Bill, Donna, Phil, Karen, and David, each facing a moral dilemma (either in the workplace or in their personal lives):

- Bill knows what he values but has not examined other alternatives. His is an unthinking stance with little or no personal involvement. He hits a foul tip.

- Donna knows what she values and cherishes this personally. She experiences self-satisfaction with her value system. She hits a single.

- Phil knows what he values, cherishes this personally, and declares his values. He publicly states his value system. He hits a double.

- Karen knows what she values, cherishes this personally, declares this publicly, and acts on her values. She takes action and accepts the consequences. Karen hits a triple.

- David knows what he values, cherishes this personally, declares this publicly, acts upon his values, and does this habitually. David exhibits full-swing living, maximum strength of character, and hits an ethical home run.

See table 2–3 for a picture description of full-swing living. Note that there is an invisible but real line separating Bill, Donna, and Phil from Karen and

TABLE 2–3   Full-Swing Living with No Values Arrest

Moral Dilemma: What to Do in a Business or Personal Moral Dilemma					
Points on the Swing	**Bill**	**Donna**	**Phil**	**Karen**	**David**
Knows values	√	√	√	√	√
Cherishes values		√	√	√	√
Declares values			√	√	√
Acts on values				√	√
Acts habitually according to value system					√
Each person except David experiences arrested development at some point on the character swing. David shows maximum strength of moral conviction and personal character development.					

David. This is a line of integrity that makes Karen and David worthy of special respect. We may love Bill, Donna, and Phil—they may even be family members—but we give highest respect to those individuals who demonstrate courage of conviction and live by their value system in actual practice.

Philosopher-psychologist Rollo May explains the importance of courage in character development:

> Courage is not a virtue or value among other personal values like love or fidelity. It is the foundation that underlies and gives reality to all other virtues and personal values. Without courage our love pales into mere dependency. Without courage our fidelity becomes conformism.
>
> The word courage comes from the same stem as the French word coeur, meaning "heart." Thus just as one's heart, by pumping blood to one's arms, legs, and brain enables all the other physical organs to function, so does courage make possible all the psychological virtues. Without courage, other values wither away into mere facsimiles of virtue.
>
> An assertion of the self, a commitment, is essential if the self is to have any reality. This is the distinction between human beings and the rest of nature. The acorn becomes an oak tree by means of automatic growth; no courage is necessary. The kitten similarly becomes a cat on the basis of instinct. Nature and being are identical in creatures like them. But a man or woman becomes fully human only by his or her choices and his or her commitment to them. People attain worth and dignity by the multitude of decisions they make from day to day. These decisions require courage.[46]

As people grow in awareness and establish individual identities, commitments are made to important values. With commitment comes inner strength to "choose one's self." This strange-sounding phrase of Danish philosopher Soren Kierkegaard means to be responsible for oneself and one's own existence. Choosing one's self is the opposite of blind momentum or routine; it is an attitude of decisiveness, meaning one accepts personal responsibility for one's own conduct and choices.[47]

Nietzsche wrote that character is not given to us by nature, but is given or assigned as a task that we ourselves must solve.[48] This is supported by theologian Paul Tillich, who believed that courage opens the way to being: If we do not have the courage to form and be true to our own character, we lose our very being.[49] The French philosopher Jean-Paul Sartre contended that human beings, in final analysis, are creatures of their own choices. In this way, each person defines and determines his own existence.[50]

There is a saying, "People are like tea bags; you don't know what they are made of until you put them in hot water." Although people are the only animals capable of moral reason, and although as a human being you may subscribe to many ethical ideals, how strong is your character? What would you do in life-and-death situations?

To personalize the subjects of personal identity and strength of character, evaluate your own values—honesty, responsibility, love, freedom, and so forth. Consider a dilemma in which your values play a part. Are you living life *full swing*, in line with your values, or do you experience *values arrest*? See table 2–4.

One way to know what values are important to you and to evaluate the strength of conviction you have shown is to complete the spaces in the next exercise. It can be a telling gauge of character formation.

TABLE 2–4   Personal Moral Strength

Sample moral dilemma: How much to charge; how much to pay; what to do about safety; what to do about discrimination—sex, race, religion.	
Points on the Swing	**Check (√) if yes**
Do you *know* what you value?	_____
Do you *cherish* your values privately?	_____
Do you *declare* your values publicly?	_____
Do you *act* on your values and accept the consequences?	_____
Do you act *habitually* on your values and accept the consequences?	_____

APPLICATION: IF I DIED TODAY . . .

Directions

If you were the editor of a newspaper and were asked to compose your own obituary, what would you have to say?

Name _____,

age _____, died today from _____.

_____ is survived

by _____.

At the time of death, principal endeavor was_____

_____.

_____will be honored for

_____

_____;

will be remembered by_____because

of_____;

will be missed by_____because

of_____;

was loved by_____.

Made contributions in the areas of_____

_____;

always hoped to_____

_____;

was most proud of_____;

_____.

Services will be_____.

Flowers may be sent_____.

In lieu of flowers,_____.

R.I.P.

How do you feel about your obituary? Could you R.I.P. (rest in peace) because you have L.W.I. (lived with integrity)? If you have pursued full-swing living in all of your dealings, your answer will be yes.

REFERENCES

1. John W. Gardner, "Building Community," prepared for the Leadership Studies Program of the Independent Sector, (Washington, DC: American Institutes for Research, 1991).

2. Harold Titus and Morton Keeton, *Ethics for Today*, 5th. ed. (D. Van Nostrand Co., 1975), 39.

3. William Hazlitt, *Lectures on the English Comedy Writers*, lecture no. 1 (Philadelphia: Lippencott, 1818).

4. Charles Darwin, *Origin of Species by Means of Natural Selection* (New York: The Modern Library, 1936), 471.

5. John W. Gardner, "The Importance of Community," (Palo Alto: American Institutes for Research, Youth and Community Research Group, 1994).

6. Charles E. Watson, *Managing with Integrity: Insights from America's CEOs* (New York: Praeger, 1991), 30.

7. Watson, *Managing with Integrity*, 100.

8. William James, *The Principles of Psychology* (New York: H. Holt, 1950).

9. Peter Drucker, "The New Society of Organizations," *Harvard Business Review* (September/October, 1992), 98.

10. Rosabeth Moss Kanter, "Values and Economics,"—notes from the editor, *Harvard Business Review* (May/June, 1990): 4.

11. Kanter, "Values and Economics," 4.

12. Leon Wieseltier, "Total Quality Meaning," *The New Republic* (July 19, 1993): 16–18, 20–22, 24–26.

13. Mary Gray, Northern Kentucky University and Jerry Jewler and Mary Stuart Hunter, University of South Carolina, 1986.

14. Gardner, "The Importance of Community."

15. Amitai Etzioni, *The Spirit of Community: Rights, Responsibilities, and the Communitarian Agenda* (New York: Crown Publishing, 1993), 26, 31, 157.

16. David Jamieson and Julie O'Mara, *Managing Workforce 2000: Gaining the Diversity Edge* (San Francisco: Jossey-Bass Publishers, 1991), 15–30.

17. Based on the work of Rosemary Hutchinson and Naomi Miller, Northern Kentucky University, 1980–1984.

18. *Oxford American Dictionary* (New York: Oxford University Press, 1980) and *Random House Dictionary of the English Language* (New York: Random House, 1968).

19. *The Reflections and Maxims of Vauvenargues*, trans. S.G. Stevens (London: Humphrey Milford, 1940).

20. Alfred North Whitehead, *Science and the Modern World*, Lowell Lectures, 1925 (New York: The Macmillan Co., 1925), 124–125.

21. Niccolo Machiavelli, *The Prince* (Chicago: University of Chicago Press, 1952), and Antony Jay, *Management and Machiavelli* (New York: Bantam Books, Inc., 1967).

22. Friedrich Nietzsche, *Thus Spake Zarathrustra*, trans. Thomas Common (New York: Modern Library, 1917), prologue, No. 3 as found in Titus and Keeton, *Ethics for Today*, 178.

23. Martin Heidigger, *Being and Time*, trans. John Macquarrie and Edward Robinson (New York: Harper and Row Publishers, Inc.), 1962.

24. Titus and Keeton, *Ethics for Today*, 67.

25. Henry David Thoreau, *Walden* (New York: C.N. Potter/Crown Publishers, 1970).

26. *The Reflections and Maxims of Vauvenargues*, 121.

27. Titus and Keeton, *Ethics for Today*, 327.

28. *Bible*, King James version, Matthew 22:37–39.

29. Radoslav A. Tsanoff, *The Great Philosophers*, 2nd ed. (New York: Harper and Row, Publishers Inc., 1953), 102–103.

30. *The Reflections and Maxims of Vauvenargues*, 115.

31. Titus and Keeton, *Ethics for Today*, 153–157; Jeremy Bentham, *An Introduction to the Principles of Morals and Legislation*, (London: Oxford University Press, 1879), chapter 10; and John Stuart Mill, *Utilitarianism* (New York: E. P. Dutton and Co., 1910), 6.

32. Titus and Keeton, *Ethics for Today*, 153–157; Bentham, *Principles of Morals and Legislation*, chapter 10; Mill, *Utilitarianism*, 6; and Anthony Quinton, *Utilitarian Ethics* (New York: St. Martin's Press, 1973), 28.

33. Titus and Keeton, *Ethics for Today*, 142.

34. "World War-Epic of the Jervis Bay," *Time* (November 25, 1940): 22–23.

35. Marie Syrkin, *Golda Meir: Woman with a Cause* (London: V. Gollancze, 1964).

36. Albert Schweitzer, *Out of My Life and Thought: An Autobiography* (New York: Holt, 1949), 157.

37. Gordon W. Allport, *The Nature of Prejudice* (Boston: Beacon Press, 1954), XIV.

38. Plato, *Dialogues of Plato*, trans. R.E. Allen (New Haven: Yale University Press, 1984).

39. John Berrill, *Man's Emerging Mind* (New York: Dodd, Mead, 1955), 1.

40. Eric Fromm, *The Sane Society* (New York: Holt, Rinehart, and Winston, 1955), 23–24.

41. C. L. James, "On Happiness," in Caesar Johnson, *To See a World in a Grain of Sand* (Norwalk, CN: C.R. Gibson Co.), 1972.

42. Erich Fromm, *The Art of Loving* (New York: Bantam Books, Inc., 1963), 20–21, 26–27, 30–31.

43. Rebecca McCann, "Inconsistency," in *Complete Cheerful Cherub* (New York: Covici, Friede, Inc./Crown Publishers, 1932), 224.

44. *The Declaration of Independence*, July 4, 1776.

45. Louis E. Raths, Merrill Harmin, and Sidney Simon, *Values and Teaching* (Columbus, OH: Charles E. Merrill Publishing, 1966), 27–36.

46. Rollo May, *The Courage to Create* (New York: W. W. Norton, 1975), 3–5.

47. Raymond F. Gale, *Developmental Behavior* (New York: Macmillan, 1969), 25, 563.

48. Gale, *Developmental Behavior*, 563–564; and Walter A. Kaufmann, *Nietzsche: Philosopher, Psychologist, Anti-Christ* (Princeton, NJ: Princeton University Press, 1979), 136.

49. Paul Tillich, *The Courage to Be* (New Haven, CN: Yale University Press, 1952).

50. Gale, *Developmental Behavior*, 5, 564.

3

Sustaining Community

An army's success depends upon its size, experience, equipment, and morale—and morale is worth more than all of the other elements combined.

Napoleon Bonaparte

In the workplace, loss of a sense of community shows itself in low morale and poor performance. On the other hand, by developing a supportive work environment, the needs of the individual and the needs of the organization can be fulfilled.[1]

Great organizations attract and keep the best people. These people, as a community, then focus on accomplishing a vision—well bodies, safe streets, good steel, a good meal, etc. These organizations have reputations for making quality products and being good places to work. A key characteristic of these organizations is a healthy culture or work climate.

This chapter presents:

- the dimensions and qualities that determine organizational climate;

- an assessment process to measure organizational health; and

- concrete suggestions for sustaining the spirit and benefits of community.

THE IMPORTANCE OF ORGANIZATIONAL CLIMATE

Most organizations resemble villages more than the finely honed, clearly focused structures they talk about in their annual reports—villages that are merging with other villages; villages that have become cross-cultural; villages that have richer and poorer parts of town. Organizations are like villages in that they have:

- methods of doing tasks established over time;

- rituals for dealing with significant events;

- a certain pace and style of working;

- unique individuals, no two of whom are alike;

- unspoken taboos;

- social structures, pecking orders, and patterns of behavior based on community values;

- aspirations, disappointments, and adjustments to make;

- habits governing dress, language, food, etc.;

- norms of behavior governing use of resources.[2]

An important element in the life of the organizational village is its psychological climate. Even if an organization creates a vision that is leader initiated, member supported, comprehensive and detailed, and worth doing, it must be sustained by key dimensions of organizational climate. Important dimensions include the reward system, organizational clarity, standards of performance, warmth and support, and leadership practices. By completing the following questionnaire, you can evaluate the climate of your organization.

APPLICATION: ORGANIZATIONAL CLIMATE QUESTIONNAIRE[3]

Directions

For each dimension of organizational climate, circle the number on the scale that represents conditions in your organization (1 is the lowest; 20 is the highest).

1. *Reward system*—The degree to which people are recognized and rewarded for good work, rather than being ignored, criticized, or punished when something goes wrong.

   1 2 3 4 5 6 7 8 9 10 11 12 13 14 15 16 17 18 19 20

Rewards are not in line with effort and performance	Effort and performance are recognized and rewarded positively

2. *Organizational clarity*—The feeling that things are well organized and that goals and responsibilities are clearly defined, rather than being disorderly, confused, or chaotic.

   1 2 3 4 5 6 7 8 9 10 11 12 13 14 15 16 17 18 19 20

The organization is disorderly, confused, and chaotic	The organization is well organized, with clearly defined goals and responsibilities

3. *Standards of performance*—The emphasis placed on quality performance and achievement of results, including the degree to which meaningful and challenging goals are set at every level of the organization.

   1 2 3 4 5 6 7 8 9 10 11 12 13 14 15 16 17 18 19 20

Performance standards are low	Performance standards are high

4. *Warmth and support*—The feeling that friendliness is a valued norm, and that people trust, respect, and support one another. The feeling that good relationships prevail in the day-to-day work of the organization.

   1 2 3 4 5 6 7 8 9 10 11 12 13 14 15 16 17 18 19 20

There is little warmth and support in the organization	Warmth and support are characteristic of the organization

5. *Leadership*—The extent to which people take leadership roles as the need arises and are rewarded for successful leadership. The willingness of people to accept leadership and direction from others who are qualified. The organization is not dominated by or dependent upon just one or two individuals.

1 2 3 4 5 6 7 8 9 10 11 12 13 14 15 16 17 18 19 20

Leadership is not provided, accepted, or rewarded; the organization is dominated by or dependent upon one or two individuals	Leadership is provided, accepted, and rewarded, based upon expertise

6. *Communication*—The degree to which important information is shared—up, down, and sideways. Communication channels are open and free-flowing between levels and areas of the organization.

1 2 3 4 5 6 7 8 9 10 11 12 13 14 15 16 17 18 19 20

Information is incorrect or unavailable	Information is accurate and available

7. *Innovation*—The extent to which new ideas are sought and used in all areas of the organization. Creativity is encouraged at every level of responsibility.

1 2 3 4 5 6 7 8 9 10 11 12 13 14 15 16 17 18 19 20

The organization is closed and unresponsive to new ideas	The organization is innovative and open to new ideas

8. *Feedback and controls*—The use of reporting, comparing, and correcting procedures such as evaluations and financial audits. Controls are used for tracking progress and solving problems, as opposed to policing and punishment.

1 2 3 4 5 6 7 8 9 10 11 12 13 14 15 16 17 18 19 20

Controls are used for policing and punishment	Controles are used to provide guidance and solve problems

9. *Teamwork*—The amount of understanding, cooperation, and support demonstrated between different levels and groups in the organization.

1 2 3 4 5 6 7 8 9 10 11 12 13 14 15 16 17 18 19 20

Teamwork is low	Teamwork is high

10. *Involvement*—The extent to which responsibility for decision making is broadly shared in the organization. People are involved in decisions that affect them.

1 2 3 4 5 6 7 8 9 10 11 12 13 14 15 16 17 18 19 20

There is little participation   Participation in decision
in decision making   making is high

Scoring

Total the scores for all of the dimensions; divide by 10. Place this number on the scale below.

TYPES OF ORGANIZATIONS

1 2 3 4 5 6 7 8 9 10 11 12 13 14 15 16 17 18 19 20

EXPLOITIVE   IMPOVERISHED   SUPPORTIVE   ENLIGHTENED

Interpretation

Results of this questionnaire can be used to reinforce strengths and improve weaknesses. High scores represent *enlightened* and *supportive* organizations. Low scores reflect *exploitive* and *impoverished* organizations. The following points should be remembered:

- An organization is as strong as its weakest link. An individual may have an excellent nervous system, sound muscular system, and good respiratory system, but if the circulation system is poor, ultimately the whole organism will fail. Similarly, an organization may be strong in performance standards, organizational clarity, and warmth and support, but if the reward system is poor, the entire organization will ultimately suffer.

- Organizational climate is important because it supports the vision and spirit of a community. It directly influences both the quality of work and the quality of life of community members. Depending on the nature of the group or organization, even life-and-death consequences can result.

  Consider an *exploitive* or *impoverished* hospital: People who can find employment elsewhere will probably leave, and these may be some of the best personnel. People who remain may spend more time complaining about working conditions and management practices than actually doing the work, with the result being poor housekeeping, unattended patients, and medical and clerical errors. *Exploitive* and *impoverished* hospitals experience unnecessary mistakes due to human factors—untrained, unqualified, and uncommitted workers.

Now consider an *enlightened* or *supportive* hospital where standards of performance are high, leadership is effective, goals and responsibilities are clear, warmth and support prevail, and the reward system reinforces good work. Given a choice, where would you want to be treated, and where would you want to work? Which type of organization provides the best quality of health care and the best quality of employment?

■ *Enlightened* and *supportive* organizations represent good investments. Because of their reputations, they attract excellent personnel, who usually outperform their demoralized counterparts in *exploitive* and *impoverished* organizations.

■ Organizations are composed of interdependent groups. The success of the total organization depends on conditions in each of its subgroups. As such, every division and unit should develop an *enlightened* or *supportive* climate to sustain *community*.

■ Leaders and followers may have different views about the climate of a group or organization. People in upper levels of responsibility often evaluate conditions more favorably than do people in lower levels. See the example in figure 3–1.

PATTERNS OF LEADERSHIP

How do communities become what they are? Who decides whether an organization will be enlightened, supportive, impoverished, or exploitive? Although members may have considerable influence, organizational climate is determined primarily by leaders. Those in charge establish the character and define norms of behaviors.

Management author Rensis Likert identifies four patterns of leadership that correspond to the four types of organizational climate. His conclusions are based on studies of thousands of managers in widely different kinds of organizations, both inside and outside the United States. A description of each of the four patterns of leadership follows.[5]

Pattern I Leadership (Exploitive)

Exploitive leadership is autocratic and hierarchical, with virtually no participation by members. Leaders make decisions and members are expected to comply without question. Leaders show little confidence or trust in others, and members do not feel free to discuss job-related problems with leaders. In a free

FIGURE 3–1   Extent to Which Leaders and Followers Agree on
Organizational Conditions[4]

Behavior	Top Staff Self-Evaluation*	First-Line Supervisor Evaluation of Top Staff Behavior	First-Line Supervisor Self-Evaluation**	Employee Evaluation of First-Line Supervisor Behavior
Always tells subordinates in advance about changes that will affect them or their work	70%	27%	40%	22%
Nearly always tells subordinates	30%	36%	52%	25%
	}100%	}63%	}92%	}47%
More often than not tells subordinates	---	18%	2%	13%
Occasionally tells subordinates	---	15%	5%	28%
Seldom tells subordinates	---	4%	1%	12%

*Top staff rated themselves 37% higher than they were rated by subordinates.
**First-line supervisors rated themselves 45% higher than they were rated by subordinates.

social and economic order, Pattern I organizations rarely survive because people avoid them as much as possible. Where they do exist, they are characterized by a lack of loyalty and recurrent financial crises.

Pattern II Leadership (Impoverished)

Impoverished leadership makes some attempt to avoid being completely autocratic. Power remains at the top, but members are given occasional opportunities for participation in the decision-making process. Pattern II organizations fall into two categories that determine their relative success. Successful Pattern II organizations are benevolent autocracies in which leaders have genuine concern for the welfare of members. Failing Pattern II organizations are autocracies that do not consider the interests or ideas of members. Some organizations are founded by autocratic, but benevolent leaders, who achieve good results. Then, as time passes and new leaders assume power, the autocratic style of leadership is maintained, but benevolence is not, and the organization fails.

Pattern III Leadership (Supportive)

Supportive leadership shows a great deal of interest and confidence in members. Power resides in leaders, but there is good communication and participation throughout the organization. People understand the goals of the organization, and commitment to achieve them is widespread. Members feel free to discuss job-related problems with leaders. This leadership pattern involves broad member participation and involvement in decision-making activities.

Pattern IV Leadership (Enlightened)

Enlightened leadership delegates power to the logical focus of interest and concern for a problem. People at all levels of the organization have a high degree of freedom to initiate, coordinate, and execute plans to accomplish goals. Communication is open, honest, and uncensored. People are treated with trust rather than suspicion. Leaders ask for ideas and try to use others' suggestions. Pattern IV leadership results in high satisfaction and productivity. Absenteeism and turnover are low, strikes are nonexistent, and efficiency is high.

Likert describes Pattern IV organizations as follows:

> A Pattern IV organization is made up of interlocking work groups with a high degree of group loyalty among the members and favorable attitudes among peers, supervisors, and subordinates.
>
> Consideration for others and skill in problem solving and other group functions are present. These skills permit effective participation in decisions on common problems. Participation is used, for example, to establish objectives that are a satisfactory integration of the needs of all the members of the organization.
>
> Members of the Pattern IV organization are highly motivated to achieve the organization's goals. High levels of reciprocal influence occur, and a high level of coordination is achieved in the organization.
>
> Communication is efficient and effective. There is a flow from one part of the organization to another of all the relevant information important for each decision and action.
>
> The leadership in the Pattern IV organization has developed an effective system for interaction, problem solving, and organizational achievement. This leadership is technically competent and maintains high performance goals.[6]

Four principles should be followed in order to develop an enlightened, Pattern IV organization: (1) view human resources as the organization's greatest asset; (2) treat every individual with understanding, dignity, warmth, and support; (3) tap the constructive power of groups through visioning and team building; and (4) set high performance goals at every level of the organization.[7]

Likert recommends that all organizations adopt the enlightened principles of Pattern IV leadership. He estimates that U.S. organizations, as a whole, are between a Pattern II and a Pattern III, and that a shift to Pattern IV would improve employee morale and productivity by 20 to 40 percent, or more.[8]

Research supports Likert's ideas. Study after study shows that when an organization moves to Pattern IV leadership, performance effectiveness improves, costs decrease, and gains occur in the overall satisfaction and health of the members of the organization. In addition, research findings show that Pattern IV leadership is applicable to every size and type of organization, including private businesses, not-for-profit organizations, and government agencies.[9]

How important are organizational climate and enlightened leadership practices? Management author John Hoerr states:

> We are in a global economy. To have world-class quality and costs and the ability to assimilate new technology, an organization must have world class ability to develop *human capabilities*. This can't be a drag on the system; it has to be a leading variable.
>
> The U.S. is moving in that direction. Participation has permanently altered the old industrial relations system that was based on the idea that mass-production inevitably breeds reluctant workers who must be bought off with high pay. The employee involvement movement has proven that assumption to be false. When jobs are meaningful and challenging, people will be committed and will perform superbly.[10]

TRADITIONAL ORGANIZATIONS

Historically, organizational structures have resembled the diagram in figure 3–2. This form of organization has been used by church, military, and government institutions down through the years because of basic assumptions people have held: Top people are smarter than bottom people; bottom people owe respect and obedience to top people; bottom people must be forced to behave; bottom people should not know about the ideas and plans of top people; and top people are more worthy and valuable than bottom people.[11]

The form and assumptions of classical organizations worked effectively in earlier times because top people *did* know more than bottom people. For the most part, only the people at the top could read and write and knew history and mathematics. Also, bottom people accepted the supremacy of nobility, religious figures, and other people in authority. Poverty and powerlessness left bottom people little choice except to conform to the wishes of powerful top people. Finally, people at the bottom were considered expendable.

As conditions changed in Western culture, particularly in the United States, traditional assumptions about human behavior became less valid. Free public education became available, providing knowledge and opportunity for more

FIGURE 3–2   Classical Organization Structure and Processes

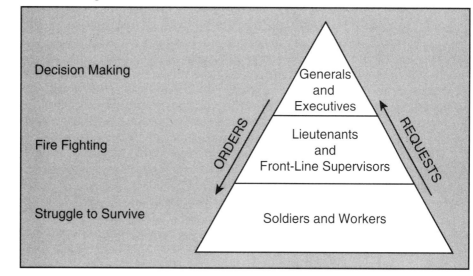

and more people, and information is now easily accessible to everyone as electronic and print media report on current affairs. Also, social status based on education and occupation has become increasingly important. An individual's status at work is a major determinant of social position in America today.[12]

Finally, the efforts of groups such as labor unions and social reform movements have decreased the absolute power advantage of those at the top. Group efforts have produced government-supported reforms such as civil rights legislation and equal employment opportunity among the races, sexes, and ages. Today, the duty of government to protect the civil rights of all people, and the equality of all people before the law, are commonly accepted social ideals.[13]

Psychologist Abraham Maslow summarizes the meaning of these social changes in American society:

> People are growing, either in their actual health of personality or in their aspirations, especially in the United States, and especially women and underprivileged groups. The more grown people are, the less well they will function in the authoritarian situation, and the more they will hate it. Partly this comes from the fact that when people have a choice between a high and a low pleasure, they practically always choose the high pleasure if they have previously experienced both. What this means is that people who have experienced freedom can never really be content again with slavery, even though they made no protest about the slavery before they had the experience of freedom. This is true with all higher pleasures; those people who have known the feeling of dignity and self-respect for the first time can never again be content with slavishness, even though they made no protest about it before being treated with dignity.[14]

In spite of changes in society and changes in the attitudes of people at work, the assumptions of some organizations remain remarkably unchanged from those held by organizations centuries ago. These organizations assume:

- The leader's job should be to set quotas, control activities, and achieve results by dispensing rewards and punishments.

- Showing respect and obedience to leaders, and keeping one's place in the pecking order, should be the duty of all members.

- Employees should not have access to the plans and budgets of the organization because they are untrustworthy or not smart enough to understand them.

- Employees need strict rules and formal discipline to keep them in line.

- Subordinates are supposed to serve their leaders. The welfare and pleasure of upper level people should be the primary concern of lower level people.

- Ideas should originate with leaders and travel downward. Creativity and change should not be expected, encouraged, or rewarded at lower levels of the organization.

- People are expendable.[15]

ENLIGHTENED ORGANIZATIONS

Contrast the assumptions of traditional organizations with today's successful organizations. Although the chart of responsibilities and reporting relationships looks similar, vastly different assumptions and practices are followed, and these result in a superior quality of work and a superior quality of work life. See figure 3–3.

The following are the assumptions and practices of enlightened organizations around important work issues. As you read these, consider your own organization—what is good about it, and what needs to be improved. Also, consider your own role. As leader or member, what can you do to enrich the climate of your organization and, in so doing, help sustain *a spirit of community*?

Customer Focused

Customers come first. Products are made and services are provided with customer interest as the number-one priority. Staff functions view line personnel as internal customers. People take the time to learn what their customers need, and then they commit themselves to fulfilling these requirements.

To reinforce a focus on the customer, Herb Kelleher, CEO of Southwest Airlines, uses wit, wisdom, and an interesting technique.

FIGURE 3–3   Enlightened Organizational Structure and Processes

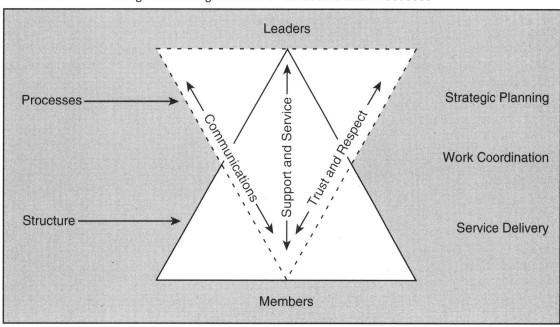

"Our checks that go to our people say, 'From our customers,' because we want to remind everyone that it's not some addition in the general office that produces that check; it's the customers."[16]

With practices like this, Southwest has been profitable twenty-one straight years.

Servant Leadership

Serving subordinates is a major commitment in successful organizations. Management author Harry Levinson describes the importance of this leadership orientation.

> People need to have access to their leaders, to be able to read their faces, to see recognition of their own existence reflected in their leaders' eyes. Managing by objectives and other rational techniques of management do not alter fundamental human needs. People need contact and support, and leaders at all levels should recognize this as one of their primary tasks.
>
> Support for members is frequently discussed, but not always delivered. The suggestion that leaders meet with their people on a regular basis is often greeted with the response that there is not enough time. But such meetings provide valuable opportunities to touch bases, lay out the work, anticipate problems, and gather momentum. They also serve to reinforce a sense of cooperative helpfulness, mutual support, and optimism.

Even in routine operations, when there is no moral or strategic crisis, people benefit from support in the form of *feedback*. As a rule, they do not get enough of it. One can ask people in almost any organization, "How do you know how well you are doing?" Ninety percent of them are likely to respond, "If I do something wrong, I'll hear about it." Too often this topic is discussed as if praise were the answer; it is not. What people are saying is that they do not have sufficient support from their leaders. Praise without support is an empty gesture.[17]

Member Empowerment

In *Flight of the Buffalo*, James Belasco and Ralph Stayer describe successful organizations as those where people agree on a common direction, are willing to assume leadership when necessary, and can rearrange the structure when the needs of the community require it. Decisions are made at the lowest possible level, and through participative vehicles such as committees and task forces, democratic leadership is practiced.[18]

In empowered organizations people experience feelings of ownership. This ensures that they will do everything in their power to create success. Not only are their egos invested in the organization, but their abilities are as well. In the end, this results in success for the person and the organization.[19]

In *Leadership and the New Science*, Margaret Wheatley describes the relationship between empowerment and ownership:

We know that the best way to build ownership is to give over the creation process to those who will be charged with its implementation. We are never successful if we merely present a plan in finished form to employees. It doesn't work to just ask people to sign on when they haven't been involved in the design process, when they haven't experienced the plan as a living, breathing thing.[20]

The typical U.S. company has put its foot in the water of member empowerment. Management author Edward Lawler reports that 80 percent of Fortune's top one thousand companies have initiated some form of participative leadership and employee involvement as a strategy for improving business performance.[21] Consider the words of Fred Smith, chairman of Federal Express:

Empowering people is the single most important element in managing the organization. Empowered people have the necessary information to make decisions and act; they don't have to wait for multiple levels of authorization. Empowered people identify problems and they fix them. They do what it takes to keep customers happy. Empowered people don't have time for turf battles, because when everyone shares power and a common goal, turf becomes irrelevant and teamwork becomes an imperative.[22]

Respect for People

Although people may accept subordinate positions in organizations, they resent being treated as inferior individuals who cannot think for themselves.

Enlightened organizations treat every person in every work classification with respect. This reflects human dignity as a basic value.

The best organizations consider the unique characteristics of each person: the needs of some for stability and others for variety; the needs of some for latitude and others for structure; the dependable delivery of some and the creative ideas of others; the open-mindedness of some and the rigid allegiances of others. What is consistent is that all people are treated with respect and dignity.

Management authors James Collins and William Lazier explain the importance of respect as a foundation of community.

> Great companies respect their customers and they respect their employees—people at all levels and from all backgrounds. Out of showing respect for others, an organization itself becomes respected. It rises in stature as a role model, and makes a positive impact on the world.[23]

Open Communication

Much of the sense of community people seek in their work lives has been lost in their towns and cities. In seeking community, people care not only for their own condition, but also for the well-being of others. This is demonstrated through constant and free-flowing communication.

Effective leaders are aware that the more people know about costs, schedules, competitive position, etc., the better quality of work they will perform. Therefore, regular communication sessions about goals, working conditions, and work-related issues are conducted throughout the organization. Communication flows freely, and information is accurate.

Work Enrichment

If a sense of community is to be achieved, work must be integrated into effective and streamlined processes. Individual tasks must match the ability, temperament, interest, and values of each member. In effective organizations, effort is made to be sure everyone has a "rich" assignment with appropriate *variety, challenge, autonomy, feedback, identity,* and *meaning*.

> In *Teaching the Elephant to Dance*, author Jim Belasco tells the story of Dr. Cooley, the famous brain surgeon. He followed Cooley on his rounds one day and, en route to the operating room, saw the surgeon stop and talk to a man mopping the hallway. They conversed for nearly 10 minutes before Cooley dashed into the operating room. His curiosity raised, Belasco commented, "That was a long conversation." The man mopping the floor replied, "Dr. Cooley talks to me quite often." The author asked, "What do you do at the hospital?" The man replied, "We save lives."[24]

To show the importance of work enrichment, ask yourself: Have you ever had a job that was boring, with no power, no challenge, no sense of accomplishment, no identity, and no meaning or importance to you? After agreement on a vision, no other element is more important for organizational success than getting the right person assigned to the right task.

Studs Terkel, author of *Working*, describes a person's work as a search for daily meaning as well as daily bread, for recognition as well as cash. "Work," he says, "is a search for a sort of life rather than a Monday-through-Friday sort of job."[25]

Innovation and Change

Successful organizations encourage new ideas at every level of responsibility and reward members who make suggestions. In this way, the organization combats inflexibility. Change is generated within the organization in a constructive manner, and responsiveness to change outside the organization is improved. Organizations do this in a variety of effective ways, from suggestion box programs rewarding individual contributions, to self-managed work teams rewarding group collaboration. In doing this, successful organizations prevent the "brain drain syndrome," where people are present physically but are absent mentally, saving their best efforts for after-work activities.

Humanistic Orientation

The members of a community-oriented organization deal with each other humanely, respect individual differences, and value the integrity of each person. There is appreciation and recognition for hard work, and an awareness that people need each other.[26]

People are recognized as multidimensional individuals who are subject to the demands and constraints of a variety of forces—family, social, and professional—all vying for time, effort, and loyalty. Therefore, policies and programs are available to accommodate a life away from the organization.

Drawing from the theories of Abraham Maslow as presented in his influential book *Motivation and Personality*, effective organizations recognize that after income has reached a level sufficient to meet economic needs, other kinds of rewards become more important to people: (1) personal security, (2) acceptance from colleagues, (3) professional recognition, and (4) creative self-expression. Policies, procedures, and programs are provided to meet these needs.[27]

Human Resources Development

Talented people are recognized as the key to success in successful organizations. As such, the highest priority is given to recruiting and developing qualified people at every level of responsibility.

Management author Peter Drucker writes, "We used to talk about 'labor.' Today we talk about 'human resources.' This change reminds us that it is the skilled and knowledgeable individual who decides in large measure what he or she will contribute to the organization, and how great the yield from his or her knowledge will be."[28]

The organization's function is to put human knowledge to work—on tools, products, and processes; on the design of work; on knowledge itself. It is the nature of knowledge, however, that it changes fast and that today's certainties can become tomorrow's absurdities. In today's organizations, it is safe to assume that anyone with knowledge will have to acquire new knowledge every four or five years, or become obsolete."[29]

Emphasizing the importance of knowledge, C. K. Prahalad and Gary Hamel write in a *Harvard Business Review* article, "The Core Competence of the Corporation":

> In the long run, competitiveness derives from an ability to build, at lower cost and more speedily than competitors, the core competencies that spawn unanticipated products. The real sources of advantage are to be found in management's ability to consolidate corporate-wide technologies and production skills into competencies that empower individuals to adapt quickly to changing opportunities."[30]

Developing a successful organization is fundamentally a learning effort. Ray Stata, CEO of Analog Devices, writes: "I would argue that the rate at which individuals and organizations learn is the only sustainable competitive advantage, especially in knowledge-intensive industries."[31]

People and organizations learn both adaptively and creatively. Conditions conducive to learning are:

1. Basic respect for the worth and dignity of all people is a cardinal value in the organization.

2. Individual differences are recognized and a variety of learning experiences are available.

3. Each person is addressed at his or her current level of development and is helped to grow to full potential.

4. Good communications prevail—people express themselves honestly and listen with respect to the views of others.[32]

Goal Setting

The goal-setting process is participative and inclusive. Task assignments and day-to-day activities are based on group objectives and strategic initiatives. These objectives and initiatives are based on organization-wide goals that are established to support the central mission or purpose of the organization. The mission exists to serve the stakeholders of the organization—customers, employees, managers, owners, etc.—and it is based on shared values. All of these elements form and reflect an organization's vision or image of its ideal state.

Organizational Control

In the most effective organizations, the emphasis is on self-control and problem solving, rather than on policing and punishment. There is a saying that people like to be led, but they hate to be controlled. Close supervision, restrictive policies, and autocratic leadership lead to resentment, resistance and rebellion. Table 3–1 shows the difference between unenlightened and enlightened organizations around issues of control.

TABLE 3–1   Different Views of Control[33]

Unenlightened Organizational Culture Is Based On:		Enlightened Organizational Culture Is Based On:
Control of others	<—<—<—>—>—>	Self-management
Obedience to authority	<—<—<—>—>—>	Vision and values
Power to punish	<—<—<—>—>—>	Trusting relationships
Position and rank	<—<—<—>—>—>	Competence and achievement
Minimal investment in people who perform fragmented jobs	<—<—<—>—>—>	High investment in people who perform whole jobs
Homogeneity	<—<—<—>—>—>	Diversity
Centralization	<—<—<—>—>—>	Decentralization
Controlled information	<—<—<—>—>—>	Free-flowing information
Many levels	<—<—<—>—>—>	Fewer levels
Fixed on stability	<—<—<—>—>—>	Open to change
Short-term profit	<—<—<—>—>—>	Long-term profit
Autocratic style	<—<—<—>—>—>	Democratic style
Concern for tasks	<—<—<—>—>—>	Concern for people
Minimum standards	<—<—<—>—>—>	Continuous improvement

Teamwork

Management author Jay Conger states that organizations of the future will increasingly utilize multifunctional project teams to address specific needs, such as better quality products and better customer service. Team members will report to a project leader as well as a functional supervisor. This deviates from the manager's traditional role as "the boss." The leader will increasingly become a teacher, coordinator, and coach.[34]

The following shows the *benefits*, *obstacles*, and *hopes* behind efforts to tap the constructive power of teams.

Benefits. Organizations are increasingly realizing productivity gains through team-based systems that allow employee participation and self-development. Studies in the automobile industry show that teams produce better quality products more efficiently than do workers in traditional work organizations.[35]

Obstacles. Despite the potential for productivity gains, many organizations have failed to adopt participative leadership practices. Much of the resistance comes from a mindset that requires workers to perform tasks defined by planners and engineers, versus work processes that are user friendly and customer focused. In addition, many managers fear the loss of authority, professional status, and personal control they associate with employee participation activities.

Hopes. Garry Berryman of Honda states: "An organization, with all its great muscle—machinery, equipment, money, facilities—can't do anything unless it has a brain. The brain is the people." No gilded-age mill owner and very few managers in the 1950s would have understood that statement. That so many organizations today have taken this principle to heart, calling upon all the members' abilities and genuinely democratizing the workplace to do so, is progress in a profound sense.

Sense of Trust

Many people have said of their organization: "Our problems are well known, and we even know what to do about them, but we are afraid to say anything. Who wants to get his head chopped off?" Effective leaders encourage constructive criticism. They use many methods—attitude surveys, suggestion systems, small-group meetings, the open-door policy, and day-to-day listening—to constantly review the appropriateness of policies and practices. In being open to criticism, the guiding light is not who said what, but what is the truth. In time and with mutually satisfying experiences, a level of trust is developed that is good for the organization and good for its people.

When the assumptions and practices of enlightened organizations are followed, both individuals and the organization benefit. Consider one example:

> A manufacturing organization decided to treat its employees more like adults. The firm was not following any behavioral theory, but simply wanted to remove conditions that made employees feel regimented and that seemed counterproductive. Time clocks, buzzers, and bells were removed, and employees were put on salary instead of hourly wages. Rigid rules were eliminated, and routine disciplinary action was replaced with counseling. Employees were encouraged to participate in decisions affecting them personally. As a result of this change in climate, absenteeism was reduced by fifty percent, and turnover declined materially. Perhaps even more important, worker resistance to change declined substantially.[36]

ORGANIZATIONAL EXCELLENCE

In their influential book *In Search of Excellence: Lessons From America's Best-Run Companies*, Tom Peters and Robert Waterman describe the nature of successful organizations:

> The findings from excellent companies amount to an upbeat message. The good news comes from treating people decently, asking them to shine, and from producing things that work. This is a timeless message that great companies of all sizes use to achieve success and must continue to use to sustain excellence.
>
> In great companies, small work units with motivated people are the norm. Precisely planned research and development efforts aimed at big bang products are replaced by armies of dedicated champions. A numbing focus on cost gives way to an enhancing focus on quality. Working according to fat rule books is avoided and replaced by everyone's contributing.
>
> Even management's job is enjoyable. Instead of isolation in an ivory tower, it is shaping values and reinforcing them through coaching and evangelism in the field—with the worker and in support of the cherished product.[37]

In *Liberation Management*, Peters states that *In Search of Excellence* is an indictment of the excesses of the "rational model" and the business paradigm that drives so many management practices even today. What he counsels instead is a commitment to timeless principles or eternal truths: attention to customers, an abiding concern for people, and the celebration of risk and experimentation.[38]

The following questionnaire evaluates strengths and weaknesses on eight attributes of excellence. With this information, an organization can create strategies for success and commitments to improve.

APPLICATION: ORGANIZATIONAL EXCELLENCE QUESTIONNAIRE[39]

Directions

Listed below are eight attributes and their characteristics common among excellent companies. Rate your organization on each characteristic using the following scale:

5—*always* present.
4—*usually* present.
3—*sometimes* present.
2—*rarely* present.
1—*never* present.

I. Risk and Experimentation (A Bias for Action)

1. _____ Concrete action is taken early.

2. _____ Prototypes are provided for customers.

3. _____ Risk taking is supported by a tolerance for failure.

4. _____ Physical layout and tools, such as conference rooms, blackboards, and flip charts, invite interaction, impromptu problem solving, and good-news-story swapping.

5. _____ Resources are willingly shifted to get the job done.

6. _____ Small teams solve problems or develop new products.

7. _____ A freewheeling informality prevails and the "glue" is a common purpose.

8. _____ Brief memos, concise proposals, and an aversion to lengthy reports create an action-oriented environment.

_____ Total

_____ Divide the total by 8.

Mark your score on the scale below.

1	2	3	4	5
1.5	2.5	3.5	4.5	
There is *not* a bias toward action.			There *is* a bias toward action.	

II. Customers Are Full Partners (Close to the Customer)

1. ____ Customer satisfaction is the number-one priority.

2. ____ Proposals are cost justifiable from the customer's standpoint.

3. ____ People put themselves in the customer's shoes.

4. ____ Product quality and customer service are measured.

5. ____ Senior leaders know and care about customers.

6. ____ Customers participate in experiments with prototypes.

7. ____ Inventions and improvement ideas come from customers.

____ Total

____ Divide the total by 7.

Mark your score on the scale below.

1	2	3	4	5
1.5	2.5	3.5	4.5	

Customers receive little consideration.
                                    Customers are treated as full partners.

III. Innovation through Entrepreneurship (Autonomy and Entrepreneurship)

1. ____ Self-initiated, self-directed experimentation is encouraged.

2. ____ The creative fanatic is tolerated.

3. ____ People who have the know-how, energy, daring, and staying power to implement ideas (the champions) are rewarded positively.

4. ____ Rewards and a share of success are provided.

5. ____ Support systems exist to get the job done.

6. ____ The burden of proof is transferred to those who want to prove that an idea will *not* work.

____ Total

____ Divide the total by 6.

Mark your score on the scale below.

1	2	3	4	5
1.5	2.5	3.5	4.5	

Innovation is *not* encouraged.
                                    Innovation *is* encouraged within the organization.

IV. Motivating People to Choose Productivity (Productivity through People)

1. ____ Respect for the individual is a basic organizational value.
2. ____ There is a dedication to developing people.
3. ____ Reasonable, clear expectations are established for each person.
4. ____ Lots of feedback and celebrating are done.
5. ____ There is a great deal of positive reinforcement.
6. ____ There is an everyday commitment to helping people become winners.
7. ____ People are involved in decisions that affect them.
   ____ Total
   ____ Divide the total by 7.

Mark your score on the scale below.

1	2	3	4	5
1.5	2.5	3.5	4.5	

There is a lack of motivation within the organization.

People are motivated to be productive.

V. Shaping a Powerful Value System (Hands-On, Values-Driven Approach)

1. ____ There is a simple, clear, compelling description of what the organization stands for.
2. ____ People do not have to change their value systems when they go home.
3. ____ The goals of the organization are not just financial.
4. ____ Leadership does not concentrate on sheer survival.
5. ____ Leaders walk around and reinforce shared values "on the floor," "with the people."
6. ____ Leaders are masters of two ends of the spectrum—abstract visioning and mundane details.
   ____ Total
   ____ Divide the total by 6.

Mark your score on the scale below.

1	2	3	4	5
1.5	2.5	3.5	4.5	

A meaningful value system to guide behavior is lacking.

A powerful value system operates throughout the organization.

VI. Staying in the Business You Know (Sticking to the Knitting)

1. ____ The majority of attention, energy, and resources is focused on the mainstream business.

2. ____ Cultures and value systems of new ventures and acquired organizations merge easily with those of the original organization.

3. ____ Credible leadership is provided for new ventures.

4. ____ Ventures into new areas are set up as manageable experiments with a commitment to divest if signs of success fail to materialize.

____ Total

____ Divide the total by 4.

Mark your score on the scale below.

1	2	3	4	5
1.5	2.5	3.5	4.5	

Mergers and acquisitions detract from the business.

Mergers and acquisitions are handled well.

VII. Structure is Simple and Leaders Lead (Simple Form, Lean Support Staff)

1. ____ Bureaucratic layers are minimal, with little red tape required to get things done.

2. ____ People are provided with an organizational structure that makes sense and works for them.

3. ____ Flexibility is fostered by creating small units and by designating short-term groups to address problems and develop innovations.

4. ____ Resources are focused on the action line. The organization is not top heavy.

5. ____ Power, energy, and decision making reside at the logical point of concern for a problem. Problem solving occurs at the lowest possible organizational level.

6. ____ Headquarters staff size is limited, and traditional central office functions are decentralized.

____ Total

____ Divide the total by 6.

Mark your score on the scale below.

1	2	3	4	5
1.5	2.5	3.5	4.5	

The company structure is complex, with first-line leaders having little influence.

The company structure is simple, and the driving force comes from first-line leaders.

VIII. Liberating Talent within Parameters (Simultaneous Tight-Loose Properties)

1. ____ Stable, well-defined expectations are provided from the top.

2. ____ A meaningful value system inherently defines appropriate behavior and is promoted throughout the organization.

3. ____ Employee involvement is allowed to function as a powerful productivity force.

4. ____ "Quality versus cost" and "efficiency versus effectiveness" arguments are denied in favor of liberating ordinary people to produce the highest quality product every time.

____ Total

____ Divide the total by 4.

Mark your score on the scale below.

1	2	3	4	5
1.5	2.5	3.5	4.5	

People feel personally constrained; at the same time, they feel organizational direction is lacking.

Central direction coexists with maximum individual autonomy.

Interpretation

Add the average scores for the eight attributes: ____

If the Total Equals: **The Evaluation is:**

32–40 Excellent; outstanding. Conditions reflect those of the best run companies.

24–31 Very good; solid. Some work is needed to attain excellence.

17–23 Below par; unsatisfactory. Improvement is needed.

8–16 Poor; failing. Much work is needed to improve.

Organizational effectiveness depends on excellence in each of the eight attributes. Low scores represent opportunities to improve and should be addressed to achieve long-term success.

Discussion

How do they do it? How do companies succeed so impressively? Peters and Waterman summarize the eight attributes that characterize companies when they are performing at their best. The same attributes apply in public sector and nonprofit organizations as well.[40]

A Bias for Action. Excellent companies are experimenters supreme. They form small bands of employees to test out ideas on customers, often with inexpensive prototypes. They appreciate the maxim that "haste makes waste"; yet they do not procrastinate.

Close to the Customer. Excellent companies provide superior quality, service, and reliability. They provide products that work and last. They get many of their best ideas from their customers. This comes from being in constant communication, discussing needs, listening intently, and responding effectively.

Autonomy and Entrepreneurship. Excellent companies foster many leaders and many innovators throughout the organization. They are a hive of what could be called "champions". They don't try to hold everyone on so short a rein that they can't be creative. Excellent organizations encourage practical risk taking, and support good tries.

Productivity through People. Excellent companies treat employees as the root source of quality and productivity gain. They do not foster "we and they" labor attitudes or regard capital investment as the fundamental source of efficiency improvement.

Hands-On, Values-Driven. In excellent companies, leaders get out with their people and communicate the company's purpose and values. Ray Kroc of McDonald's regularly visited stores and assessed them on the factors the company holds dear: QSC & V—Quality, Service, Cleanliness, and Value. Sam Walton was as famous for his bone-deep concern for people as he was for his immense economic success.

Stick to the Knitting. Former Johnson & Johnson CEO Robert Johnson put it this way: "Never acquire a business you don't know how to run." While there are exceptions, excellent companies stay reasonably close to the work they know.

Simple Form, Lean Staff. The underlying structural forms and systems are elegantly simple. Top-level staffs remain lean.

Simultaneous Tight-Loose Properties. Excellent companies are both decentralized and centralized. For the most part, they have delegated decision making to the shop floor or product development team. On the other hand, they are committed centralists around the few core values they hold dear.

The authors go on to write that the attributes of excellent organizations are not startling. They also note that these are attributes that organizations may stray from, but not without consequences. The successful company of today may be tomorrow's failure. Indeed, many of the companies initially included in the "excellence list" have slipped over time and have been replaced by companies more effective in *living* the attributes of "close to the customer," "productivity through people," "bias for action," and "hands-on, values-driven."

ORGANIZATIONS IN PROGRESS

Figure 3–4 shows five phases in the life of an organization. Each phase includes a period of evolution when growth takes place and a period of revolution when crisis threatens the continued development and possibly the existence of the organization.

The following is a description of the typical periods of growth and crisis for each of the five phases:

- *Phase 1: Growth through Creativity.* In its earliest period, an organization's activities are usually centered around the development of products and markets. Top leadership is devoted to these goals. Communication between leaders and followers is frequent and informal. People may work long hours for low pay in anticipation of future benefits.

  Crisis of Leadership. As the organization grows, it becomes increasingly difficult to handle the rapidly swelling staff using the old, informal methods. Leaders become overworked and harried by administrative details. A "crisis of leadership" leads to the first revolution. Founders, frequently incapable or unwilling to change habits and styles, may have to step aside in favor of individuals who can focus and organize the organization's activities.

- *Phase 2: Growth through Direction.* Under strong and capable organizers, the organization may experience a period of sustained growth. A functional structure is introduced. Accounting systems, budgets, and personnel policies are adopted. Communication becomes more formal with policies, reports, and memos replacing word-of-mouth customs. Responsibilities are divided between upper level policy makers and lower level specialists.

  Crisis of Autonomy. Lower level leaders, however, become increasingly frustrated and demand more autonomy and room to exercise their own initiative. With upper level leaders reluctant to give up authority, a new revolutionary period is at hand.

FIGURE 3–4   Five Phases of Organizational Development

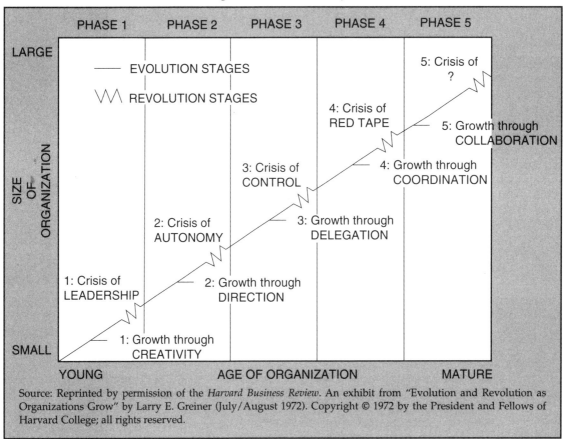

■ *Phase 3: Growth through Delegation.* The successful organization will install effective decentralization and empowerment activities in answer to the crisis of autonomy. Greater responsibility is given to lower-level leaders. Top executives stay out of day-to-day operations, often concentrating on acquiring new units for the organization. Communication from the top is less frequent.

   Crisis of Control. Decentralized leaders are able to penetrate new markets, respond faster to customers, and develop new products. Eventually, however, top leaders may attempt to return to a centralized structure because of a sense of loss of control. This attempt brings on a new revolution, the "crisis of control." The organization must find a new solution to coordination problems.

■ *Phase 4: Growth through Coordination.* This evolutionary period is characterized by the installation of systems for achieving organizational efficiencies and economies. Under the initiation of top leaders, decentralized units are merged into clusters and groups, each of which is expected to show satisfactory return on invested capital. Central staff personnel are added to initiate, control, and review programs for line managers.

Crisis of Red Tape. These changes encourage more efficient use of company resources, and field leaders learn to justify their actions more carefully to headquarters. Tension gradually builds, however, between line and staff and between headquarters and the field. A revolution develops as rules and regulations begin to interfere with problem-solving activities.

■ *Phase 5: Growth through Collaboration.* In response to the crisis of red tape, a flexible and pragmatic approach to management develops. Groups and interdivisional teams perform tasks and solve problems. Headquarters' staff is held to a minimum, and the focus of their efforts is to support and facilitate the success of field personnel. Leaders are trained in behavioral skills so they can improve organizational performance. Many of today's organizations are in this stage of evolution.

Crisis Unknown. Revolution and crisis may center around the psychological saturation of members who become emotionally and physically exhausted by the intensity of teamwork and the heavy pressure for innovative solutions. There may also be pressure for representation on organization boards, as already exists in many European countries. At present, the situation is "crisis unknown."

LEADERSHIP CHALLENGE

At each phase of an organization's development, effective leadership is necessary to resolve crises and sustain community.

Herman Maynard, Jr., and Susan Mehrtens, authors of *The Fourth Wave*, identify the challenges facing today's leaders: 1) creating work environments where people feel safe; 2) fostering truth-telling in all dealings; 3) articulating clear and consistent goals, as well as explicit values to guide member behavior; and 4) facing and resolving dysfunctional practices within the community. To meet these challenges, the authors prescribe a structure based on community, a locus of control based on personal commitment, and an atmosphere that supports freedom of expression, respect for all people, and lifelong learning.[41]

What is the key factor that leaders must remember in order to build and sustain community? Ren McPherson, past president of Dana Corporation, states: "Almost everybody agrees, 'people are our most important asset.' Yet almost no one really lives it. Great companies live their commitment to people."[42] This, in essence, is the nature of an enlightened organization, and it is the secret of true *community*. It is an old truth that applies today: The human side counts.

In his work on servant leadership, Robert Greenleaf proposes that the world can be saved as long as three truly great institutions exist—one in the private sector, one in the public sector, and one in the nonprofit sector. He believes that these organizations will achieve success through a culture of civility supported by a spirit of community, and that their success will serve as a beacon for the world.[43]

REFERENCES

1. John W. Gardner, *On Leadership* (New York: The Free Press, 1990).

2. Geoffrey M. Bellman, *Getting Things Done When You Are Not In Charge: How to Succeed from a Support Position* (San Francisco: Berrett–Koehler, 1992), 50–51.

3. Steve Martin and Terry Almond, Northern Kentucky University, based on Rensis Likert, *The Human Organization* (New York: McGraw–Hill, 1967); also George H. Litwin and Robert A. Stringer, Jr., *Motivation and Organizational Climate* (Boston: Harvard University, Graduate School of Business Administration, Division of Research, 1968), 66–88.

4. Rensis Likert, *New Patterns of Management* (New York: McGraw–Hill, 1961).

5. Likert, *New Patterns of Management*, 222–236.

6. Likert, *New Patterns of Management*, 99, 197–211.

7. Likert, *New Patterns of Management*, 197–211; and David G. Bowers, *Systems of Organization: Management of the Human Resource* (Ann Arbor: University of Michigan Press, 1976), 106–107.

8. Rensis Likert and Jane Gibson Likert, *New Ways of Managing Conflict* (New York: McGraw-Hill, 1976), 52, 98.

9. Likert, *New Ways of Managing Conflict*, 17.

10. John Hoerr, "The Payoff from Teamwork," *Business Week* (July 10, 1989): 56–62.

11. "The Corporate Dropout," *Iron Age* (January 1, 1970).

12. "The Corporate Dropout."

13. Robert J. Harris, *The Quest for Equality: The Constitution, Congress and the Supreme Court* (Westport, CN: Greenwood Press, 1977), 1.

14. Abraham H. Maslow, "The Necessity for Enlightened Management Policy," *Eupsychian Management: A Journal* (Homewood, IL: Irwin/Dorsey Press, 1965), 261.

15. Likert, *New Patterns of Management*.

16. Herb Kelleher, address to the National Press Club, Washington, June 8, 1994.

17. Harry Levinson, *Executive* (Cambridge, Mass: Harvard University Press, 1981), 187–189.

18. James A. Belasco and Ralph C. Stayer, *Flight of the Buffalo: Soaring to Excellence, Learning to Let Employees Lead* (New York: Warner Books, 1993).

19. David Condon, Tastemaker International, Cincinnati, OH, 1993.

20. Margaret Wheatley, *Leadership and the New Science: Learning About Organization from an Orderly Universe*, (San Francisco: Berrett/Koehler, 1992), 66–67.

21. John Greenwald, "Is Mr. Nice Guy Back?" *Business Week* (January 27, 1992): 42.

22. Frederick W. Smith, "Creating an Empowering Environment for all Employees," *Journal for Quality and Participation* (June 1990).

23. James C. Collins and William Lazier, *Beyond Entrepreneurship* (New York: Prentice-Hall, 1992), 220.

24. James A. Belasco, *Teaching the Elephant to Dance: Empowering Change in Your Organization* (New York: Crown, 1990).

25. Studs Terkel, *Working* (New York: Pantheon, 1974).

26. John W. Gardner, "Building Community," prepared for the Leadership Studies Program of the Independent Sector, (Washington, DC: American Institutes for Research, 1991).

27. Abraham Maslow, *Motivation and Personality*, 2nd ed. (New York: Harper and Row, 1970).

28. Drucker, "The New Society of Organizations," 101.

29. Drucker, "The New Society of Organizations," 96.

30. C. K. Prahalad and Gary Hamel, "The Core Competence of the Corporation," *Harvard Business Review* (May 1990).

31. Ray Stata, "Organizational Learning—The Key to Management Innovation," 30, no. 3, *Sloan Management Review* (September 1989): 63–64.

32. E. L. Thorndike, *Human Learning* (New York: Century, 1931).

33. David Condon, Tastemaker International, Cincinnati, OH, 1993.

34. Jay A. Conger, "The Brave New World of Leadership Training," *Organizational Dynamics* (Winter 1993): 52.

35. John Hoerr, "Is Teamwork a Management Plot? : Mostly Not," *Business Week* (February 20, 1989).

36. "The Unregimented Workforce," *Management in Practice* (AMA, September 1974), 1–2 in Keith Davis, *Human Behavior at Work: Organizational Behavior*, 6th ed. (New York: McGraw-Hill, 1981), 108.

37. Thomas J. Peters and Robert H. Waterman, Jr., *In Search of Excellence: Lessons from America's Best Run Companies* (New York: Harper and Row, 1982), xxv.

38. Tom Peters, *Liberation Management* (New York: Knopf, 1992), xxxi.

39. Tim Baker and Teresa Waterman, Northern Kentucky University, 1984, based on Peters and Waterman, *In Search of Excellence*.

40. Peters and Waterman, *In Search of Excellence*, 14–16.

41. Herman Maynard, Jr. and Susan Mehrtens, *The Fourth Wave: Business in the 21st Century* (San Francisco: Berrett/Koehler, 1993), 161.

42. Peters and Waterman, *In Search of Excellence*, 16.

43. Robert K. Greenleaf, *Servant Leadership: A Journey into the Nature of Legitimate Power and Greatness* (New York: Paulist Press, 1991).

PART 2

Interpersonal Skills Development

4

Effective Human Relations

Relationships have a rhythmic variation: openness and sharing of feelings, then assimilation; flow and change, then a temporary quiet; risk and anxiety, then security.

Carl Rogers

In a healthy community there is a sense of belonging and respect, and a spirit of mutual responsibility. There is altruism that is consistently urged by all of the major religions and by secular humanists as well.[1]

How do you build community between people? What are the foundation behaviors of good human relations? These are the central concerns of this chapter. How will the answers be discovered? By experience; by doing. Confucius wrote:

> I <u>listen</u> and I hear;
> I <u>see</u> and I remember;
> I <u>do</u> and I understand.
>
> Confucius (551–479 B.C.)

Human relationships preoccupy us and fascinate us. They can be our undoing or the joy of our lives. It isn't easy or automatic to do what it takes to develop and maintain good human relations. Yet the reward is worth the effort. Indeed, good relationships are the essence of community.

People can't learn *trust* and *respect*, the essential ingredients of a good relationship, from a lecture; and they can't learn *trust* and *respect* by reading a book. These concepts of community are truly learned in the doing. In *I and Thou*, Martin Buber reflects this thought when he writes, ". . . What is real is you and what is real is me; but what is really real is the experience of we." This is what is meant by **community**. Topics in this chapter include:

- the importance of human relationships;

- basic beliefs about people;

- the need for interpersonal trust and mutual respect;

- how to deal with difficult people; and

- the role of civility in building community.

PEOPLE AS SOCIAL BEINGS

History has witnessed a changing definition of what it means to be human. The evolution of Western civilization is the result of many forces:

- Prehistoric groups struggled for survival in a hostile world.

- The ancient Greeks were concerned about virtue and reason.

- Hebrew culture emphasized the importance of law and social order.

- During the first thirteen hundred years A.D., Christianity added the concepts of love, sin, and holiness.

- Major themes of the Renaissance were power, will, and creativity.

- The Protestant "work ethic" took root during the sixteenth and seventeenth centuries.

- The eighteenth and nineteenth centuries saw the emergence of "economic man" as wealth, money, and possessions became dominant goals; "political man," concerned with the rights of individuals, the power of states, and their relationships; and "scientific man," in pursuit of knowledge and the mastery of technology.

- The twentieth century has been both macro-nationalistic (consider the impact of world wars and national governments) and micro-psychological (consider the interest in personal growth and interpersonal relations).

Through all of these periods, there has been a common thread—people as social beings. Humankind, in essence, is social product, social producer, and social seeker.[2]

A case from history shows that social interaction is necessary for the very survival of the young human being. In the thirteenth century, Emperor Frederick II conducted an experiment recorded by a medieval historian in these terms:

> His folly was that he wanted to find out what kind and manner of speech children would have when they grew up if they spoke to no person beforehand. So he bade foster mothers and nurses to suckle the children, to bathe and wash them, but in no way to play with them or to speak to them; for he wanted to learn whether they would speak the Hebrew language, which was the oldest; or Greek, Latin, or Arabic; or perhaps the language of their parents, of whom they had been born. But he labored in vain, because all of the children died. They could not live without the petting and the joyful faces and loving words of their foster mothers.[3]

This example, as well as results from modern studies, shows that life itself depends on social relationships.

THE IMPORTANCE OF HUMAN RELATIONSHIPS

Human relations are important to the individual and the society. John Donne, the seventeenth-century English poet, wrote in the language of his time:

> No man is an Iland, intire of it selfe;
> Every man is a peece of the Continent,
> A part of the maine;
> If a Clod be washed away by the Sea, Europe is the lesse,
> As well as if a Promontorie were,
> As well as if a Mannor of thy friends, or of thine owne were;
> Any man's death diminishes me,
> Because I am involved in Mankinde;

And therefore;
Never send to know for whom the bell tolls;
It tolls for thee.[4]

In *A Different Drum*, Scott Peck writes: "We are all, in reality, interdependent. Throughout the ages, the greatest leaders of all of the religions have taught us that the journey of growth is the path away from self-love, and toward a state of being in which our identity merges with that of humanity."[5]

HUMAN RELATIONS IN THE WORKPLACE

Psychologist William Menninger explains the importance of human relationships in the world of work:

> The only hope for man to be fulfilled in a world of work is that he get along with his fellowmen—that he try to understand them. He may then be free to contribute to their mutual welfare—theirs and his. Insofar as he fails, he fails himself and society.[6]

The first empirical evidence of the importance of human relations in the workplace was provided by studies conducted at Western Electric's Hawthorne Plant outside Chicago, Illinois, in the period between 1927 and 1932. These studies were conducted by Elton Mayo and other research personnel from Harvard University. The original purpose of the studies was to discover the effect of working conditions—noise, lighting, etc.—on employee performance. The final result was to demonstrate the critical role of human relations, particularly employee recognition and management support.[7]

The Hawthorne studies followed a period of American history marked by massive industrialization, exploitation of workers, and the use of scientific management to improve employee efficiency. As epitomized by Charlie Chaplin in the film *Modern Times*, the worker had been dehumanized in the pursuit of production and profit.

With the published results of the Hawthorne studies, the industrial community awakened to the fact that the worker must be treated as more than a machine, and that humanism in the work place is both good for people and good for business. Participative work groups, enlightened leadership practices, and meaningful job assignments were recognized as important to prevent worker alienation, and a human relations movement began to take root.

Today it is a recognized fact that people have greater satisfaction and produce more when they are involved in their work, when they feel they are doing something important, and when their work is appreciated. The quality of work and quality of work life are greatest when people are treated with dignity, trust, and respect.

Human relations are increasingly important in today's workplace for four important reasons.

1. In previous periods, more people worked alone and therefore did not have to concern themselves with interpersonal relationships. In today's workplace, people work with physical, financial, and human resources to accomplish tasks. Of the three, human factors are the most important.[8]

2. Today more people are employed in service occupations, where success depends on how well the customer is served. Writing in *Liberation Management*, Tom Peters states, "All business decisions hinge, ultimately, on conversations and relationships; all business dealings are personal dealings in the end."[9]

3. Higher productivity is the key to improved profit and an increase in the standard of living. In order to build superior work teams, people need greater competence in human-relations skills. In 1982 the National Science Foundation reported that Japanese companies of the period were more productive than American companies primarily because of collaborative work relationships.[10]

4. In his essay, *Building Community*, John Gardner describes the modern work force as composed of a more varied mix of personalities and cultures; thus the necessity—and challenge—of building strong human relations with all kinds of people. It is interesting to note that the most common cause of supervisory failure is poor human relations.[11]

TRUST AND RESPECT IN HUMAN RELATIONS

Trust and respect are the key elements of any good relationship, and they are the foundation of community. Trust is expressed by an openness in sharing ideas and feelings. Respect is demonstrated by a willingness to listen to the ideas and feelings of others. Without trust and respect, human relations break down.

The following exercise examines the level of trust and respect you have with other people. This exercise can be completed individually or with another person. It is a useful tool for building community between people in any environment.

APPLICATION: STYLES OF HUMAN RELATIONS[12]

Directions

Following is a 5-point scale to be used in evaluating yourself and another person on the use of twenty-four behaviors important for good human relations. Read each behavior and determine how much it is like you or the person you are rating. Select a value from the scale and enter the number in the appropriate space at the right.

Scale Value	Meaning
5	Extremely characteristic; almost always does this
4	Quite characteristic; usually does this
3	Somewhat characteristic; occasionally does this
2	Quite uncharacteristic; seldom does this
1	Extremely uncharacteristic; almost never does this

HUMAN RELATION BEHAVIORS

                                                                Self   Partner

This Person:

(T) 1. States opinions in an uncensored manner.   _____   _____

(R) 2. Invites ideas from others; does not
         dominate discussion.   _____   _____

(T) 3. Admits to confusion or lack of knowledge
         when uncertain.   _____   _____

(R) 4. Shows interest in what others have to say
         through body posture and facial expressions.   _____   _____

(T) 5. Expresses self openly and candidly.   _____   _____

(R) 6. Gives support to others who are struggling
         to express themselves.   _____   _____

(T) 7. Admits to being wrong rather than attempting
         to cover up or place blame.   _____   _____

(R) 8. Keeps private conversations private; does not
         reveal confidences.   _____   _____

(T) 9. Tells others what they need to know, even
         if it is unpleasant.   _____   _____

(R) 10. Listens to others without being defensive.   _____   _____

(T) 11. Is honest with his or her feelings.   _____   _____

(R) 12. Shows respect for the feelings of others.   _____   _____

(T) 13. Shares concerns, hopes, and goals with others.   _____   _____

(R) 14. Does not make others feel like they are
         wasting his or her time.   _____   _____

(T) 15. Shares thoughts, no matter how "far out"
         they may seem.   _____   _____

(R) 16. Does not fake attention or merely pretend to listen.
                _____ _____

(T) 17. Speaks truthfully; refuses to lie.
                _____ _____

(R) 18. Does not act hurt, angry, or mistreated when others disagree.
                _____ _____

(T) 19. Is sincere; does not pretend.
                _____ _____

(R) 20. Values suggestions from others.
                _____ _____

(T) 21. Uses language and terms others can understand.
                _____ _____

(R) 22. Tries to prevent interruptions, such as telephone calls and people walking in during important discussions.
                _____ _____

(T) 23. Tells others when they are wrong or need to change.
                _____ _____

(R) 24. Encourages others to express themselves.
                _____ _____

Scoring

Step One. Total the scores you gave yourself for the odd-numbered questions—all questions with (T) in front of them. This total represents your *willingness to express* yourself. Record the score on the TRUST axis in figure 4–1. Next, total the scores you gave yourself for the even-numbered questions—all questions with (R) in front of them. This is your *willingness to listen to others*. Record this score on the RESPECT axis. Then find the point where the two scores intersect and shade in the enclosed area back to "0."

Step Two. You are now ready to analyze the scores you gave your partner. Total the scores you gave your partner for all odd-numbered questions—all questions with (T) in front of them. Record this score on the TRUST axis in figure 4–2. Next, total the scores you gave your partner for all even-numbered questions—all questions with (R) in front of them. Record this score on the RESPECT axis. Then find the point where these two scores intersect and shade in the enclosed area back to "0."

Step Three. Exchange evaluations with your partner.

Step Four. Compare your self-evaluation and your partner's evaluation with the four styles of human relations in figure 4–3. Which style are you most like? Does your partner see you as you see yourself?

FIGURE 4–1   Self-Evaluation

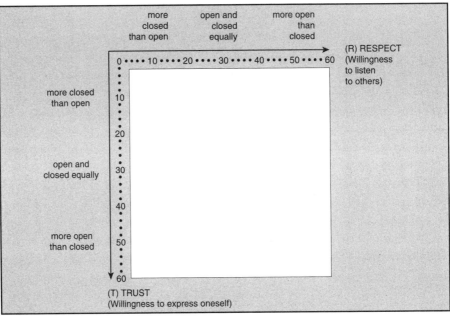

FIGURE 4–2   Partner Evaluation

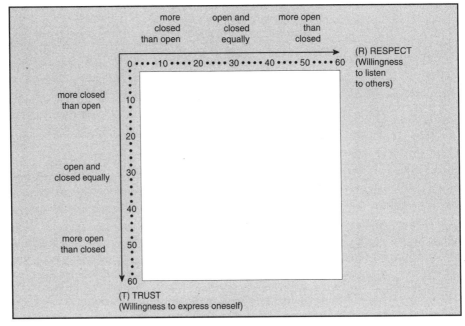

FIGURE 4–3   Human Relations Styles—Turtle, Owl, Bull-in-a-China-Shop, and Picture Window

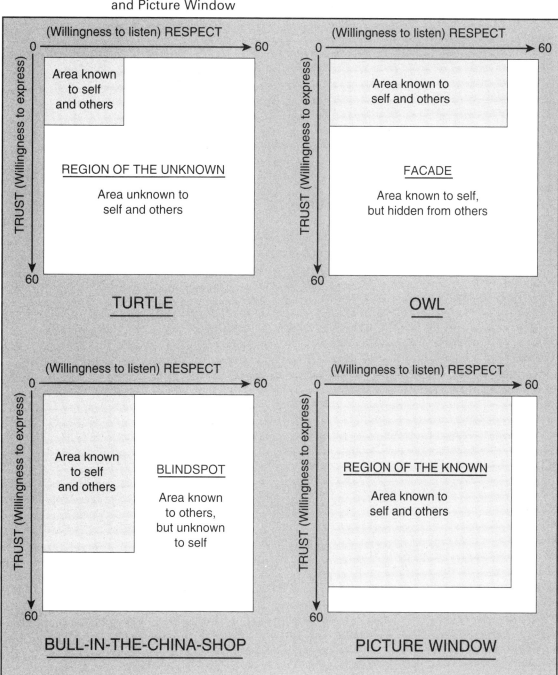

Step Five. Go back to the questionnaire and discuss with your partner what can be done to raise low scores.

Step Six. Discuss the importance of self-expression (showing trust) and listening (showing respect) as these relate to your partnership. Consider the importance of these two traits in your relations with others on the job and in the home.

FOUR STYLES OF HUMAN RELATIONS

The degree of trust and respect a person shows results in a style of human relations. The following is a description of each style.

Turtle—Low Trust/Low Respect

The turtle is reluctant to express ideas or feelings to others; nor does the turtle listen to others. The turtle is in a shell. Whether meaning to or not, the turtle communicates low trust in the motives of others and low respect for their opinions. The result is a large *region of the unknown.* Misunderstanding, frustration, untapped creativity, and unresolved problems live in this region.

People who have turtle relationships find them to be cold, impersonal, and unsatisfying. Just as partners may experience turtle styles of human relations, so may whole groups. Turtle relationships may exist within a work group, between management and employees, and between an organization and its public. Such *communities* are characterized by low morale and poor performance.

Turtle relationships can be improved if people are willing to listen to the ideas and feelings of others and are willing to openly express their own ideas and feelings. This process can be started by one, but it takes two to improve a turtle relationship. Someone must take the initiative, and someone must respond favorably.

Owl—High Respect/Low Trust

The owl style of human relations is better than the turtle, because respect is shown toward the opinions of others. The owl gives time and attention, thus showing concern for the ideas and feelings of others. However, when someone listens, listens, listens, but does not share ideas and feelings in return, a *facade* develops, with two corresponding drawbacks: an impression of role playing and insincerity; and the suppression of conflict, with a resulting decrease in creativity and problem-solving potential.

The owl avoids self-expression and relies too much on listening. Ultimately, this is not satisfying for either partner because the relationship is one-sided. The solution is to demonstrate trust in others by becoming more self-expressive.

It takes two to improve an owl relationship. The owl gradually must become more open. This takes time, because change is difficult for many people to accept, and dealing with confrontation and being honest in self-expression can be threatening. Also, the owl's partner must show respect by listening as ideas, hopes, goals, and feelings are shared.

Bull-in-a-China-Shop—High Trust/Low Respect

The bull-in-a-china-shop is, like the owl, one-dimensional. The good part is that the bull is open and honest with feelings and ideas. Whether they are right or wrong, popular or not, you always know where bulls stand. By open self-expression, the bull says, "I trust you and I believe you will not use what I say to hurt me." This is the good part. The bad part is the enormous *blind spot* the bull creates by not listening to others. Perhaps unintentionally, the bull is demonstrating that other people's feelings and ideas are unimportant.

Whether the bull-in-a-china-shop style develops as a result of ego striving, natural aggressiveness, or actual superiority, it is often destructive in human relationships. The blind spot typically contains negative data—the frustration, resentment and anger of others—that may one day erupt. Negative feelings could also be turned inward and result in low self-esteem for the bull's partner and friends.

The solution is for the bull-in-a-china-shop to become a better listener. The bull must realize that others need to express themselves too, and should show respect for them by listening. People who rarely ask for others' opinions or listen to their problems, have a bull-in-a-china-shop style of human relations, and they have a large blind spot. By listening, they can reduce this blind spot and improve the quality of their relationships on the job and in the home.

Picture Window—High Trust/High Respect

The most effective style of human relations is characterized by dialogue, and it is symbolized by the picture window. Scores of 48 or higher on both trust and respect reflect this profile. With this style, people show mutual respect as each listens to the ideas and feelings of others, and they demonstrate interpersonal trust as ideas and feelings are shared openly and honestly.

The *region of the known* is the dominant feature of picture window relationships, and what goes on in this area is candid and free-flowing discussion about issues, events, and experiences. By no means is dialogue tame. Indeed, opposing points of view and diverse values sometimes clash. Conflict is viewed positively, however, as all parties recognize that they are not identical twins, that disagreement is natural, and that out of diversity can come increased creativity and intense satisfaction. Picture window relations are characteristic of true feelings of community. For a summary of each style of human relations, see table 4–1.

TABLE 4–1   Summary of Human Relation Styles

	TURTLE	OWL	BULL-IN-A CHINA SHOP	PICTURE WINDOW
FEATURES OF THE RELATIONSHIP	"Region of the unknown" dominates	"Facade" dominates	"Blind spot" dominates	"Region of the known" dominates
SKILLS USED: Listening Expressing	Minimal Minimal	Often used Rarely used	Rarely used Often used	Often used Often used
EFFECTS ON THE INDIVIDUAL	Distrust; overconcern with self-protection; detachment	Self-censure; relationships important but guarded; lack of spontaneity	Need to assert self; unaware of impact on others and their responses	Trust and respect for others and self
EFFECTS ON THE RELATIONSHIP	Misunder-standing; aversion to risk taking; untapped creativity; impersonal relationships; low satisfaction	Suspicion; avoidance of conflict; reduced problem solving	Resentment; reduced quality; lack of cooperation	Consensus out of discussion; creative pro-blem solving; emotional support; stimulating and satisfying relationship

PICTURE WINDOW RELATIONSHIPS

How can people create picture window relationships? How can fear and disre-gard be replaced by trust and respect? First, look at some situations in which interaction takes place. Normally, people are unwilling to engage in self-disclosure if they feel that what they say or do will be used against them. Sometimes a buyer-beware climate may require distrust. On the other hand, trust and respect are appropriate in a climate of good will.

To create a good relationship, someone must show an initial demonstration of trust toward the other. If this expression is met with respect, a positive atti-tude will develop that leads to further trust and further respect, and so on, until a picture window relationship is achieved. This process works because experi-ences shape attitudes, which influence experiences, which shape attitudes, and so on. The concern isn't whether or not a relationship is currently a picture window, but whether people are willing to take the actions necessary to create one.

More than twenty years ago, psychologist Carl Rogers identified five characteristics of good human relationships. To some degree, these characteristics are present in all picture window relationships and all true communities.

1. *Sensitivity*: Satisfying relationships depend on the willingness of each party to understand the other's emotions and experiences. This takes time, energy, and, most importantly, the desire to know how the other person feels and understand that person's needs.

2. *Open communication*: Thoughts and feelings, including negative ones, are expressed, so they do not block closeness, and so that each person has an opportunity to decide whether he or she wishes to change.

3. *Honesty*: Even though it is difficult to achieve, the strongest bond between people is a large component of self-disclosure. We are able to say with honesty what we want and those emotions we feel, such as fear, guilt, resentment, anger, and worry, without worrying about the impression we are making. We are willing to be ourselves.

4. *Respect for the individual*: While the relationship is characterized by openness on both sides, there is acceptance of the rights of each individual to believe and behave according to his or her own standards. We do not require that the other person, in order to be valued, must meet our conditions for thoughts, feelings, and actions. In this sense, positive regard is unconditional.

5. *Rhythm*: Relationships have a rhythmic variation to them. There is openness and sharing of feelings, then a period of assimilation of these experiences. There is flow and change, then a temporary quiet. There is risk and anxiety, then security.[13]

Think of a relationship that is important to you and ask, "Are you doing all you can to demonstrate *sensitivity*, are you *open in communication*, are you *honest* with your feelings, do you show *respect* for the other person, is there *rhythm* in the relationship?"

TRUST AND RESPECT IN THE WORKPLACE

As shown in table 4–2, human relationships are important in the workplace. Early in the interview, the executive depicted speaks with *turtle camouflage* as she describes the operation of the company's executive committee. Later in the interview, she speaks with *picture window openness*.

Trust and respect are especially important between levels of responsibility in organization life. Unfortunately, many people work in environments characterized by suspicion and disregard. A recent survey showed that only 20 percent

TABLE 4–2   Turtle Camouflage Versus Picture Window Openness[14]

During the first part of the interview, the executive said:	Yet later in the same interview, she said:
The relationship among executive committee members is "close" and "friendly," based on years of working together.	I do not know how my peers feel about me. That's a tough question to answer.
The strength of this company lies in its top people. They are a dedicated, friendly group. We never have the kinds of disagreements and fights that I hear others do.	Yes, the more I think of it, the more I feel this is a major weakness of the company. Management is afraid to hold someone accountable; to say, "You said you would do it. What happened?"
I have an open relationship with my superior.	I have no idea how my superior evaluates my work or feels about me.
Group discussions are warm and friendly, not critical.	We trust each other not to upset one another.
We say pretty much what we think.	We are careful not to say anything that will antagonize anyone.
We respect and have trust in each other.	People do not truly know each other, so they are careful in what they say.
The executive committee tackles all issues.	The executive committee tends to spend time talking about relatively unimportant issues.
The executive committee makes decisions quickly and effectively.	A big problem of the executive committee is that it takes forever and a day to make important decisions.
The executive committee makes the major policy decisions.	On many major issues, decisions are really made outside the executive committee meetings. The executive committee convenes to approve a decision and have "holy water" placed on it.

of employees feel trust and respect are placed in them by management. Clearly, there are significant opportunities to build good will and develop a sense of community.[15]

At one company, management was considering sharing quality and cost performance data with all employees. Some of the managers were hesitant because the information contained poor performance data that could be damaging if it fell into the wrong hands. A decision was made, however, to take the chance and share the data. As a result, employees suggested a number of cost-saving actions that resulted in millions of dollars worth of savings. Not only did the employees treat the information appropriately, but, in fact, the approach was so successful that it has become a regular part of the company's operating practices.[16]

Scott Peck describes the sense of community that is experienced in all picture window workplaces:

> In genuine community there are no sides. It is not always easy, but by the time they reach community, the members have learned how to listen to each other in a respectful way, and how to express themselves honestly without fear. Sometimes community is reached with miraculous rapidity. But at other times it is arrived at only after lengthy struggle. Just because it is a safe place does not mean community is a place without conflict. It is, however, a place where conflict can be resolved without physical or emotional bloodshed and with wisdom as well as grace. A community is a group that can fight together gracefully.[17]

SUCCESSFUL HUMAN RELATIONSHIPS

The goal of human relations in true community is the maximum well-being of all people involved. Management educators John Jones and William Pfeiffer describe the dynamics of win/lose situations in the article on the following page.

Since win/lose situations are common, it is important to know how to cope with them. Also, since the predominant trend of win/lose contests is toward lose/lose outcomes, it is important to know how to redirect them toward "win/win" results. Management author Wendy Leebov presents twelve principles and techniques for obtaining win/win results.[18]

1. *Agree upon goals.* Objectives should be understood and agreed upon by all parties.

2. *Be on the lookout for competitive behavior.* If you feel under attack, or feel yourself lining up support, you are probably in a win/lose contest for power.

3. *Listen to understand.* Stop thinking about counterarguments while the other person is speaking. Pay genuine attention to what people are saying. Seek first to understand, then to be understood.

4. *Avoid absolute statements.* Absolutes leave no room for compromise. "I think this is one way . . ." is better than, "This is THE ONLY way. . . ."

5. *Admit mistakes.* Admit it openly when you have made a mistake, overlooked something, or made a poor decision; and then apologize. Remember that mistakes can be valuable learning experiences for future use.

The Dynamics of Win/Lose Situations

Win/lose situations pervade American culture. We use the adversary system in our courts. Political parties compete to win elections and to win points in legislatures. Debates are common in schools, universities, and in the media. The put-down is generally regarded as wit. Defeating an opponent is the most widely publicized aspect of a good deal of our sports and recreation.

The language of business, politics, and even education is filled with win/lose terms. A person "wins" a promotion and "beats" the competition. Students compete to "top the class" or "outsmart" the teacher. Although we recognize the importance of cooperation, it seems that we put enormous value on winning.

In an environment that stresses winning, it is no wonder that competitive behavior persists where it is inappropriate. Imagine a typical business meeting to decide a suitable plan, program, policy, or procedure. Members interrupt each other to introduce their own ideas. Proposals are made that other members do not even acknowledge. Partnerships and power blocs are formed to support one idea against proponents of another.

When members of such a group analyze the behavior of the group, they commonly agree that they failed to listen to each other because they were thinking of ways to state a case or to counter the proposal of someone else; or they were interrupting to get their own points across before another speaker clinched the sale of his idea. In these ways, they were acting as competing individuals, rather than as a cooperative group. They had started out to reach the best decision on a common problem, but had slipped into a win/lose contest. Very often, the original purpose is completely overshadowed by the struggle to win.

Win/lose contests can develop within any organization. Individuals may strive for dominant positions, and battles can rage between groups of people. For example, a planning department might develop a new production procedure. When it is introduced to production employees, they might resent it and lock horns with planners. It is easy to interpret the situation in win/lose terms. The planners are showing that they know more and can design a procedure better than the workers on the job. If the new procedure works well, the planners "win." On the other hand, if the innovation does not improve production, the planners "lose" and, in a sense, the workers "win" because their normal operation proved superior. Seen in this light, it should be expected that the production employees will not be committed to giving the innovation a fair trial. In extreme cases, people may even sabotage new methods, "to show those theoretical snobs in Planning." In fact, all efforts to plan for others are plagued by win/lose traps. In some companies and institutions, internal win/lose rivalries absorb more effort than the main production or service.

The following are problems that may arise from win/lose situations. Win/lose may:

- Divert time and energy from main issues.
- Delay decisions.
- Create deadlocks.
- Drive unassertive people to the sidelines.
- Interfere with listening.
- Obstruct exploration of alternatives.
- Decrease sensitivity.
- Cause people to drop out, either physically or mentally.
- Arouse anger.
- Decrease creativity.
- Leave losers resentful.
- Cause underdogs to sabotage.
- Provoke personal abuse.
- Cause defensiveness.
- Reduce productivity.

Source: Reproduced from *The 1973 Annual Handbook for Group Facilitators* by J.E. Jones and J.W. Pfeiffer (Eds.). Copyright © 1973 by Pfeiffer & Company, San Diego, CA. Used with permission.

6. *Involve people.* Whenever possible, people should have influence on decisions that affect them.

7. *Use decision making by consensus.* Avoid vote-taking without discussion and void autocratic fiat.

8. *Live up to agreements.* Follow through on every promise.

9. *Draw a continuum line.* Have people place themselves on a continuum line regarding issues. It often occurs that different "sides" are not far apart.

10. *Be alert to selling or winning strategies.* Note these in others, and avoid using them yourself. "Any intelligent person can see the advantages . . . " would be a danger signal.

11. *Respect differences.* See things from the other person's view. Try to understand the other person's needs, goals and problems.

12. *Think positive.* Beliefs have a way of influencing reality. If you think a problem or relationship is impossible to solve, it probably will be.

The key for turning win/lose situations into win/win results is to strive for what is best for all. In this way, everyone comes out on top, and this represents the human relations ideal. It should be noted that win/win agreement is not automatic, and may even be difficult to achieve, but the experience of community makes it worthwhile.

Management author Stephen Covey provides a useful model to understand the ingredients required for win/win relationships. Figure 4–4 shows that the quality of a relationship is in direct proportion to the amount of *consideration* and *courage* expressed by the parties. The higher the level of consideration shown toward each other, and the higher the amount of courage shown to live by one's convictions, the greater the benefit will be to the partners involved. Consider your own relationships: Do you demonstrate the consideration and courage required for win/win relationships?

BASIC BELIEFS ABOUT PEOPLE

The quality of human relations in any workplace reflects first of all its members', and particularly its leaders', views of the essential nature and value of humanity itself.

Human Nature

It makes a great deal of difference whether those involved view people, in general, as good or evil. If we assume that people are basically good, we can believe that misbehavior is a reactive response rather than a manifestation of character. This will lead to a search for causes in experience rather than in nature.

FIGURE 4–4   Ingredients of Win/Win Relationships[19]

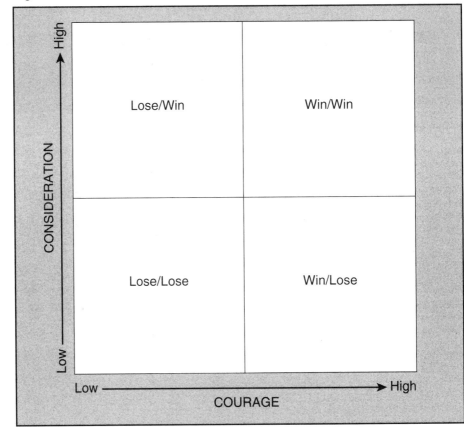

If, on the other hand, we assume that people are inherently bad, then we are prone to assume that misbehavior is caused by something within the person that cannot be altered directly. Accordingly, our attention will focus on limiting freedom to choose and act through external restrictions and controls.

Human Value

What is the basic value of human beings? This is a question as old as written history and probably as old as society itself. It stems from the debate as to whether people are ends in themselves or merely means to ends. Reduced to its simplest terms, we treat people as *ends* when we allow them to establish their own purposes and to choose and decide for themselves. When we view people as ends, we reflect a humanistic view. In contrast, when we treat people as *means*, we limit their choices and utilize them primarily as instruments for our own purposes. This is an antihumanistic view.

Table 4–3 illustrates how attitudes about human beings range from pessimism at one extreme to optimism at the other.

The Pessimistic Pole—Four Views of Human Nature

We begin by examining the attitude that people are inherently selfish and uncooperative. An early giant in the history of Western thought, Niccolo Machiavelli, in *The Prince* (1515), urged that, because of man's selfish and uncooperative nature, people must be strictly and ruthlessly controlled by anyone who seeks to gain or maintain a position of power. A ruler must put aside any question of morality and must achieve control at any price and by whatever means available, including fear and force. Machiavelli wrote:

> It is much safer to be feared than loved. For it may be said of men in general that they are ungrateful, voluble dissemblers, anxious to avoid dangers, and covetous of gain.[21]

Thomas Hobbes wrote in *The Leviathan* (1651) that human beings covet power and material goods, and will attempt to attain these even at the expense of others. They live in perpetual competition with their neighbors. He states, "If any two individuals desire the same thing, which nevertheless they cannot both enjoy, they must become enemies. Law must therefore define what is moral. But, in order for law to be effective, an authority must exist to enforce it." Hobbes believed that people recognize the need for laws and law enforcement out of fear of loss of life and property. As a consequence, they enter into a social contract, giving up the individual rights possessed in nature to a central authority. In this way, people bring about the creation of a commonwealth ruled by a sovereign.[22]

According to Sigmund Freud, the father of psychoanalysis, we are motivated by innate instincts and drives that we must constantly struggle to pacify. These instincts and drives have been identified with aggression and

TABLE 4–3   Attitudes About Human Beings[20]

The Pessimistic Pole (−)	The Optimistic Pole (+)
People are: • selfish and uncooperative • power-hungry and materialistic • aggressive and sex-driven • possessive and warlike	People: • value goodness over evil • are inclined toward reason and mutual support • have a natural tendency toward cooperation • seek affection and are naturally capable of development

sex. Freud observed, in *Civilization and Its Discontents* (1930), that society itself is threatened by the underlying hostilities that exist between human beings. To the extent that society curbs these animal forces, we become civilized and our energies can be turned toward socially acceptable goals. But, said Freud pessimistically:

> Psychoanalysis has concluded that the primitive, savage, and evil impulses of mankind have not vanished in any individual, but continue their existence, although in repressed state; and they wait for opportunities to display their activity.[23]

A predisposition of human beings to be possessive and warlike was noted by the philosopher Henri Bergson, who wrote:

> The origin of war is ownership, individual or collective, and since humanity is pre-destined to ownership by its structure, war is natural. So strong, indeed, is the war instinct, that it is the first to appear when we scratch below the surface of civilization in search of nature. We all know how little boys love fighting. They get their heads punched. But they have the satisfaction of having punched the other fellow's head.[24]

The Optimistic Pole—Four Views of Human Nature

Now let us turn to a more positive view that emphasizes the human tendency to be helpful and cooperative. In *On the Commonwealth* (51 B.C.), Marcus Tullius Cicero argued that people by nature believe in goodness and abhor savagery and baseness. On the assumption of mutual advantage, they come together by social instinct. When enough individuals are gathered, they form a democratic association or commonwealth for the benefit of all. Out of this group emerges a leader who governs voluntary subjects through a moral claim to their allegiance rather than through regulation based on force.[25]

The philosopher John Locke argued that the human being's fundamental inclination is to use reason, and that *reason itself* establishes cooperation as the basis for human relationships. In *The Second Treatise of Government*, Locke wrote that people of reason are inherently disposed toward mutual support and cooperation:

> Nature has a law to govern it, which obliges everyone; and reason, which is that law, teaches all mankind that, being all equal and independent, no one ought to harm another in his life, health, liberty, or possessions.[26]

In *Cooperation Among Animals*, W.C. Allee reported research evidence showing that cooperative relationships increase the probability of survival for any single individual, as well as for a species as a whole. One of his experiments showed that it takes proportionately less toxic colloidal silver to kill a single goldfish in an aquarium than if the aquarium holds a number of goldfish. He suggested that the ability of a group of goldfish to neutralize a poison increases faster than that of a single goldfish. As Allee explored further evidences of cooperation in higher animals, he came to the following conclusion:

All through the animal kingdom—from amoeba, to insects, to man—animals show automatic unconscious proto-cooperation and even true cooperation. There is much evidence that the inclination toward natural cooperation is stronger than the opposing tendency toward competition.[27]

The psychologist Karen Horney believed that all individuals in their natural development seek affection and approval from others. Where interpersonal relationships are not supportive, anxiety develops and this interferes with the growth of a healthy personality. In such cases, people tend to respond in three basic ways: 1) "moving toward people"—feeling inadequate, they become attached and dependent; 2) "moving against people"—rejected, they become rebellious and aggressive; and 3) "moving away from people"—they seek comfort for rejection in symbolic substitutes and fantasy.[28]

Horney did not believe people are doomed by predetermined instincts, nor that patterns of behavior are eternally established by early life experience. Her concept of human existence is hopeful and optimistic. She believed a person is born neither a devil nor a saint, but that from the time of birth the course of a person's development reflects the nature of relationships with significant people in the person's environment. Also, she viewed the human being as a proactive pilot, not as a reactive robot. What is needed is not a method of controlling innately selfish or even predatory drives toward competition and conflict with other people, but a means of tapping the human potential for joining in productive relationships with others.[29]

Where Do You Stand?

Personal history draws each of us toward some primary tendency that determines the general pattern of our human relations. Small changes may occur to accommodate the various roles we play, but there seems to be a core pattern that represents our basic beliefs concerning human nature. We view people along the continuum of evil or good, depending on our personal experiences. Is your own view of human nature primarily positive or negative? What experiences and factors have influenced your view? As a result, what principles and practices do you follow in your relations with others?

DEALING WITH DIFFICULT PEOPLE

Achieving *community* is not always easy. Sometimes we cannot avoid dealing with difficult people. With some people, difficult behavior is deeply ingrained, and the best answer is to avoid them. If this is not possible or desirable, there is only one alternative, and that is to endure with grace just like you would the weather. Sometimes it can help if you reframe the situation. Instead of focusing on the negative aspects of the person, find the good. Consider the positive qualities the person possesses.

Most difficult behavior is situational. This is good because something can usually be done about it. The options are to change the situation, change the person, or leave. Every effect has a cause and if the cause can be discovered, the problem behavior can be corrected.

The leading sources of situation-based dysfunctional behavior are pressure, conflict, and frustration. This trilogy can be caused by others or caused by self, but the effect is the same—failed relationships and harmful wear and tear on all parties.

Specific causes of difficult behavior include:

- Feelings of insecurity and inadequacy.

- Feelings of being unappreciated and unloved.

- Bad habits developed from poor role models.

- Displacement of personal frustrations onto safe and convenient targets.

- Never having learned to be nice or considerate of others.

A difficult person may need help from others to identify and solve problems. Heavy doses of education, encouragement, and patience can be helpful as the individual attempts to replace negative patterns of behavior with healthy and effective ways of living.

An important point to remember is that the difficult person must *want to change*. If not, the problem behavior will continue. Of course, all behavior has consequences, and the difficult person will learn this.

You can tell if you are dealing with a difficult person if:

- You think about him or her often.

- You tense up at the mention of his or her name.

- Ordinary coping techniques have failed.

- Your emotional health is deteriorating.

- Your job or personal performance is suffering.

- You are entertaining bizarre thoughts.

So how do you deal with difficult people? Here are ten steps or principles for dealing with difficult behaviors.

1. Be sure the best person available addresses the problem. Difficult people typically won't listen to just anybody.

2. Choose battles carefully. People have just so much accommodation and flexibility in their makeup. Be sure any behavior change will be worth the effort.

3. Pick the right place. Address problems in private so that all parties can share thoughts and feelings in an uncensored way. Only when people are *fully* honest can problems be *truly* solved.

4. Pick the right time. Deal with problem behavior as soon as possible. Otherwise memories fade and the impact of actions is filtered by time. One note: Balance timeliness with being cool and calm. If a person is overly emotional, the wrong message could be sent or received.

5. Be specific with feedback. Focus on the behavior, not the person. Don't say, "You're a jerk!" But do tell the person exactly what he or she has done and the impact as you see it. Be direct, specific, and constructive.

6. Tell and show how you feel. If the person knows you care, your criticism will get a better hearing. Do you remember when you were corrected as a child? When *you really listened* was when you knew *they really cared*.

7. Manage your emotions. If you find yourself losing control, try biting your lip, counting to ten, taking "time out," or imagining yourself in a pleasant environment. Keeping a sense of humor will be an asset.

8. Stop talking. Let the person vent. It is only natural to want to respond when someone gives criticism. There may be good reasons for the person's behavior, and these can be learned only when you listen. Remember, most behavior, functional or dysfunctional, can be traced to normal human needs—needs for security, belonging, respect, and self-expression. By listening carefully, underlying causes and feelings behind the facts can be understood.

9. Take the time to talk things over until there is agreement on appropriate future behavior. It is important to focus on creating a better future instead of reliving the past. In reaching agreement, be sure the person knows that, although the behavior may have been unacceptable, the person as an individual is valued and respected. There are two important corollaries to gaining agreement on future behavior: a) Don't block all exits; allow face-saving behavior; b) ask for changes that are possible to achieve.

10. When the person takes steps to change or improve, reinforce this with honest appreciation and sincere encouragement. Even small steps in the right direction should be recognized.[30]

By following this *ten-point plan*, behavior can be modified. As a last important point, remember that difficult behavior is in the eye of the beholder, and unless a person believes what he is doing is wrong, he will not change happily or wholeheartedly. Any change will be accompanied by resentment that at some point and in some way may present a problem.

THE ROLE OF CIVILITY IN BUILDING COMMUNITY

In *A World Waiting to Be Born*, Scott Peck writes that in true community, "The sum is greater than its parts," but that this occurs only when civility reigns. He argues that civility must be rediscovered in today's human relationships and in our organizations. The essence of his message is that people must recommit to the Golden Rule. This means treating others with the same regard with which they themselves want to be treated. The degree to which this sounds either quaint or novel is the measure of how far many aspects of modern society have strayed from this basic and universal maxim for decent living.[31]

Peck states that to be healthy does not mean that a group or organization must be in a state of genuine community at all times. To the contrary, groups repeatedly lose this genuine state and fall out of community—perhaps to emptiness, perhaps to chaos, perhaps even to pseudo-community. Two characteristics of a truly healthy group are the quickness with which its members recognize that they have lost community, and their willingness to expend the effort to rapidly regain it.[32]

People can't just build community one time; they must nurture it for as long as they continue to be together. This is an ongoing process of "maintenance and renewal." A homeowner immediately understands the concept. If a physical structure must be continually worked on for upkeep and repair, why shouldn't the same be true for a community of people?[33]

Peck describes an interesting process used in his own efforts to build and sustain community:

> When a group achieves an obviously deep level of community, there are always a few people who do not feel it—who do not feel "in community" with the rest. Yet their evaluations are generally as favorable as those of the majority. It would seem that *under the right circumstances* people can benefit as much from their failures as their successes. In fact, we know this to be the case. Frequently, a "Dots Exercise" will be used. Each person is given six large dots to color either red or blue—red for a moment when they experienced intense community and blue for a moment of intense frustration, resistance, or isolation. Breaking into smaller groups to discuss their dots with each other, most people come to realize that while they enjoyed their red dot moments, they actually learned more from their blue dot ones. Indeed, they will often start recoloring them to end up with dots that are both red and blue. It is good to avoid developing a special language, but one of the phrases that has crept into community building is "the Blessing of the Blue Dot."[34]

Peck identifies the configuration of personality and power within a group or organization to be a potential obstacle to creating community. Specifically, no matter how deeply those at the bottom or middle of the organization desire it, community will be difficult to achieve if those at the top are resistant. Conversely, if the top leaders are the kinds of people who want community, they can probably have it. They may have to work hard for it. They may have to plan carefully. It may require time and resources. But if top leaders want to achieve a positive and healthy human environment, it can be done under almost any circumstances.[35]

Peck believes community building is an ideal vehicle for teaching civility to individuals and organizations. The development of community is an excellent means to create and maintain a truly healthy person and organization.[36]

Along these lines, in an article entitled "The Brave New World of Leadership Training," Jay Conger describes *building community* as the most important task facing leaders today. He views this as a special assignment that combines two basic leadership competencies—visioning and empowerment. Both of these are related since vision itself must be empowering. The vision's purpose is not only to achieve a meaningful strategic or company goal, but also to create a dedicated community of people.[37]

BUILDING COMMUNITY—AN EXPERIENTIAL APPROACH

The rules for good relationships are to *show respect by listening in a responsive manner*, and *show trust by expressing oneself honestly and openly*. These rules are too seldom taught and practiced. Consequently, many people do not know how to relate with each other—one on one, or group to group. The following exercise provides an effective way to develop trust and respect, the foundation behaviors of good human relationships and building community.

APPLICATION: THE DYADIC ENCOUNTER[38]

Introduction

A theme frequently thought and occasionally voiced when people meet or work together is, "I'd like to get to know you, but I don't know how." This sentiment often is expressed in work groups and emerges in marriage and other dyadic (two-person) relationships. Getting to know another person involves a learnable set of skills and attitudes—self-disclosure, trust, listening, acceptance, and nonpossessive caring.

Through the Dyadic Encounter, a unique learning experience, people who need or want to communicate more effectively can create "picture windows." They can learn trust and respect "by doing," as they build relationships and skills that can be applied both on the job and in the home.

The conversation that you are about to have is intended to result in more effective human relations. Tasks are accomplished more effectively if people have the capacity to exchange ideas, feelings, and opinions freely.

In an understanding, nonjudgmental manner, one person shares information with another, who reciprocates. This results in a greater feeling of trust, understanding, and acceptance, and the relationship becomes closer.

Directions

The following ground rules should govern this experience:

- Each partner responds to each statement before continuing to the next statement.

- Complete the statements in the order they appear, first one person responding and then the other.
- Do not write your responses.
- If your partner has finished reading, begin the exercise.

A. My name is _____

B. My hometown is _____

C. Basically, my job is _____

D. The reason I am here is _____
_____

E. Usually, I am the kind of person who _____
_____

F. The thing I like most is _____
_____

G. The thing I dislike most is _____
_____

H. My first impression of you was _____
_____

I. On the job I am best at _____
_____

J. My greatest weakness is _____
_____

K. The best boss I ever had was _____
_____

L. The worst boss I ever had was _____
_____

M. I like people who _____
_____

N. I joined this organization because _____
_____

O. The next thing I am going to try to accomplish is _____

_____

_____

P. Away from the job, I am most interested in _____

_____

_____

Q. Society today is _____

_____

_____

R. What concerns me is _____

_____

_____

S. My most embarrassing moment was _____

_____

_____

T. I believe in _____

_____

_____

U. I would like to _____

_____

_____

V. What I like about you is _____

_____

_____

W. What I think you need to know is _____

_____

_____

X. You and I can _____

_____

_____

Y. During our conversation:

a. your face has communicated _____

_____

_____

b. your posture has conveyed _____

_____

_____

c. your hands and arms have indicated _____

_____

_____

Z. Have a brief discussion of your reactions to this conversation. Time permitting, you may wish to discuss other topics of your own choosing. Several possibilities are projects at work, leadership practices, societal needs, and future goals. _____

_____

_____

_____

REFERENCES

1. John W. Gardner, "Building Community," prepared for the Leadership Studies Program of the Independent Sector, (Washington, DC: American Institutes for Research, 1991).

2. Bernard Berelson and Gary Steiner, *Human Behavior* (New York: Harcourt, Brace, and World, Inc. 1964).

3. Peter Farb, *Humankind* (Boston: Houghton-Mifflin Co., 1978), 7.

4. John Donne and William Blake, *The Complete Poetry and Selected Prose of John Donne and the Complete Poetry of William Blake* (New York: Random House, Inc. 1941), 332.

5. M. Scott Peck, *The Different Drum*, (New York: Simon & Schuster, 1987) 288.

6. William C. Menninger. For a more detailed explanation of this concept, see William Menninger and Harry Levinson, *Human Understanding in Industry* (Chicago: Science Research Associates, 1956).

7. Elton Mayo, *The Human Problems of an Industrial Organization* (New York: Macmillan, Inc., 1946), 56–59, 129–130.

8. M. R. Hensen, "Better Supervision from A to Z," *Supervisory Management* (August 1985): 5, in Robert N. Lussier, 2nd ed., *Human Relations in Organizations: A Skill Building Approach* (Homewood, Ill.: 1990), 4.

9. Tom Peters, *Liberation Management* (New York: Knopf, 1992).

10. Ken Macher, "The Politics of People," *Personnel Journal* (January 1986): 50.

11. Gardner, "Building Community."

12. Joseph Luft and Harrington Ingram, "The Johari Window: A Graphic Model of Interpersonal Awareness," *Proceedings of the Western Training Laboratory in Group Development* (University of California, Los Angeles: Extension Office, 1953); Joseph Luft, *Group Processes: An Introduction to Group Dynamics*, 2nd ed. (Palo Alto , CA: National Press, 1970); Jay Hall, *Team Effectiveness Survey* (Conroe, Texas: Teleometrics International, 1968); and Naomi Miller, Northern Kentucky University, 1982.

13. Carl Rogers, *A Way of Being* (Boston: Houghton-Mifflin Co., 1980); and Carl Rogers, "The Necessity of Sufficient Conditions of Therapeutic Personality Change," *Journal of Consulting Psychology*, 21 (1957): 95–103.

14. Chris Argyris, "Interpersonal Barriers to Decision-Making," *Harvard Business Review* (March/April, 1966): 84-97.

15. Education and Personnel Research Department, Personnel and Staff, Ford Motor Company, *A Guide for Managers and Supervisors on Participative Management and Salaried Employee Involvement* (May 1984), 12.

16. Ford Motor Company, *A Guide for Managers and Supervisors on Participative Management and Salaried Employee Involvement*, 12.

17. Peck, *The Different Drum*, 71.

18. Wendy Leebov, *Positive Co-Worker Relationships in Health Care* (Chicago: American Hospital Publishing, 1990).

19. Stephen R. Covey, *The Seven Habits of Highly Effective People* (New York: Simon & Schuster, 1989), 218.

20. Based on the work of Henry P. Knowles and Borje Saxberg, "Human Relations and the Nature of Man," *Harvard Business Review* (March/April 1967).

21. Niccolo Machiavelli, *The Prince and the Discourses* (New York: Random House, Modern Library Edition, 1950), 61.

22. Thomas Hobbes, *Leviathan* (Indianapolis: Bobbs-Merrill Co. Inc., The Library of Liberal Arts Edition, 1958), 105.

23. Letter from Freud to Dr. Van Eeden, quoted in Ernest Jones, *The Life and Work of Sigmund Freud*, 2 (New York: Basic Books, Inc. Publishers, 1957), 368.

24. Henri Bergson, *The Two Sources of Morality and Religion* (Garden City, New York: Doubleday & Co., Inc. Anchor Book Edition, 1935), 284.

25. Based on Knowles and Saxberg, "Human Relations and the Nature of Man."

26. John Locke, *The Second Treatise of Government* (New York: The Liberal Arts Press, Inc., 1952), 5.

27. W. C. Allee, *Cooperation Among Animals* (New York: Henry Schuman, 1951), 29.

28. Karen Horney, *Neurosis and Human Growth: The Struggle Toward Self-Realization* (New York: W. W. Norton & Co., Inc., 1950).

29. Horney, *Neurosis and Human Growth.*

30. Raymond K. Tucker, *Fighting It Out with Difficult—If Not Impossible—People* (Dubuque: Kendall/Hunt, 1987), 5–6.

31. M. Scott Peck, *A World Waiting to be Born: Civility Rediscovered* (New York: Bantam Press, 1993), 271–298.

32. Peck, *A World Waiting to be Born*, 340–341.

33. Peck, *A World Waiting to be Born*, 339.

34. Peck, *A World Waiting to be Born.*

35. Peck, *A World Waiting to be Born*, 298.

36. Peck, *A World Waiting to be Born.*

37. Jay A. Conger, "The Brave New World of Leadership Training," *Organizational Dynamics* (Winter 1993): 56.

38. Adapted from John E. Jones and Johanna J. Jones in J. William Pfeiffer and John E. Jones, ed., *A Handbook of Structured Experiences for Human Relations Training* (San Diego: University Associates, Inc. 1974), 1.

5

The Miracle of Dialogue

Dialogue occurs when the being of a person is present in the words spoken. One dares to share with another the real person one is.

Gordon Lippitt

Communication is the anchoring concept required to build and sustain community. The essential processes of communication are *effective expression* and *effective listening*. These are skills that can be learned and they are the primary subjects of this chapter.

Building community requires the will to do so. People have to want to express themselves, and they have to want to listen to others. In the final analysis, it is a free and personal choice. If you want to build community with people, you should:

- express yourself honestly, to demonstrate *trust* in your own worthiness and in the goodwill of others; and

- listen for understanding, as opposed to making judgments, to demonstrate *respect* for the ideas and needs of others.

The path to community goes through the forest of communication, and the seeds of communication are trust and respect. These together represent *the miracle of dialogue.* **Dialogue** is an old idea valued by the ancient Greeks and practiced in many tribal societies such as the Native American. Yet it is all but lost to the modern world.[1]

THE IMPORTANCE OF COMMUNICATION

Each of the following questions can be answered with one word—*communication*.

- How do you create and convey a vision?

- How do you teach and reinforce values?

- What is the basis of good relationships?

- How do you deal with different types of people?

- How do you solve conflict when values collide?

- How do you tap the constructive power of groups?

- How do you build and sustain community?

Communication is important throughout our lives. Consider the story of Helen Keller. Although she was unable to see or hear the world around her, Helen Keller learned to communicate at the age of seven. This ability gave her an understanding of an environment that had been almost meaningless to her and allowed her to enrich the world by her words (see the following page).

The Importance of Communication

The most important day I remember in all my life is the one on which my teacher, Anne Mansfield Sullivan, came to me. . . . She led me into another room and gave me a doll. . . . When I had played with it a little while, Miss Sullivan slowly spelled into my hand the word "d-o-l-l". . . . In the days that followed, I learned to spell in this uncomprehending way a great many words, among them pin, hat, cup, and a few verbs like sit, stand, and walk. But my teacher had been with me several weeks before I understood that everything has a name.

One day, while I was playing with my new doll, Miss Sullivan put my big rag doll into my lap also, spelled "d-o-l-l," and tried to make me understand that "d-o-l-l" applied to both. Earlier in the day, we had a tussle over the words "m-u-g" and "w-a-t-e-r." Miss Sullivan had tried to impress it upon me that "m-u-g" is mug and that "w-a-t-e-r" is water, but I persisted in confounding the two. In despair, she had dropped the subject for the time, only to renew it at the first opportunity.

I became impatient with her repeated attempts, and seizing the new doll, I dashed it upon the floor. I was keenly delighted when I felt the fragments of the broken doll at my feet. Neither sorrow nor regret followed my passionate outburst. I had not loved the doll. In the still, dark world in which I lived, there was no strong sentiment or tenderness. I felt my teacher sweep the fragments to one side of the hearth, and I had a sense of satisfaction that the cause of my discomfort was removed. She brought me my hat, and I knew I was going out into the warm sunshine. This thought, if a wordless sensation may be called a thought, made me hop and skip with pleasure.

We walked down the path to the well-house, attracted by the fragrance of the honeysuckle with which it was covered. Someone was drawing water, and my teacher placed my hand under the spout. As the cool stream gushed over one hand, she spelled into the other the word water, first slowly, then rapidly. I stood still, my whole attention fixed upon the motions of her fingers. Suddenly I felt a misty consciousness as of something forgotten—a thrill of returning thought; and somehow the mystery of language was revealed to me. I knew then that "w-a-t-e-r" meant the wonderful cool something that was flowing over my hand. That living word awakened my soul; gave it light, hope, joy, and set it free.

I left the well-house eager to learn. Everything had a name, and each name gave birth to a new thought. As we returned to the house, every object I touched seemed to quiver with life. That was because I saw everything with a strange, new sight that had come to me. On entering the door, I remembered the doll I had broken. I felt my way to the hearth and picked up the pieces. I tried vainly to put them together. Then my eyes filled with tears; for I realized what I had done, and for the first time, I felt repentance and sorrow.

I learned a great many new words that day. I do not remember what they all were; but I do know that mother, father, sister, teacher, were among them—words that were to make the world blossom for me. . . . It would have been difficult to find a happier child than I was as I lay in my crib at the close of that eventful day. I lived over the joys it had brought me, and for the first time, longed for a new day to come.[2]

One of the most difficult problems of life is communication between people. This is the process by which one can, to a degree, know what another thinks and feels. Communication is the source of all human growth and the key to human relatedness. Through communication, the basic loneliness of the self can be overcome and the need for community can be satisfied. The words "communicate" and "community," although verb and noun, come from the same root. The principles of good communication are also the basic principles of community building.[3]

The importance of communication is not new. The Bible tells how the people of Shinar constructed a great tower so they could reach the heavens. Because God did not want them to succeed, He caused them to speak in different languages. With the resulting inability to communicate, their efforts at construction failed and the Tower of Babel crashed to the earth.

COMMUNICATION IS UNDERSTANDING

Communication takes many forms—written, oral, verbal, and nonverbal. Similarly, there are many standards by which we can judge the effectiveness of communication. Is it clear or unclear, prosaic or poetic? There is one standard, however, that takes precedence over all others: Does communication lead to *understanding*? The overall purpose of communication is to lower the walls of misunderstanding that unduly separate people from each other.[4]

Communication does not require conformity. Even if it were possible, would we want a world where every person had the same thoughts and wanted the same things? Harry Truman described the value of differences: "All progress begins with differences of opinion and moves onward as the differences are adjusted through reason and mutual understanding."[5]

Complete agreement may not be desirable, but understanding is. Without understanding, people experience failed relations and accomplish little. The communication process can be compared to a pair of scissors. Sometimes the blades go toward each other, and there is agreement; sometimes they go apart, and there is disagreement. But the scissors never make progress—they never create anything worthwhile—unless they are held together with a pin. Communication is the linchpin of good relationships and the foundation of community.

POWER OF THE SPOKEN WORD

Dialogue requires the expression of one's true self. An arc of distortion results if a person sends a message that is not intended. The greater the arc, the greater the degree of misunderstanding. See figure 5–1.

Effective self-expression depends on ten key rules. By using these rules, one can overcome communication barriers that prevent community.

FIGURE 5–1   The Arc of Distortion—Sending the Wrong Message[6]

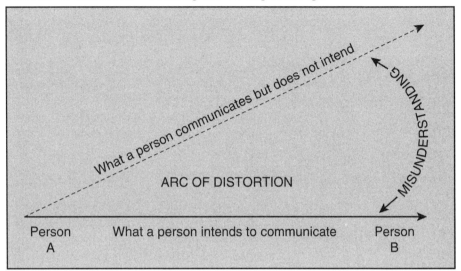

- Build vocabulary strength.
- Use the right words.
- Know when to stop talking.
- Balance enthusiasm with control.
- Think before speaking.
- Make actions support words.
- Ask questions for understanding.
- Give feedback effectively.
- Develop writing skills.
- Consider the audience.

Build Vocabulary Strength

A deficient vocabulary can cause communication problems. Words, as symbols, are tools for both thought and expression. If we do not know the exact meaning of words, we cannot think and communicate with precision.

The vocabularies of many people are poorly developed. Modern languages such as English, French, and Russian have approximately half a million words. But a mere nine words constitute 25 percent of the daily vocabulary of the average American age twenty-five or older. These words are *the, be, to, have, will, it, and, you, of.* Add thirty-four more words for a total of forty-three, and you have fully one-half of the average person's daily vocabulary.[7] Is it any wonder that people have trouble communicating their ideas and feelings to others?

Many masters of speech—Shakespeare, Robert Burns, Charles Dickens, and Abraham Lincoln—began with only ordinary vocabularies and received little or no formal education. Each was able to achieve enormous success through hard work and practice. The effort to develop a good vocabulary is one of the best investments a person can make.

The excerpt from *The Autobiography of Malcolm X* on the following page is a contemporary and dramatic example of the importance of vocabulary.

Use the Right Words

We must use the correct words or the audience will not be listening. Avoid words that are above or below the vocabulary level of listeners. Instead, use words that capture their interest. To attract the attention of others, use the following attention-gaining phrases: *I want to help you. What do you need? Thank you. We.*[8]

Stephen Covey, famous for *The 7 Habits of Highly Effective People*, notes that some words are self-defeating and depressing, while others are uplifting, energizing, and bridge-building:[9]

Self-Defeating/Depressing Words	Uplifting/Energizing Words
■ There is nothing we can do	■ Let's look at the choices
■ They won't allow that	■ We can try something new
■ I can't	■ I will
■ I must	■ We can
■ If only	■ Forward

If someone were to ask, "Why are you speaking?" you would probably reply that you want to accomplish something, help someone, or solve a problem. Remember that the words we use sometimes work against our intended goals. Keep in mind that a small part of the human body—the tongue, no more than four inches long—has the power to destroy a person six feet tall. Before speaking, be sure every word passes three important tests: (1) Is it *true*? (2) Is it *necessary*? (3) Is it *kind*? If all of your words qualify, you are more likely to accomplish your communication goals.[10]

The Autobiography of Malcolm X

Every book I picked up had sentences that contained anywhere from one to nearly all of the words that might as well have been in Chinese. When I just skipped those words, of course, I really ended up with little idea of what the book said. So I had come to the Norfolk Prison Colony still going through only book-reading motions. Pretty soon, I would have quit even these motions, unless I had received the motivation that I did.

I saw that the best thing I could do was get hold of a dictionary—to study, to learn some words. I was lucky enough to reason also that I should try to improve my penmanship. It was sad. I couldn't even write in a straight line. It was both ideas together that moved me to request a dictionary along with some tablets and pencils from the Norfolk Prison Colony school.

I spent two days just riffling uncertainly through the dictionary's pages. I'd never realized so many words existed! I didn't know which words I needed to learn. Finally, just to start some kind of action, I began copying. In my slow, painstaking, ragged handwriting, I copied into my tablet everything printed on that first page, down to the punctuation marks. I believe it took me a day. Then, aloud, I read back to myself, everything I'd written on the tablet. Over and over, aloud to myself, I read my own handwriting.

I woke up the next morning, thinking about those words—immensely proud to realize that not only had I written so much at one time, but I'd written words that I never knew were in the world. Moreover, with a little effort, I also could remember what many of these words meant. I reviewed the words whose meanings I didn't remember. Funny thing, from the dictionary's first page right now, that "aardvark" springs to my mind. The dictionary had a picture of it, a long-tailed, long-eared, burrowing African mammal, which lives off termites caught by sticking out its tongue as an anteater does for ants.

I was so fascinated that I went on—I copied the dictionary's next page. And the same experience came when I studied that. With every succeeding page, I also learned of people and places and events from history. Actually the dictionary is like a miniature encyclopedia. Finally the dictionary's A section had filled a whole tablet—and I went on into the B's. That was the way I started copying what eventually became the entire dictionary. It went a lot faster after so much practice helped me to pick up handwriting speed. Between what I wrote in my tablet, and writing letters, during the rest of my time in prison I would guess I wrote a million words.

I suppose it was inevitable that as my word base broadened, I could for the first time pick up a book and read and now begin to understand what the book was saying. Anyone who has read a great deal can imagine the new world that had opened. Let me tell you something: from then until I left prison, in every free moment I had, if I was not reading in the library, I was reading on my bunk. You couldn't have gotten me out of books with a wedge. Between Mr. Muhammad's teachings, my correspondence, my visitors—usually Ella and Reginald—and my reading of books, months passed without my even thinking about being imprisoned. In fact, up to then, I never had been so truly free in my life.

I have often reflected upon the new vistas that reading opened to me. I knew right there in prison that reading had changed forever the course of my life. As I see it today, the ability to read awoke inside me some long dormant craving to be mentally alive. Not long ago, an English writer telephoned me from London, asking questions. One was, "What's your alma mater?" I told him, "Books."

Know When to Stop Talking

Have you ever known a person who talked so much that other people quit listening? These individuals overwhelm their listeners with conversation until they become confused, bored, or both. The following story makes the point:

> Mark Twain was attending a meeting where a missionary had been invited to speak. Twain was deeply impressed. Later, he made the following comment.
>
> "The preacher's voice was beautiful. He told us about the sufferings of the natives, and he pleaded for help with such moving simplicity that I mentally doubled the fifty cents that I had intended to put in the plate."
>
> "He described the pitiful misery of those poor people, and I raised the amount again. Then that preacher continued, and I felt that all the cash I carried on me would be insufficient, so I decided to write a large check."
>
> "Then he went on. That preacher went on and on about the dreadful state of those poor natives, and I abandoned the idea of a check. Still he went on. And I got back to one dollar, then fifty cents. And still he went on. And when the plate came around . . . I took ten cents out of it."[11]

It is interesting to note that the Lord's Prayer has 56 words, the Gettysburg Address has 266 words, the Declaration of Independence has 300 words, and a recent government ruling on cabbage prices contains 26,911 words.[12] You can reduce the arc of distortion by knowing when to stop speaking.

Balance Enthusiasm with Control

If you want to express yourself effectively, be emotionally involved in what you are saying. Enthusiasm helps gain and keep the listener's attention. But if emotions rise beyond an optimum point, the ability to communicate is reduced.

Have you ever been so angry that you could not express yourself effectively? Or have you ever been so happy that you could not describe your feelings? Figure 5–2 shows the relationship between over- or understimulation and self-expression. For optimum self-expression, seek balance in your emotional involvement—neither too low, nor too high.

Think Before Speaking

For communication effectiveness, think things through before beginning to speak. A good technique is to picture the audience in your mind; then mentally go over what you want to say, how you want to say it, and, most importantly, why you want to say it. Henry David Thoreau raised this issue nearly a century and a half ago when he wrote: "We are in great haste to construct a magnetic telegraph from Maine to Texas; but Maine and Texas, it may be, have nothing important to communicate."[13] In our urge to communicate, we have to ask, for what purpose?

FIGURE 5–2   The Relationship Between Emotion Level and the Ability
to Express Oneself

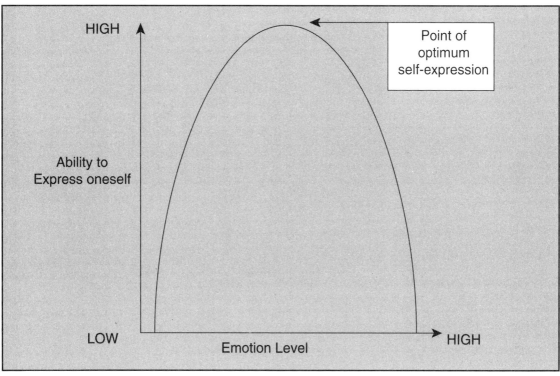

Make Actions Support Words

The majority of interpersonal communication is done without speaking. As Shakespeare wrote in *Macbeth*, "Your face is as a book, where men may read strange matters." People use nonverbal cues, such as facial expressions, hand and arm gestures, body posture, clothing, status symbols, and the use of space to convey messages. Commonly accepted interpretations of various forms of nonverbal communication in American culture are presented in table 5–1.

The manner used to express oneself gives meaning to words. Ralph Waldo Emerson put it this way: "What you *do* speaks so loudly, I cannot hear what you *say*." Indeed, studies show that meaning is communicated according to the following percentages: 55 percent body, 38 percent voice, 7 percent words. Thus, nonverbal behavior accounts for fully 93 percent of what is communicated.[15]

TABLE 5–1   Commonly Accepted Interpretations of Nonverbal Communication in American Culture[14]

Nonverbal Communication	Interpretation
Facial Expressions	
Frown	Displeasure, unhappiness
Smile	Friendliness, happiness
Raised eyebrows	Disbelief, amazement
Narrowed eyes	Anger
Blushing	Embarrassment
Eye Contact	
Glancing	Lack of interest
Steady	Active listening, interest, seduction
Hand and Arm Gestures	
Pointing finger	Authority, displeasure, lecturing
Folded Arms	Not open to change, preparing to speak
Arms at side	Open to suggestions, relaxed
Hands uplifted outward	Disbelief, puzzlement, uncertainty
Body Postures	
Fidgeting, doodling	Boredom
Hands on hips	Anger, defensiveness
Shrugging shoulders	Indifference
Squared stance or shoulders	Problem-solving, concern, listening
Biting lip, shifting, jingling money	Nervousness
Sitting on edge of chair	Listening, great concern
Slouching in chair	Boredom, lack of interest
Clothing	
Business dress	Authoritative, conservative
Sloppy attire	Disrespect, lack of responsibility
Casual clothes	Relaxation
Proxemics (Physical Space)	
From physical contact to 18 inches	Intimate space
From 18 inches to 4 feet	Personal space
From 4 feet to 8 feet	Social space
From 8 feet outward	Public space
Voice Characteristics	
Speaking loudly, quickly, and with clipped enunciation	Anger
Monotone and downward inflection	Boredom
High pitch, fast rate, loud volume, and upward inflection	Joy
Status Symbols	
Rare or expensive possessions	High status
Prestigious titles	High status

Succinctly put, actions speak louder than words, as the nonverbal experiments in the box below reveal.

Because people respond to nonverbal cues, it is important that verbal and nonverbal messages be congruent. Be sure your actions communicate the meaning you intend. For example, supervisors who value their employees must demonstrate this by listening to their ideas. Because other people cannot read your mind, be sure to say what you mean and reinforce your words with action. Remember, there is more to communication than meets the ear; nonverbal signals are vitally important.

Nonverbal Leakage

People often communicate their inner feelings more accurately by gesture and action than by speech. There are many occasions when you would like to hide your true feelings, but are unable to do so.

A set of experiments that examined changes in behavior of a group of nurses forced into a situation where they were told to tell lies proved that actions do, indeed, speak louder than words. The nurses tried hard to conceal their lies, because they were told that skill at deception was an important attribute for their future careers. But when lying, the nurses:

- Decreased the frequency of simple gestures they made with their hands. The hand actions they would normally use to emphasize verbal statements—to drive home a point, or to underline an important moment—were significantly reduced. The experienced observer is not fooled by this; if the hands don't move, there is something amiss.
- Increased the frequency of touching their faces and heads. Everyone touches the face from time to time during a conversation, but the number of times these simple actions are performed rises dramatically during moments of deception. Deception favorites include: the *chin stroke*, the *lips press*, the *mouth cover*, the *nose touch*, the *cheek rub*, the *eyebrow scratch*, the *earlobe pull*, and the *hair groom*. During deception attempts, any of these may show a marked increase, but two in particular receive a special boost: the *nose touch* and the *mouth cover*.
- Showed an increase in the number of body shifts they made as they spoke. A child who squirms in the chair is obviously dying to escape, and any parent recognizes these symptoms of restlessness immediately. In adults, they are reduced and suppressed, but they do not vanish. These unobtrusive body shifts are saying, "I wish I were somewhere else." They are actually inhibited movements of escape.
- Made greater use of the *hand shrug*. While many body gestures decreased in frequency, this became more common. It is almost as if the hands were disclaiming any responsibility for the verbal statements being made.
- Displayed facial expressions that were *almost* indistinguishable from those given during truthful statements. Untrained observers were unable to detect them. However, after special training, using slow-motion films, observers were able to spot them in normal-speed films of interviews. To a trained expert, even the face cannot lie.[16]

Ask Questions for Understanding

If you are truly interested in communication effectiveness, ask questions to see if your listener has understood your message. If you have given instructions, ask the listener to repeat them. If you have expressed an opinion, ask the other person to summarize it in his or her own words. Testing for understanding reduces the arc of distortion and avoids misunderstanding.

It can be argued that the six most important words a person can use are *who, what, why, when, where,* and *how.* Each is a type of question:

- informative, such as "Who does . . . ?"

- hypothetical, such as "What if . . . ?"

- justifying, such as "Why do we . . . ?"

- clarifying, such as "When do you . . . ?"

- directive, such as "Where do I . . . ?"

- open-ended, such as "How do you . . . ?"

By asking these basic questions and listening to the response, you achieve three important goals: You discover things you may have never known, you build goodwill by showing respect for the ideas of other people, and you help others grow as they learn to concentrate and put their thoughts into words.

Give Feedback Effectively

A common cause of communication breakdown is the tendency to evaluate or pass judgment. This may result in resentment and defensiveness on the part of the listener and may undermine the speaker's good intentions.
Effective feedback:

- *Focuses on description, not judgment.* To tell a person he or she is "dominating" will probably not be received as constructively as to say, "Just now, when we were discussing the issue, you did not appear to listen to what others said, and I felt I had to agree with your arguments or face an attack from you."

- *Focuses on behavior rather than personality.* You should refer to what a person does, rather than what you think or imagine the person is like. You might say that a person "talked more than anyone else in the meeting," rather than the person "is a loudmouth."

- *Takes into account the needs of the receiver.* Feedback can be destructive when it serves only the needs of the person giving feedback and fails to consider the needs of the person who is receiving it. Feedback should be given to help, not to hurt or merely vent one's feelings.

- *Addresses behavior that the receiver can do something about.* Frustration is only increased when people are reminded of shortcomings over which they have no control or physical characteristics about which nothing can be done. When confronted with this kind of feedback, people typically shut down and clam up.

- *Shares ideas and information rather than making demands.* By sharing ideas and information, you leave others free to decide whether and how to change in accord with their own needs and values. When you make demands, you tell others what must be done and typically raise resentment to some degree.

- *Is well timed.* When feedback is given at an inappropriate time, it may do more harm than good. The reception and use of feedback involves many possible emotional reactions, depending on a person's readiness to hear it, the amount of support available from family and friends, and other factors. In general, feedback is most useful at the earliest opportunity after the behavior occurs.

- *Gives information the receiver can understand and use.* Overloading a person with feedback reduces the possibility that the feedback can be used effectively. When you give more information than can be used, you may be satisfying some need of your own rather than helping the other person.

- *Concerns what is said or done and how, not why.* The "why" takes you from the observable to the inferred and involves assumptions regarding motive or intent. Telling others what their motivations or intentions are may alienate them. Besides, it is dangerous to assume that you know why a person says or does something, or what they "really" mean, or what the person is "really" trying to accomplish. In general, you should provide feedback only on what you observe.[17]

Why is it so difficult to give feedback to others?

- People want to be liked.

- People are too busy.

- People do not want to hurt or embarrass anyone.

But there are greater reasons to do so:

- The person receives important and useful information.

- Future communication problems can be prevented.

- A positive relationship based on trust and respect is developed.

Develop Writing Skills

The failure to communicate is not limited to oral communication. Poor writing habits can result in significant arcs of distortion, as the examples in the box below show.

Abraham Lincoln was a master of writing skills. When he wrote proclamations, speeches, and letters, he was communicating with his pen. As a youth, he split logs with a single, well-aimed blow from his ax. Later in life, the sharp edge of his prose found its mark just as efficiently, laying the truth bare with resounding whacks.

Lincoln wrote with analogy and explained difficult concepts by using stories, maxims, tales, and figures. He almost always colored his lesson or idea with some story that was plain and near to people, that they might instantly see the force and bearing of what he said.

Consider the Audience

You can improve the likelihood of being understood by tailoring what you say and how you say it to the audience. The effective communicator learns the special needs, interests, and concerns of the listener before speaking.

Groups may develop unique words or phrases that only members understand. This special language may give a feeling of cohesiveness; however, it can result in communication problems when new members or outside people are involved.

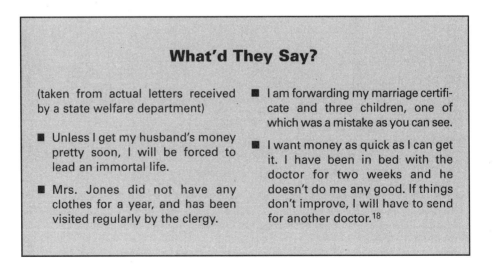

What'd They Say?

(taken from actual letters received by a state welfare department)

- Unless I get my husband's money pretty soon, I will be forced to lead an immortal life.

- Mrs. Jones did not have any clothes for a year, and has been visited regularly by the clergy.

- I am forwarding my marriage certificate and three children, one of which was a mistake as you can see.

- I want money as quick as I can get it. I have been in bed with the doctor for two weeks and he doesn't do me any good. If things don't improve, I will have to send for another doctor.[18]

THE ART OF LISTENING

Figure 5–3 illustrates the arc of distortion that results if a person receives the wrong message.

Poor listening is a major cause of communication breakdown. The Roman philosopher Cicero wrote, "God gave us two ears and only one mouth. In view of the way we use these, it is a good thing this is not reversed." More recently, psychologist Carl Rogers wrote, "The biggest block to personal communication is the inability to listen intelligently, understandingly, and skillfully to another person. This deficiency in the modern world is widespread and appalling."[20]

There are two patterns of listening—active and passive. The achievement of dialogue requires *active listening*. At this level, people refrain from evaluating the speaker's words and place themselves in the other's position, attempting to see things from the other person's point of view. Some characteristics of this level include acknowledging and responding, not letting oneself be distracted, paying attention to the speaker's nonverbal messages, and suspending one's own thoughts and feelings to give attention solely to listening. Active listening requires that you listen not only for the content of what is being said, but, just as importantly, for the intent and feelings of the message as well.[21]

FIGURE 5–3   The Arc of Distortion—Receiving the Wrong Message[19]

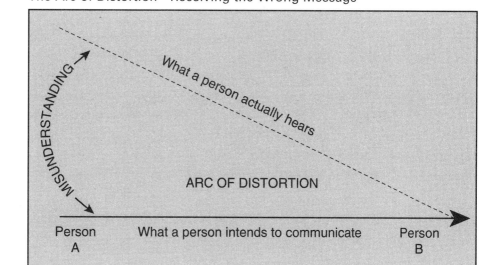

Passive listening is the enemy of community. With passive listening, one hears sounds and words, but does not really listen. At this level, people stay at the surface of communication and do not listen to the deeper meaning of what is being said. They aren't making an effort to understand the speaker's intent. They tend to be more concerned about content than feeling; they remain emotionally detached from the conversation. At this level, misunderstanding may occur since the listener is only slightly concentrating on what is said. Also, speakers could be lulled into a false sense of security that they are, in fact, being listened to and understood. Communication expert Alan Zimmerman explains: "You can be a gift to another person, but you are only a present if you are present."[22]

To achieve active listening, use the *"ladder"* approach:

- *L*ook at the person talking
- *A*sk questions to understand
- *D*on't interrupt
- *D*on't distract
- *E*stablish trust
- *R*espond[23]

Poor listening is a problem that affects many people. Studies of listening effectiveness show that 40 percent of the average white-collar worker's day is spent in the listening process, yet listening comprehension typically is only 25 percent.[24] Most people would be upset if their pay were reduced by 30 percent (75 percent of 40 percent), yet the misunderstanding and mistakes resulting from inadequate listening can be critical (particularly in occupations with life-and-death consequences, such as medicine, transportation, justice, and the military), and this is precisely what would happen to a blue-collar laborer who produced poor quality work.

What can be done to improve listening effectiveness? Ralph Nichols, pioneer and most recognized authority on the art of listening, outlines ten principles of effective listening. These principles apply on the job, in the home, and in the greater community.[25]

- Capitalize on thought speed; use spare thinking time to advantage.
- Listen for ideas; don't miss the forest for the trees.
- Reduce emotional deaf spots; beware of "red flag" words.
- Find an area of interest; listen for usability.
- Judge content; not delivery.
- Hold your fire; go easy on argument.

- Work at listening; give full attention.

- Resist distractions; concentrate.

- Hear what is said; avoid denial.

- Challenge yourself; seek to improve.

Capitalize on Thought Speed

Most people talk at a speed of 125 words per minute. Yet people think at a much faster rate—around 500 words per minute.[26] It is difficult—almost painful—to slow down thinking speed. Therefore, you usually have about four times as much thinking time as you need for every minute you are in conversation. What you do with this extra thinking time depends on whether you are a poor listener or an effective listener.

If you are a poor listener, you usually start to listen to the speaker, then realize there is time to spare. So, you briefly turn your thoughts to something else. These side trips of thought continue until you tarry too long on some enticing but irrelevant subject. When your thoughts return, you find the speaker is far ahead of you. At this point, the conversation is harder to follow, making it easier to take more mental side excursions. Finally, you stop listening entirely. The speaker is still talking, but your mind is in another world.

If you are a good listener, you will use thought speed to advantage—by applying spare thinking time to concentrating on what is being said. To capitalize on thought speed, you should:

- Anticipate what the speaker is going to talk about on the basis of what has already been said. Ask: "What is this person trying to get across?"

- Mentally summarize what the speaker has been saying. What point, if any, has already been made?

- Weigh evidence by mentally questioning it. If facts, stories, and statistics are used, consider: Are they accurate? Am I getting the full picture? Is this person telling me only what will prove a point?

- Take a few helpful notes on major points. As an old saying goes, "The strongest memory is weaker than the palest ink." Research shows that you will gain 20 percent more if you take notes and 35 percent more if you put notes into a summary of how you will use what you have heard.[27]

- Listen between the lines. People don't put everything important into words. The changing tone and volume of the speaker's voice may have meaning; so may facial expressions, hand and arm gestures, and other body movements.

Listen for Ideas

Do you ever say, "When I listen, I concentrate on details"? If so, you may be a poor listener. Suppose someone is giving you information composed of points A through Z. The person begins to talk. You hear point A and think, "Point A, point A, point A. . . . I have to remember it." Meanwhile, the person is telling you about point B. Now you have two things to memorize. You are so busy memorizing point A and point B that you miss point C completely. And so it goes up to point Z. You catch some information, confuse other information, and completely miss the rest.

Good listeners focus on main ideas. As information is presented, weigh one point against the other. Try to find a relationship between them. The person talking usually will put several points together to develop or support a central idea. If you want to comprehend and remember the speaker's message, listen for main ideas, not for a series of memorized details.

Reduce Emotional Deaf Spots

Parallel to the blind spots that affect human vision are emotional deaf spots that impair one's ability to listen and understand. These deaf spots are the dwelling places of our most cherished notions, convictions, and complexes. Often, when a speaker invades one of these areas with a word or phrase, the mind turns to familiar mental pathways that crisscross the invaded area of sensibility. When emotional deafness occurs, listening efficiency drops rapidly to zero.

To show how emotional deaf spots work, suppose your tax accountant calls and says, "I have just heard from the Internal Revenue Service, and . . . " Suddenly, you breathe harder and think, "Auditors. Can't they leave me alone?" You have stopped listening. Meanwhile, your accountant is saying there is a chance you can save 1,000 dollars this year. But you don't hear this, because the words "Internal Revenue Service" have created emotional deafness.

Emotional deaf spots are common to almost everyone. An ardent Republican, for example, may become temporarily deaf on hearing the names of Jimmy Carter and Bill Clinton; and many Democrats quit listening when they hear the names of Ronald Reagan and George Bush. Other "red flag" words that cause emotional deafness include *government agency*, *tax increase*, *downsizing*, and *mother-in-law*.

For more effective listening, identify the words that bother you and analyze why they upset you. A thorough examination may reveal that they really shouldn't bother you at all.

Find an Area of Interest

Studies of listening effectiveness support the importance of being interested in the topic under discussion. Poor listeners usually declare a subject dry after the first few sentences. Once this decision is made, it serves to rationalize any and all further inattention. Good listeners follow different tactics. Although their first thought may be that the subject sounds boring, a second thought immediately follows, based on the realization that to get up and leave would be awkward. The final reflection is that, being trapped anyway, it would be good to learn if anything is being said that can be put to use.

The key to the whole matter of interest in a topic is the word *use*. Whenever you wish to listen carefully, ask yourself, "What is the speaker saying that I can use? What worthwhile ideas are being expressed? Is the speaker reporting any workable procedures? Is there anything of value to me or anything I can use to make myself happier?" Such questions help keep attention on the subject as you screen what is said in a constant effort to sort out elements of value.

Judge Content, Not Delivery

Many listeners justify inattention to a speaker by thinking to themselves, "Who could listen to such a character? What an awful voice. Will the speaker ever stop reading from those notes?" The good listener reacts differently. The good listener may well look at the speaker and think, "This person has a problem. Almost anyone ought to be able to communicate better than that." But from this initial similarity, the good listener moves on to a different conclusion, thinking, "But wait a minute . . . I'm not interested in the speaker's personality or delivery. I want to find out if this person knows something that I need to know."

Essentially, people listen with their own experiences. Should a speaker be held responsible because a listener is poorly equipped to receive the message? Even if you cannot understand everything you hear, one way to improve communication effectiveness is to assume responsibility to be a good listener by judging content, not delivery. Can you remember a time when you withheld judgment of delivery and benefitted by the content?

Hold Your Fire

Albert Einstein wrote, "If A equals success, then the formula is A equals X plus Y plus Z. X is work, Y is play, and Z is keep your mouth shut."[31] Overstimulation is almost as bad as understimulation, and the two together constitute the twin evils of inefficient listening. We don't have to agree with what is being said, but we do have to hear it if we hope to benefit from communication.

The overstimulated listener gets too excited or excited too soon by the speaker. You must learn not to get worked up about a speaker's point until you are certain you thoroughly understand it. The secret is contained in the principle that you should withhold judgment until comprehension is complete. You must overcome the tendency to evaluate, pass judgment, and agree or disagree with statements until you learn what is meant. This means you should hold your fire.

Some people are greatly addicted to overstimulation. For them, a speaker can seldom talk for more than a few minutes without touching on a pet bias or conviction. Occasionally, they are aroused in support of the speaker's point, but often the reverse is true. In either case, overstimulation reflects the desire to enter into argument. This can be especially harmful if it occurs with family members, friends, and colleagues.

The aroused person usually becomes preoccupied by trying to do three things simultaneously: calculate the harm being done to personal ideas, plot an embarrassing question to ask the speaker, and mentally enjoy all the discomfort the speaker will experience once a devastating reply is launched. With these three things happening, subsequent passages go unheard.

Carl Rogers and Fritz Roethlisberger state: "The tendency to react to any emotionally meaningful statement by forming an evaluation of it from our own point of view is the single biggest barrier to interpersonal communication."[28] Silence really can be golden. It shows people that you respect them and you want to understand their point of view. So, *hold your fire.*

Work at Listening

Listening is hard work. It is characterized by faster heart action, quicker blood circulation, and a small rise in body temperature. To be a good listener, you must be an active participant. Too few people get involved and work at listening.

One of the most striking characteristics of poor listeners is their unwillingness to spend energy in a listening situation. People, by their own testimony, frequently enter school, community, or business meetings worn out physically, assume postures that only seem to give attention to the speaker, and then proceed to catch up on needed rest or reflect on purely personal matters.

Faking attention is one of the worst listening habits. It is particularly prevalent when you are listening to someone you know very well, such as family members or a friend. You think you know what the speaker is going to say anyway, so you just appear to tune in. Then, feeling conscience-free, you pursue any of a thousand mental tangents.

You will be forgiven almost every listening mistake but one. A listener must be present. No sidelong glances, squirming, or signs that you are being driven to distraction. For selfish reasons alone, one of the best investments you can make is to give each speaker your full attention. You should establish and maintain eye contact and indicate by body posture and facial expression that the occasion and the speaker's efforts are of concern to you. React with raised eyebrows, head nods, and smiles when appropriate. When you do these things, you help the speaker express thoughts clearly, and you, in turn, profit by better understanding. This does not imply acceptance of the speaker's point of view or favorable action on the speaker's arguments. Rather, it is an expression of interest.

Resist Distractions

Ours is a noisy age. People are distracted not only by what they hear, but also by what they see. Poor listeners tend to be influenced readily by all types of distractions, even in an intimate face-to-face situation. Often they create distractions themselves by tapping feet, drumming fingers, and clicking pens.

A good listener fights distraction. Sometimes the fight is easily won—by closing a door, turning off the radio, moving closer to the person talking, or asking the person to speak louder. If distractions cannot be solved easily, then your task becomes one of concentrating.

One of the best counselors at our university likes to listen to music when working alone. When a student comes by, he reaches over and shuts the radio off; then, turning directly toward the student, he gives his full attention. This is a powerful message that communicates respect for people and interest in what they have to say.

Hear What Is Said

People often fail to hear what is said, even when spoken to directly. An employee may be ordered to improve performance or be released; or a supervisor may be criticized for poor leadership practices. Later, when the employee is discharged or the supervisor is relieved of leadership position, both may be surprised, claiming never to have known of impending trouble.

In such instances the mechanism of *denial* serves to shut out unfavorable messages. This poor listening habit is common to many people who use selective listening and hear only what they want to hear. By hearing only what is satisfying and by denying negative messages, people fail to hear what is said, and the consequences can be great.

Some people are masters of denial. Do you have a tendency toward selective hearing? What messages might you be blocking or denying?

Challenge Yourself

Good listeners develop an appetite for hearing a variety of presentations difficult enough to challenge their mental capacities. Perhaps the one word that best describes the poor listener is *inexperienced*. Although you may spend 40 percent of your day in the listening process, in contrast to 9 percent writing, 16 percent reading, and 35 percent talking, you may be inexperienced at hearing anything mentally tough, technical, or expository; you may be conditioned to light, recreational material (television programs, radio shows, sports events, gossip, etc.). This problem can be significant because it lowers performance on the job and in the classroom.[29]

Inexperience can be difficult to overcome. It takes recognition of your weakness, a desire to improve, and effort. You are never too old to meet new challenges, particularly when the challenge is meaningful and the rewards are great. Seek opportunities to challenge your listening skills.

An important capstone or corollary to effective listening is to *be responsive*. People will continue to communicate only if their words are taken seriously. When a person makes a request or suggestion, the best thing to do is to respond as soon as possible. Disregard or delay, and this confirms the other person's worst fear—his ideas don't matter.

PSYCHOLOGICAL SIZE AND TWO-WAY COMMUNICATION

One of the best ways to achieve two-way communication is to use, not abuse, psychological size. In essence, psychological size is the nonphysical power one person has over another. If psychological size is abused, communication breaks down and the overall potential for building community is reduced.[30]

Any person perceived as having power over the freedom, success, or income of others, or who has the ability to make others appear ridiculous, incompetent, or weak, must guard against the abuse of psychological size. This concept has special relevance for people in authority positions. The individual who determines careers, decides wages, and makes job assignments has considerable power over others, and this can influence the communication process.

Subordinates are in a weaker, less powerful position, dependent to some degree on the authority figure to protect them and watch out for their well-being. Some will deny this observation, but one has only to observe the typical work environment to see how differences in psychological size can affect relationships and determine the way things are done. Deference and paternalism are not uncommon.[31]

People in positions of authority are often surprised to discover that others may fear their power and inhibit behavior accordingly. A graphic representation of a leader with big psychological size and the one-way communication that can result is presented in figure 5–4.

One-way communication presents three problems:

- *People may be reluctant to say or do anything that might offend the powerful figure.* According to George Reedy in *The Twilight of the Presidency*, even people who had enjoyed two-way communication with Lyndon Johnson when he was in the Senate began to censure their behavior once he assumed the presidency. Because of his increased psychological size, a subtle shift from two-way dialogue to one-way communication developed.[32]

- *People may become dependent on the leader to make all the decisions.* Unwilling to risk making a mistake and being criticized, people may fail to take initiative. The leader must then solve all of the problems and make all the decisions. This underuses the subordinates and overburdens the leader.

FIGURE 5–4   Abuse of Psychological Size

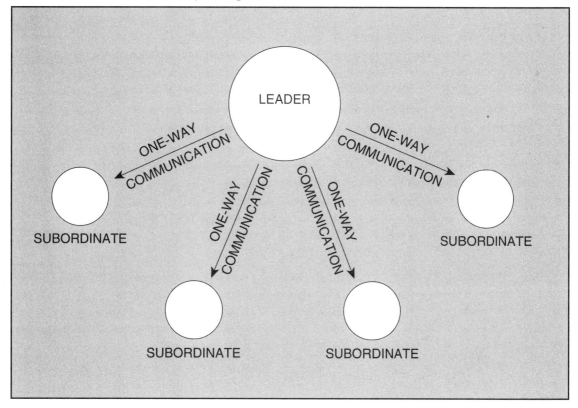

- *People may become resentful of the leader.* The leader is seen as autocratic and arrogant, and this may cause hostility, rebellion, and even sabotage. Consider the case of the infamous Captain Queeg in the film classic *The Caine Mutiny.* The captain's abusive behavior eventually led to tragedy for everyone.

How can people avoid the abuse of psychological size and develop the two-way communication that is necessary to create community? First, they must recognize the factors that contribute to psychological bigness:

- High status position
- Power to evaluate performance
- Power to hire, fire, and assign work
- Power to dispense and withhold rewards
- Use of sarcasm and ridicule

- Use of terminal statements, so that no disagreement is possible
- Job competence
- Formal, distant manner
- Cruel and punishing remarks
- Know-it-all, superior attitude
- Ability to talk fluently
- Commanding physical appearance
- Interrupting others
- Shouting at others
- Distinctive or privileged clothing
- Power to make decisions
- High social standing
- Material wealth
- Rewards of office—automobile, parking privileges, etc.
- Public criticism

Some of the items on this list are distinctly positive. For example, job competence and the ability to express oneself are desirable traits. Also, some of the factors causing psychological bigness are attributes of the person or the office, and it may be difficult or undesirable to change them. For example, neither a supervisor's physical size nor the power to make decisions should be changed.

Other factors of psychological bigness, however, serve no purpose except to alienate people and result in one-way communication:

- Use of sarcasm and ridicule
- Use of terminal statements, so that no disagreement is possible
- Formal, distant manner
- Cruel and punishing remarks
- Know-it-all, superior attitude
- Interrupting others
- Shouting at others
- Public criticism

As a rule, people should avoid any behavior that demeans or intimidates another person. The solution is to equalize psychological size. A picture of the proper use of psychological size and good two-way communication is presented in figure 5–5.

Many leaders mistakenly think that the best way to equalize psychological size is to reduce their own size. In doing so, however, they may reduce their size so low that respect is lost and cannot be regained. Few individuals have the ability to go from large psychological size to small psychological size and back again without losing effectiveness. Therefore, the most effective approach is not for leaders to lower their own psychological size, but to raise the size of others.

The best way to raise psychological size is to show genuine interest in people. Through attention and sincere listening, the leader shows that others are important. This builds pride and commitment, and increases the productivity of the group as a whole.

Leaders should keep in mind three important points to develop two-way communication and build community. First, model an honest and open style of communication. Some people will take longer than others to respond with honesty and openness in return. Still, the leader should set a good example and stick with it.

FIGURE 5–5   Effective Use of Psychological Size

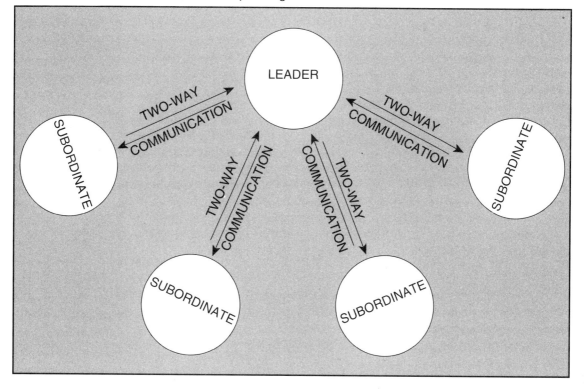

Second, be patient and allow time for people to change. It usually takes time and patience to create dialogue between people, and too rapid a change from one style of operating to another may be interpreted as insincerity or may confuse people. Each person comes to each new relationship carrying the baggage of past experiences. Individuals who have been conditioned to be protective and reserved will usually be slow to express themselves.

Third, make a sincere effort to draw people out without constantly evaluating their remarks. This will usually be seen as a demonstration of respect and will help create true dialogue. The following guidelines can help accomplish this goal.[33]

- *Stop talking.* You cannot listen to others if you are talking. Shakespeare wrote, "Give every man thine ear, but few thy voice."[34]

- *Put the talker at ease.* Help the other person feel free to talk. This is called a supportive environment or atmosphere. Sit or stand in a relaxed manner.

- *Show the person that you want to listen.* Look and act interested. Don't read your mail while the other person is talking. Listen to understand, rather than to oppose. Maintain eye contact.

- *Remove distractions.* Don't doodle, tap, or shuffle papers. Turn off the TV. Hold telephone calls. Will it be quieter if you shut the door?

- *Empathize with the person.* Try to put yourself in the other person's place to understand the speaker's point of view.

- *Be patient.* Allow time. Don't interrupt. Don't walk toward the door or walk away while the other person is talking. Some people take longer to make their point.

- *Hold your temper.* An emotional person may misinterpret a message or may say something unintended. If you are angry, cool off before responding. Take a walk or try counting to ten.

- *Go easy on argument and criticism.* This puts the speaker on the defensive and may result in a "blow-up"; or it may cause the person to "shut down."

- *Ask questions.* This encourages the speaker and shows you are listening. It also helps develop additional points. Few actions demonstrate respect as much as asking others for their opinion.

- *Encourage clarification.* When the speaker touches on a point you want to know more about, simply repeat the statement as a question. This will allow clarification and elaboration.

- *Stop talking.* This is the first and last point, because all others depend on it. You cannot do a good job of listening while you are talking. As Shakespeare wrote, "Give thy thoughts no tongue. . . ."[35]

REFERENCES

1. Peter Senge, *The Fifth Discipline: The Art and Practice of the Learning Organization* (New York: Doubleday, 1990), 239.

2. Helen Keller, *The Story of My Life* (New York: Doubleday, 1903).

3. M. Scott Peck, *The Different Drum: Community-Making and Peace* (New York: Simon and Schuster, 1987), 83.

4. Peck, *The Different Drum*, 257.

5. Harry S. Truman, Address to the United Nations Conference (April 25, 1945).

6. Warren Bennis, Kenneth D. Benne, and Robert Chin, *The Planning of Change* (New York: Holt, Rinehart, and Winston, 1971).

7. Wilfred Funk and Norman Lewis, *30 Days to a More Powerful Vocabulary* (New York: Pocket Books, 1971), 219.

8. Will Forpe and John McCollister, "The Most Important Words," *The Sunshine Book* (Middle Village, NY: Jonathan David Publishers, Inc. 1979), 216.

9. Stephen R. Covey, *The Seven Habits of Highly Effective People* (New York: Simon and Schuster, 1989).

10. "Three Gates that Test Our Words," Forpe and McCollister, *The Sunshine Book*, 220.

11. "The Price of Over-Talk," Forpe and McCollister, *The Sunshine Book*, 220.

12. William Henry as quoted in Michael LeBeouf, *Working Smart* (New York: McGraw-Hill, Inc., 1979), 179.

13. Walter Kiechel III, "How We Will Work in the Year 2000," *Fortune* (May 17, 1993), 48.

14. James Higgins, *Human Relations: Concepts and Skills* (New York: Random House, Inc., 1982), 88.

15. Albert Mehrabian and Morton Wiener, "Decoding of Inconsistent Communications," *Journal of Personality and Social Psychology*, 6, no. 1 (1967): 109–114; and Albert Mehrabian and Morton Wiener, "Inference of Attitudes and Nonverbal Communication in Two Channels," *Journal of Consulting Psychology*, 31, no. 3 (1967): 248–252.

16. Desmond Morris, *Manwatching* (New York: Abrams, 1977), 108–110.

17. "Characteristics of Effective Feedback," *EEO Newsletter*, Washington (DC) Metropolitan Transit Authority (April 1982).

18. Higgins, *Human Relations*, 83; and Robert M. Fulmer, *The New Management* (New York: Macmillan, Inc., 1974).

19. Bennis, Benne, and Chin, *The Planning of Change.*

20. Carl Rogers and Frederick Roethlisberger, "Barriers and Gateways to Communication," *Harvard Business Review* (July–August 1952), 52.

21. Alan Zimmerman, ed., "We've Got to Keep Meeting Like This," *Communi-Care* (Winter 1991).

22. Zimmerman, "We've Got to Keep Meeting Like This."

23. Gail Gregg, "They Have Ears, But Hear Not," *Across the Board* (September 1983): 56–61.

24. John Hasling, *Group Discussion and Decision-Making* (New York: Thomas Crowell/Harper and Row, 1975), 55.

25. Ralph Nichols, *Are You Listening?* (New York: McGraw-Hill, 1957), 77–101, 128–140; Hasling, *Group Discussion and Decision-Making*, 57–60; and Keith Davis, *Human Behavior at Work*, 6th ed. (New York: McGraw-Hill, 1981), 412–414.

26. Andrew Wolvin and Carolyn Coakley, *Listening*, 4th ed. (Dubuque: W.C. Brown, 1992), 243.

27. Zimmerman, "We've Got to Keep Meeting Like This."

28. Rogers and Roethlisberger, "Barriers and Gateways to Communication."

29. Hasling, *Group Discussion and Decision-Making*, 55; and Clark Caskey, "The Vision of Supervision," *Supervision* (August 1985), 3.

30. The concept of "Psychological Size" was adapted from a course developed by the Ford Motor Company, Training and Development Department.

31. Levinson, *Executive*, 44–46.

32. George E. Reedy, *The Twilight of the Presidency* (New York: World Publishing Co., 1970), 11–15, 76–83.

33. Davis, *Human Behavior at Work*, 413.

34. Hamlet 1.3.68, *The Quotable Shakespeare: A Topical Dictionary*, compiled by Charles DeLoach (Jefferson, NC: McFarland, Inc., 1988).

35. Hamlet 1.3.59, *The Quotable Shakespeare*.

6

Interpersonal Styles

There is a great deal of human nature in people.

Mark Twain

T his chapter features the role of personality in the community building process. We have personalized the subject, so you can assess your *interpersonal style* and the influence it has in your relationships with others. The message of this chapter is:

- understand the unique characteristics of different types of people;

- appreciate their special contributions; and

- be wise, caring, and flexible to meet their needs.

PERSONALITY PLAYS A PART

Even as obvious as some differences are—age, sex, race—none of these is the major cause of communication breakdown. That distinction goes to personality conflict. When communication fails at work, rarely is it caused by lack of technical skill or the lack of desire to do the job; often it is because of personality differences. When people approach a common task from different points of view, barriers can occur that lower performance and reduce opportunities for all.

We have all seen the phenomenon where you know Ann and I know Bill. You think Ann is great and I think Bill is great; but they don't get along with each other. They may have the same high values and the same good intentions, but they have personality differences that make them uncomfortable with each other and may even affect their work.

We have also seen the case where a group is led by a leader with a certain personality, and things go well. Along comes another leader with a different personality, and the group deteriorates. The leaders are equally qualified and equally motivated to do a good job, but the relationship is poor between the second leader and the group. Personality conflict can destroy morale and lower group performance.

The following questionnaire measures *style of interpersonal relations*, an important element in the human side of work. It will allow you to better understand yourself and the people in your world. This understanding can help communications, teamwork, and the community building process.

APPLICATION: INTERPERSONAL STYLE QUESTIONNAIRE[1]

Directions

This questionnaire consists of twenty-six statements. There are no right or wrong answers. The best answers are your true opinions.

For each statement, indicate which of the three alternatives, *a*, *b*, or *c*, is most true or most important to you by circling *a*, *b*, or *c* in the MOST column.

Then choose the least true or least important of the three alternatives and circle its letter in the LEAST column.

For every statement, be sure you circle one alternative in each column. If *a* is circled under MOST, then either *b* or *c* should be circled under LEAST.

Do not skip any questions and do not debate too long over any one statement. Your first reaction is desired.

	MOST			LEAST		
	T	P	I	T	P	I

1. When I enter new situations, I let my actions be guided by:
  a. my own sense of what I want to do
  b. the direction of those who are responsible
  c. discussion with others
	b	c	a	b	c	a

2. When faced with a decision, I consider:
  a. precedent and traditions
  b. the opinions of the people affected
  c. my own judgment
	a	b	c	a	b	c

3. People see me as:
  a. a team player
  b. a free spirit
  c. a dependable person
	c	a	b	c	a	b

4. I feel most satisfied when:
  a. I am working on personal goals
  b. I do things according to standards
  c. I contribute to a project
	b	c	a	b	c	a

5. I try to avoid:
  a. not being myself
  b. disappointing those in authority
  c. arguments with my friends
	b	c	a	b	c	a

	MOST			LEAST		
	T	P	I	T	P	I

6. In my opinion, people need:
   a. guidelines and rules for conduct
   b. warm and supportive human
      relationships
   c. freedom to grow

	a	b	c	a	b	c

7. Over time, I have learned:
   a. no person is an island
   b. old paths are true paths
   c. you only pass this way once

	b	a	c	b	a	c

8. I want to be treated:
   a. as a unique person
   b. as an equal
   c. with respect

	c	b	a	c	b	a

9. I avoid:
   a. not meeting my responsibilities
   b. compromising my personality
   c. the loss of good friends

	a	c	b	a	c	b

10. What the world needs is:
    a. more people who think independently
    b. more understanding among diverse people
    c. more people who respect and abide
       by the law

	c	b	a	c	b	a

11. I am most happy when:
    a. I am free to choose what I want to do
    b. there are clear guidelines and rewards
       for performance
    c. I share good times with others

	b	c	a	b	c	a

12. I am most responsible to _____ for my actions:
    a. family and friends
    b. higher authorities
    c. myself

	b	a	c	b	a	c

13. In order to be a financial success, one should:
    a. relax; money is not important
    b. work in cooperation with others
    c. work harder than others

	c	b	a	c	b	a

14. I believe:
    a. there is a time and place for everything
    b. promises to friends are debts to keep
    c. he who travels fastest travels alone

	a	b	c	a	b	c

	MOST			LEAST		
	T	P	I	T	P	I

15. I want the value of my work to be known:
    a. soon after completion
    b. with the passage of time
    c. while I am doing it

	MOST			LEAST		
	b	a	c	b	a	c

16. A group member should support:
    a. the decisions of the majority
    b. only those policies with which he or she
       personally agrees
    c. those who are in charge

	MOST			LEAST		
	c	a	b	c	a	b

17. I believe feelings and emotions:
    a. should be shared with discretion
    b. should be shared openly
    c. should be kept to oneself

	MOST			LEAST		
	c	b	a	c	b	a

18. The people I enjoy working with are:
    a. free thinking
    b. well organized
    c. friendly

	MOST			LEAST		
	b	c	a	b	c	a

19. I value:
    a. teamwork
    b. independent thinking
    c. order and organization

	MOST			LEAST		
	c	a	b	c	a	b

20. I believe in the saying:
    a. all work and no play makes Jack a
       dull boy
    b. united we stand, divided we fall
    c. there are no gains without pains

	MOST			LEAST		
	c	b	a	c	b	a

21. My work day goes best when I:
    a. have freedom of operation
    b. know what is expected of me
    c. experience fellowship with good colleagues

	MOST			LEAST		
	b	c	a	b	c	a

22. If I suddenly received a large sum of money,
    I would:
    a. use most of it now for the things I want
    b. invest most of it for the future
    c. spend half of it now and save the rest

	MOST			LEAST		
	b	c	a	b	c	a

23. I grow best by:
    a. following established truths
    b. interacting with others
    c. learning from personal experience

	MOST			LEAST		
	a	b	c	a	b	c

	MOST			LEAST		
	T	P	I	T	P	I

24. It is important that I:
    a. plan a year or two ahead
    b. live my life to the fullest now
    c. think about life in a long-range way

| c | a | b | c | a | b |

25. I am known for:
    a. making my own decisions
    b. sharing with others
    c. upholding traditional values

| c | b | a | c | b | a |

26. I work best:
    a. with structure and organization
    b. as a member of a team
    c. as an independent agent

| a | b | c | a | b | c |

Scoring

Step 1. Add the total circled for each column, and put these totals in the boxes marked T, P and I. Each section total should equal 26.

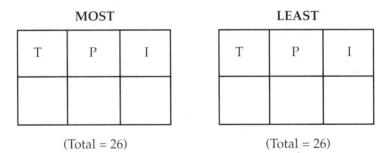

MOST

T	P	I

(Total = 26)

LEAST

T	P	I

(Total = 26)

Step 2. Determine your scores for T, P and I by using the following formula: Score = 26 + MOST – LEAST. For example, if your T MOST was 20 and if your T LEAST was 12, your T score would be: 26 + 20 – 12 = 34. Complete the following:

T Score = 26 + _____ – _____ = _____
                     T MOST   **T LEAST**

P Score = 26 + _____ – _____ = _____
                     P MOST   **P LEAST**

I Score = 26 + _____ – _____ = _____
                     I MOST   **I LEAST**

(Your total should equal 78) TOTAL = _____

Interpretation*

The letters T, P, and I represent three styles of interpersonal relations.

T = Traditional
P = Participative
I = Individualistic

If your highest score is T, you are *traditional*. If your highest score is P, you are *participative*. If your highest score is I, you are *individualistic*. If you are within one point of the same score for all three, you have built-in versatility for dealing with different types of people. If your two high scores are T and I, this means there are two opposite forces in your world asking you to be two different ways. One force is saying, "Be traditional," and the other is saying, "Be individualistic." Although this can present problems, it can also be good if it allows you to accomplish your values and goals in life. Values and goals are more important than style of interpersonal relations. Note that occasionally it may be difficult for others to understand you because of the different signals you send.

TYPES OF PEOPLE AND TYPES OF CULTURE

One way to show that all styles of interpersonal relations have equal value is to identify people in history who represent distinctly different styles and who are each held in high esteem.

Traditional

When historians identify people who have had the most impact on humankind, the name of Moses always makes the top ten. His leadership style exemplified *traditional* behavior.

A woman in history who was *traditional* was the longest reigning monarch of all the European monarchs. Indeed, a whole era or period of history was named after Queen Victoria, known for her moral strength and high standards of conduct.

---

*Interpretation Note: There are many interesting models and well-developed instruments that can be used in the community building process. Self-report questionnaires can help people learn more about themselves, understand other people, and improve human relations. However, no questionnaire should be used as a basis for decision making unless proven to be fake-proof, valid, and reliable: (1) answers may be inaccurate (an unemployed parent may feel justified lying on an employment test); (2) the relationship between test scores and other behaviors may be unknown or lack dependability (there may be no relationship between test scores and job performance); (3) different days may produce different results (mood and recent experience may influence scores).

Also note that no questionnaire can capture the full flavor and uniqueness of a single human being. There is no one just like anyone else anywhere in the world. Each individual is biologically different in that we are products of millions of ancestors, no two of whom were exactly alike, and each person is unique in his or her experiences, resulting in perceptions and judgments that are different from every other person's.

Participative

A woman in history who was *participative* was Eleanor Roosevelt. She was people-caring and people-serving. Always concerned with the welfare of others, she focused her life on the betterment of society.

Some of the best products of the United States have been the ideas and accomplishments of *participative* Benjamin Franklin. Indeed, without Franklin the United States would not exist as we know it today.

> There were few activities in which Benjamin Franklin did not excel. Philosopher, inventor, diplomat, printer, scientist—he was all of these and more. By his many achievements, including discovering electricity and helping to write the Constitution, Franklin left his mark upon the face of America and the world.[2]
>
> Frederick A. Birmingham

Individualistic

One of America's most influential thinkers was the *individualist* Henry David Thoreau, who wrote:

> If a man does not keep pace with his friends,
> perhaps it is because he hears a different drummer.
> Let him step to the music he hears,
> however measured or far away.[3]

An example of a woman who was *individualistic* is Joan of Arc, who led the French people by her conviction and brave example.

If you were an employer, you would probably have trouble deciding which of these individuals to hire. Each has special qualities and would make valuable contributions. However, each is different in style of interpersonal relations, and each would require different treatment to be both happy and productive.

People are products of culture—family, town, and country. As such, style of interpersonal relations is influenced by how we are raised. Societies teach and reinforce behavior traits, so that just as individuals are traditional, participative, and individualistic, so are whole groups of people.[4]

Because personality is a social construct, it involves cross-cultural variations. Studies across cultures show that style of interpersonal relations is a basic dimension or characteristic.[5] Traditional social orientations put the needs and interests of the group above the individual. Individualistic social orientations involve separating the self from others. Participative social orientations seek a middle ground between individualistic and traditional styles with an emphasis on warm and supportive human relations.[6]

Traditional cultures tend to be formal and structured, such as those of old England, Germany, and Hungary. Many nonwestern cultures, including those of Japan, China, and India, are traditional in nature.[7] Participative cultures develop in melting-pot societies: The United States is about 20 percent traditional,

60 percent participative, and 20 percent individualistic. Individualistic cultures include the French, Italian, and Greek.

It is important to note that there are exceptions to these generalizations. For example, it is possible for an individual Frenchman to be more traditional than the most traditional German; and there may be a Hungarian who is more individualistic than the most individualistic Italian. It is also important to note that human traits vary in degrees, so that *a person typically is a mixture of all three styles.* While you may be primarily participative, you probably have a few traditional and individualistic characteristics as well.

Describing whole groups of people according to interpersonal style should not obscure the extensive diversity and variation that characterize each individual person. Also, it should be noted that certain qualities belong potentially to all people, such as basic honesty, concern for others, and open-mindedness.[8]

UNDERSTANDING OTHERS

Certain characteristics distinguish each style of interpersonal relations. As you read the following descriptions, think about the people with whom you live and work. The descriptions will help explain why some people are easy for you to understand, although you may not always agree with them (they are like you), and why other people are difficult for you to understand (they are different from you). Think also about the ways these different types of people should be treated to bring out their best in building community.

Form of Control

Traditionals are comfortable with rules, policies, and procedures. They believe that without such guidelines, social breakdown occurs.

Participatives prefer interpersonal commitment as a form of control. The participative says, "I will do this. Will you do that?" Social ties are their preferred form of control.

For individualists, control is a negative word. They dislike the idea of restricted freedom. In this spirit, Thoreau wrote, "The only obligation I have a necessity to assume is to do at any time what I think is right."[9]

Basis of Action

The basis of action for traditionals is direction from authorities in which they believe. These authorities may be parental, supervisory, governmental, or religious. In any case, traditionals believe those in charge should determine the course of action to be taken.

Discussion and agreement with others are the basis of action for participatives. Democracy is their preferred form of government, and participative management is their favorite style of leadership.

The basis of action for individualists is direction from within. The individualist has an internal compass to establish direction and a personal yardstick to measure the rightness and wrongness of behavior. There is a concept in psychology called *locus of control* that asks, "Who is in charge, the world or me?" The individualist says, "Me."

To Be Avoided

Traditionals avoid deviation from authoritative direction. Therefore, systems and procedures to guide behavior should be available. They appreciate job descriptions with responsibilities clearly defined. Business plans, life plans, and road maps for travel are important to them.

Participatives avoid confrontation and strive to reach agreement if at all possible. Interpersonal conflict and misunderstanding are particularly painful. Abraham Lincoln, who had both traditional and individualistic moments, was mostly participative. In this fashion he wrote, "Am I not destroying my enemies when I make friends of them?"[10]

Individualists avoid not being themselves. Congruency is important to them. They strive to be true to their own essential nature. Individualists realize that life is a progression of social roles, but they insist on choosing their own parts.

Perception of Responsibility

Traditionals believe highest allegiance should go to superordinate powers. These powers may be in the church, community, workplace, or home.

Participatives feel responsibility to help others. They try not to disappoint family, friends, and colleagues. Participatives relate to the little boy who told Father Flanagan of Boys Town, "He ain't heavy, he's my brother." They see themselves as their brothers' keeper.

"To thine own self be true and thou cannot be false to any man," advises Polonius, in *Hamlet*. This is an individualistic principle. Individualists assign first responsibility for their own actions to their own conscience.

Goals Desired

Traditionals value organization and order. They believe the mission, goals, and objectives of an organization should be identified, and that each person's role should be made clear. Work plans and organization charts are helpful job aids for traditionals.

Participatives value group consensus and smooth human relations. By interpersonal style, they make good personnel officers, counselors, and work group supervisors. Participatives are harmonizing agents. A quote from Lincoln makes the point well:

> A drop of honey catches more flies than a gallon of gall. So it is with men as well. If you would win a man to your cause, first convince him that you are his friend. It is a drop of honey that catches his heart, which, say what he will, is the highroad to his reason.[11]

Individualists value independence and freedom. "Give me wings and let me fly" and "no rules for me" are interpersonal needs felt by individualists. They are especially uncomfortable with close supervision. Assignments that allow as much freedom as possible are ideal for individualists (assuming they have the ability and desire to accomplish the work). Consider Patrick Henry, the individualist, who said, "Give me liberty, or give me death." You will also recall that some people sought to kill him.

Basis for Growth

Traditionals believe there is a time and place for everything, and the best way to grow is by following the established order. They value traditions in all areas of life—family, work, and religion. Philosophically, traditionals relate to Ecclesiastes 3:1–2: "To every thing there is a season, and a time to every purpose under the heaven: A time to be born, and a time to die; a time to plant, and a time to pluck up that which is planted."

Participatives enjoy human interaction and prefer to grow in this manner. A participative would make a poor Robinson Crusoe—stranded on a deserted island—until Friday came along. Participatives like to teach others and learn from them as well. Sharing is a basic interpersonal value. In the work setting, they especially appreciate group involvement activities. Staff meetings and collaborative work teams are seen as growth opportunities by participatives.

Individualists prefer growth through introspection and self-analysis. It is important for them to get away occasionally and think, "How do I feel about this; what is my philosophy on that, and what are my beliefs on this?" Individualists grow best through personal experience and self-discovery. A sentiment that reflects their nature is expressed by the poet Robert Frost, who wrote:

> I shall be telling this with a sigh
> Somewhere ages and ages hence:
> Two roads diverged in a wood,
> And I—
> I took the one less traveled by,
> And that has made all the difference.[12]

Position in Relation to Others

Traditionals are comfortable as members of the hierarchy. Whether at the top, in the middle, or on the first rung of the ladder, they value structure and organizational clarity. Many people who are in top positions in organizations are traditionals. Note that George Washington was traditional in his style of interpersonal relations.

Participatives are comfortable as members of the team. In fact, the **team** acronym, **T**ogether **E**veryone **A**ccomplishes **M**ore, is a participative concept. Participatives make good work group and committee members, because they enjoy working with and through others. Indeed, committees are creatures of the participative personality. They are tools not only to get the job done, but also to meet social needs.

Individualists are most comfortable as separate people. For all of their lives, they have seen the group go one way, and, almost instinctively, they have gone the other. By personality type, individualists are the pioneers of society—the first to do this and the first to go there. If Daniel Boone were to complete the Interpersonal Style Questionnaire, he would be an individualist—as would Christopher Columbus, the explorer and navigator. For their needs to be met, individualists must express themselves as the unique individuals they see themselves to be, not as members of a group or bureaucracy.

Material Goods

The traditionals are the world's best competitors. Witness the success of the Germans and Japanese in the international marketplace. And witness the New England Yankee, who came from Puritan stock and formed the basis of the American free market system.

Participatives collaborate to get material goods. Teamwork comes naturally, as the participative says, "If we help each other, together we will accomplish more." Barn building, potluck suppers, and the volunteer fire department are participative activities.

Individualists tend to take material goods for granted, thinking that everyone should have them.

Identification and Loyalty

The traditional's first loyalty is to the organization—the U.S. Marine Corps, the FBI, the Catholic church. Pride in the organization is especially important to them. This is the reason organizations need legends, logos, and other means to build "Yankee spirit" and achieve "Celtic pride."

The participative's first loyalty is to the group—the shoulder-to-shoulder work group, team, or department. Inclusion and a sense of belonging are important values for participatives. Edwin Markham's short verse captures the essence of the participative personality:

> He drew a circle that shut me out,
> Heretic, rebel, a thing to flout;

But Love and I had the wit to win—
We drew a circle that took him in.[13]

Loyalty is not a major value for individualists, but when they have it, they have it intensely for the person or ideal they deem worthy.

To show how this works, imagine three Marine Corps privates—traditional, participative, and individualistic: The traditional's highest loyalty will be to the corps and all it represents; the participative's first loyalty will be to his comrades-in-arms, the platoon; and the individualist's primary allegiance will be to those individuals and ideals who have earned his respect and support. Indeed, when the traditional thinks of patriotism, he imagines an old Uncle Sam, finger pointing, saying, "I want you"; while service for the participative is based on such ideas as "united we stand, divided we fall"; and the individualist's ideal is to preserve "the land of the free."

One can see these orientations surface when personalities clash. If you ever have an argument with a traditional, realize the importance placed on responsibility and duty. If you ever have an argument with a participative, know that what is valued is brotherhood and love. If you ever have conflict with an individualist, know that what is important is freedom and liberty.

This example explains why people can fail to communicate and still respect each other at a basic level. Participatives and individualists realize that traditionals uphold an important quality with *commitment to responsibility*, while traditionals and individualists recognize the universal value in the participative's *commitment to love*. Finally, traditionals and participatives see the importance of the individualist's *dedication to freedom*.

Time Perspective

The time perspective for traditionals is the future. Because of this, they often have supplies, tools, and money when others do not.

For participatives, the time perspective is the near future—tomorrow or next week; they can wait that long.

The time perspective for individualists is the present—today. Don't talk to them about the past; they will say, "The past is gone." And don't talk to them about the future; they will say, "The future may never come." Individualists are primarily interested in here-and-now experience and living life fully in the moment.

It is interesting to see the influence of all three styles—traditional, participative, and individualistic—in American culture. It can be argued that this diversity gives strength to the society. Consider the tenets that reflect each style. America is a nation of laws (*traditional*), conceived by and for people (*participative*), and dedicated to freedom and the rights of individuals (*individualistic*).

A short interpretation of styles of interpersonal relations is seen in table 6–1.

TABLE 6–1   Interpersonal Styles—Short Interpretation

Behavior/Value	Traditional	Participative	Individualist
Form of control	rules, laws, and policies	interpersonal commitments	what I think is right or needed
Basis of action	direction from authorities	discussion and agreement with others	direction from within
To be avoided	deviation from authoritative direction	failure to reach agreement	not being one's self
Perception of responsibility	superordinate powers	colleagues and self	self
Goals desired	compliance	consensus and smooth human relations	individual freedom
Basis for growth	following the established order	human interaction	introspection and personal experience
Position in relation to others	member of hierarchy	peer group member	separate person
Material goods	competition	collaboration	taken for granted
Identification and loyalty	organization	group	individual
Time perspective	future	near future	present

DEALING WITH DIFFERENT TYPES OF PEOPLE

Differences in personality can result in perceptions and judgments that are poles apart. You have undoubtedly seen individuals and groups who should be working together smoothly, but are not. An awareness of the nature and needs of different types of people is the first step in building relationships. This enables new levels of cooperation and success.

Although each person is unique and should be treated according to individual makeup, the following guidelines are useful for meeting the needs and bringing out the best in each style of interpersonal relations. Remember that most people have characteristics of all three styles but tend to develop a preference for one or two over the other(s). The most ardent individualist will have traditional moments, and vice versa.

Meeting the Needs of Traditionals

Provide work rules and job descriptions with duties spelled out in priority order. Provide an organization chart showing reporting relationships; respect the chain of command. Respect traditions and established ways; appeal to historical precedent. Avoid changes when possible; if impossible, introduce changes slowly. Accentuate reason over emotion when handling problems. Mind your manners and language; be courteous. Establish a career plan with benchmarks for progress, rewards expected, and time frames. Provide tangible rewards for good performance, preferably money. Recognize good work with signs of status, such as diplomas, uniforms, medals, and titles. Reinforce company loyalty through service pins, award banquets, and personal appreciation. Communicate the mission, goals, and objectives of the organization, and provide an action plan. Keep work areas organized, clean, and safe. Finally, be clear and logical when giving orders.

Meeting the Needs of Participatives

Include them in the decision-making process; use participative management. Provide opportunity for off-the-job social interaction—company picnics, recreation programs, and annual meetings. Emphasize teamwork on the job through task forces, committee projects, quality improvement teams, and other group involvement activities. Have regular, well-run staff meetings; provide ample opportunity for sharing ideas. Ask for opinions, listen to what is said, and then demonstrate responsiveness. Get to know the person—family makeup, off-the-job interests, and personal goals. Appeal to both logic and feelings when dealing with problems; emphasize a joint approach and talk with, not at, the person. Use communication vehicles such as bulletin boards, newsletters, focus groups, telephone hot lines, and the open-door policy to exchange information. Allow people skills to shine in public relations, teaching, and mediation projects. Provide growth opportunities through in-service training and staff development programs. Finally, keep human relations smooth; consider personal feelings.

Meeting the Needs of Individualists

Recognize independence and personal freedom; don't supervise too closely. Provide immediate reward for good performance; don't delay gratification. Talk in terms of present; de-emphasize past and future. Provide opportunities for growth through exploration and self-discovery. Keep things stimulating; keep things fun. Focus on meaningful personal experiences, satisfying interpersonal relationships, and important social causes. Provide individual job assignments, and assign work by projects when possible. Accentuate feelings over logic when handling problems. Reward good performance with personal time off and personal fulfillment activities. Keep things casual; minimize formality. Avoid rigid controls; allow for questions and creativity. Finally, treat the individualist as a separate person, not as a member of a group or organization.

The concept of interpersonal style is like being right-handed or left-handed. Although people are able to use either hand, they usually prefer one over the other. The preferred hand is generally better developed, making it more efficient and effective to use. You can demonstrate this for yourself by first writing your name as you normally would. Then change hands and sign your name. You can do it, even though it is difficult and feels unnatural to do.

SOLVING PERSONALITY DIFFERENCES

Differences in personality can result in communication problems unless there is tolerance between people. Unless the idea is accepted that it is OK to be different, misunderstanding can develop over any dimension of interpersonal style. When differences occur, there are four steps you can take to improve communication and build community.

Step One: Talk It Out

Silence results in emotional wear and tear on everyone. At the same time, it prevents any possibility of solving problems. The silent treatment is a negative treatment; anyone can be negative. Use the positive approach and talk it out.

- *Where* to talk it out is in private, so that all parties can communicate in an uncensored and honest way. Unless the truth is known, a problem will never be fully resolved.

- *When* to talk it out is when people are fresh. Otherwise, they won't be able to think clearly, much less express themselves clearly.

- *How* to talk it out is to be sure every word spoken passes three important tests—is it *true*, is it *necessary*, is it *kind*?

Step Two: Be Understanding

Look at things from the other person's view. As an old saying goes: "You can't understand another person until you have walked in his shoes." So, see things from the woman's point of view; see the man's side. See things from the boss's perspective; see it through the customer's eyes. See things as grandpa does. Empathy can go a long way to promote understanding.

Also, try to understand the forces—past and present—in another person's life that may have influenced and helped shape the personality. You may understand Mary better if you know what it was like to be raised as an only child in the 1960s. You may understand John better if you know what it was like to be raised in a large family in the 1940s. If you do not know this information, you should ask.

Step Three: Give a Little

Be willing to compromise. If people are frozen in different styles or points of view, no amount of talking will result in good relations. Remember, everyone must be flexible. If one party is always the one to compromise, a sense of fairness is violated and the relationship will ultimately deteriorate. People may stay in a relationship physically, but leave it emotionally.

Step Four: Be Tolerant

Recognize that differences in personality are unavoidable, that few people live or work with their identical twin, and that tolerance of different styles—traditional, participative, and individualistic—is necessary if *community* is to be achieved.

ORGANIZATIONAL STYLES

Organizational styles are partly a product of the personality of the founder or head of the organization, who embodies a certain style of behavior and sets up a particular kind of structure, thereby attracting similar types of people. They, in turn, attract more of their own kind. As the company establishes policies and practices with which these people are comfortable, a corporate style is developed. Over time, people who do not fit the company profile are eliminated, and an organizational style becomes well established. In his book, *Executive*, Harry Levinson describes corporate styles.

> Employees of American Telephone and Telegraph (AT&T) traditionally looked upon "Ma Bell" as *maternalistic*. The company always provided good benefits and could be counted on to take care of its own. Its public image reflected this dependability: AT&T was traditionally the soundest of the "widows-and-orphans" stocks. It also tried to be a model of service, as shown in a well-known advertisement in which a telephone operator sits at her switchboard while flood waters rise around her. The psychological contract between the company and its employees historically was one of support and dependency, although this has changed in recent years as a result of social and economic pressures; employees have been forced into early retirement, jobs have been eliminated by attrition, and there is pressure on executives to be more competitive.
>
> International Business Machines (IBM) has a different organizational style. Once *paternalistic* like its founder, Thomas Watson, Sr., over time it developed the aggressive characteristics of a marketer. People in marketing perform in a free enterprise

environment and are thus competition-driven. The path to success at IBM is through sales, and there is intense competition among salespeople, reinforced by a system of quotas. In years past, IBM represented marketing at its best, because of the high-quality products, guaranteed service, and a powerful ideal of integrity that backed up its marketing efforts. Currently the company is striving to regain its former luster.

At Sears, Roebuck, and Company, the organizational style was historically *egalitarian*. The company was originally set up to give a great deal of responsibility and flexibility to store managers. Sears had an unusually "flat" organizational chart, with only three levels of management. As many as 30 store managers would report to a single person. Because they were not closely supervised, managers had great freedom to use their own judgment. Over the years, Sears succumbed to pressures to economize by centralizing and computerizing nationwide sales and promotion. These and other business decisions did not serve Sears well, in contrast to the customer orientation and popular personnel practices of more aggressive competitors. Currently, Sears is seeking to recapture its earlier standing. Whether it can succeed by going back to its successful roots is an unanswered question.[14]

Just as most people find their own families more congenial than others, so are they more at home with a certain kind of organizational style. Someone from a traditional Italian family may feel comfortable as a second-in-command to an authoritarian boss, whereas a person with a different background might not. In a traditional Italian family, sons respect the father and know they will eventually take over if they patiently bide their time. Similarly, a rigid German upbringing may serve a person well in the highly disciplined atmosphere typical of machine tool factories, where precision and quality control are essential.

An interesting example of "fit" between individual and organizational style was the Federal Bureau of Investigation during the Hoover years. The FBI traditionally attracted many lawyers and accountants who grew up in families with traditional values and strict rules, partly because they felt at home within the agency's rigid structure and organization, which was a lot like that of their families and schools.[15]

INTERPERSONAL STYLES AND ORGANIZATIONAL EFFECTIVENESS

An important point to remember is that different types of people need different treatment to be healthy and achieve their full potential. The absence of planning and clear guidelines is particularly upsetting to traditionals. Conflict and impersonal relationships take an especially heavy toll on participatives. Strict rules and close supervision represent a hostile environment for individualists. The most effective organizations honor the needs of all three types of people. They establish structure and high standards for traditionals, provide warmth and social interaction for participatives, and encourage creativity and personal growth for individualists.

Although different communities may attract different types of people—the structure and order of the military may appeal to traditionals, human interaction and service to others may meet participative needs, and freedom of action and creative expression may appeal to individualists—it should be remembered that each interpersonal style has positive qualities, and that a community with variety can benefit by the balance.

- *Traditionals* bring roots, stability, and discipline that every community needs if it is going to grow and prosper. They provide systems and procedures that allow a lot of people to work together in an organized way.

- *Participatives* are interactive and friendly. They provide the glue that holds the community together. As leaders, they are participative; as followers, they are good team players. Participatives are the harmonizing agents needed by every family, work group, and organization. Participatives provide warmth and support by their very nature.

- *Individualists* provide new ideas and creativity. They are independent and resist close supervision, but when personally motivated, they are dynamic and creative. A community needs creativity within to remain vibrant and develop new markets, new products, and new initiatives, especially if it exists in a competitive environment.

MIXING PERSONALITIES TO STRENGTHEN COMMUNITY

In building a team, some people select "in their own image." They choose associates with personalities similar to their own. This can limit the potential of the group in meeting its goals. The following shows how each style of interpersonal relations can add balance, flexibility, and overall effectiveness to a group or organization.

What Can Individualists and Participatives Gain from Traditionals?

TRADITIONALS:

- Provide clarity of direction
- Organize efforts
- Give attention to detail
- Adhere to standards
- Appreciate traditions
- Show patience

- Remember facts and figures
- Give structure and order
- Provide consistency

What Can Traditionals and Individualists Gain from Participatives?

PARTICIPATIVES:

- Care about people
- Bring harmony and peace
- Teach and give counsel
- Give encouragement to others
- Instill team spirit
- Persuade and motivate
- Are sensitive to others and aware of their needs
- Provide warmth and support

What Can Participatives and Traditionals Gain from Individualists?

INDIVIDUALISTS:

- Challenge the system
- Find flaws in procedures
- Tackle problems with zest
- Provide reform where needed
- Generate new ideas
- Focus on the present
- Accentuate possibilities
- Celebrate the individual

In addition to assets, each style has potential liabilities that can affect relations with others. In many cases, these are strengths that have been overdeveloped. Just as too many muscles can be a hindrance to an athlete, too much of a given personality trait can be a hindrance in interpersonal relations. The following exercise can be used to draw a profile of your interpersonal style.

APPLICATION: INTERPERSONAL STYLE ASSESSMENT

Directions

The following are positive qualities and negative potentials for each interpersonal style. A profile can be obtained for one's personal style by reviewing the qualities and potentials with an eye toward development.

TRADITIONAL

Positive Qualities		*Negative Potentials*
Organizational ability	+ + + + + − − − − −	Rigid about schedules
Grounded in reality	+ + + + + − − − − −	Closed to opportunity
Attention to details	+ + + + + − − − − −	Mired in minutia
Task-oriented	+ + + + + − − − − −	Insensitive to people
High standards	+ + + + + − − − − −	Can't relax
Values tradition	+ + + + + − − − − −	Stuck in the past
Concrete and factual	+ + + + + − − − − −	Misses "the big picture"
Fulfills responsibility	+ + + + + − − − − −	Lacks spontaneity

PARTICIPATIVE

Positive Qualities		*Negative Potentials*
Concern for others	+ + + + + − − − − −	Neglects oneself
Attention to people	+ + + + + − − − − −	Inattention to tasks
Adaptable	+ + + + + − − − − −	Loss of direction
Multiple commitments	+ + + + + − − − − −	Scattered efforts
Grace under pressure	+ + + + + − − − − −	Too easygoing
Tolerant of diversity	+ + + + + − − − − −	Lack of standards
Loves people	+ + + + + − − − − −	Can't say no
Consensus builder	+ + + + + − − − − −	Group conformity

INDIVIDUALISTIC

Positive Qualities		*Negative Potentials*
Quick and responsive	+ + + + + − − − − −	Wasteful
"Big picture" thinker	+ + + + + − − − − −	Overlooks details
Self-motivated	+ + + + + − − − − −	Inconsiderate of others
Creative ideas	+ + + + + − − − − −	Impractical application
Highly committed	+ + + + + − − − − −	Overextended
In touch with self	+ + + + + − − − − −	Out of touch with others
Value driven	+ + + + + − − − − −	Too many causes
Loves choice	+ + + + + − − − − −	Can't decide

Table 6–2 provides an overall description of each style of interpersonal relations.

The case on the following page shows how a variety of styles can add to the effectiveness of a work community.

As a community experiences greater diversity, there is need for greater tolerance. With sufficient tolerance, the different positive qualities of traditional, participative, and individualistic types of people can help the community achieve its full potential. By nature, traditionals provide needed structure and organization, participatives add warmth and supportive human relations, and individualists bring creativity and the capacity for change from within.

TABLE 6–2   An Overall Description of Each Style of Interpersonal Relations.

Issue/Subject	Traditional	Participative	Individualistic
Preferred Social Form:	Formal organization	Group interaction	Individualism
Leadership Style:	Organizer, director	Participative, inclusive	Entrepreneurial, creative
Strategic Emphasis:	Stability and standards	Communication and teamwork	Innovation and change
Behavioral Norms:	Rules, policies, procedures	Warmth and support	Independent effort
Decision Making:	Leader decides	Group decides	Individual decides
Core Value:	Responsibility	Love	Freedom
Public Persona:	Conservative, traditional	Collegial, flexible	Liberal, unconventional
Leadership Needs:	Clarity, predictability, dependability	Encouragement, involvement, appreciation	Meaningful work and freedom to act
Special Characteristics:	Prepares for the future	Needs to be needed	Lives life fully in the moment

Variety Makes a Difference

Background

Of all the probation and parole offices in the state, Lancaster was the most critical. It serviced the most populated county and city of the state; its parolees and probationers had the worst offender records; and it was the largest office in the state, both for personnel and budget.

Also, of all the offices in the state, Lancaster seemed best equipped to accomplish its mission. Its personnel had the best education and most experience; the leadership was considered exceptional; and extra funds had been provided to support the office in its critical assignment.

The Situation

With so many factors working in its favor, the Lancaster probation and parole office was expected to be successful, yet it was failing. Employee turnover was the highest in the state; there was constant staff conflict over procedures and policies; and the recidivism rates for parolees and probationers were the worst in the state.

Evaluation

An evaluation of the staff of fifty officers and supervisory personnel revealed that there were forty-eight individualists, one traditional, and one participative in the group: (1) The forth-eight individualists were all probation and parole officers—well-meaning and talented to a person. But each was doing his or her own thing, often to the detriment of others in the office. (2) The single traditional was the supervisor over approximately one-half of the officers. He was well-respected because of his ability and years of experience, but his basic reaction to all of those individualists was just to shake his head. They were too loose and too independent-minded to suit him. (3) The participative was the director of the office—the single factor holding the entire group together. Evaluation showed the primary cause of the organization's problems to be *too many individualists*.

The Solution

First, all staff members recognized the need for increased cooperation in day-to-day operations. They realized that there were too many people who wanted to do their own thing, but who by doing so, were often counterproductive to the work of others. The entire staff resolved to be more cooperative in their daily behavior. Thus, regular staff meetings were scheduled, and everyone attended them on time. Also, rules were developed for the use of telephones, cars, and copy machines, as well as secretarial services; and everyone made a conscientious effort to adhere to them.

In addition, each staff member took concrete steps to understand and appreciate the different duties, personalities, and methods of the rest of the people in the organization. This was accomplished not only over differences in style of interpersonal relations, but also over differences in case-load management, counseling techniques, and philosophy of criminal justice. The information shared and ideas generated upgraded the quality of work of the entire office. Interpersonal conflicts decreased, and the performance of the office improved.

Finally, as new people were hired to fill vacancies, traditional and participative candidates were selected to help balance the work force when other qualifications were equal. The traditionals introduced clarity and consistency, which all organizations need; the participatives added the human or charismatic element so that employees enjoyed working in the organization and clients felt supported. Individualists were retained to provide creativity and new ideas. It was recognized that all three were required in order to perform the best quality of work.[16]

INTERPERSONAL STYLES AND LEADERSHIP EFFECTIVENESS

For a practical application showing that all three styles of interpersonal relations are important for community success, consider the case of four organization presidents:

- The first president was *individualistic*. He was a creative visionary whose genius was to found and physically create the organization. He was innovative and entrepreneurial.

- The second president was *traditional*, combining courtly southern ways with a basic goodness of character. His concern for people became a model and standard for others who would continue to serve the organization.

- The third president was *participative*, a master of diplomacy and persuasion. Gifted at finding the middle ground in disputes and the high ground in direction, he brought stability to the organization.

- The fourth president was *versatile* with roughly equal amounts of all three styles. His administrative approach was traditional or chain of command, his manner in dealing with people was participative, and his international initiatives were individualistic.

How can four people be so different, yet be so effective? The answer is that as important as interpersonal style is, there are other factors that are even more important. These are **character**, **leadership**, and **tolerance of diversity**.

- *Character*. Each of the four presidents told the truth as he believed it to be, and in any moral dilemma, consideration of others came first. Think about it: We will forgive a person anything—odd dress, strange habits, even personality differences—when *character* is good.

- *Leadership*. All four presidents employed universal principles of effective *leadership*. Each had a vision and a plan. Each kept job knowledge current to solve problems and develop others. Each demonstrated a humanistic approach in dealing with people.

- *Diversity*. All four presidents showed understanding, responsiveness, and flexibility in relating to all types of people—young and old, black and white, male and female, and even traditional, participative, and individualistic. Each was tolerant of differences and *valued diversity*.

In building community, the challenge is to understand and value different types of people, and to be wise, caring, and flexible to meet their needs. If we meet this challenge, individuals will be served and the community will grow by the gifts they bring.

What will it take to meet this challenge? First, a sincere belief that the greatest good for all individuals can best be achieved through community. Second, the knowledge that diversity enriches individuals and groups. Third, the day-to-day practice of considering the interests and meeting the needs of others. Ask yourself how you are doing in these three key areas, and what you can do to improve.

REFERENCES

1. Adapted from Thomas E. Bier, "Contemporary Youth: Implications of the Personalistic Life Style for Organizations" (doctoral diss., Case Western Reserve University).

2. Frederic A. Birmingham, "The Infinite Riches of Ben Franklin," *The Saturday Evening Post* (January/February 1982): 50.

3. Henry David Thoreau, *Walden* (Chicago: The Lakeside Press, 1930), 285–286.

4. C. Kagitcibasi and J. W. Berry, "Cross-Cultural Psychology: Current Research and Trends," *Annual Review of Psychology*, 40, (1989).

5. G. Hofstede, *Culture's Consequences* (Newbury Park, CA: Sage, 1980).

6. Hofstede, *Culture's Consequences*.

7. C. H. Hui and M. J. Villareal, "Individualism-Collectivism and Psychological Needs," *Journal of Cross-Cultural Psychology*, 20 (1989):310–323; C. Kagitcibasi, "Diversity of Socialization and Social Change" in P. R. Dasen, J. W. Berry, and N. Sartorius, eds. *Health and Cross-Cultural Psychology*, (Newberry Park, Ca.: Sage, 1988); and H. Triandis, "Collectivism vs. Individualism: A Reconceptualization of a Basic Concept in Cross-Cultural Social Psychology," in C. Bagley and G. K. Verman, eds. *Personality, Cognition, and Values* (London: Macmillan, 1985).

8. B. Schwartz, "The Creation and Destruction of Value," *American Psychologist*, 45 (1990): 7–15.

9. Stephen M. Joseph, *The Me Nobody Knows* (New York: Avon, 1969).

10. Emanual Hertz, *Lincoln Talks—A Biography in Anecdotes* (New York: Viking Press, 1939), 367.

11. Archer H. Shaw, *The Lincoln Encyclopedia* (New York: Macmillan, 1950), 149.

12. Robert Frost, *The Road Not Taken: A Selection of Robert Frost's Poems* (New York: Holt, Rinehart, and Winston, 1985), St. 4.

13. Edwin Markham in Raymond F. Gale, *Developmental Behavior* (New York: Macmillan, 1969), 192.

14. Harry Levinson, *Executive* (Cambridge: Harvard University Press, 1981), 76, 139–141.

15. Levinson, *Executive*.

16. Case from the authors' files—Kentucky Corrections/Probation and Parole.

CHAPTER

7

Understanding
People

There are only two or three human stories, and they
go on repeating themselves as fiercely as if they
never happened before.

Willa Cather

People are the originators of community, the means to its attainment, and the purpose for its existence. Building community requires an understanding of *why people do what they do*. This chapter provides a primer on this fascinating subject. Topics include:

- the personal and social nature of personality;
- the importance of self-concept;
- personality structure and dynamics;
- personality defense mechanisms; and
- stages and tasks of personality development.

PERSONAL AND SOCIAL NATURE OF PERSONALITY

Psalm 8 asks, "What is man, that thou art mindful of him?" The scientist answers, "Man is a product of internal and external forces." Each person is the result of interaction between biological heritage and cultural history. The kind of person you are and what you do depend on both raw material (heredity) and what is done with this raw material (how it is shaped and grown). We must eat to live; but whether we eat rice or meat, and whether we use fingers or utensils, are influenced by culture and experience.[1]

The Dutch philosopher Baruch Spinoza describes the *personal* nature of personality: "To be what we are and to become what we are capable of becoming is the ultimate end of life."[2] More than a century ago, Soren Kierkegaard emphasized that the most common despair is the unwillingness to be oneself, and that the deepest form of despair is choosing to be other than oneself.

> Even the richest personality is nothing before he has chosen himself. On the other hand, even what one might call the poorest personality is everything when he has chosen himself; for the great thing is not to be this or that, but to be oneself."[3]

Personality is also *social*, a series and integration of social roles. Shakespeare wrote:

> All the world's a stage,
> And all the men and women merely players;
> They have their exits and their entrances,
> And one man in his time plays many parts,
> His acts being seven ages.[4]

Throughout our lives, we define ourselves as leaders, parents, citizens, and other social beings, adopting the goals, values, and characteristics of these roles. Social roles can be so important that the individual may break down when roles are changed. Imagine the successful businessman who, on losing his fortune and prestige, commits suicide. Or imagine the homemaking mother who, having raised her children, becomes depressed and physically ill.[5]

Studies of boys' gangs show how social roles influence the behavior of young people:

Leaders. As a result of physical strength, intellectual ability, courage, or some other characteristic, one individual in the group tends to emerge as the leader. The leader gives instructions, settles disputes, coordinates activities, sets an example for the others, and often serves as a group conscience. When a member of the gang gets into trouble with outsiders, he may justify his behavior by blaming the leader: "He told me to do it."

Advocates. These are youngsters who are more facile with words or ideas than the leader, but who lack organizing ability or boldness in action. These group members may be cast in the role of negotiators with rival gangs or defenders of the group against adult disapproval. They are expected to be masters of the alibi and skilled at rationalization and clever negotiation. They play a role roughly analogous to that of lawyer or diplomat.

Clowns. Many juvenile groups have their court jester—one who is expected to be funny. Sometimes this person differs from the others in physical appearance (for example, very tall, thin, or heavy), and sometimes the person is below par in other skills demanded by the group. By combining humor and self-display, the clown can gain status in the group and the affectionate regard of other members.

Fall guys. Often there is a member whose alleged ineptness, mistakes, or simply bad luck get him blamed for almost everything that goes wrong for the group. The presence of such a scapegoat tends to relieve the others of feelings of inferiority and insecurity that would otherwise result from group failures.

Mascots. In some cases, the group adopts a mascot—an individual who is younger, physically handicapped, or otherwise different from other members of the group in a way that they consider inferior. The mascot is usually well accepted by the group as long as he sticks to his role and does not attempt to participate in the group as a full-fledged member. It is not unusual for male groups to adopt female mascots.[6]

THE IMPORTANCE OF SELF-CONCEPT

Self-concept is that constellation of central ideas and attitudes we have about ourselves. Prescott Leckey, a psychologist early in this century, explained the importance of self-concept in human behavior: "Every person's central mission in life is the preservation and enhancement of his concept of himself."[7]

This was put another way years later by educator S.I. Hayakawa, "The primary goal of a human being is not self-preservation, but preservation of the symbolic self. Why else would a man spend hundreds of dollars a year to catch a few fish? Or why would a woman skip lunch for years to buy a fur coat? Or why would a soldier throw his body on a live grenade, killing himself to save comrades he might not even know? We do what we do in order to be consistent with who we think we are."[8]

People know their self-concept, dimly or clearly, and can usually justify why they do what they do in a word or phrase. Comedian Steve Martin says,

"I'm a wild and crazy guy." Oliver North explained his motives to a congressional committee, "I did what I did because I am a patriot." As author Jack Bickham explains, people begin forming a self-concept early in life. They test it, and if it seems reasonably accurate, they begin to define themselves more specifically by it. To themselves and others, they may say, "I'm a man of action." Or, "I'm a lady of quality." Or, "I'm a brilliant writer, but I can't do math." Or, "I'm a Danforth, and every Danforth is a lawyer."[9]

Whatever the roots of people's perceptions, once they start making judgments about themselves, the die is cast and it is hard to alter. People appear dedicated to become more of what they think they already are. This can be seen throughout one's life. The quiet and assuming man who rushes into a burning building to save a child may never have considered himself to be a hero, but he probably always considered himself to be a man who loved children, and he could have told you earlier, "I'm a person who does what he must."[10]

A few lines by John Masefield illustrate the multiple yet unifying nature of self-concept:

Three men went down the road,
As down the road went he;
The man they saw, the man he was,
And the man he wanted to be.[11]

Self-concept is the guiding light in the interaction between forces within and forces outside the person. People are thinking creatures who not only react to the world, but are capable of originating behavior and making free choices. Indeed, as does no other known being, people influence the world and create themselves.[12] The story on the next page is a touching illustration of the importance of self-concept.

PERSONALITY STRUCTURE AND DYNAMICS

The psychologist Kurt Lewin once said, "There is nothing quite so practical as a good theory; it explains so much." Historically, the most important theory of personality has been that of Sigmund Freud. Some of Freud's ideas have had lasting influence in explaining why people do what they do, including 1) the importance of the subconscious in determining behavior, and 2) the dynamic relationship among the id, the ego and the superego.

The Importance of the Subconscious

Freud compared the human personality to an iceberg. Below the waterline is the mass of the iceberg, and below our level of consciousness is the mass of personality. See figure 7–1.

The Mask

An ancient legend tells of a king who conquered and ruled over a vast domain. He was brave and respected, but no one loved him. This made him lonely, and his face reflected his inner bitterness. Deep, ugly lines developed around his mouth, and he never showed a smile.

One day the king saw a beautiful young lady and fell in love with her immediately. He decided to marry her. He clothed himself in his finest robes and placed a glittering crown on his head. But when he looked into the mirror, he saw only a cruel, hard face.

He was terribly distressed until he thought of a wonderful idea. He called for his magician and said: "Make me a mask, and paint it with your magic paints, so that it will make my face look kind and pleasant."

"This I can do," said the magician. "But on one condition: you must keep your real face in the same lines that I paint; one frown or display of anger, and the mask will be ruined."

"I will do anything you say in order to win the love of my lady. Tell me how to keep the mask from cracking."

"You must think kind thoughts," replied the magician, "and to do this, you must do kind deeds. You must strive to make your people happy rather than to acquire more territory. Be kind and courteous to all of your subjects."

The king agreed, so the magician made a mask of very thin wax which he painted skillfully. The king tried it on and he looked very handsome indeed. He had little difficulty in winning the hand of the woman he loved.

The king was very careful not to spoil his mask, and his subjects were amazed at the change that had come over him. They gave all the credit to his wife who, they said, had made him over to be like herself.

Years went by, and as gentleness and thoughtfulness for others became a habit and part of his personality, the king was convinced that he should be more honest and not just pretend to be so.

He began to regret that he had deceived his beautiful wife with his magic mask, and he called for his magician, "Remove this mask," he said. "Take it away. This false face is not my true one."

"If I do, I can never make another mask like it," warned the magician, "and you will have to remain with your own real face as long as you live." Still the king was true to his desire to be honest.

The magician took off the mask, and the king ran to the mirror, full of fear and anguish over what he might see. To his amazement, he saw that his eyes were bright and his lips were curved into a radiant smile. The old ugly lines around his mouth and the old frown had disappeared, and his face was the exact likeness of the mask he had worn for so long.

The king's wife never noticed the difference. She saw only the familiar features of the man she loved so dearly.[13]

Just as you can only see the tip of the iceberg, so is conscious behavior only the "tip" of the human personality. Below the waterline lies the subconscious, the dwelling place of things forgotten because of poor memory and things repressed because they are unpleasant or threatening. Both positive and negative experiences and feelings live in the subconscious.

Freud was fascinated by the past and loved the stories and themes of earlier civilizations. Indeed, the contemporary he seemed to admire the most was

FIGURE 7–1   Conscious and Subconscious Personality

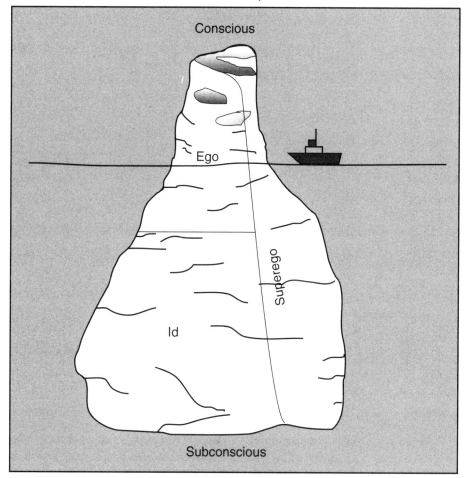

Heinrich Schliemann who, in Freud's youth, discovered and began to dig up the lost city of Troy. The parallel was apparent when in his own work he would admonish his patients to search for repressed memories and unearth buried experiences layer by layer, not unlike the technique of excavating a buried city.[14]

If we are to fully understand and deal with human behavior—our own and others—we should recognize that people often do what they do for subconscious reasons unknown to themselves. A person may dress or speak in a certain manner, and the subconscious motive may be to be accepted by others; a person may shout or make an emotional display, and the subconscious purpose may be to gain attention; a person may distrust others, and the subconscious reason may be to avoid being hurt.

The Relationship Among the Id, Ego, and Superego

Freud identified three structures within the personality and assigned to each one certain functions and energies.[15]

One of these is the *id*, which is composed of two powerful drives: 1) a constructive drive leading to love, growth, and integration of the personality; and 2) a destructive drive leading to feelings of hate, constriction of the personality, and death. One of the major tasks of the personality is to fuse these drives so that the constructive drive is dominant. Also the site of repressed memories, wishes, and impulses, the id comprises the uncivilized core of the person that continually struggles for expression.

The job of the *ego*, considered to be the executive part of the personality, is to control and guide the powerful drives of the id. The ego is made up of the five senses, together with the abilities to concentrate, form concepts, think reflectively, and act. The ego seeks to master the outside world so that the person can survive.

The third structure of the personality is the *superego* or the conscience—an internal, self-governing agent with four functions:

1. *Rules.* As part of growing up, children identify with their parents and other important figures in their environment. In doing so, they assimilate many rules for living, including basic rules about expressing aggressive impulses and about giving and receiving love.

2. *Values.* By the same process of identification, children adopt certain values. Examples of values include the sanctity of life, honesty in all matters, and respect for other people.

3. *Ideals.* The conscience spurs people to attain an ideal state of being, a concept of oneself at one's best. This ideal is constructed from expectations held by others, aspirations people develop for themselves, and from identification with important figures in the environment. Mark Twain said, "It may be called the Master Passion, the hunger for self-esteem." The concept of "self-esteem" refers in part to a person's efforts to satisfy the superego. The superego, like a distant mountain peak, may be beyond one's capacities to fully attain; yet it continues to serve as a goal toward which one is constantly striving. Various role models, ranging from scholars and saints on the one hand to con artists and drug dealers on the other, may influence the superego. Their roles are reinforced by history, literature, religion, and myth.

4. *Judgments.* The fourth function of the superego is the one that evaluates and makes judgments. Everyone has experienced pangs of conscience or twinges of guilt after having violated rules or values by which one lives or when one has not met the ideals of the superego.

More than two thousand years before Freud described the roles and relationships among the id, ego, and superego of the human personality, the philosopher Plato recognized the importance of a three-way struggle within the individual. In *Dialogues*, Plato describes *Reason* (ego) as driving a chariot, the *Soul* (the human being) with arms straining to control two steeds, *Spirit* (superego), and *Appetite* (id), who often pull in opposite directions. The goal of *Reason* is to achieve balance between these two powerful internal forces in all human beings. Plato believed that only through reason could one achieve the moral ideal and become a fully developed person.[16]

PERSONALITY DEFENSE MECHANISMS

People use defense mechanisms to preserve both biological and emotional health. Biological protection ranges from the large muscle movements that allow us to fight off physical attack, to the microscopic efforts of white blood corpuscles that enable us to combat infection and disease. In a healthy person, such biological defenses are natural and automatic reactions to physical threat.

In a similar way, emotional well-being is preserved through psychological defense mechanisms. These often subconscious behaviors are brought into operation to protect our feelings of self-worth and our positive self-concept.

Everyone uses defense mechanisms, and they can be helpful as we adjust to life's demands. However, psychological defenses can be overused and can actually be harmful by distorting reality and preventing us from dealing with problems effectively. The following is a discussion of defense mechanisms used by individuals and groups.[17]

Denial

If the truth is too threatening, you can deny it. Although this can give needed comfort in the short term, it is the equivalent to lying to oneself. If carried to extreme, denial of reality can be harmful. For example, people can deny physical illness, and this can help them get through the day. But at some point, they must face and correct the reality of physical illness, or greater harm may result. In human relations, a person may refuse to face the faults of self or others by denying data that conflicts with idealistic dreams and personal wishes.

Fantasy is a common form of denial and this can be a pleasant escape. Through fantasy we can deny unpleasant experiences and conditions and can imagine the world as we would like it to be. Although a certain amount of fantasizing is normal and healthy, it can be harmful over the long term if we substitute the easier path of make-believe for the more difficult path of dealing with the truth and real-life endeavor. Constant denial of important facts, faults, or failures prevents people from coping successfully with reality. Denial may be seen in individuals and groups under stress.

Projection

Projection involves blaming others for our own failures and difficulties, or attributing to others our own unacceptable urges. Thus, if a person likes to dominate in every situation, she may accuse others of being authoritarian. If a person is dishonest, he may proclaim, "You can't trust anybody." People who crusade militantly against loose morals or the evil of alcohol may be doing so as a subconscious defense or safeguard against their own errant desires.

Sublimation

If a person has goals or desires that are unacceptable, a psychological defense is to redirect behavior into more acceptable areas. In this way, we preserve self-respect, social reputation, and emotional health. People of all ages and in all areas of life use sublimation. A tackle executed on the football field may represent sublimated aggression; an abstract painting may represent sublimated sexuality; working in an orphanage may represent sublimated parental urges for the person who does not have children.

Displacement

If we transfer negative emotions from one person or thing to another person or thing, we are using displacement as a defense mechanism. Sometimes this is subconscious, and sometimes not. Sometimes it can be constructive, and sometimes not. It would not be constructive to shout at your spouse, strike your children, or kick the cat because you are upset about your work. However, it may be helpful to relieve your frustration by hitting a punching bag or lifting weights. Activities such as bowling and body-contact games can serve to displace emotions in socially acceptable ways.

Fear may be displaced from an actual source to related situations, as in the case of irrational phobias—fear of animals, open spaces, heights, etc. It is usually best to deal with the source of emotional concern, even when this is difficult or unpleasant. If a person upsets you, channel your energy into solving problems together, rather than displacing negative emotions onto innocent bystanders.

Regression

Regression is a retreat from a currently unpleasant situation to a more pleasant one in the past. If we retreat to childhood, we do not have to feel as responsible for our actions or for other people. We can be playful, spontaneous, irresponsible, and even selfish without feeling guilty.

Regression is a common defense mechanism of people under stress. Psychologist Bruno Bettelheim describes the general regression to infantile behavior seen in many of the prisoners at Dachau and Buchenwald during World War II:

> The prisoners lived, like children, only in the immediate present. They became unable to plan for the future or to give up immediate pleasure or satisfactions to gain greater ones in the near future. They were boastful, telling tales about what they had accomplished in their former lives, or how they succeeded in cheating foremen or guards, and how they sabotaged the work. Like children, they felt not at all set back or ashamed when it became known that they had lied about their prowess.[18]

More common examples of regression are the wife who goes home to her mother every time she and her husband quarrel, the manager who resorts to temper tantrums when he doesn't get his way, and the student who indulges in candy and ice cream when the going gets tough, grades are low, and the world seems generally overwhelming.

As a defense mechanism, regression can be beneficial to the extent that it results in spontaneity and other healthy traits associated with childhood, and harmful to the extent that it results in selfishness or other unhealthy behavior.

Withdrawal

Emotional withdrawal, up to a certain point, is a highly effective method of defending ourselves from unnecessary disappointment and pain. Unfortunately, individuals who have been badly bruised by life's blows may withdraw from any further involvement in which they might be hurt. Thus, the sensitive man who has been shaken by a failed love affair may insulate himself to such a degree that he finds it difficult to achieve a close relationship again.

This reaction is especially common among people who have been rejected and hurt in childhood and who by adulthood have insulated themselves with a protective shell of detachment that makes it nearly impossible for them to give or receive love or to participate enthusiastically and fully in life. An important benefit of the experience of *community* is to help people relate to others in a healthful way.

Identification

The mechanism of identification can be a constructive agent for emotional health. We can feel good about ourselves through identification with the family, country, company, or team we identify as our own. Self-worth can be enhanced as we take satisfaction and pride in the group's success. For example, by identifying with one's father, a child can recognize the qualities that make the father so effective and can gain personal confidence needed to attempt similar exploits.

When practiced in moderation, identification is normal and healthy. However, when exercised to an extreme, or when used in place of personal experience and earned self-worth, identification can be harmful. The father who lives life vicariously through his child's achievements places an undue burden on the child for his own happiness and fails to experience life firsthand. People who rely solely on the success of others for their own sense of worth usually experience frustration and dissatisfaction in the long run.

Repression

Repression can protect people by submerging painful memories or desires that threaten self-esteem. A person with strong feelings of hostility may have these so repressed that the person is unaware of them. Similarly, sexual desires that the individual considers to be immoral may be blocked from consciousness. Sometimes repressive defenses may be bolstered by other defenses such as displacement.

Repressing thoughts and feelings is a defense mechanism that can be helpful. For example, if it is not helpful to dwell on some embarrassing incident or failure, why do it? Better to keep it repressed and free your mind for constructive activities. In this way, the personality remains undamaged.

Some experiences can be so traumatic that one represses them into the subconscious to prevent personality breakdown. This is the case of the battle-fatigued soldier who can remember everything up to the point of physical combat but who has repressed the experiences of fear, killing, and death.

On the other hand, repression can be very harmful if you fail to deal with negative thoughts and feelings satisfactorily before repressing them, or if you repress so much of your personality that you do not know who you are, where you have been, or where you are going. In such cases, repression can affect physical health and harm personality development.

Undoing

Undoing is a defense mechanism designed to negate or atone for some disapproved desire, idea, or act. Sometimes you are sorry for the harmful things you do. By going through the process of undoing, you can feel better about yourself and thus preserve psychological health. For example, you may cause another person pain, extra work, or unhappiness. In order to undo this, you may take extraordinary steps to help them or to otherwise make up for your misdeeds.

The unfaithful husband may suddenly shower his wife with gifts to atone for his behavior, the businessperson may seek to undo unethical business practices by giving large sums of money to the church or community, or the selfish mother may try to compensate by buying expensive presents and toys for her children.[19]

The process of undoing can be harmful if it becomes habitual behavior. People lose patience and respect for the person who constantly makes mistakes and seeks forgiveness by undoing.

Rationalization

Three common rationalizations are "it wasn't important anyway," "what is meant to be will be," and "if only. . . ." Rationalization is often used to justify actions, explain failures, and alleviate frustrations. We may use rationalization to soften the disappointment of thwarted desires. Examples include the rejected lover who says, "I wasn't ready to settle down anyway"; the job applicant who says, "It would have been a terrible job," after learning that someone else has been selected; and the man losing his hair, who reminds you that Don Juan was completely bald.

In some instances, rationalization can be helpful if it helps to preserve self-worth or self-confidence. However, rationalization can be used to justify unsatisfactory behavior and mistakes in judgment, and this can be harmful. Examples are the person who justifies cheating by pointing out that everyone does it and the individual who rationalizes speeding in a car to make a business appointment on time.[20]

When used to extreme, rationalization can result in a person who constantly justifies mistakes, takes no responsibility for personal actions, and, ultimately, has low social respect and self-esteem. We may suspect we are rationalizing when we must hunt for reasons to justify our beliefs, can't explain inconsistencies in our words and actions, and become overly emotional when reasons for our behaviors are questioned.

People are vulnerable creatures, and personality defense mechanisms can serve a protective purpose. However, these mechanisms can also become disruptive and self-defeating. In general, defense mechanisms distort reality and can lure individuals and groups into inaccurate perceptions and inappropriate behavior. If certain defenses become habitual, they can impair personal growth, interpersonal effectiveness, and the experience of community.

STAGES AND TASKS OF PERSONALITY DEVELOPMENT

How is personality formed and grown? Psychologist Erik Erikson identified eight stages of personality development from birth to old age. During each stage, the individual is challenged to accomplish certain physical, psychological, and social tasks of life. The successful completion of these developmental tasks results in happiness and a positive self-concept. Failure to meet the tasks of any of life's stages can lead to low self-esteem and difficulty with later personality development. Figure 7–2 shows the eight stages and tasks of personality development.

FIGURE 7–2　　　Stages and Tasks of Personality Development[21]

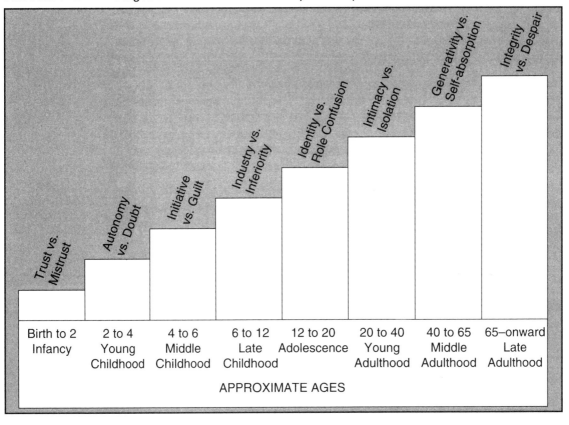

At every stage of life, we are faced with three objectives: (1) resolve unfinished issues from previous stages, (2) accomplish the critical tasks of the present stage, and (3) prepare for the next stage. Just as constructing a solid base provides a firm foundation for a building-block structure, meeting the developmental tasks of each stage of life provides a foundation for further development. The eight stages and developmental tasks of personality formation are as follows:[22]

Stage 1—Trust vs. Mistrust

The first stage of personality development occurs during infancy (the first one or two years of life). A newborn needs stimulation and affection. If these needs are satisfied, the infant will develop *trust*—a sense that the world is a safe and secure place and that other people (particularly parents) will provide protection.

On the other hand, if a baby's needs for stimulation and affection are not satisfied and the child is ignored or abused, *mistrust* will result. The baby will learn to view the world as a hostile place, requiring self-protective behavior rather than openness toward others.

The major developmental tasks of infancy are (1) giving and receiving affection, and (2) achieving a loving, reliable relationship with the mother and other primary caretakers. Successful completion of these tasks results in feelings of security and well-being.

Stage 2—Autonomy vs. Doubt

The second stage of personality development usually occurs during young childhood (from about two to four years of age). If a young child learns to explore and do things independently during this period, self-confidence and a sense of *autonomy* will develop—the sense that "I can do it myself."

On the other hand, if the child does not succeed at such tasks as eating or controlling body functions and is continually criticized for making a mess, shame and *doubt* will result.

The major developmental tasks of this period are (1) achieving physical self-control, and (2) viewing oneself as an independent and worthy person. The young child who has learned trust and autonomy is better prepared for all subsequent stages of life.

Stage 3—Initiative vs. Guilt

The third stage of personality development is associated with the preschool years (from about four to six years of age). Language develops and motor skills and physical coordination improve during this stage. It is an extension of the previous stage, when autonomy can develop into *initiative*, or doubt can deteriorate into *guilt* and fearfulness. If a five-year-old proclaims, "I am going to climb that tree," and succeeds in this initiative, self-confidence and mastery of the environment are reinforced.

On the other hand, if the child is discouraged from trying, or is ridiculed for failing, the child may feel guilt and may be reluctant to attempt anything new or difficult again. The small child has dreams of being a giant and a tiger, but may, in these same dreams, run in terror for dear life.[23]

Important developmental tasks of this period include (1) learning personal care, (2) learning to be a member of a family or social group, and (3) beginning to distinguish right from wrong. The favorable outcomes of satisfying these tasks are constructive personal habits and self-approval.

Stage 4—Industry vs. Inferiority

The fourth stage of personality development usually occurs during later childhood (from about six to twelve years of age). If scholarship, craftsmanship, and social skills are learned successfully during this period, a child develops a sense of *industry* and feelings of accomplishment. Tremendous self-worth can be created by succeeding in schoolwork, animal care, athletics, music, hobbies, and other activities.

On the other hand, feelings of *inferiority* (the feeling that "I can't do anything right") can result from failure. This is why it is important for a child to be encouraged and to receive recognition in the areas of their greatest aptitude during this period of life.

Feelings of industry or inferiority formed during this period represent either an advantage or a handicap for all subsequent personality growth. The sphere of activity during this stage of personality development usually extends beyond the family and includes the neighborhood, school, and other social institutions. Scouting, sports, and hobby clubs are examples of important childhood communities.

Important developmental tasks of this period include (1) developing a conscience and a system of values, (2) learning mental, physical, and interpersonal skills, (3) learning to compete and cooperate with age-mates, and (4) learning how to win and lose gracefully. Satisfying these tasks successfully results in personal competence and effective work and social habits.

Stage 5—Identity vs. Role Confusion

The fifth stage of personality development usually occurs during adolescence (from about twelve to twenty years of age). The greatest task of this period is to develop a sense of personal *identity*. The feeling that "I know and like who I am" is the goal. Included in the definition of "self" is a healthy sexual identity (there are boys and girls, and I am glad I am a girl), moral identity (there is right and wrong, and I believe I know what is right), and a life plan (I want to work with my hands, have a family, and live in the country).

The concern with discovering and being oneself occurs concurrently with the concern for establishing satisfying human relationships and sharing with others. Belonging to a peer group and giving and receiving affection are important to the adolescent.

The young person who suffers from either *role confusion* or a lack of love wanders through the teen years without self-understanding, without clear goals, and in an unhappy state. Adolescence is a critical period of life and is often filled with stress, not only for the individual, but for family and friends. This is due primarily to the teenager's natural efforts to escape from parental dominance and to establish an independent identity.

Important developmental tasks of this stage include (1) adjusting to body changes, (2) achieving emotional independence from parents, (3) making new friends of both sexes, (4) developing intellectual skills, and (5) selecting and preparing for an occupation. The satisfactory completion of these tasks results in feelings of self-esteem, fidelity in human relations, and optimism toward life.

Stage 6—Intimacy vs. Isolation

The sixth stage of personality development is usually associated with young adulthood and includes the ages from about twenty to forty. During this period, the individual typically "leaves the family nest" psychologically and economically. During this stage, balance must be found between two opposing challenges. The many possibilities of adult life must be explored, keeping options open; at the same time, the young adult must achieve basic occupational success.

Meaningful relationships are sought with people outside the family during this period. A major goal of these relationships is to establish a sense of *intimacy*, a feeling of closeness and commitment with another person. A relationship in which one can be oneself and can experience unconditional acceptance is what is meant by intimacy. For most young people, intimacy consists of a loving relationship with a person of the opposite sex.

Economically, the young adult begins earning a livelihood. As this is done, assets developed during earlier periods (autonomy, initiative, industry, and identity) will be of immense help, while doubt, guilt, inferiority, and role confusion will be liabilities as a career is pursued. Without a loving relationship and meaningful work, the young adult typically experiences a sense of *isolation* and feelings of being unimportant. Freud identified the central issues of this stage of development to be love and work.[24]

Also, during the period of young adulthood, important personal and social values solidify as the individual considers the purpose of existence and the meaning of life. Finally, young adulthood is usually a period of starting a family and nurturing children. Concern for an independent self expands to include concern for dependent others.

Important developmental tasks of this stage include (1) finding a satisfying social group, (2) selecting and learning to live with a mate, (3) starting a family and meeting the physical and psychological needs of young children, (4) getting started in an occupation, and (5) defining personal and social values. Successfully meeting these challenges results in loving relationships, social responsibility, and economic independence.

Stage 7—Generativity vs. Self-Absorption

The seventh stage of personality development is associated with middle adulthood, approximately forty to sixty-five years of age. With personal affairs in order, the adult who achieves *generativity* directs attention toward other people—family and friends, as well as the larger community. The person becomes concerned about the state of the world and the well-being of future generations. There is the need to be needed and the desire to contribute to the welfare of others. Productivity, creativity, and responsibility are important values for the person who exhibits generativity during middle adulthood.

In contrast, a person who has not developed generativity experiences *self-absorption*, the feeling that "I come first before anyone or anything else." Oscar Wilde portrayed such self-absorption in *The Picture of Dorian Gray*, a story about a vain young man who received his wish to remain young forever. He used other people and was cruel to those who loved him. A self-portrait reflected all of his misdeeds, and this evil image haunted him. In the end, he stabbed the picture, then died. Wilde's story is a parable that illustrates the disaster of self-absorption.[25]

Developmental tasks of middle adulthood include (1) making productive contributions, (2) relating to other people as people, (3) helping young people become happy and self-sufficient, (4) adjusting to aging family members, (5) establishing economic security for one's remaining years, (6) developing leisure activities, (7) providing leadership in social, economic, religious, and other institutions, and (8) adjusting to the physical changes of aging. The satisfactory resolution of these tasks leads to a sense of contribution, social stability, and peace of mind.

Stage 8—Integrity vs. Despair

The last stage of personality development occurs during later adulthood, from about sixty-five years of age onward. This is the period of reflection, summing up, and ending life. The central task of this stage is to achieve *integrity* and inner peace. The older person with integrity feels that life has been good and the years have been used well. There is a sense of fulfillment.

On the other hand, the elderly person who has not achieved integrity feels that life has been wasted, is filled with regret, and feels personal *despair*. The older person with integrity cares about future generations and seeks to help other people, while the older person with despair dwells on personal problems of the past, thinking, "If I could only live my life over, I would do things differently."

The developmental tasks of later adulthood include (1) adjusting to decreasing physical strength, (2) adjusting to retirement and a reduced income, (3) maintaining interests beyond oneself, (4) adjusting to the deaths of family and friends, and (5) accepting one's own impending death. The satisfactory accomplishment of these tasks results in a sense of equanimity, fulfillment, and inner peace.

Erikson's model of personality development provides a review of past development, a diagnosis of present conditions, and a preview of future tasks. It helps explain why a person at any age may feel happy and fulfilled, and another person may feel inadequate and depressed.

An important point to remember is that although developmental tasks tend to be age related, people can accomplish unfinished tasks of earlier periods at any point in time. The late bloomer is a phenomenon we all have witnessed. Also a shooting star may fall and a personality may diminish. A good way to view this is to see personalities like books. Each is in the process of being written, and every life is worth a novel.

WHAT IS HE?

In this chapter, we have discussed the nature of personality, its structure and dynamics, personality defense mechanisms, and the stages and tasks of personality development. We have learned that each person adopts a concept of self that can be consistently lived. This concept is carried into all of life's activities. Thus we go through our days expressing ourselves, each in our own way. In this spirit, we conclude with D.H. Lawrence's thought-provoking poem "What is he?"

> What is he?
> —A man, of course.
> Yes, but what does he do?
> —He lives and is a man.
> Oh quite. But he must work. He must have a job of some sort.
> —Why?
> Because obviously he's not one of the leisured classes.
> —I don't know. He has lots of leisure. And he makes quite beautiful chairs.
> There you are then! He's a cabinet maker.
> —No, no!
> Anyhow a carpenter and joiner.
> —Not at all.
> But you said so.
> —What did I say?
> That he made chairs, and was a joiner and carpenter.
> —I said he made chairs, but I did not say he was a carpenter.
> All right then, he's just an amateur.
> —Perhaps! Would you say a thrush was a professional flautist, or just an amateur?
> I'd say it was just a bird.
> —And I say he is just a man.
> All right! You always did quibble.

Source: "What is he?" by D. H. Lawrence from *The Complete Poems of D. H. Lawrence* by D. H. Lawrence, edited by V. de Sola Pinto & F. W. Roberts. Copyright © 1964, 1971 by Angelo Ravagli and C. M. Weekley, executors of the estate of Frieda Lawrence Ravagli. Used by permission of Viking Penguin, a division of Penguin Books USA Inc.

REFERENCES

1. William C. Menninger and Harry Levinson, *Human Understanding in Industry* (Chicago: Science Research Associates, 1956), 21.

2. Baruch Spinoza as quoted in Will Forpe and John McCollister, *The Sunshine Book: Expressions of Love, Hope and Inspiration* (Middle Village, NY: Jonathan David Publishers, Inc., 1979), 41.

3. Soren Kierkegaard in Raymond F. Gale, *Developmental Behavior* (New York: Macmillan, 1969), 25.

4. Shakespeare, *As You Like It*, 2.7.139.

5. James C. Coleman, *Personality Dynamics and Effective Behavior* (Glenview, IL: Scott, Foresman and Company, 1960), 63–64.

6. Fritz Redl and W. W. Wattenberg, *Mental Hygiene in Teaching* (New York: Harcourt Brace Jovanovich, Inc., 1951).

7. Prescott Lecky, *Self-Consistency: A Theory of Personality* (New York: Island Press, 1945).

8. Jack M. Bickham, "The Core of Characterization," *Writers Digest* (November 1989), 26–30.

9. Bickham,"The Core of Characterization," 26–30.

10. Bickham,"The Core of Characterization," 26–30.

11. John Masefield in Gale, *Developmental Behavior*, 490.

12. Clark E. Moustakes, ed., *The Self-Explorations In Personal Growth* (New York: Harper and Row, Publishers, Inc., 1956), 91.

13. Forpe and McCollister, *The Sunshine Book*, 35.

14. Helen Dudar, "The Unexpected Private Passion of Sigmund Freud," *The Smithsonian* (August 1990).

15. Harry Levinson, *Executive* (Cambridge, Mass.: Harvard University Press, 1981), 18–19.

16. Plato, *Dialogues of Plato*, trans. R. E. Allen (New Haven: Yale University Press, 1984).

17. Coleman, *Personality Dynamics and Effective Behavior*, 198–207; Anna Freud, *The Ego and the Mechanisms for Defense* (London: Hogarth Press and the Institute for Psychoanalysis, 1937); Sigmund Freud, *Civilization and Its Discontent* (London: Hogarth Press, 1930); Sigmund Freud, *The Problem of Anxiety* (New York: W. W. Norton & Co., Inc., 1936); and James F. Calhoun and Joan Ross Acocella, *Psychology of Adjustment and Human Relationships* (New York: Random House, Inc., 1978), 66–68.

18. Coleman, *Personality Dynamics and Effective Behavior*, 200.

19. Coleman, *Personality Dynamics and Effective Behavior*, 203.

20. Coleman, *Personality Dynamics and Effective Behavior*, 198–199.

21. Coleman, *Personality Dynamics and Effective Behavior*, 90; E. H. Erickson, *Childhood and Society*, 2nd ed. (New York: W. W. Norton & Co., Inc., 1963); and Robert J. Havighurst, *Developmental Tasks and Education* (New York: Longman's , Green and Co., 1952).

22. Coleman, *Personality Dynamics and Effective Behavior*; Havighurst, *Developmental Tasks and Education*; Ernest R. Hilgard and Richard C. Atkinson, *Introduction to Psychology* 4th ed., (New York: Harcourt, Brace & World, 1967), 74; and Louis H. Janda and Karen E. Klenke-Hamel, *Psychology: Its Study and Uses* (New York: St. Martin's Press, Inc., 1982), 205–207.

23. Erikson, *Childhood & Society.*

24. Coleman, *Personality Dynamics and Effective Behavior*, 81–91.

25. Oscar Wilde, *The Picture of Dorian Gray* (New York: Modern Library, 1985).

PART 3

Valuing Human Diversity

Culture and Values

We are not born with values, but we are born into cultures and societies that promote, teach, and impart their values to us. The process of acquiring values begins at birth. But it is not a static process. We are formed largely by the experiences we have, and our values form, grow, and change accordingly.

Maury Smith

Each person is the product of other people—family, community and society. Culture explains how so many creatures of one species (more than 5.6 billion people are alive at present) can be so dissimilar in appearance and behavior. Culture explains why some people wear clothing and others do not, why some people honor children and others abuse them, why some people are industrious and others are not, and why some people love peace and others make war.[1]

This chapter discusses the role of culture and value formation in the experience of community. Points this chapter makes are:

- culture influences all that we are and do;

- there are distinctive values and social themes in American culture;

- values conflict can occur due to different cultural experiences;

- the values of different generations can enrich a community; and

- tomorrow's communities are created by today's values.

THE IMPORTANCE OF CULTURE

From birth onward the young human being is like a book, and what will be written for three score and ten years will be largely determined by culture. Human beings are nature's most flexible creatures and the ones most capable of growth. Human drives are less rigid and the brain less developed at birth than in any other species, and the human childhood is the longest.[2] Anthropologist Margaret Mead explains the importance of culture in shaping our lives:

> The functioning of every part of the human body is molded by the culture within which the individual has been reared—not only in terms of diet, sunlight, exposure to diseases, overstrain, occupational hazards, and traumatic experiences, but also by the way he, born into a society with a definite culture, has been fed and disciplined, fondled and put to sleep, punished and rewarded. Culture is a principal element in the development of the individual that will result in his having a structure, a type of functioning, and a pattern of behavior different in kind from that of individuals who have been socialized within another culture.[3]

Culture refers to the distinctive ways of life of a group of people. Culture is a way of thinking, feeling, and believing. It is the group's knowledge stored up for future use. Every culture is designed to perpetuate the group and its solidarity, and to meet the demands of individuals for an orderly way of life.[4]

THE ROLE OF VALUES

Values are one of the most important elements of culture, because they affect everything a person does or is. Values are those things we hold dear. Before we fully value something, certain criteria must be met. What we value must be freely chosen, personally cherished, publicly declared, overtly demonstrated, and worthy of sacrifice. The more you understand your values, the clearer you can be in your ideas about life and the more confident you can be in your actions.

In *The 7 Habits of Highly Effective People,* Stephen Covey describes how values are interrelated and influence important aspects of life. See table 8–1.

VALUES IN AMERICAN CULTURE

John Gardner describes the influence of culture on value systems:

> In any community, the process of value generation goes on continuously in face to face groups such as family and neighborhood. One must include school, church, and workplace as well, as these are, in fact, communities. The community teaches. If it is healthy and coherent, the community imports a positive value system. If it is fragmented or sterile or degenerate, lessons are taught anyway—but not lessons that heal and strengthen. It is a community and culture that hold the individual in a framework of values; if the framework disintegrates, individual value systems disintegrate.[6]

Distinctive values in American culture have been enterprise, independence, humanitarianism, cooperation, and honesty.[7]

Enterprise and hard work are viewed as basic American values. These traits have been associated with need, especially in pioneer America, when daring, courage, and determination were assets for survival itself. As long as there are frontiers to challenge us—industrial, scientific, intellectual, or otherwise—we are likely to value the enterprising and hardworking individual. A primary motivation in our society is the urge to "get ahead," to make something of ourselves. This is the reason we value aggressiveness, especially in competitive situations.

Independence and love of freedom are characteristics that the majority of Americans believe describe themselves. Liberty and freedom have long been associated with America's founding fathers and also with the immigrants who have come to this land. Americans use individual characteristics and achievements to define who they are, and they expect, indeed demand, a large measure of independence and freedom to determine these.

Humanitarianism, or concern for others, has been a basic feature of our national self-image. No people in all of history have been more sensitive to appeals at home and abroad in behalf of needy and underprivileged people. Influenced by Judeo-Christian ideals, acts of kindness and humanitarianism are viewed as fundamental values in the American character.

Cooperation has a distinct place in the American value system. People helping people has been essential to the survival both of the individual and the

TABLE 8–1   How Values Influence Important Aspects of Life[5]

If your value is ...	... these are ways you may perceive other areas of your life:					
	Family	Work	Possessions	Pleasure	Friends	Principles
Family	• The highest priority	• A means to provide for family needs	• Family comfort, status, and opportunities	• Family oriented or unimportant	• Friends of the family or threat to family life	• Rules that keep family unified and strong
Work	• Help or interruption to work • People to instruct in work ethic	• Main source or fulfillment and satisfaction • Highest ethic	• Tools to increase work effectiveness • Fruits of labor	• Waste of time unless work-related	• Developed in work setting or otherwise unimportant	• Ideas that result in work success
Possessions	• Possession to use, dominate, smother, control • Showcase	• Opportunity to obtain status, authority, and recognition	• Source of economic status and security	• Buying, shopping, joining clubs	• Personal objects • Usable	• Concepts that enable the acquisition of possessions
Pleasure	• Vehicle or interference to personal satisfaction	• Work to live • "Fun" work OK	• Objects of fun • Means to have fun	• Supreme end in life • Main source of satisfaction	• Companions in fun	• Natural drives and instincts to be satisfied
Friends	• Help or obstacle to developing friendships • Social status symbol	• Social opportunity	• Means of buying friendship • Means of entertaining or providing social recognition	• Enjoyed with friends • Primarily social events	• Critical to personal happiness • Belonging, acceptance, popularity are important	• Basic laws that enable one to get along with others
Principles	• Opportunity for service, contribution, and fulfillment • Opportunity for intergenerational help	• Opportunity to use talents and abilities in a meaningful way • Means to provide economic resource	• Enabling resources • Responsibilities to be properly cared for • Secondary to people in importance	• Joy that comes from a focused life • Recreation as a part of a balanced lifestyle	• Confidants; those to share with, serve, and support	• Immutable natural laws that cannot be violated with impurity • When honored, leads to integrity, growth, and happiness

community. Just as we value the individual entrepreneur, we value teamwork and productive group effort as well. Indeed, Americans tend to view enterprise and cooperation as mutually supportive behaviors that should be learned and exercised by every individual if the community is to succeed.

Honesty is viewed as the best policy in our society; it is required of all who measure up to the image Americans have of themselves. It is taught to our children and respected in our leaders. Indeed, Americans identify honesty as the number-one quality admired and wanted in a leader. Our first president, George Washington, is honored because he was considered to be honest, and we consider our best leaders to be those who always tell the truth as they believe it to be.

With the above values as backdrop, there are five social themes that have had primary influence in defining American culture.[8]

- *The heroic individual* with quests and discoveries. One can think of Christopher Columbus, Daniel Boone, Amelia Earhart, and other famous figures in American history.

- *Hordes at the door*, each bringing gifts but demanding resources from those already present. One can think of wave after wave of immigrant populations that have helped shape America.

- *Giants of the earth* and their struggle to bring forth a living from the land and from the factory. One can think of all who persevered and overcame adversity through hard work.

- *Rot at the top*, a term that could only be coined by independent people abhorrent of authority. One can think of Tammany Hall and machine politics, the Teapot Dome and influence peddling, the Watergate affair and illegal cover-up, and other examples of political corruption.

- *Creation of community* where neighbors help neighbors and every person is his brother's keeper. One can think of the "American town hall," the "one-room school house," and the "volunteer fire department."

Our trials and triumphs around these themes have largely determined the American experience. To understand the concept of community in this country and its workplaces, consider the play and interplay of these five themes.

- Americans *celebrate the individual*, so within the group, organization, or broader community, it is only natural for each person to want to be treated like the unique individual he sees himself to be.

- The theme of exclusion and inclusion is constantly being played out as *new members arrive* and are assimilated into the community. They bring gifts, but they also use resources, so tension can occur until a balance is reached.

- Americans *value hard work* and reward those who work hard with community membership, recognition, and support. Communities typically must struggle, build, and maintain themselves. In doing these activities, hard work is a necessity.

- Americans *don't like bosses*, so woe to those who like the top too much or put self-interest ahead of community welfare. True leadership is an elected matter in the American community.

- Transcendence of self to *serve* others is an American ideal played out in parenthood and volunteerism. American communities value respect for the individual, it is true, but self-interest before the common good is not acceptable.

The basic character of a group of people is defined by its value system and the willingness of its members to make personal sacrifice to uphold these values. The primary measure of American society has been the actions of its people to live up to moral ideals when they are tested. Its ideals have been persistent hard work in the face of adversity, individual freedom in contrast to subservience, a basic concern for fellow human beings, cooperation and goodwill with others, and honesty in all dealings.

PERIODS OF LIFE AND VALUE FORMATION

Working effectively with different kinds of people is increasingly important in the modern workplace. Achieving community in a world of diversity begins with understanding how values are formed and shaped.

Values are developed during four periods of life, as summarized in table 8–2.

Imprinting—Ages 1 through 7

The family is the major influence during the first period of life, as children learn such skills as how to eat, talk, and walk. Habits are formed, and the right and wrong ways to do things are learned by example, direction, and reinforcement.

TABLE 8–2   Cultural Periods[9]

Period	Ages	Source of Influence
Imprinting	1–7	Family
Identification	8–12	Heroes and villains
Socialization	13–20	Peer group members
Adulthood	21 onward	Value system firm unless there is a significant emotional experience

To understand the importance of the imprinting period, consider that a child who is fed when hungry, held when frightened, and played with often will learn to behave differently from one who is fed according to a rigid schedule, left to cry it out when frightened, and rarely held just for fun.[10]

The following summarizes the powerful and long-lasting influence the family can have during the imprinting period:

> In interactions with father, mother, and siblings, the young child begins differentiations of self as liked or unliked, wanted or unwanted, acceptable or unacceptable, able or unable, worthy or unworthy, adequate or inadequate.
>
> The more positive the self-concept a child acquires, the greater is the feeling of adequacy and happiness; conversely, the more negative the self-concept acquired, the more frustrated and unhappy the child becomes.
>
> Experience later in life may change the concepts developed as a product of family living, but never easily or quickly. The most basic of self-concepts may be so deeply rooted in the individual's organization that they are difficult to alter, even by the most drastic of later experiences.[11]

The role of the family as it affects work experiences is especially interesting. For example, a highly mechanized or isolated work setting in which employees cannot talk to one another because of noise level or distance between them will hardly meet the needs of people who are accustomed to warm family relationships or a high degree of contact with others.[12]

Identification—Ages 8 through 12

During the identification period, the young person identifies heroes and villains. These people may be family members or others outside the family. In any case, the young person is attracted by the behavior of heroes (association) and repelled by the behavior of villains (aversion). The theory is that the central characters and favorite fantasies of childhood can become dominant themes of one's life. These identifications tend to solidify and are important determinants of adult behavior.[13]

> Imagine favorite stories and heroes of childhood, and think of the personal characteristics and lifestyles they imply: Peter Pan (the boy who never grew up); Wendy (who looked after others); Tarzan (strong and brave); Jane (beautiful and loving toward animals); and the Lone Ranger (who did good works and always left a silver bullet).
>
> "The human being is a featherless, storytelling animal," says Sandor McNab. We tell stories about who we are, where we come from, and where we are going. Personal myths formed during childhood can influence us all of our lives. Often, in order to change our lives, we have to edit our mythology.[14]

Sports figures, movie celebrities, and music stars are often heroes for young people in our society. Through the things they say and do, how they look and act, and the ideas they promote, they become models for the young person who tries to be like them.

Socialization—Ages 13 through 20

Friends exert a major influence on teenagers. The peer group affects everything they do, from dress and hairstyle to study and dating habits. If you ask teenagers why they are doing something, they are likely to say, "Because *everyone* does." Although basic religious and political values are shaped primarily by parental example, the things teenagers care about most—music, cars, dress—are usually influenced more by members of their own generation. Consider the following statement made by one adolescent girl:

> Peer pressure is extremely influential in my life. The closest friend I have had is a lot like me in that we are both sad and depressed a lot. I began to act even more depressed than before I was with her. I would call her up and try to act even more depressed than I was because that is what I thought she liked. I felt pressured to be like her.[15]

The adolescent years are especially important because it is during this period that a person normally becomes capable of making independent value judgments. Although teenagers typically rely heavily upon the opinions of friends and others whom they like or respect, they are biologically capable of complex reasoning and independent thought, and in this sense, they are mature. It is only natural that they want to be treated as adults.

Whether it is formed independently or as a result of social influence, when a teenage point of view is reached, it is usually difficult to alter. Often, these values remain with them for the rest of their lives.

Adulthood—Age 21 Onward

By the time a person has lived through imprinting, identification, and socialization, the value system is fairly firm. Ideas about what is right and wrong and good and bad are well established and are unlikely to change—unless a *significant emotional experience* takes place, an experience so emotional and so dramatic that it changes the person's entire life. For most people, few experiences are significant or emotional enough to disrupt the basic value system formed during their early years.

Typically, values and beliefs solidify at about the age of twenty-one, and when people are thirty, fifty, seventy, and ninety years of age, they continue to do what they do largely because of the forces and events that occurred in their lives from birth to age twenty-one. As a rule, if a person changes basic values during the adult years, it is only because a situation is met that previous values cannot resolve.

Think of your own life and consider: Have you ever had a significant emotional experience that has changed your values and beliefs? It may have been a brush with death, or the loss of someone or something important to you; it may have been a book you read or a film you saw; it may have been a person you met or an adventure you had. Any of these experiences can have an effect on you that is significant and emotional enough to change your values.

CULTURAL FORCES—THEN AND NOW

The following is a discussion of important cultural forces and how they shape our values. It helps explain why different age groups think and act the way they do. There are several points to keep in mind:

- Although culture can help explain the behavior of groups of people, the behavior of individuals must be evaluated individually, since each person is a unique human being.

- Culture has more influence on some people than others. Some are more externally directed, listening to social echos, while others are more internally directed, listening to an inner voice.

- The influence of cultural forces can usually be seen as people interact.

- No person is culture free. From the moment of birth to the moment of death, each of us is influenced by our environment.

Family

The family is the first and most important cultural force influencing human behavior. As the French author Marcel Proust writes, "After a certain age, the more one becomes oneself, the more obvious one's family traits become." Everything the family does affects the growing person. How the family earns and spends money, how it distributes and accomplishes household chores, and how it celebrates birthdays and holidays are all important determinants of the behavior of its members.

Basic attitudes toward people are influenced to a large degree by a person's family experiences, especially during the imprinting and identification periods. The little girl who attracts her daddy's attention by acting cute and feminine is later likely to relate to her male age-mates in the same way; the little boy who grows up resenting his father's autocratic manner will probably always feel uncomfortable with strict or close supervision from other authority figures—teachers, employers, or military officers; and whoever has seen a male employee act as if his immediate supervisor were nonexistent, or refuse to listen to advice, should know that this pattern of behavior is common among men who grow up fatherless.[16]

A family is a densely woven fabric made up of innumerable threads such as race, religion, income, and health, each influencing the developing child. An important thread can be a person's position in the family, especially if it results in a consistent pattern of interaction with other family members. Consider the following account.

> As my brother led me on a tour of his building, past works of corporate art, through conference rooms and executive dining rooms while I trailed along with my untied shoelace flapping on the marble floor, it occurred to me that even in childhood—when he was Jimmy and I was Stevie—somehow I had already perceived him as J.P.
>
> In order to avoid the hopeless task of competing against Jim, I became in many ways his opposite. Where he was authoritative, I was cunningly acquiescent. Where he was athletic, I was bookish. Without either of us consciously knowing it, I conceded him the title of standardbearer, conservator, defender of the realm—then scouted out the terrain and found my own dreamy path.[17]

The importance of birth order and whether or not one is an only child was first described by the psychologist Alfred Adler, when he wrote, "A person's position in the family can leave an indelible stamp on his or her style of life."[18]

- There is evidence that firstborn children are typically more serious and reliable than later born children. They are generally well organized and goal directed with a penchant for control.[19] Firstborns tend to be the focus of their parents' attention and expectations. Therefore, they are likely to be demanding and responsible in their relations with others. As adults, they tend to gravitate toward leadership positions and serious-minded work.[20]

- Middle-born children tend to have a knack for mediation and peacemaking. They are usually well liked by friends and peers. In family matters, they are often mavericks with the fewest pictures in the family album. Although they may experience confusion in childhood—not knowing whether to act old, not knowing whether to act young—they tend to be the best adjusted adults. By the time they are out of childhood, they are typically seasoned diplomats.[21]

- Last-born children are typically people-oriented charmers. They are carefree spirits with a tendency to blame people and events outside themselves for problems they encounter. They are engaging and persuasive and are most comfortable when seen as "special." Often, by the time they are born, their parents have exhausted expectations and energy on the siblings ahead of them, and are prone to lighten up and even pamper them. Last-borns typically have a zest for life and love to laugh.[22]

- Only children tend to be viewed either as self-starters, independent thinkers, and strong leaders, or as self-centered and aloof.[23] They usually develop verbal abilities earlier and to a greater degree than do children from larger families. Having been the center of attention in their families, they tend to be dominant and demanding in their relationships, and have trouble taking orders from others.[24]

As the founding father of birth-order theory, Adler believed that the idea could be taken too far. More important than birth order and number of siblings is the way parents and other family members interact with firstborn, later born, and only children as they are growing up. He wrote, "There has been some misunderstanding of my custom of classification according to position in the family. It is not, of course, the child's number in the order of successive births that influences his character, but the situation into which he is born and the way he interprets it."[25]

The structure of the family has changed in American society. After World War II, the dominant pattern was for women to remain at home, particularly during the child-raising years. This was the norm during the 1950s and 1960s. Today women are working outside the home in increasing numbers—some by choice and some by necessity. Currently, almost 60 percent of all women in America are working or looking for work. There are literally millions of working mothers with children under six years of age. Four out of five single mothers with children under the age of three work.[26] These young children are learning social and economic roles from Mom and Dad that differ from those taught in other eras.

Socioeconomic Class

Socioeconomic class has a major impact on everything about a person, from occupational choice (lawyer or laborer) to entertainment preference (theater or baseball) to clothing worn (Brooks Brothers or Sears).

A person's status can even have life-and-death consequences. This is largely because of nutritional, medical, and other advantages that money and position can provide. Consider the fate of the passengers of the luxury ship *Titanic*, which struck an iceberg in the North Atlantic in 1912 and sank, causing the loss of more than 1,500 lives. Not all classes had an equal chance to survive. Only 3 percent of the female passengers traveling in first class were drowned, whereas 16 percent in second class, and 45 percent in third class lost their lives.[27]

Socioeconomic status can also make a difference in legal justice. It can influence whether a person is arrested, indicted, convicted, and sent to jail, and if jailed, how long the person will stay. White-collar criminals in America spend less time in jail than do offenders from lower socioeconomic groups because they can afford to post bond while they await trial. If convicted, they tend to receive lighter sentences than do blue-collar people.[28] Indeed, studies show that a person driving a prestigious car is much less likely to be stopped for speeding than is a person driving a low-prestige car.[29]

Socioeconomic levels especially influence living standards and educational attainment:

Living standards. The wealth of the upper class tends to be self-perpetuating; there is some truth in the saying that "it takes money to make money." Lack of wealth in the lower class tends to be self-perpetuating as well, as seen in the following downward spiral: Low family income leads to early entry into the work force for children; leaving school early restricts later job opportunities and qualifications for job advancement; limited job opportunities and advancement lead to low family income.[30]

Educational attainment. Educational opportunities available to members of the upper class provide advantages throughout their lives. This upward spiral begins early in life: Advantaged children benefit from better elementary and secondary educations; this makes it possible for them to enter more prestigious colleges; graduation from these colleges results in advantages upon entering the labor market; this provides the means that enable them to afford superior educations for their children; this, in turn, allows the children to continue as members of the upper class.

Education

Throughout the identification and socialization periods, the behavior of young people is heavily influenced by schools, as knowledge, skills, and attitudes are conveyed. This includes what is taught (the curriculum), how it is taught (the teacher), and with whom the child learns (other students).

- *The curriculum.* A person's view about reality, truth, and values is influenced by what is learned in school. For example, the Bible and the *Origin of Species* teach two entirely different conceptions of the creation of man.

- *The teacher.* Whether a person is taught in terms of absolutes, or that reality exists in shades of gray, will influence beliefs and human relationships throughout a person's life.

- *Other students.* Whether or not a person goes to a school that is multicultural can have a lot to do with attitudes toward people who are *different*. Dealing with different types of people at an early age usually makes it easier to do so later in life.

The culture of the school has a profound impact on what young people learn and how they learn it. There is a saying that people learn less by what is taught, than by what is caught. Schools have changed over the years, and these changes have impacted the workplace. Differences in older and younger generations' management practices, work habits, and social attitudes support this point.

- *Management practices.* In the past, students were taught to follow instructions without question, and teachers tended to be autocratic in their relations with students. Today young people commonly challenge ideas to which they are exposed, and teachers are more democratic in their relationships. An increasing demand for employee involvement in the workplace and an increasing tendency to question rules and orders are the natural consequences of this shift.

■ *Work habits*. In the past, students were not promoted to the next grade until they had mastered the material of their present grade. Today young people may be graduated from high school without the knowledge and skill expected of eighth graders. As a result, many younger employees expect pay raises and job advancement without a great deal of effort on their own part.

■ *Social attitudes*. In recent years, new subjects have been added to the school curriculum in addition to reading, writing, and arithmetic. Children are learning about computers, human sexuality, and ecology. As a result, value gaps are common between younger workers, who think computers are as natural as lightbulbs, who are sexually sophisticated, and who are deeply concerned about the relationship between business and the environment, and older workers, who have a basic distrust of computers, who do not agree with new sexual mores, and who see environmentalists as irrational people responsible for slowing economic growth and putting people out of work.

Media

Communication media can have significant impact on values and attitudes.

■ *Books*. A few examples make the point—the Bible (Christianity), the Koran (Islamic), and the Bhagavad Gita (Hinduism) prescribe moral tenets for millions of people.

■ *Newspapers and magazines*. Consider the role of the American press in reporting the Watergate political affair and publishing the government's Pentagon papers, which detailed U.S. involvement in the Vietnam War.

■ *Radio*. Virtually every American home has a radio that transmits ideas and alters moods. Think of the impact of Orson Welles' radio show "War of the Worlds," which terrified audiences and even drove some to suicide. Consider Franklin D. Roosevelt's radio intonation, "The only thing we have to fear is fear itself," that helped many Americans to gain confidence and recover from the Great Depression. Finally, think of how radio music, news broadcasts, and talk shows today can lift your spirits or depress you as you listen in your home or car.

■ *Film*. Impressionable audiences have been influenced by "good guy" heroes (Roy Rogers, Gary Cooper, John Wayne, Luke Skywalker, and Indiana Jones) as well as by "antiheroes" (where the rascal gets the girl), and have attempted to emulate the behavior portrayed as glamorous and successful. Whether a person identifies with forces of good or forces of evil can be influenced by films.

- *Television.* Television is the dominant communication medium in America today. Fully 99 percent of U.S. homes have television sets. Contrast this with the fact that only 96 percent have indoor toilets. In just a little more than forty years, television has graduated from a fuzzy image on a small screen that fascinated the viewer, to an electronic medium that the average person watches nearly seven hours a day.[31]

  Television has significant influence on how communication and learning take place in the modern workplace. For example, video presentations are a popular medium for employee education, and leaders of organizations are increasingly using computer networks and teleconferencing as means of communicating with their employees.

Music

Music has always been an important cultural force. Rhythm, notes, and lyrics evoke moods and convey messages that affect the listener. Consider the impact of Elvis Presley, the Beatles, and Michael Jackson on the dress and behavior of several generations of young people. It seems that every month a new star emerges to influence the young.

Different values are programmed into different generations through music. Think about the values represented in five popular songs of five different periods:

- "How Much Is That Doggy in the Window" of the 1950s, dealing with economic conditions;
- "Bridge Over Troubled Waters" of the 1960s, dealing with human relationships;
- "Another Brick in the Wall" of the 1970s, dealing with social conditions;
- "Do You Think I'm Sexy" of the 1980s, dealing with sexuality; and
- Ice-T's 1990s album featuring rape with a flashlight and a cop-killing song that goes, "Die, die, die, pig, die!"

New social values and new ways of expressing sexuality, racism, and violent behavior are being taught through music and music videos. Yet how many adults are conscious of this, and how many simply say: "Turn that thing off. Who could listen to such noise?"[32]

Religion

Religion is an important element of culture, having a significant influence on values and beliefs. It is most likely to be brought into play during major life events, such as birth, marriage, war, and death. The more uncertainty that surrounds an event, the more likely it is that religion will play a part. In a study of the Trobriand Islanders, anthropologist Bronislaw Malinowski observed that the villagers did not extend their magical rituals to fishing the safe and reliable inner lagoon, but did use magical ceremonies in the case of open-sea fishing:

> It is most significant that in lagoon fishing, where man can rely upon knowledge and skill, magic does not exist; while in open-sea fishing, full of danger and uncertainty, there is extensive magical ritual to secure safety and good results.[33]

Religion can have a major influence on community in the workplace. At different times and locations in America, if you were not of a certain faith, you might even have been denied a job. Even today, in some work environments, there is a tendency to discriminate in favor of one religious group over another.

Institutions

The institutions of society are important cultural forces, since they preserve and shape human values. Some, such as schools, have their primary influence during the formative years of identification and socialization, while others affect people all of their lives. In American society the goals of the YMCA, Scouts, Junior Achievement, and 4-H clubs are to influence the beliefs and skills of young people in the areas of physical fitness, outdoor life, commercial enterprise, and farming. Also, each of these organizations attempts to teach such universal values as resourcefulness, honesty, and concern for others. On the other hand, government, as an institution, exerts influence on people throughout their lives as laws are made and executed, and transgressors are judged.

Conflict between the generations can occur within and about institutions, particularly if young people view them as self-serving, bureaucratic, and irrelevant entities administered by people who are out of touch. If alienation develops, young people will tend to avoid society's institutions; either physically or mentally, they will drop out. The best way to prevent alienation is for leaders to manage institutions so that they are genuinely responsive, nonbureaucratic, and, above all, relevant for the people they are designed to serve. All institutions—school systems, churches, businesses, social groups, and political parties—face this problem.

Table 8–3 identifies forces and events that have influenced the values of different age groups in modern American culture.

HOW GENERATIONS DIFFER

Different age groups form basic values while living through different periods. Imagine a person raised during the Depression of the 1930s, another raised during the social changes of the 1960s, and another raised during the 1990s. If these

TABLE 8–3 Forces and Events That Have Influenced American Values[34]

People Who Are in Their 80s	When Their Values Formed: 1920s
Influence Factors	

- World War I
- Close family ties
- Radio
- Automobiles (Model T)
- Prohibition
- Speakeasies
- Flappers
- Stock market crash
- Rural society

People Who Are in Their 70s	When Their Values Formed: 1930s
Influence Factors	

- The Great Depression
- Federal income taxes begin
- FDR
- The "3 Rs" taught in school
- Boogie-woogie music
- Government legislation
- The work ethic
- *Gone with the Wind*
- Fireside chats
- Chautauqua

People Who Are in Their 60s	When Their Values Formed: 1940s
Influence Factors	

- Great Depression ends
- World War II
- Victory gardens
- Atomic bomb
- Air travel
- Family car
- Big-band music
- Work ethic
- Patriotism

People Who Are in Their 50s	When Their Values Formed: 1950s
Influence Factors	

- Korean War
- Rock-and-roll music
- Television arrives
- Short hair
- James Dean
- Elvis Presley
- The gray flannel suit
- Unions gain strength
- "I Like Ike"
- Ozzie and Harriet

People Who Are in Their Late 40s	When Their Values Formed: 1960–1964
Influence Factors	

- Sputnik
- U.S. space program
- The Kennedy years
- The Beatles
- Small sports cars
- Business booms
- Cuban missile crisis
- John Kennedy assassinated
- Interstate highways
- Civil Rights Act

TABLE 8–3   Forces and Events That Have Influenced American Values (continued)

People Who Are In Their Early 40s	When Their Values Formed: 1965–1969
Influence Factors	
• Civil rights movement • Vietnam War • British rock invasion • Miranda case • Increase in drug use, especially marijuana • The pill	• Churches relax moral standards • Hippie movement • Dr. Spock • Long hair • Robert Kennedy and Martin Luther King assassinated

People Who Are in Their 30s	When Their Values Formed: 1970s
Influence Factors	
• Kent State • Watergate • Explicit movies • Computers • Feminism • Two-career families	• Mobile society • Divorce rate increases • "Me" generation • *Star Wars* • Acid rock • Fast food

People Who Are in Their 20s	When Their Values Formed: 1980s
Influence Factors	
• Violent crime • Cocaine/crack • Reaganomics • Cable television • MTV, music videos • The Moral Majority	• Million dollar athletes • Wall Street greed • Japanese products • Gay rights • AIDS epidemic

People Who Are in Their Teens	When Their Values Formed: 1990s
Influence Factors	
• Fall of Communism • Breakup of Soviet Union • Desert Storm • Information technology explosion • Single-parent families • AIDS crisis	• Radio/TV talk shows • Clinton presidency • Sexual abuse publicized • Health-care problems • Homeless people • Global products and markets

people live or work together, they will have to put forth extra effort to understand and appreciate each other's views. The observation of one octogenarian makes the point well:

> I am one of the "older generation." Born in 1913, I could not have selected a better period of time to live my life. I witnessed the end of World War I and the horse and buggy era. I drove a Model T Ford, picked blackberries and gathered black walnuts. I smoked corn silk, learned how to make sausage, and attended church services regularly.
>
> I respected my elders and was taught to say "Yes, ma'am" and "No, sir." I witnessed the births of new inventions and the progress of technology that made this twentieth century a most interesting time to live. Great advances in science, transportation, and communication have enriched our lives. But I find it enigmatic that values have declined at an equal pace with our technical progress.[35]

Different values can help explain conflict between older and younger people on a variety of important subjects. Flashpoints between the generations include "motivation to work," "reaction to change," "gratification of needs," "attitude toward authority," "personal appearance," "respect for property," and "gender role changes."

Motivation to Work

Older people tend to work for money and security. Having lived through two world wars and the Great Depression, they know what it is like to be out of a job and to do without material goods. They do not want to do this again. Therefore, they are inclined to define "success" in economic terms. On the other hand, younger people tend to work for social and self-fulfillment goals, and they want work to be fun.

Young people also work in order to have leisure. As recently as 1969, the majority of Americans believed that hard work always "paid off." Yet, in less than ten years, most people no longer believed this to be true. This shift in thinking is due primarily to the attitudes of younger people, many of whom work to live as opposed to live to work.[36] When young employees are given a three-day layoff for making mistakes on the job, they are likely to respond, "Great, I'll take five." This attitude is unthinkable to most older people. For older generations, a three-day layoff is likely to be viewed as a severe economic punishment.

Figure 8–1 shows the inverted order of priorities among younger and older Americans. In general, older Americans feel the need for survival first, relationships second, and personal growth third, while younger Americans invert this order—first comes personal growth, then relationships, and survival is taken for granted. The older person's focus on money and security has been accentuated in recent years due to turbulent economic conditions and an uncertain employment outlook.

FIGURE 8–1 The Motivational Needs Felt by Older and Younger Americans[37]

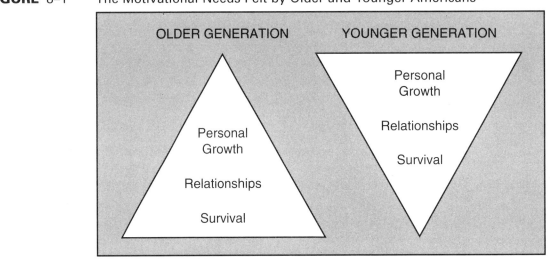

Reaction to Change

Older people have created the world as it is today, therefore their typical reaction to change is to oppose it. On the other hand, younger people have little sense of ownership of things they did not help create; in addition, they are used to new experiences, having grown up in a world of seemingly constant technical innovation. In general, younger people are less resistant to change, are more adaptive when it occurs, and will often be the creators of change.

Gratification of Needs

Relatively few older people are accustomed to the immediate gratification of personal needs. As children they may have been forced to make do with few toys and almost no luxuries—quilts were made from outgrown clothes cut into squares. When they became adults, self-gratification generally took a back seat to the needs of younger family members. Contrast this with the fact that many young people in the United States today have not wanted for many things for very long. A common saying is that old folks worked all of their lives to have what young people start out with today.

Since the start of the Industrial Revolution, each generation has wanted to give its children all of the things Mom and Dad wanted, but never had. But it wasn't until the 1950s that this goal could become a reality for large numbers of people. From this time onward, most American parents had more money and resources to spend on their children than their parents had, and it became common to hear, "My kids are going to have it better than I did."

Now, in the work setting and in the home, the children of the fifties, sixties, seventies, and eighties have grown up expecting, and often demanding, immediate gratification of personal desires. Self-sacrifice and the postponement of satisfaction are resisted by many younger people—a fact that is upsetting to many older adults. In place of an ethic of self-denial and sacrifice, an ethic of self-absorption has been programmed into large numbers of Americans.[38]

Attitude Toward Authority

Older generations were taught, "Children should be seen and not heard," and "Children should obey their elders." Respect and obedience to authority figures were developed from an early age in these generations. In contrast, younger people tend to question what they hear and decide for themselves. They may have concluded from observation or personal experience that respect must be earned. The task of leadership today is more challenging than it used to be because obedience, either at home or on the job, is not automatically given.

Personal Appearance

For older people, two world wars fought by short-haired heroes reinforced the idea that if you were a man, you had to have short hair. For more than half a century, young men were encouraged to wear their hair short and to dress neatly if they wanted to be considered masculine and respectable.[39]

Then came the 1950s, and young people found that long hair and unconventional dress distinguished them from their elders. Indeed, hairstyle and clothing became symbols of rebellion against the older generation. In the work setting today, dress, hairstyle, and other elements of personal appearance continue to be sources of conflict between the generations, as older people wish younger people would be more tasteful in their appearance and young people wish older people would relax.

Respect for Property

It is not unusual for older people to put scraps of paper in their pockets until they find a trash can to dispose of them. On the other hand, younger people are often careless and even destructive to property. This reflects the fact that many young people have not had to clean, fix, or replace the things they damaged or lost while growing up. If they made a mess, someone else would clean it up; if they broke something, someone else would fix it; if they lost something, someone else would buy a new one.

If a person does not have to work for something in the first place and is not held responsible for what is broken or lost, there is little incentive to take care of property. Property is often not valued simply because it appears to be so easily replaced. This point is important in the work setting because of the need to care for tools, equipment, buildings, and grounds. Often, there is no way to repair or replace something once it is gone.

Gender Role Changes

Older people tend to be stereotyped in their thinking concerning male and female social roles. Many older men are opposed to women working outside the home and would do almost anything to avoid having to report to a female supervisor. In contrast, younger people are more flexible about who does what; increasingly in recent years, younger people have learned nondiscrimination and sexual equality so that who is the subordinate and who is the supervisor is not as emotional a question.

Consider that the average person's attitude about whether a wife should work outside the home reversed between the years 1938 and 1978 in favor of women working. An increasing tendency for young men to drop out of the work force at the same time more women enter employment is evidence of further shifts in attitudes regarding sex roles. Between 1947 and 1977, the exodus from the work force of men in their prime working years doubled.[40] Recently, a young man's criteria for a wife—she has to be attractive, have good values, and have a good job—came as a shock to his older father who would have never considered a woman's occupational status as a factor for consideration in marriage.

VALUES AND COMMUNITY—FIVE IMPORTANT POINTS

The different values of different people can enrich a community. But when values collide, communication can break down. Misunderstanding can occur on the job, in the home, and in society at large. What can be done? Keep in mind the following points to improve communication and build community:

- *The values people have are based on what they were exposed to during their formative years—ages one through twenty.* Some values may be more positive and constructive than others, but all values are normal in the sense that culture creates them.

- *To understand the values of another person, try to see things through her or his "cultural eyes."* Consider the forces and events that were in effect during the imprinting, identification, and socialization periods. Is materialism the result of being forced to do without things while growing up? Is intolerance the product of being taught that "black is black and white is white"? Is difficulty adjusting to a female supervisor the result of having only known women as mothers, sisters, and girlfriends, never as bosses? Is inability to show emotion due to the belief that a man should be strong and that the display of emotion is a sign of weakness? Is preference for rock-and-roll music the result of having been socialized during the 1950s?

■ *Once values are formed, they do not change easily.* What people are like during young adulthood tends to remain unchanged for the rest of their lives. In fact, it is very difficult for one person to alter another person's values once they have developed. If you are over twenty-one, consider your own values—has anyone ever tried to change you? Were they successful? Typically, people change their values only through *significant emotional experiences.* You should remember this if you seek to change others; otherwise, you must learn to live with them as they are.

■ *The positive values of different generations should be recognized.* A business leader describes the need for the different generations to appreciate each other:

> A company needs to be constantly rejuvenated by the infusion of young blood. It needs young people with the imagination and the guts to turn everything upside down if they can. It also needs old fogies to keep them from turning upside down those things that ought to be right side up. Above all, it needs young rebels and old conservatives who can work together, challenge each other's values, yield or hold fast with equal grace, and continue after each hard-fought battle to respect each other.[41]

■ *Values are communicated primarily by actions, less by words.* For example, young people who see elected leaders convicted of crimes and then pardoned will form their own attitudes toward public officials and criminal justice regardless of the speeches they hear.

At the family level, parents who say to their children, "We believe in respect for people, good health habits, and personal honesty," are teaching the opposite values when they disregard people's feelings, smoke cigarettes, and cheat on taxes.

Human beings long for meaning and the first web of meaning comes from one's culture. Young people are bombarded by value instruction every waking hour. The school teaches; the playground teaches; television teaches; the home teaches—insistently and in many voices—good lessons and bad.[42]

Because tomorrow's communities are created by today's values, it is important for each person to consider, "What are my values and how can I communicate these by my actions?" To evaluate your own values and your efforts to communicate them, complete the following exercise.

APPLICATION: WHAT ARE YOUR VALUES—HOW DO YOU COMMUNICATE THEM?

What do you value and what behaviors communicate your values to others? What are your views on:

A. Marriage _____

_____

_____

_____

B. Family _____

_____

_____

_____

C. Work _____

_____

_____

_____

D. Government _____

_____

_____

_____

E. Education _____

_____

_____

_____

F. Religion _____

_____

_____

_____

What are your views on:

A. Acceptable language_____

_____

_____

_____

B. Dress_____

_____

_____

_____

C. Sex_____

_____

_____

_____

D. Money_____

_____

_____

_____

E. Guns_____

_____

_____

_____

F. Television_____

_____

_____

_____

G. Any other issue regarding values_____

_____

_____

_____

REFERENCES

1. U.S. Bureau of Census, "World Population Profile—Table 1351," *Statistical Abstract of the U.S.—1994* (Washington, DC: U.S. Department of Commerce, 1994).

2. James C. Coleman, *Personality Dynamics and Effective Behavior* (Chicago: Scott, Foresman and Co., 1960), 44–73.

3. Margaret Mead "The Concept of Culture and the Psychosomatic Approach," *Contributions Toward Medical Technology*, ed. Arthur Weider (New York: Ronald Press, 1953), 1: 377–378.

4. Clyde Kluckhohn, "Cultural Factors in Personality" in Warren R. Baller, *Readings in the Psychology of Human Growth and Development* (New York: Holt, Rinehart and Winston, 1962), 324–325.

5. Based on the work of Stephen R. Covey, *The Seven Habits of Highly Effective People* (New York: Simon & Schuster, 1989).

6. John W. Gardner, *On Leadership* (New York: The Free Press, 1990), 113.

7. Warren R. Baller and Don C. Charles, *The Psychology of Human Growth and Development* (New York: Holt, Rinehart and Winston, 1961), 184–185.

8. Robert B. Reich, *Tales of a New America* (New York: Times Books, 1987), 3–19, 235–253.

9. This and the following sections (Cultural Forces—Then and Now; How Generations Differ; and Values and Communication—Five Important Points) are based on *The People Puzzle: Understanding Yourself and Others* by Morris Massey (Reston, Va.: Reston Publishing Co., 1979). This excellent book provides the conceptual framework for understanding values and gives many examples that help explain why people do what they do.

10. Massey, *The People Puzzle.*

11. Arthur W. Combs and Donald Snygg, *Individual Behavior* (New York: Harper & Brothers, 1959), 136.

12. Harry Levinson, *Executive* (Cambridge, Mass.: Harvard University Press, 1981), 31.

13. Sigmund Freud, *The Ego and The Id*, ed. James Strachey, (New York: W. W. Norton and Co. Inc., 1960).

14. Sandor McNab, "The Stories We Live By," *Psychology Today* (December 1988): 44.

15. Massey, *The People Puzzle.*

16. Levinson, *The Executive*, 30.

17. Stephen Harrigan "Places Everyone," *Health* (November/December, 1992): 67.

18. Alfred Adler, *Understanding Human Nature* (New York: Greenberg, 1927).

19. Julius and Zelda Segal, "The First Born Child," *Parents* (67, No. 5, May 1992).

20. Harrigan, "Places Everyone," 67.

21. Harrigan, "Places Everyone," 70.

22. Harrigan, "Places Everyone," 70.

23. Zick Rubin and Elton B. McNeil, *The Psychology of Being Human*, 3rd ed. (New York: Harper & Row, Publishers, Inc., 1981), 360–364; and Didi Moore, "The Only Child Phenomenon." *The New York Times Magazine* (Jan. 18, 1981): 26.

24. Moore, "The Only Child Phenomenon," 26, and Rubin & McNeil, *The Psychology of Being Human*, 360–364.

25. Adler, *Understanding Human Nature.*

26. Louis Richman, "Why the Middle Class is Anxious," *Fortune* (May 21, 1990): 106–112; and U.S. Bureau of Census, "Employment Status—Tables 614, 617, 619, 621, 624, 625, and 626," *Statistical Abstract of the U.S.—1994* (Washington, DC: U.S. Department of Commerce, 1994).

27. Peter Farb, *Humankind* (Boston: Houghton-Mifflin, Bantam, 1978), 359.

28. Farb, *Humankind*, 338.

29. Farb, *Humankind*, 350.

30. Coleman, *Personality Dynamics & Effective Behavior.*

31. "Generations," *Cincinnati Enquirer* (March 21, 1993): H–2.

32. Massey, *The People Puzzle*, 97. and James Bowman, "Plain Brown Rappers," *National Review* (July 20, 1992).

33. Bronislaw Malinowski, *Magic, Science, and Religion and Other Essays* (Garden City, NJ: Doubleday & Co., Inc., 1954), 14.

34. Based on Massey, *The People Puzzle.*

35. Tom Henry, "The Olden, Golden Decades," *Cincinnati Enquirer* (March 21, 1993): H–1.

36. Massey, *The People Puzzle.*

37. Daniel Yankelovich, *New Rules: Searching for Self-fulfillment in a World Turned Upside-Down* (Toronto: Bantam, 1982), 33.

38. Massey, *The People Puzzle*; and Yankelovich, *New Rules.*

39. Massey, *The People Puzzle.*

40. Yankelovich, *New Rules*, xv.

41. Karen Holly Horrell, *Speech—Outstanding Women In Business Conference*, Cincinnati, OH, 1992.

42. John W. Gardner, "Reinventing Community," address delivered to the Carnegie Council on Adolescent Development, Washington, DC: December 11, 1992.

CHAPTER 9

Social Tolerance

The Cold Within

Six human beings were trapped one day
In black and bitter cold.
Each one possessed a stick of wood,
Or so the story's told.

With dying fire in need of logs,
The first one held hers back;
For of the faces around the fire,
She noticed one was black.

The next one looking across the way
Saw one not of his church,
And couldn't bring himself to give
The fire his stick of birch.

The third one sat in tattered clothes;
He gave his coat a hitch.
Why should he give wood to use
To warm the idle rich?

The richest man sat back and thought
Of the gold he had in store,
And how to keep what he had earned
From the lazy, shiftless poor.

The black man's face bespoke revenge
As the fire passed from his sight;
For all he saw in his stick of wood
Was a chance to spite the white.

And the last man of this forlorn group
Did naught except for gain.
Giving only to those who gave
Was how he played the game.

The logs held tight in death's still hands
Was proof of human sin.
They didn't die from the cold without;
They died from the cold within.

Alexander Pope

A major requirement in the creation of community is **social tolerance**. Too often, lack of tolerance leads to discrimination, exclusion from opportunity, and other forms of social injustice. This can be seen on a large scale in relations between nations, and it can be seen on a personal scale in relations in the workplace.

This chapter discusses the role of tolerance in building community, the causes and consequences of prejudice, and how to deal with social differences. Important points include:

- the harm that discrimination can bring—you wouldn't want anyone to be a victim; and

- the power of beliefs to create reality—people tend to live up or down to their own self-image, and this image is heavily influenced by the attitudes of others.

THE NATURE OF COMMUNITY

Community is integrative. It involves bringing together people of different cultures, personalities, and stages of development, and integrating them into a whole that is greater than the sum of its parts. This integration is not simply a melting down process; rather, it is a building up in which the identity of the individual is preserved, yet simultaneously transcended. Community does not eliminate diversity. Instead, it welcomes other points of view, embraces opposites, and seeks to understand all sides of every issue.[1]

A healthy community is a safe place precisely because no one is attempting to heal, convert, or fix others. People accept each other as they are. They tolerate individual foibles as good families do. They value each other, not as objects or means to other ends, but as precious beings in their own right. In community, people are free to be themselves. They are free to discard defenses and disguises, free to grow and achieve their full potential, free to become their whole and true selves.[2]

Scott Peck, author of *The Different Drum*, describes the diversity that is fundamental in the very concept of community.

Because a community includes members with many different points of view and the freedom to express them, it comes to appreciate the whole of a situation far better than an individual, couple, or ordinary group can. Incorporating the dark and the light, the sacred and the profane, the sorrow and the joy, the conclusions of the community can be well rounded. Nothing is likely to be left out. With so many frames of reference, community can approach *reality* more and more closely. Realistic decisions, consequently, are more often guaranteed in community than in any other human environment.[3]

HOW SOCIAL ATTITUDES ARE FORMED

A subtle, psychological cause of the breakdown of community is intolerance—an unwillingness to accept people and ideas other than one's own. The greater the level of intolerance, the more difficult it is to understand other people, and the harder it is to adapt to new situations involving other points of view. Another word for intolerance is closed-mindedness. Economist Paul Samuelson's tongue-in-cheek description of working women reflects intolerance in the workplace.

> Women are built by nature to tend babies in the home. They are emotional. They have monthly ups and downs. They cannot carry heavy weights. They lack self-confidence. Men will not work under a woman. Man-to-man talk will be inhibited by the presence of women. Even women prefer a male physician to a female one. Women lack imagination and creativity. If you mix men and women on the job, they will carry on to the detriment of efficiency and good morals. By the time you have trained a woman, she'll get married and leave you, or have a baby; or alternatively, you won't ever be able to get rid of a woman once you've hired her. If a woman does turn out to be a superlative economic performer, she's not feminine; she's harsh and aggressive with a chip on her shoulder against men and the world. (And she's killing her chances of getting married.) Women workers, seeking pin money, take bread from the mouths of family breadwinners.[4]

Where do such ideas come from? How is such intolerance developed? Intolerance results from attitudes formed both in the home and in the larger community.

Home

Nothing innate in children causes them to prefer a certain color of skin or a certain shape of eyes. Small children learn such preferences by association and imitation. They observe the behavior of role models, particularly their parents, as they interact with others, and they begin to copy attitudes and ways of behaving. Preferences for social customs, such as eating, speaking, and living habits, are developed early as a result of home and family influence.[5]

More than two hundred years ago, Thomas Jefferson recognized the importance of the home environment for shaping attitudes when he wrote, ". . . for man is an imitative animal. This quality is the germ of all education. From cradle to grave, people learn to do what they see others do."[6] As early as age three and usually by age five, children notice ethnic differences, and social stereotyping begins to develop.[7]

In our society, boys and girls are typically treated differently from the time they are born. Boys are dressed in blue and given cars and trucks for toys, while girls wear pink and are encouraged to play with dolls and dishes. Boys are usually allowed more freedom, while girls are treated more protectively. Role stereotyping is not a new phenomenon as shown in the following nursery rhyme from England, 1844:

> What are little boys made of?
> Frogs and snails
> And puppy dogs' tails.
>
> What are little girls made of?
> Sugar and spice
> And all that's nice.[8]

By the age of three, most children know whether they are male or female, and they have distinct, if not exaggerated, ideas of what masculinity and femininity should involve.[9] Through conditioning (a system of rewards and punishments), imitation (copying the behavior of those perceived to be most like themselves), and self-definition (categorizing people into two sexes and then deciding to which group they belong), children establish sexual identity, a critical task for normal growth and development.[10]

Just as attitudes toward sex roles are influenced by home and family, so are other social attitudes, including broad views on work, health, and government, as well as specific opinions about food, language, dress, and other people.

Community

Social attitudes continue to develop throughout later childhood and during the early teens, as *school*, *religion*, *social custom*, and *community stereotypes* play important roles. The socialization that most people experience during this period has tremendous influence on their values and their likes and dislikes for particular types of people. By late adolescence, attitudes usually solidify around the norms of the community and groups with whom the person associates.[11]

School. To see how schools can influence social attitudes, consider that textbooks historically have portrayed males more favorably than females. A study of books awarded prizes for excellence by The American Library Association found that male characters outnumbered females eleven to one, and, in the case of animals with sex identities, ninety-five to one. Throughout these books, males were typically shown in adventurous and varied roles, while females were usually shown in supportive and homemaker roles.[12]

In another study, social researcher Marjorie U'Ren found that only 15 percent of schoolbooks with illustrations of people included pictures of women. She writes: "We tend to forget the fact that the female sex is half the human race, that women are not merely the ladies' auxiliary to the human species."[13]

Religion. Religious teachings are important in shaping attitudes toward types and groups of people. Consider the implications of the following prayer all male Orthodox Jews are supposed to say every morning:

Blessed art thou, O Lord our God, King of the Universe, that I was not born a gentile. Blessed art thou, O Lord our God, King of the Universe, that I was not born a slave. Blessed art thou, O Lord our God, King of the Universe, that I was not born a woman.[14]

Similar antifeminist bias is reflected in Christianity due largely to the teachings of Saint Paul, who viewed the inferior role of women as part of a divine natural order. In I Corinthians 11:7–9, Paul writes:

A man is in the image of God and reflects God's glory; but woman is the reflection of man's glory. For man did not come from woman; woman came from man. And man was not created for the sake of woman, but woman was created for the sake of man.

Social custom. The role of social custom in forming attitudes is shown by the different roles played by men and women in different societies. Anthropologist Margaret Mead spent the years 1931–1933 in New Guinea studying the contrasting attitudes of societies toward the sexes. Among three groups—the gentle Arapesh, the cannibalistic Mundugumor, and the head-hunting Tchambuli—living within a radius of only about a hundred miles, she found strikingly different ideas about masculinity and femininity.

Social Custom and Sex Roles

Among the Arapesh, men and women are regarded as equally gentle and are equally likely to initiate sexual relations. In fact, parents are more inclined to warn their sons than their daughters against getting into situations in which they might be seduced. Males take as much delight as females in those many aspects of parenthood that the North American and European stereotypes regard as "maternal" behavior. So little distinction is made between parental roles that the Arapesh verb that translates as "to bear a child" refers equally to males who have become fathers and to females who do the actual bearing. When Mead remarked to a group of Arapesh that a certain middle-aged male was handsome, they agreed, and then one added, "But you should have seen him before he bore all those children."

The nearby Mundugumor also apply the same standards of behavior to both sexes, but their ideal is the direct opposite to that of the gentle Arapesh. Both male and female Mundugumors are taught from infancy to be independent and competitive. As adults, females are expected to be every bit as aggressive in sexual encounters, and no less violent, jealous, and quick to avenge insults as are males.

Among the third group, the Tchambuli, the sexes exhibit definite behavioral differences, but with an exact reversal of the roles expected of them in most other societies. The males spend much of their time playing the flute and cultivating the arts; they take care in choosing their attire each day and in adorning themselves with jewelry; and most of the work they do consists of shopping and trading. The females, on the other hand, are assertive and practical; they show little interest in clothing or jewelry; and it is they who, by fishing and by manufacturing utensils for trade, largely provide for the family.[15]

The influence of social custom on the roles played by men and women in American society was recently discussed at a prejudice reduction workshop conducted by the National Council of Christians and Jews. Participants were asked to give an example of an incident in which they had experienced prejudice firsthand. One young man reported that the school nurse had called to say his daughter was sick—was his wife home? When he answered "no," the nurse thanked him and hung up—even though he was obviously home!

Community stereotypes. National and ethnic stereotypes are important determinants of social attitudes. Consider Russian author Leo Tolstoy's characterization of people from different parts of Europe, as described in *War and Peace*:

> A Frenchman is self-assured, because he regards himself personally, both in mind and body, as irresistibly attractive to men and women. An Englishman is self-assured, as he sees himself as being a citizen of the best-organized state in the world. An Italian is self-assured, because he is excitable and easily forgets himself and other people. A Russian is self-assured, just because he knows nothing and does not want to know anything, since he does not believe that anything can be known. The German's self-assurance is worst of all, stronger and more repulsive than any other, because he imagines that he knows the truth—science—which he himself has invented, but which is, for him, the absolute truth.[16]

Social attitudes that develop in the home and in the community tend to remain with us all of our lives and they play important roles in human relations. Once formed, these attitudes are difficult to change. In *The Nature of Prejudice*, psychologist Gordon Allport reports the following conversation:

> Mr. X: The trouble with the Jews is that they only take care of their own people.
>
> Mr. Y: But the record of the community chest campaign shows that they give more generously, in proportion to their numbers, to the general charities of the community, than do non-Jews.
>
> Mr. X: That shows they are always trying to buy favors and intrude into Christian affairs. They think of nothing but money; that is why there are so many Jewish bankers.
>
> Mr. Y: But a recent study shows that the percentage of Jews in the banking business is negligible, far smaller than the percentage of non-Jews.
>
> Mr. X: That's just it; they don't go in for respectable businesses; they are only in the movie business or they run night clubs.[17]

In effect, Mr. X is saying, "Don't confuse me with the facts; my mind is made up," and he will create one rationalization after another to support his basic attitudes.

Besides attitudes toward specific groups and customs, people acquire an orientation toward the world in general through family, friends, school, and other cultural influences. Some may develop a world view that is "black and white," with no tolerance for differences. Others may develop a view that is neither black nor white, but a reality in between, so that opinions are tentative and open to new information and new interpretation. A person's view of the world affects one's entire life, because it is carried into every relationship one has.

WHY TOLERANCE IS IMPORTANT

By nature, people are opinionated. Opinions add vitality to human relationships as satisfying allegiances are formed and exciting debates are held. The extremes of community—love and hate—have their origin in shared and opposing opinions. Tolerance is important because no two people are exactly alike. Sometimes, when people have opposing views, trust and respect can be developed and goodwill can be experienced only through tolerance.

Tolerance is also important because intolerance can lead to discrimination, and discrimination can have harmful effects. Put yourself in the shoes of writer-psychiatrist Alvin Poussaint:

> A white policeman yelled, "Hey, Boy, come here." Somewhat bothered, I retorted: "I'm no boy," He then rushed at me, inflamed, and stood towering over me, snorting, "What d'ja say, Boy?" Quickly he frisked me and demanded, "What's your name, Boy?" Frightened, I replied, "Dr. Poussaint. I'm a physician." He angrily chucked and hissed, "What's your first name, Boy?" When I hesitated, he assumed a threatening stance and clenched his fists. As my heart palpitated, I muttered in profound humiliation, "Alvin." He continued his psychological brutality, bellowing, "Alvin, the next time I call you, you come right away, you hear? You hear?" I hesitated. "You hear me, Boy?"[18]

Poussaint was humiliated and, in his words, "psychologically castrated." Frustration and powerlessness are burdens prejudiced people may intentionally or unknowingly place on others. Poussaint was the victim of discrimination born of intolerance.

Being discriminated against can result in feelings of worthlessness and inferiority. In studies of young children of color, psychologist Kenneth Clark discovered that severe emotional stress can occur as a result of feelings of inadequacy and inferiority, to the extent that children will reject black dolls and black customs in favor of white dolls and white norms.[19]

Discrimination can even have life-and-death consequences. Discrimination against Jews, Poles, and Gypsies in Nazi Germany during World War II resulted in genocide for many millions of people. Although the death ovens of Auschwitz, Dachau, and Buchenwald were instruments of destruction, intolerance was the cause. In *Mein Kampf*, Adolph Hitler wrote:

If the Jews were alone in this world, they would stifle in filth and offal; they would try to get ahead of one another in hate-filled struggle and exterminate one another.[20]

It is hard to believe that horrible atrocities traced to intolerance continue in modern times. Consider Southeast Asia, Africa, Eastern Europe, the Middle East; yes, and in the United States too.

If you have ever been the minority in a majority group, you know firsthand the importance of tolerance. Have you ever been the different one? Have you ever been the only:

- handicapped person in a group?
- older person in the company of young people?
- child among adults?
- poor person among the wealthy?
- person of color in a predominantly white school setting?
- visitor in a foreign country?
- Asian or Hispanic in a black neighborhood?
- male in a traditionally female occupation?
- female in a traditionally male occupation?
- tall, heavy, or smart one in the class?

Whether you enjoyed being different or not, and whether you were helped or harmed by the experience, you can see that tolerance can have a powerful influence on human relationships, and the experience of community.

CAUSES AND CONSEQUENCES OF PREJUDICE

Certain practices are both the cause and consequence of prejudice. They often occur in relations between majority and minority members of a group, and usually serve to harm communication and the experience of community. Included are chauvinism, stereotyping, double standards, formula relations, jokes and segregation, powerlessness and rebellion, self-fulfilling prophecy, rallying, and censorship.[21]

Chauvinism

People may consider themselves to be superior and more important than others. The names American Indians give their own tribes usually translate as "The People" or "The Human Beings," implying they consider other tribes to belong to a subhuman species. Similarly, the English name for people living around the Arctic Circle is Eskimo, meaning "eaters of raw meat," although the name these people use for themselves is Inuit or Inupik, "The Real People."[22] The following shows the tendency for people of all types and different times to be chauvinistic.

Social Superiority and the Eye of the Beholder

During the past several centuries, light-skinned Europeans have been able to convince most of the world that a dark skin indicates inferiority in one way or another. The assumption of superiority by western Europeans, though, is a recent development that is largely due to the colonial adventures of the industrialized nations. Certainly, no such superiority could have been even claimed until the earliest beginnings of the Industrial Revolution.

About two thousand years ago, for example, the Roman statesman and orator Cicero recommended against taking a Briton into one's house because, he said, more stupid slaves were not to be found in the entire Roman Empire. Ancient Greek art, literature, and mythology often portrayed dark-skinned people with respect. The Umayyad dynasty that ruled the Moslem Empire in the seventh and eighth centuries proudly referred to its members as "the swarthy people," in contrast to "the ruddy people," their Persian and Turkish subjects.

Nor did Africans feel inferior because of their dark skins until after long contact with Europeans. Early European explorers in Africa reported that many Africans regarded light skin as repulsive—and, in fact, both Stanley and Livingstone felt a sense of shame at their own lightness in contrast to the richly dark-skinned people around them.

It is interesting to note that no single population has ever had exclusive control over achievement. Any scientific racist who happened to be living about ten thousand years ago would have had to conclude that a superior race inhabited the Near East, where domestication, settled village life, trade, and advanced technology were already in existence. Clear evidence would also have been found of the inferiority of northern Europeans, who would not cross the threshold between hunting-gathering and village life for many more thousands of years.

After the fall of Rome, China emerged as the greatest power and technologically the most sophisticated civilization in the world. As recently as 1793, the British sent a delegation to China to beg the mighty Emperor Ch'ien-lung for permission to open trade. But the emperor replied to King George III that China had no need to enter into trade with the "red-faced barbarian," since, in his words, "our dynasty's majestic virtue has penetrated into every country under heaven, and kings of all nations have offered their costly tribute by land and sea. As your Ambassador can see for himself, we possess all things."

In fact, any objective survey of the past ten thousand years of human history would show that during almost all of it, northern Europeans were an inferior barbarian race, living in squalor and ignorance, producing few cultural innovations.[23]

The French philosopher Vauvenargues explains mankind's general tendency to be chauvinistic:

> It is a misfortune that men cannot ordinarily possess a talent without some desire to disparage all others. If they have subtlety, they decry force; if they are geometrists or physicians, they attack poetry and rhetoric. And the mass of mankind, who forget that those who have won distinction in one field may be bad judges of a different kind of talent, allow themselves to be prejudiced by their verdicts. So, when metaphysics or algebra are the fashion, it is metaphysicians or algebraists who make the reputation of poets and musicians, and vice versa; the dominating mind compels others to submit to its own judgments, and generally to its errors.[24]

Stereotyping

Stereotyping is sorting people into rigid types or forcing them into concrete molds that have little or nothing to do with them as individuals. Stereotyped individuals are automatically assumed to possess traits common to the group to which they belong. All blacks have rhythm, all women want a man, all Latins are good lovers, all blondes are dumb, and all smart people wear glasses are examples of stereotyping. Stereotyping ignores individuality and keeps human relations on a superficial, unsatisfying plane. As the story on the following page shows, stereotyping can begin at an early age.

The lists in table 9–1 show how Americans tend to stereotype large groups of people.

TABLE 9–1   Four Characteristics Ranked Highest for Nine Ethnic Groups[25]

Germans	**Irish**	**Italian**
Scientific	Quick-tempered	Artistic
Industrious	Witty	Impulsive
Stolid	Honest	Passionate
Intelligent	Sentimental	Emotional
Chinese	**English**	**Japanese**
Superstitious	Sportsmanlike	Organized
Patient	Intelligent	Industrious
Conservative	Conventional	Aggressive
Tradition-loving	Tradition-loving	Competitive
Jews	**Turks**	**Americans**
Intelligent	Religious	Intelligent
Mercenary	Warlike	Materialistic
Industrious	Sensual	Democratic
Acquisitive	Zealous	Freedom-loving

What Do You Want to Be When You Grow Up?

Preschool ideas about adult-life occupations are already ossified stereotypes. Consider the story of a woman who took a childrearing leave of absence from her job as a newspaper reporter. One day, when her three-year-old, Sarah, expressed interest in a TV story about a crime reporter, the woman decided to explain her own career: "Before you were born, I used to have a job like that," the mother said, building to a simple but exciting description of journalism. "I went to fires or to the police station, and the stories I wrote were printed in the newspaper with my name on them."

After listening attentively, Sarah asked, "Mommy, when you had this job before I was born, did you used to be a man?" Obviously, the child had not yet developed the concept of gender constancy; but what necessitated the magical thinking that turned her mother into a man was Sarah's inability to associate the exciting job of a newspaper reporter with the female sex.

Seventy Wisconsin children, ages three to five, had much the same problem. When asked, "What do you want to be when you grow up?" the boys mentioned fourteen occupations: fireman, policeman, father/husband, older person, digger, dentist, astronaut, cowboy, truckdriver, engineer, baseball player, doctor, Superman, and the Six-Million-Dollar Man. Girls named eleven categories: mother/sister, nurse, ballerina, older person, dentist, teacher, babysitter, baton twirler, ice-skater, princess, and cowgirl.

Next, the children were polled on their more realistic expectations: "What do you think you *really* will be?" they were asked.

The girls altered their choices toward even more traditional roles—changing from ballerina, nurse, and dentist to mother—while the boys changed to more active, adventurous futures—for instance, from husband to fireman.

Pittsburgh children of the same ages were asked, "What do you want to be when you grow up?" followed by, "If you were a boy (girl), what would you be when you grow up?" For the first question, most chose stereotyped careers: policeman, sports star, cowboy, and one "aspiring spy" for the boys; nursing and the like for the girls. To the second—what they would be if they were the "opposite" sex—the children answered with stereotyped other-sex occupations as well. But their reactions to the second question were striking. The boys were shocked at the very idea of being a girl. Most had never thought of it before, some refused to think about it, and one put his hands to his head and sighed, "Oh, if I were a girl, I'd have to grow up to be nothing."

The girls, on the other hand, obviously had thought about the question a great deal. Most had an answer ready. Several girls mentioned that their other-sex occupational ambition was their true ambition, but one that could not be realized because of their sex. More poignantly, the gender barrier had become so formidable that it even blocked out fantasies and dreams. Thus, one girl confided that what she really wanted to do when she grew up was to fly like a bird. "But I'll never do it," she sighed, "because I'm not a boy."[26]

TABLE 9–2   Stereotypes: Not Always False[27]

When individuals in different countries were asked to describe their own and each others' national character, a high level of agreement was found. French, Italians, and Americans generally were seen as being easygoing, while English, Russians, and Germans were described as being just the opposite.

Respondents who liked a country tended to give positive labels to those traits that had been labeled negatively by respondents who disliked the country.

English, Russians, and Germans		French, Italians, and Americans	
Positive	**Negative**	**Positive**	**Negative**
Thrifty	Stingy	Generous	Extravagant
Serious	Grim	Fun-loving	Frivolous
Skeptical	Distrustful	Trusting	Gullible
Cautious	Timid	Bold	Rash
Selective	Choosy	Broad-minded	Undiscriminating

Although there was general agreement that the English, Germans, and Russians have a tight style of relating, the choice of a positive word like *thrifty* or a negative word like *stingy* depended on whether the nationality was liked or disliked. Americans, French, and Italians were seen as being loose in style, but a positive judgment, like *spontaneous*, as opposed to a negative judgment, like *impulsive*, for example, also depended on the feelings of the judges.

Although character stereotypes may be agreed on by the people rating and those being judged, the actual words used to describe people depend on positive or negative attitudes held about the group (see table 9–2).

Double Standards

Minority members may have to be more competent than majority members of a group or society in order to be accepted by the dominant group. This double standard can be seen when mistakes made by males are tolerated, but mistakes made by females are not tolerated, and when, to be promoted, a black must be clearly superior to every white candidate. Table 9–3 shows how double standards can be used to judge the behavior of men and women in business.

Formula Relations

There is a tendency to handle certain types of people and situations in certain set ways, regardless of the circumstances or the individuals involved. Examples are (1) old-timers—leave them alone, (2) chronic complainers—give them more responsibility, and (3) troublemakers—make examples out of them. Sometimes

TABLE 9–3   Judging the Same Behavior Based on Double Standards[28]

Man	Woman
A businessman is aggressive.	A businesswoman is pushy.
He is careful about details.	She's picky.
He loses his temper because he's so involved in his job.	She's a complainer.
He follows through.	She doesn't know when to quit.
He's firm.	She's stubborn.
He makes wise judgments.	She reveals her prejudices.
He is a man of the world.	She's been around.
He isn't afraid to say what he thinks.	She's opinionated.
He exercises authority.	She's tyrannical.
He's discreet.	She's secretive.
He's a stern taskmaster.	She's difficult to work for.

these formulas work and sometimes they do not, because each person and circumstance is unique.

A related practice is *haloing*, or classifying people as either all good or all bad, with no provision for a middle ground. The judgment is often based on only one aspect of the person, while other aspects are ignored. Examples are (1) unjustified high ratings for the athlete, (2) unjustified low ratings for the shop steward, and (3) unjustified high ratings for the personal friend.

Sometimes people are lumped into categories of "good" minorities or "bad" minorities based on the haloing concept. When people are judged to be "good" minorities, other people may constantly try to make them fail or look bad. In any case, haloing reduces personal growth and harms interpersonal relations.[29]

Jokes and Segregation

Members of a majority may whisper and tell jokes behind the backs of minority people. This often happens to overweight children or to new kids in school. Telling Polish, Italian, and other ethnic jokes is also common. Often, these jokes are painful to the person or group who is the object of the "humor."

Perceived differences can cause people to dislike or avoid each other even though they should work together to accomplish a mission. This can happen on an individual scale or on a group scale. Such was the case in the United States with separate "Negro" fighting units during World War I and World War II.[30]

Powerlessness and Rebellion

People may lack influence and opportunity because of limited numbers and little power. They may have little recourse but to conform to the wishes of the powerful majority. In this situation, they may suppress their feelings and individuality, choosing to "go along to get along"; or they become resentful and erupt in defiance when the opportunity arises. Consider the 1831 revolt of Nat Turner and the tragic deaths he and his fellow slaves dealt their former masters:

> By the early part of 1830, Nat Turner was "writhing in his shackles" and looking forward to the time when he could rise up and "slay the enemy with their own weapons." In August 1831, Turner and a band of seven other slaves set out in their struggle for freedom. In their first attacks, he ordered his men not to leave a single white man, woman, or child alive. He killed his own master and his family, and took arms, ammunition, and horses, and moved on to the next house. They gathered more slaves there and continued on with their slaughter, killing fifty-seven white people within forty hours. He is quoted as saying, "It was my objective to carry terror and devastation wherever we went," and "I viewed the mangled bodies as they lay, in silent satisfaction."[31]

In recent times, frustration and anger were shown by Malcolm X when he said, "If someone puts a hand on you, send him to the cemetery." This was his advice to fellow blacks in the urban ghettos in the early 1960s.[32]

Self-Fulfilling Prophecy

If a person or group is seen as inferior, little is expected of them. If little is expected, there is a tendency for them to withdraw. If one does not try, achievement will be low. If achievement is low, self-esteem will be low. Low self-esteem results in low social esteem . . . and the downward spiral continues.

It is a proven fact that expectation of failure can help bring about failure. Conversely, expectation of success can help bring about success. Children have been found to score from two to three points higher when an IQ test is administered by a teacher who conveys expectation for success, than when the same test is given by a teacher who does not convey high expectations. This phenomenon is called the "Pygmalion effect."[33]

A classic example of the power of the self-fulfilling prophecy is the story of Eliza Doolittle in the George Bernard Shaw play *Pygmalion*, the inspiration for the celebrated musical *My Fair Lady*. Responding to the high expectations of her teacher, Professor Higgons, Eliza *became* a *lady*. Her explanation was profound. She said, "The difference between a flower girl and a lady is not what she is, it is how she is treated."[34]

Rallying

By introducing a minority person into the presence of a majority, the commonality of the majority is accentuated. This newly discovered uniformity of the majority creates an energy that is often expended against the minority. This can be seen when a different type of person joins the work group or moves into the neighborhood.

> In Hyde Park, a suburb of Cincinnati, Ohio, about twenty people filed suit against a resident home for the mentally retarded, challenging the constitutionality of Cincinnati's zoning code. Their lawyer argued that the home is "incompatible" with the "family uses" in that residential zone. In response, the Assistant Attorney General representing the Ohio Department of Mental Retardation and Development Disorders stated that, "The heart of the case is fear of things and people who are different."[35]

Censorship

People sometimes censor their remarks and behavior, not out of politeness, but because of fear of criticism. They become inhibited and hide their true feelings. Minorities may resort to the following coping mechanisms.[36]

- They become standout minorities through high achievements in order to show the majority just how competent they are.

- They strive to blend in with the majority and suppress individuality by taking on the appearance of the majority as much as possible. For example, a woman may act like a man in a man's world, or an older person may act much younger in the presence of young people.

- They seek the protection and support of powerful members of the majority. The saying, "Behind every great man, there is a good woman" reflects this coping behavior.

THE SOLUTION

What is the solution to problems that occur as a result of social differences?

- Make an equal number of all types of people, so there will be no majority or minority group members? No. Even if one wanted to, this feat would be impossible to accomplish.

- Eliminate all differences between people? No. Differences enrich people. We would not want a world where everyone is exactly the same. In *The Rhinoceros*, Eugene Ionesco showed that conformity can be an evil tyranny, just as great as discrimination:

One by one, all but one member of a small French province turned into a rhinoceros. They came to perceive the lifestyle and condition of the growing majority to be better than their own, and were willing to give up their own identities to become a part of it.[37]

■ Recognize that differences among people are inevitable, that minority members will be present in almost every social grouping, that both positive and negative feelings toward different types of people are normal, but one must not discriminate in a harmful way? Yes. The answer is yes when dealing with different types of people and when the best communications and human relations possible are the goals.

Specifically, how should people handle social differences in building community?

■ First, we should try to *understand ourselves*. Each person should ask:
"How were my social attitudes formed?"
"What are my feelings toward other types of people and different types of behavior?"
"Do I express my attitudes in any way that could harm others? Do I overprotect, stereotype, unfairly treat, or make jokes about other types of people?"

■ Second, we should try to *understand others*, recognizing that every person has a different perspective. Each should ask:
"How does it feel to a member of the minority or a member of the majority?" Then listen to the answer.
"What are the problems of being different, either as a minority or a majority member?" Then listen to the answer.

■ Third, we should *tell each other what helps* and harms our relationship. We should deal with behaviors rather than motives. We should express our true selves, and listen to understand.

■ Fourth, we should *agree on basic values* that will guide our relationships, such as truth, trust, and respect.

■ Fifth, we should emphasize and *build on ideas held in common*, particularly goals we can share. We should take steps to downplay differences and highlight areas of agreement.

■ Sixth, we should *"lighten up."* There is a time to be demanding, and a time to be tolerant. As Benjamin Franklin once said: "Keep your eyes wide-open before marriage, and half-shut afterwards." This idea applies in all human relationships.

The following is a true story about extreme attitude change. It reflects the six steps for dealing with social differences and developing goodwill between people.

Attitudes Can Change

Claiborne P. Ellis describes his journey from childhood to becoming president of the Durham, North Carolina chapter of the Ku Klux Klan to becoming the regional business manager of the International Union of Operating Engineers. The story illustrates a series of attitude changes. Ellis began by hating blacks, Jews, and Catholics and ended by evaluating members of these groups by their individual behavior.

Ellis was born in Durham, North Carolina. His family struggled constantly with poverty, and many of his early memories involve the economic depression of the 1930s. He was very close to his father, who worked during the week in a textile mill, but drank a great deal on weekends. When C.P. was around seventeen years old, his father died. C.P. had to leave school to help support his family. He took a series of low-skilled jobs and eventually borrowed 4,000 dollars to buy a service station. By then he had married and was working ". . . my butt off and just never seemed to break even." Two months before the final loan payment was due, he had a heart attack. Despite his wife's efforts, the service station was lost. He had been taught ". . . to abide by the law, go to church, do right and live for the Lord, and everything will work out." But it didn't work out. The continuing failure to lift his family into minimal economic security turned a smoldering bitterness into hatred. He wanted to blame something or someone for his failures and soon found a convenient group as a target.

While Ellis owned the service station, he was invited to join the Ku Klux Klan. It was an opportunity he seized eagerly because, "It gave me an opportunity to be part of something." Not only did he enjoy belonging to a group, but also his longstanding sense of inferiority began to disappear. His father had been a member of the Klan, and Ellis was well versed in their attitudes. The Klan hated blacks, Jews, and Catholics. And so did Ellis. He quickly rose through various offices to the presidency of the local chapter. Because the civil rights movement was becoming active in Durham at this time, Ellis's hatred was directed mostly at blacks. In particular, he despised a woman named Ann Attwater, who seemed involved in every boycott and demonstration he went to watch.

Although the Klan is notorious for protecting the anonymity of its members, Ellis unashamedly brought the local chapter out into the open. He began attending meetings of the city council and county commissioners to represent the Klan's point of view. He and his group had numerous confrontations with representatives of the black community at various board meetings. Members of these boards would not publicly agree with the attitudes of the Klan, but they privately shared these views. The people who called to praise him also avoided him in public. While searching for an explanation for this inconsistency, Ellis began to reconsider his role. It struck him that he was being used. "As a result of our fighting one another, the city council still had their way. They didn't want to give up control to the blacks, nor to the Klan." It was at this point that Ellis recalled doing ". . . some real serious thinkin'." Although he was becoming convinced of the correctness of his beliefs about being used, he could not persuade other Klansmen. He had to struggle with the inconsistency on his own, and it caused him many a sleepless night.

During this period, a critical event occurred. The state AFL-CIO received a federal grant to assist them in finding solutions to the racial problems in the public schools. To his amazement, Ellis was asked to join a citizens' panel to

Attitudes Can Change (continued)

discuss these problems. As soon as he learned that members of the black community would also be invited, he refused the invitation by saying, "I am not going to be associated with those types of people." On a whim, however, he attended the first evening meeting. Many of the participants, including Ann Attwater, were familiar to him because of past confrontations. The moderator of the meeting was a black man who encouraged everyone to speak freely. During the meeting, Ellis did just that, repeating his extreme antiblack attitudes. To his surprise, some of the black members, who did not agree with a single one of his attitudes, praised him for his honesty in expressing his views. Ellis's involvement in the group began to grow. On the third night, with backing from some of the black participants, he was elected cochairperson of the group, along with Ann Attwater.

Despite mutual reluctance, Ellis and Attwater agreed to put aside their personal differences and to work together toward the common goal of finding solutions. Through their joint work, they began to see many similarities between themselves. Their efforts to recruit more panelists from among members of their respective groups were met with the same suspicion and rejection. Furthermore, the children of both had come home from school in tears. Ellis's child was ridiculed by his teacher for being the son of a Klansman,

while Attwater's child was ridiculed by her teacher for being the daughter of an activist. The discovery of such commonalities and their joint work led Ellis to a feeling of respect and liking for Attwater. Through their leadership, the panel agreed on a number of resolutions. Although the school board did not implement all of them, the panel members had worked together effectively.

Ellis's attitudes did not change immediately. His initial justification for working on the panel was that school integration was the law and that all people should be law-abiding. In the hope of implementing the panel's recommendations, he ran for the school board. He was still associated with the Klan, but he did not campaign for Klan themes. His platform was simply that before making any decisions, he would listen to the voice of all of the people. The campaign brought him into contact with many blacks. At long last, he began seeing people as individuals. With this change came a sense of rebirth. He no longer had sleepless nights and enrolled in an evening program that resulted in his receiving a high school equivalency diploma. During this period, he helped to organize the first labor union at his place of employment. When the opportunity arose, he gladly switched his career to labor-union work, where he felt he could help the poor, both black and white.[38]

What does science have to say about racial differences? Geneticists Luca Cavalli-Sforza, Paolo Mennozi, and Alberto Piazza state in their scholarly book, *The History and Geography of Human Genes*:

Once the genes for surface traits such as coloration and stature are discounted, the human "races" are remarkably alike under the skin. The variation among individuals is much greater than the differences among groups. In fact, the diversity among individuals is so enormous that the whole concept of race becomes meaningless at the genetic level. The authors say there is "no scientific basis" for theories touting the genetic superiority of any one population over another.[39]

POINTS TO REMEMBER

In the *community-building* process, keep in mind the following points about social tolerance.

- Social tolerance is different from personal patience. It is possible for a person to be open-minded toward different types of people and forms of behavior, but to be inflexible when it comes to certain personal habits or situations. In this case, such a person is like the snake who says, "Don't tread on me."

- Attitudes are hard to conceal. Few people are professional actors, so when intolerance exists, it is usually no secret.

- Intolerance can be stressful. Even if one is able to hide intolerance from others, it will probably exact a toll in the form of physical and emotional problems.

- Social tolerance can help explain many human relations dynamics. Imagine two people, one with low tolerance and one with high tolerance. Who usually makes decisions in this relationship? The low tolerance person does, because he has strong opinions and is less flexible; he thinks he is right and is intolerant of alternative views. Besides, the high tolerance person is thinking, "What difference does it make?" The question is, is this a good situation? The answer is that it is normal, and it can be good as well, as long as two things are true:

  a. The low tolerance person must have the correct answer. Because what if he is wrong? What if he believes, "Junior should be raised one way," when he really should be raised another? Or what if he says, "Sell," when they really should buy? And so on.

  b. The high tolerance person must remain tolerant. Every well has a bottom, and every person's tolerance has its limit. If someone gives in on every issue with nothing seemingly returned, the relationship usually becomes dissatisfying. Even the most tolerant person has limits.

Now, imagine two people with low tolerance who live or work together. What would you predict for their relationship? If they have the same goals and agree on how to achieve them, they will probably accomplish what they set out to do, no matter how difficult. If, however, they do not see eye to eye, major conflict can be expected, since intolerance makes compromise difficult, if not impossible. In this case, they are likely to fail.

As a last example, imagine two people with high tolerance who live or work together. Their mutual flexibility would probably result in an easygoing relationship, no matter how different their personal views. However, they must be careful not to overvacillate. Their best course of action would be to agree on a plan as early as possible, and then use their natural tolerance of differences to work together to accomplish these goals.

From this discussion, it can be seen that people with low tolerance tend to have more stress in human relations than people with high tolerance. Also, decision making in a relationship often depends on who has the strongest views, and has little to do with the facts or with how much people care about each other.

- Introducing dramatic change is the only way to alter attitudes. Once formed, attitudes continue unless something new, major, and emotional happens. A woman who is uncomfortable with strangers will remain that way unless she has new experiences that are positive and rewarding. A man who is prejudiced against certain types of people because of their age, sex, race, etc., will remain that way unless he has new and satisfying experiences that change his mind.

THE OPEN COMMUNITY

In the open community, social differences do not divide people. Instead, diversity is welcome. There is a wonderful wholeness that incorporates the wide variety and richness of human experience.

People need social tolerance and a "live and let live" attitude when absolutes do not apply and when positive relations among different types of people are desired. This attitude creates a sense of belonging and respect, and it results in the greatest good for all people. Consider Thomas Jefferson's views on religious tolerance:

> No person shall be compelled to frequent or support any religious worship, place, or ministry whatsoever, nor shall be enforced, restrained, molested, or burdened in body or goods, nor shall otherwise suffer on account of religious opinions or beliefs; but all people shall be free to profess, and by argument to maintain, their opinions in matters of religion, and this shall in no way diminish, enlarge, or effect their civil capacities.[40]

Another American came to the same conclusion. The Native American leader Tecumseh advised: Trouble no man about his religion—respect him in his views, and require that he respect yours.[41]

REFERENCES

1. M. Scott Peck, *The Different Drum: Community Making and Peace* (New York: Simon & Schuster, 1987), 234.

2. Peck, *The Different Drum*, 68.

3. Peck, *The Different Drum*, 65.

4. Paul Samuelson, *Economics*, 10th ed. (New York: McGraw Hill, Inc., 1976), 790.

5. John Lambert, *Social Psychology* (New York: Macmillan, Inc., 1980), 11–13.

6. Thomas Jefferson, *Notes on the State of Virginia*, 1782.

7. S. K. Thompson, "Gender Sex-Role Development," *Child Development* 46 (1975), 339–347.

8. J. O. Halliwell-Phillipps, *Popular Rhymes and Nursery Tales* (Detroit: Singing Free Press, 1968).

9. Catherine Garvey, *Play* (Cambridge, Mass.: Harvard University Press, 1977).

10. Lawrence Kohlberg, "A Cognitive Developmental Analysis of Children's Sex-Role Concepts in Self-Analysis," in E. Maccoby, ed., *The Development of Sex Differences* (Palo Alto: Stanford University Press, 1966), 82–173.

11. Jeffery H. Goldstein, *Social Psychology* (New York: Academic Press, 1980), 82–115; Sueann Robinson Ambron, *Child Development*, 3rd ed. (New York: Holt, Rinehart, & Winston, 1981), 508–513.

12. Lenore J. Weitzman, Deborah Eifler, Elizabeth Hokada, & Catherine Ross, "Sex Role Socialization in Picture Books for Preschool Children," *American Journal of Sociology* (May 1972).

13. Marjorie B. U'Ren, "The Image of Women in Textbooks," in V. Gordnick and B. K. Moran, ed., *Women in Sexist Society: Studies in Power and Powerlessness*, (New York: New American Library, 1971), 318–346.

14. *A daily morning prayer for men who are Orthodox Jews*. For an interpretation of this prayer, see Joseph H. Heitz, *Authorized Daily Prayer Book* (New York: New American Library, 1971), 318–346.

15. Margaret Mead, *Sex and Temperament in Three Primitive Societies* (New York: Morrow, 1935).

16. Leo Tolstoy, *War and Peace*, trans., Louise and Alymer Maude (New York: Simon & Schuster, Inc., 1942), 9:709.

17. Gordon W. Allport, *The Nature of Prejudice* (Reading, Mass: Addison-Wesley Publishing. Co., 1954), 13–14.

18. Alvin Poussaint, "A Negro Psychiatrist Explains the Negro Psyche," in ? , *Confrontation* (New York: Random House, Inc., 1971), 183–184.

19. Kenneth Clark and Maimie Clark, "Racial Identification and Preference in Negro Children," in *Readings in Social Psychology*, ed., T. M. Newcomb & E. L. Hartley (New York: Holt, Rinehart and Winston, 1947), 169–178.

20. Adolph Hitler, *Mein Kampf* (Cambridge Mass: Riverside Press, 1943), 302.

21. Rosabeth Moss Kanter & Barry A. Stein, *A Tale of "O"* (Cambridge, Mass, Goodmeasure, Inc., 1980).

22. Farb, *Humankind*, 266.

23. Farb, *Humankind*, 264–265.

24. *The Reflections and Maxims of Vauvenargues*, trans., S.G. Stevens (London: Humphrey Milford, 1940), 99.

25. D. Katz and K. W. Braly, "Racial Stereotypes of One Hundred College Students," *Journal of Abnormal and Social Psychology* (1933): 280–290.

26. Letty Cottrin Pogrebin, *Growing Up Free* (New York: McGraw-Hill, Inc., 1980).

27. Based on Dean Peabody, *National Characteristics* (Cambridge, Mass.: Cambridge University Press, 1985). (Cambridge, Mass.: Cambridge University Press, 1985).

28. Robert M. Fulmer, *Practical Human Relations*, (Homewood, IL: Richard D. Irwin, 1977).

29. Edward L. Thorndike, "A Constant Error in Psychological Ratings," *Journal of Applied Psychology*, 4 (1920): 25–29; and Elliot McGinnes, *Social Behavior: A Functional Analysis* (Boston: Houghton-Mifflin Co., 1970), 162.

30. Richard M. Dalfiume, "The Forgotten Years of the Negro Revolution," in *The Negro in Depression and War*, ed., Bernard Sternsher (Chicago: Quadrangle Books, 1969), 300.

31. Ruth Wilson, *Our Blood and Tears* (New York: G. P. Putnam's Sons, 1972), 103–107.

32. Allen J. Matusow, "The Struggle for Civil Rights," in *The Social Fabric: American Life from the Civil War to the Present*, eds. John H. Gary and Julius Weinberg (Boston: Little, Brown & Company, 1978), 297–298.

33. Farb, *Humankind*, 271; Robert K. Merton, "The Self-Fulfilling Prophecy," *Antioch Review*, 8 (1948): 193–210; and Robert Rosenthal, *Pygmalion in the Classroom* (New York: Holt, Rinehart and Winston, 1968).

34. From Frederick Loew's, "My Fair Lady," with lyrics by Alan J. Lerner.

35. "Fear Lies at the Heart of Suit, Attorney Says," *The Cincinnati Enquirer* (February 18, 1981): sec. D3.

36. Kanter and Stein, *A Tale of "O."*

37. Eugene Ionesco, *Rhinoceros and Other Plays*, tran., Derek Prouse (New York: Grove Press, Inc., 1960).

38. Studs Terkel, *American Dreams: Lost and Found* (New York: Pantheon Books, Inc., 1980).

39. Luca Cavalli-Sforza, Paolo Menozzi, and Alberto Piazza. *The History and Geography of Human Genes* (Princeton: Princeton University Press, 1994).

40. Henry C. Dethloff, ed., *Thomas Jefferson and American Democracy* (Lexington, Mass.: D.C. Heath & Co., 1971), 12.

41. Dan Gibbons, *Compendium of Quotations & Anecdotes* (Cincinnati: Audio Visual Network, 1993).

10

Valuing Diversity

Always give a word or sign of salute when meeting or passing a friend, or even a stranger if in a lonely place. Show respect for all of mankind.

Tecumseh

In true community, there is a philosophy of pluralism, an open climate for dissent, and a relentless effort to eliminate racism, sexism, and other discriminations. Where community exists, all people have reason to believe that they are accepted and respected and that their voices will be heard.[1]

This chapter addresses the invisible but real walls that separate people and ultimately reduce the human potential. The prescription is to turn walls in our minds and hearts into bridges that join and make a structure that is stronger than its individual cells. The prescription is to value diversity in building *community*. To this end, remember:

- all people should be treated with respect and dignity—we must have an *eyes-level* approach rather than an *eyes-up or eyes-down approach* in our dealings with people, regardless of social status;

- every person should model and reinforce an essentially democratic character and humanistic approach to life; and

- valuing diversity provides strength and a positive advantage for organizations operating in multicultural environments.

DIVERSITY IN THE WORKPLACE

The word *corporation* conjures up images of authority, bureaucracy, competition, control, and power. The word *community* evokes images of democracy, diversity, cooperation, inclusion, and common purpose. The model under which an organization chooses to operate can determine its survival in a competitive and changing world. The idea of community at work is particularly satisfying to the makeup and challenges of today's diverse work force.[2]

If there is one word that characterizes America's workplace, that word is "diversity." The U.S. work force is composed of more minorities, recent immigrants, and women than ever before, and this pattern is expected to continue and increase considerably by the year 2000 and beyond.

An overview of census figures from 1980 to 1990 shows that the Asian or Pacific Islander population increased over 100 percent, Hispanic Americans increased their numbers by more than 50 percent, Native Americans increased by nearly 40 percent, and African Americans by more than 10 percent. All of these figures contrast sharply with a 6 percent growth of the non-Hispanic white population during the same period.[3]

In addition to racial and ethnic diversification, the American population also is growing older. The 1980 median age was 30. In 1990 it was 33, and it is projected to increase to 36 by the turn of the century.[4]

As table 10–1 shows, the twenty-first century work force is expected to see a continued increase in numbers of females, minorities, and immigrants in comparison to white males.

TABLE 10–1   Work Force Participation (in percentages)—1988 and 2000[5]

Year	1988 (actual)	2000 (projected)
Total Employment	65.9	67.8
Men	76.2	74.7 (down)
Women	56.6	61.5 (up)
Whites	66.2	68.2
Men	76.9	75.3 (down)
Women	56.4	61.5 (up)
African Americans	63.8	66.0
Men	71.0	70.7 (down)
Women	58.0	62.1 (up)
Asians (and other)	64.9 (1986)	65.8
Men	74.9 (1986)	72.4 (down)
Women	55.9 (1986)	60.1 (up)
Hispanics	67.4	68.7
Men	81.8	80.4 (down)
Women	53.2	56.9 (up)

Enormous change is going on in the American workplace. No longer pre-dominantly white and male, three out of every five American employees are women and 25 percent are minorities. Now, for the first time in history, white males constitute the minority class.[6]

Tomorrow's leaders face a formidable challenge in learning to manage many different ethnic groups. They will have to develop the ability to com-municate across cultures. This will require an understanding of the issues surrounding diversity and a tolerance of diverse viewpoints. They will have to create plans and goals that incorporate the needs of a multicultural work-place, and do this in such a way that all members may feel a sense of ownership.[7]

MANAGING DIVERSITY

Although diversity is the new reality, many managers are unprepared to han-dle it. Many grew up having little personal contact with other cultures. In this sense, they are actually "culturally deprived." Often their previous experi-ences have not covered the kinds of situations that arise in today's multi-cultural settings.[8]

One short example gives diversity a human feel, showing how difficult it can be for employer and employee as well:

> An American nursing supervisor gave a directive to one of her Filipino nurses, and the supervisor wanted it to be done stat! For the supervisor, that meant now, immediately, before anything else. The Filipino nurse, meaning no disrespect but with a different time orientation, completed what she had been doing and then complied with the supervisor's request—five to ten minutes later than expected. To the nurse, stat meant soon. A few minute's delay was acceptable. She could complete her work in a short time, then take care of the supervisor's request. She certainly did not see her behavior as insubordinate. The supervisor saw this situation differently. The nurse was either casual about her duties or disrespectful of authorities.[9]

In addition to different perceptions about time, people can have different ideas about work habits, communication patterns, social roles, and a myriad of other workplace issues. For example, employee motivation practices continue to reflect white male experiences and attitudes. Some of these methods can be highly dysfunctional when applied to women or to African Americans, Asians, Hispanics, or Native Americans. Consider a few examples:[10]

- A manager was pleased with a new breakthrough achieved by one of his Native American employees. Therefore, he recognized her with great fanfare and personal praise in front of all of the other employees. Humiliated, she didn't return to work for days.

- After learning that a friendly pat on the back would make employees feel appreciated, a manager took every chance to pat his subordinates. His Asian employees, who hated being touched, avoided him like the plague.

- Concerned about ethics, a manager declined a gift offered him by a new employee, an immigrant who wanted to show gratitude for her job. He explained the company's policy about gifts. She was so insulted, she quit.

- A new employee's wife, an Eastern European, stopped by the office with a bottle of champagne, fully expecting everyone present to stop and celebrate her husband's new job. When people merely said "hello" and then returned to work, she was mortified. Her husband quit within a few days.

The concept of managing diversity is conceptually different from equal employment opportunity, which was designed in this country primarily as an attempt to reduce racism and sexism. Dealing with diversity means behaving in a way that creates *community* among people and gains benefits from their differences. An analogy makes the point well: If you were planting a garden and wanted to have a variety of flowers, you would never think of giving every flower the same amount of sun, the same amount of water, and the same type of soil. Instead, you would cultivate each flower according to its needs. This means that neither the rose nor the orchid is more or less valuable because they require different treatment. Along these lines, an even better term than managing diversity is *achieving inclusivity*.[11]

Leaders of diverse work groups may wonder, "How can I possibly learn about all of these people?" The answer is that while you can't learn all there is to know about every culture, the more you know, the more successful you will be because people will appreciate your efforts. If you understand very little about the background and characteristics of others, how can you hope to interact effectively with them?

In working with different types of people, it is important to understand one's own cultural background as well, whatever it is—Native American, Asian, Hispanic, African American, or European. It is interesting that many whites don't think of themselves as having a culture. They think "culture" is something that only minorities have. A model showing the philosophical orientations of different cultural groups is presented by educator Edwin Nichols. See table 10–2.

TABLE 10–2   Philosophical Orientations of Different Cultural Groups[12]

Cultural Groups/World Views	Value Orientation	Knowledge Orientation	System of Thought	Way of Living
European Euro-American	*Person—Object* The highest value is in objects or in the acquisition of objects.	*Cognitive* One knows through counting and measuring.	*Dichotomous* Either/Or	*Technology* All behavior is repeatable and reproducible
African African-American Hispanic Arabian	*Person—Person* The highest value is in relationships between people.	*Affective* One knows through feeling and rhythm.	*Diunital* The union of opposites.	*Ntuology* All behavior is interrelated through human and spiritual networks.
Asian Asian-American Native American Polynesian	*Person—Group* The highest value is in group unity.	*Conative* One knows through self-transcendence.	*Nyaya* The objective world is independent of thought and mind.	*Cosmology* All behavior is interrelated in the harmony of the universe.

DIVERSITY IN THE CORPORATION

It has been the pattern in the American workplace to expect women, minorities, and others outside the mainstream to do all of the adapting. This should be a two-way street. While women and minorities should build relationships, learn the prevailing norms of behavior, and work to become effective members of the community, leaders should share the rules, accommodate cultural differences, and create climates that allow all types of people to succeed.

As an example of this, David Kearns, CEO of Xerox Corporation, states that, "At Xerox, we identified successful white males and studied where they had been and what they had done to be successful. Then we set targets and put in place processes to ensure that women and minorities got the same types of experiences."[13]

Dealing with diversity requires changing old habits. In doing this, four principles or practices should be followed:

- *Be aware*. Occasionally stop and ask, "What is happening?" Don't be like the ostrich with its head in the sand.

- *Be sure everyone is given the opportunity to participate*. Go for inclusion and openness as community values.

- *Share the rules*. Communicate the customs of the community and be willing to change them in order to nurture diverse types of people.

- *Be sensitive to differences*. Appreciate the uniqueness of every individual.[14]

Writing in *Training and Development*, Barbara Jerish, director of work force diversity at Honeywell, makes the following suggestions:

1. Organizations must effectively manage diversity to remain competitive, both internationally, as well as in the American marketplace.

2. Organizations should create environments that are conducive to the growth and development of all employees. We should have a policy that says we aren't going to tolerate any type of behavior that degrades personal dignity or disrupts working relationships.

3. People may have stereotypes and prejudices that convey a message of nonacceptance or exclusiveness that are acted out because of fear. We need to eliminate this through educating people and showing how biases and stereotypes get communicated in our day-to-day conversations and the way we conduct our work relationships.

4. Organizations need to help their members achieve their potential. It is an issue of empowerment. It is listening to people, not being so arrogant to assume we know the needs of all other people.[15]

In *The New Leaders: Guidelines on Leadership Diversity in America*, Ann Morrison reports results of her study on diversity practices in U.S.-based private and public organizations. The practices considered most important are:

1. top management's personal involvement;
2. targeted recruitment;
3. internal advocacy groups;
4. emphasis on Equal Employment Opportunity statistics;
5. inclusion of diversity in performance evaluations;
6. inclusion of diversity in promotion decisions;
7. inclusion of diversity in management succession;
8. diversity training groups;
9. networks and support groups; and
10. work and family policies that support diversity.[16]

Many companies have embraced the concept of diversity and have made enormous efforts to change. Consider the experiences of Apple™ Computer, table 10–3.

TABLE 10–3   Apple™ Computer[17]

Santiago Rodriquez, manager of multicultural diversity for Apple™ Computer, notes that implementing a diversity program is a slow process. But for the computer maker, the benefits have made it worth the wait.

Several factors have contributed to creating a diversity program, including the need to attract, develop, and retain the best talent possible in a highly competitive industry, and the need to involve diverse viewpoints into the design and development of products.

Apple™ has been able to incorporate diversity at every level of the organization. Key components include:

- *Communication*—between employees and senior management about diversity issues. For example, African-American employees have met with upper level officers to discuss empowerment strategies, networking, and ways to assist the company in meeting its business goals.
- *Involvement*—with multicultural communities through company-sponsored and employee volunteer groups.
- *Celebration*—of multicultural holidays and events. Festivities are open to everyone, and these are held on the corporate campus.
- *Recruitment*—of talent from multicultural communities. Apple™ has formed ongoing relationships with minority, women's, and disability-oriented organizations.
- *Education*—about the meaning and benefits of diversity. Each manager is provided guidance that outlines what constitutes good management behavior from a multicultural perspective.

These programs and others have raised diversity as a highly visible issue at every level of the corporation. "People talk about it a great deal. Many volunteer to help on various programs and initiatives, and the concept as a corporate value has gained major acceptance," says Rodriquez.

BENEFITS OF DIVERSITY

What are the benefits organizations receive by valuing diversity and achieving inclusivity? Ray Benedict, vice-president of employee development at Great American Insurance Companies, reports the following:

- Increase in work force creativity

- Broader range of knowledge and skill

- Better decisions based on different perspectives

- Better services provided to diverse populations

- Ability to recruit excellent talent from the entire labor pool

- In essence, creating an environment that nurtures the multicultural fabric of community.[18]

Benedict explains that, far from being a stumbling block, diversity in the workplace can be a springboard for opportunity and excellence.

STRATEGIES, TECHNIQUES, AND TOOLS TO CHANGE

Dealing with diversity is no easy task, and it never ends. But it is the right thing to do and it is worth the effort for all involved. The following are effective strategies and techniques that can help individuals and organizations overcome cultural differences and achieve true community.[19]

What Individuals Can Do

- Connect with and value your own culture. Assess how your background translates into your own lifestyle, values, and views.

- Think about how it feels to be different by remembering times when you felt that you were in the minority. Examine how you felt and its impact on your behavior.

- Try to understand each person as an individual, rather than seeing the person as a representative of a group.

- Participate in educational programs that focus on learning about and valuing different cultures, races, religions, ethnic backgrounds, and political ideologies.

- Make a list of heroes and heroines in music, sports, theater, politics, business, science, and so forth. Examine your list for its diversity.

- Consider the difficulties you might face if you were physically handicapped.

- Learn about the contributions of older people and people with visual or hearing impairment. Consider how their contributions have helped us all.

- Learn more about other cultures and their values through travel, books, and films, and by attending local cultural events and celebrations.

- Continually examine your thoughts and language for unexamined assumptions and stereotypical responses.

- Model behavior that is inclusive and not prejudging. By including a wide variety of people in your world, you can more easily serve as a model to others.

- Include people who are different from you in social conversations, and invite them to be part of informal work-related activities, such as going to lunch or attending company social events.

- Include employees from a variety of backgrounds in decision-making and problem-solving processes. Use differences as a way of gaining a broader range of ideas and perspectives.

- When dealing with people, try to keep in mind how you would feel if your positions were reversed.

What Organizations Can Do

- Develop mentoring and partnering programs that cross traditional social and cultural boundaries.

- Develop specific strategies to increase the flow of applicants from a variety of backgrounds. For example, if you commonly recruit students from college campuses, ensure that the student populations represent a diversity of backgrounds.

- Be willing to hire employees with nontraditional backgrounds and skills.

- Use referrals from employees within your organization to help you identify promising candidates for recruitment.

- Look at the career paths and opportunities in your area with an open mind. Aggressively eliminate intentional or unintentional discrimination.

- Describe to all employees the specific promotional routes and the skills required for them to succeed.

- Look for opportunities to develop employees from diverse backgrounds and prepare them for positions of responsibility. Tell them about the options in their present careers, as well as other career opportunities within the organization.

- Evaluate the holidays your organization officially recognizes to see whether they accommodate a diverse work force.

- Show sensitivity in your physical work environment. Display artwork and literature representing a variety of cultures, and make structural changes to ensure accessibility.

- Research the demographics of your organization. Determine the level of diversity that currently exists.

- Form a group to address issues of diversity. Invite members who represent a variety of backgrounds.

- Celebrate differences through team-building activities.

- Implement training programs that focus on diversity in the workplace—programs designed to develop a greater awareness and sensitivity to differences.

- Pay attention to company publications such as employee newsletters. Do they reflect the diversity of ideas, cultures, and perspectives present in the organization?

- Evaluate official rules, policies, and procedures of the organization to be sure all employees are treated fairly.

- Talk openly about diversity issues, respect all points of view, and work cooperatively to solve problems.

It can be difficult to change the habits of people. Those in power tend to have established or been rewarded by conditions as they are, so it is natural to resist efforts to change. Two excellent videos that can raise consciousness, influence people to value diversity, and help build community are *A Class Divided* and *Valuing Diversity.*[20]

A Class Divided is a dramatic account of an experiment on prejudice performed by grade school teacher Jane Elliot, in which eye color became the basis for discrimination. This theme is played out in the adult world as well with live interaction in a prison institution. The two primary lessons of the tape are 1) to recognize the evil of discrimination, and 2) to realize the power of the self-fulfilling prophecy whereby beliefs can create reality. The prescription for the viewer is to adopt an *eyes-level approach* in all human dealings—never look up and never look down at anyone on the basis of age, race, sex, or any other physical attribute. Also, because people tend to fulfill the expectations of others and live up or down to their image, stack the cards and expect the best. On a 1 to 10 scale, this video is a 10 for impact. This film connects on a human plane with all audiences.

Situations dramatized in the *Valuing Diversity* tapes expose viewers to typical problems associated with discrimination. In one, a female executive's intelligent suggestions are ignored by a group of men. In another, a Hispanic employee's comic touches fall flat in a business meeting. A third is about a bright Asian technician who is up for a promotion, but whose self-effacing manner will probably prevent him from getting it. Another Asian man is seen at a disadvantage when he can't keep up in a brainstorming session, because its impulsive and frenetic nature is alien to him.

Education is only the first step toward changing behavior. Remaining sensitive to differences in others is an ongoing process that is never fully completed. Lennie Copeland, coproducer of *Valuing Diversity*, says, "Even working with this stuff all of the time, I still have to focus on tolerance; I have to look beyond stereotypes and learn the person. . . . I recently hired an editor I wouldn't have thought of hiring ten years ago. Fresh from Japan, he was as stiff as a board and barely spoke English. But his work was beautiful. I've learned to look carefully at someone's work. Later, I found out that the stiffness was due to back surgery."[21]

LEADERSHIP AND PERSONAL EXAMPLE

Leadership plays a pivotal role in dealing with diversity. Leaders should:

- *Empower others.* As a leader, share power and information, solicit input, and reward people; encourage participation and share accountability.

- *Develop people.* Provide opportunities for growth, then model and coach desired behaviors; delegate responsibility to those who have the ability to do the work; individualize training and development efforts.

- *Value diversity.* See diversity as an asset; understand diverse cultural practices; facilitate integration among people; help others identify their needs and options.

- *Communicate.* Clearly communicate expectations, ask questions to increase understanding, show respect through listening; develop communication across cultures and language differences; provide ongoing feedback with sensitivity to individual differences.[22]

As important as leadership is, in the final analysis, it falls on each person to do the right thing. In *The Meaning of Our Success*, Marian Wright Edelman states:

Remember that the fellowship of human beings is more important than the fellowship of race and class and gender. Be decent and fair and insist that others be so in your presence. Don't tell, laugh at, or in any way acquiesce to racial, ethnic, religious, or gender jokes, or to any practices intended to demean rather than enhance another human being. Walk away from them; stare them down; make them unacceptable. Through daily moral consciousness, face up to rather than ignore voices of division. Remember that we are not all equally guilty, but we are all equally responsible for building a decent and just society.[23]

GENDER DIVERSITY IN THE WORKPLACE

The participation of women in the workplace continues to increase. The male labor force is projected to grow at 12 percent. This rate compares with a 25 percent gain projected for women. By the year 2000, women are expected to be 47.5 percent of the work force, up from 38.1 percent in 1970, 42.5 percent in 1980, and 45.8 percent in 1990. By the year 2000, 61.1 percent of American women are expected to be working outside the home. At this rate, they will constitute three-fifths of new entrants into the labor force between 1985 and 2000.[24] See table 10–4.

With the changing role of women in American society from wife and mother, to wife and mother and career person as well, there has been a merging of the sexes in the workplace. This has brought the need for better understanding between men and women. Social attitudes play an important part in this equation.

Stereotyping can have significant influence on working relationships between men and women. Traditional ideas about "a woman's place" are held by many people of both sexes. While these ideas are changing, they can be strong enough to cause strain between men and women working side by side.

The following exercise addresses attitudes toward women working. To understand its relevance, imagine the role of attitude when a man has to adjust

TABLE 10–4   Women's Growing Share (in Thousands) of the Work Force[25]

	1950	1960	1970	1980	1990	Projected 2000
Women in the work force	18,389	23,240	31,543	45,487	57,230	66,670
Female labor force participation rate (%)	33.9	37.7	43.3	51.5	57.5	61.5
Female share of the work force (%)	29.6	33.4	38.1	42.5	45.8	47.5

to a woman as his boss, or a woman has to adjust to a workplace dominated by male values and customs that are foreign to her early social conditioning.

APPLICATION: ATTITUDES TOWARD WOMEN WORKING[26]

Directions

This questionnaire consists of twenty statements concerning sex roles and the impact they have on the work setting. Circle the response that most closely describes your attitude toward each statement.

1. Generally speaking, the mother of a financially sound family should not work outside the home.
   a. strongly agree
   b. agree
   c. undecided
   d. disagree
   e. strongly disagree

2. Women do not need as much formal education as men.
   a. strongly agree
   b. agree
   c. undecided
   d. disagree
   e. strongly disagree

3. A man can be just as good a homemaker as a woman.
   a. strongly agree
   b. agree
   c. undecided
   d. disagree
   e. strongly disagree

4. Truck driving is a man's job.
   a. strongly agree
   b. agree
   c. undecided
   d. disagree
   e. strongly disagree

5. A woman who wants a career, but feels obligated to be a housewife, has a damaging, rather than preserving, effect upon the family unit.
   a. strongly agree
   b. agree
   c. undecided
   d. disagree
   e. strongly disagree

6. The principal breadwinner should have the final authority in making family decisions.
   a. strongly agree
   b. agree
   c. undecided
   d. disagree
   e. strongly disagree

7. Women are too emotional to effectively manage other people.
   a. strongly agree
   b. agree
   c. undecided
   d. disagree
   e. strongly disagree

8. Men do not have the patience and compassion needed to deal with the sick and elderly.
   a. strongly agree
   b. agree
   c. undecided
   d. disagree
   e. strongly disagree

9. Women have not been absorbed into the work force at the same rate and levels of employment as men because of role definitions and discriminations, not because of any lack of intelligence or ability.
   a. strongly agree
   b. agree
   c. undecided
   d. disagree
   e. strongly disagree

10. If a military draft is in effect, both men and women should be drafted into the armed services.
    a. strongly agree
    b. agree
    c. undecided
    d. disagree
    e. strongly disagree

11. Some jobs are more suitable for males, while others are more suitable for females.
    a. strongly agree
    b. agree
    c. undecided
    d. disagree
    e. strongly disagree

12. It is more appropriate for men to play contact sports than it is for women.
    a. strongly agree
    b. agree
    c. undecided
    d. disagree
    e. strongly disagree

13. Men and women are essentially equal in the ability to do physical work.
    a. strongly agree
    b. agree
    c. undecided
    d. disagree
    e. strongly disagree

14. To me, it does not matter whether my supervisor is a man or a woman.
    a. strongly agree
    b. agree
    c. undecided
    d. disagree
    e. strongly disagree

15. Men are basically superior to women.
    a. strongly agree
    b. agree
    c. undecided
    d. disagree
    e. strongly disagree

16. Family leave benefits should be available to the father as well as to the mother.
    a. strongly agree
    b. agree
    c. undecided
    d. disagree
    e. strongly disagree

17. Whether my doctor is a man or a woman makes no difference to me.
    a. strongly agree
    b. agree
    c. undecided
    d. disagree
    e. strongly disagree

18. God created man first; therefore, the male is more important.
    a. strongly agree
    b. agree
    c. undecided
    d. disagree
    e. strongly disagree

19. I would not mind if the next U.S. president is a woman.
    a. strongly agree
    b. agree
    c. undecided
    d. disagree
    e. strongly disagree

20. Environmental influences are more important than biological factors in determining the masculinity or femininity of a person.
    a. strongly agree
    b. agree
    c. undecided
    d. disagree
    e. strongly disagree

Scoring

Use the following work sheets to obtain total scores. Give 1 point for each A response, 2 points for each B response, etc., for Group I questions. Give 5 points for each A response, 4 points for each B response, etc., (reverse) for Group II questions. Total each column, and then add these to get composite totals. Add the two composite totals to obtain a grand total.

GROUP I QUESTIONS

	a 1	b 2	c 3	d 4	e 5	
1						
2						
4						
6						
7						
8						
11						
12						
15						
18						Composite Total
Totals						

GROUP I I QUESTIONS

	a 5	b 4	c 3	d 2	e 1	
3						
5						
9						
10						
13						
14						
16						
17						
19						
20						Composite Total
Totals						

Group I Questions Composite Total	
Group II Questions Composite Total	
Grand Total	

Interpretation

20–36 Points: *Strict traditional*

Your attitudes are extremely traditional and are based on the concept that "a woman's place is in the home." You see a man's role as breadwinner and figure of strength and authority in the family, as well as in the world of work. You see men and women as entirely different and unequal beings, not because of socialization, but because they are born to be so.

37–52 Points: *Conservative*

Your attitudes tend to be conservative, and you find it difficult to accept many of today's new practices. You believe that a man should protect a woman, "the weaker sex," and that the two should not work at the same jobs or be treated in the same manner.

53–68 Points: *Semiconservative*

You can accept today's changing ideas and agree that women are mistreated in many ways. At the same time, you hold essentially conservative attitudes, probably acquired through upbringing, that cause you to feel uncomfortable at the thought of women mixing on an equal basis with men in the workplace.

69–84 Points: *Semiliberal*

You are broad-minded concerning the treatment of men and women. You agree that changes must take place in the overall attitude of our society so that equal rights may be protected. Still, you have some undeniable feelings that, as a man or woman, you fill a different position in the social structure from someone of the opposite sex.

85–100 Points: *Liberal*

You are as liberal as they come on the subject of male-female sex roles and relationships in today's world. You feel that men and women are equal, and that any difference in job placement or social treatment is the exclusive result of social conditioning, not inborn characteristics.

Although it is popularly believed that chauvinistic attitudes are the domain of males in society, the passage on the following page from Anne Roiphe's *Confessions of a Female Chauvinist* shows this to be untrue.

IMPROVING COMMUNICATION ACROSS GENDERS

What is the solution for improving communications between the sexes? The answer has three parts:

1. Recognize the different characteristics and needs of the different sexes.

2. Recognize that men and women are more alike than they are different.

3. Recognize that each person is a unique individual.

Recognize the Different Characteristics and Needs of the Different Sexes

Two interesting areas where men and women are different are *attitudes toward success* and *communication habits*.

Attitudes toward success   In a conversation among friends, a complaint is lodged by two sixth-grade girls against another girl:

Shannon: She's gotta wear Polo every *day*.
Julia: I know, well I like *Polo*, but *God!*
Shannon: Every *day!*
Julia: *Really!*
Shannon: Just think how much—and sh-she's putting herself *up*.[28]

Confessions of a Female Chauvinist

Listen to any group that suffers materially and socially. They have a lexicon with which they tease the enemy: ofay, goy, honky, gringo. "Poor pale devils," said Malcolm X loud enough for us to hear, although blacks had joked about that to each other for years. Behind some of the women's liberation thinking lurk the rumors, the prejudices, the defense systems of generations of oppressed women whispering in the kitchen together, presenting one face to their menfolks and another to their card clubs, their mothers and sisters. All this is natural enough but potentially dangerous in a situation in which you hope to create a future that does not mirror the past. The hidden antimale feelings, a result of the old system, will foul us up if they are allowed to persist.

When I was a child, we believed boys were less moral than we were. They appeared to be hypocritical, self-seeking, exploitative, untrustworthy, and very likely to be showing off their precious masculinity. I never had a girl friend I thought would be unkind or embarrass me in public. I never expected a girl to lie to me about her marks or sports skill or how good she was in bed. Altogether—without anyone's directly coming out and saying so—I gathered that men were sexy, powerful, very interesting, but not very nice, not very moral, humane, and tender, like us. Girls played fairly while men, unfortunately, reserved their honor for the battlefield.

Minorities automatically feel superior to the oppressor because, after all, they are not hurting anybody. In fact, they feel morally better. The old canard that women need love, men need sex—believed for too long by both sexes—attributes moral and spiritual superiority to women and makes of men beasts whose urges send them prowling into the night. This false division of good and bad, placing deforming pressures on everyone, doesn't have to contaminate the future. We know that the assumptions we make about each other become a part of the cultural air we breathe and, in fact, become social truths.

Women who want equality must be prepared to give it and believe in it, and in order to do that it is not enough to state that you are as good as any man, but also it must be stated that he is as good as you and both will be humans together. If we want men to share in the care of the family in a new way, we must assume them as capable of consistent loving tenderness as we.

Aggression is not a male-sex-linked characteristic: brutality is masculine only by virtue of opportunity. True, there are one thousand Jack the Rippers for every Lizzie Borden, but that surely is the result of social forces. Women as a group are indeed more masochistic than men. The practical result of this division is that women seem nicer and kinder, but if the world changes, women may have a fuller opportunity to be just as rotten as men and there will be fewer claims of female moral superiority.

I remember coming home from school one day to find my mother's card game dissolved in hysterical laughter. The cards were floating in black rivers of running mascara. What was so funny? A woman named Helen was lying on the couch pretending to be her husband with a cold. She was issuing demands for orange juice, aspirin, suggesting a call to a specialist, complaining of neglect, of fate's cruel finger, of heat, of cold, of sharp pains on the bridge of the nose that might indicate brain involvement. What was so funny? The ladies explained to me that all men behave just like that with colds, they are reduced to temper tantrums by simple nasal congestion, men cannot stand any little physical discomfort—on and on the laughter went.

The point of this is the nature of the laughter—us laughing at them, us feeling superior to them, us ridiculing them behind their backs. If they were doing it to us we'd call it male chauvinist pigness; if we do it to them, it is inescapably female chauvinist sowness and, whatever its roots, it leads to the same isolation.[27]

Appearing better than others is a violation of the girls' egalitarian ethic. Girls are conditioned to stress their connections and similarity. Studies of girls' conversations show that girls fear rejection by their peers if they appear too successful, while boys do not. Girls learn that by displaying differences, they will not get what they want—acceptance by their peers. For this, they have to appear the same as, not better than, their friends. In contrast, boys, from the earliest age, learn that they can get what they want—higher status—by displaying differences, especially superiority.[29]

Communication habits Studies suggest that boys and girls in America grow up in what are essentially different cultures, so that talk between men and women is cross-cultural communication. In *You Just Don't Understand: Women and Men in Conversation*, linguist Deborah Tannen builds a strong case for her hypothesis that boys and girls grow up in different worlds of words. Tannen notes that boys and girls play differently, usually in same-sex groups, and that their ways of using language in their games are separated by a world of difference:

> Boys tend to play outside, in large groups that are hierarchically structured. Their groups have a leader who tells others what to do and how to do it, and resists doing what other boys propose. It is by giving orders and making them stick that high status is attained. Another way boys achieve status is to take center stage by telling stories and jokes, and by sidetracking or challenging the stories and jokes of others. Boys' games have winners and losers and elaborate systems of rules that are frequently the subjects of arguments. Finally, boys are frequently heard to boast of their skill and argue about who is best at what.
>
> Girls, on the other hand, play in small groups or in pairs; the center of a girl's social life is her best friend. Within the group, intimacy is the key, and differentiation is measured by relative closeness. In their most frequent games, such as jump rope and hopscotch, everyone gets a turn. Most of girls' activities, such as playing house, do not have winners or losers. Although some girls are certainly more skilled than others, they are expected not to boast about it, or show that they think they are better than the others. Girls don't give orders; they express their preferences as suggestions, and suggestions are likely to be accepted. Whereas boys say, "Gimme that!" and "Get outta here!" girls say, "Let's do this," and "How about doing that?" Anything else is put down as "bossy." They don't grab center stage—usually, they don't want it—so they don't challenge each other directly. Much of the time, they simply sit together and talk. Girls are not accustomed to jockeying for status in an obvious way; they are more concerned with being accepted and liked.[30]

Tannen believes differences developed in childhood cast a long shadow into adulthood. When men and women talk to each other about troubles, for example, there is a potential problem because each expects a different response. Men may ignore or avoid dealing with feelings and emotions, preferring instead to attack underlying causes. Women, expecting to have their feelings supported, may misconstrue men's aggressive approach and feel that they themselves are being attacked. In general, where men seek status, women seek connection.[31]

Tannen explains that from childhood, there is a tendency for men to use conversation to negotiate status; women talk to create rapport. The clash of the two styles can lead to frustration—in personal relations, of course, but in the office as well, from the female manager who feels she isn't heard in meetings, to the male executive who is baffled when his gruff orders spark resentment or anger.[32]

To the question, "Who talks more, women or men?", seemingly contradictory evidence is reconciled by differences between public speaking and private speaking. Men generally are more comfortable doing "public speaking," whereas women usually feel more comfortable doing "private speaking."

Another way of capturing these differences is by using the terms *report talk* and *rapport talk*. For most men, report talk is primarily a means of preserving independence or negotiating and maintaining status in a hierarchical social order. To the man, talk is for information that can equate to power. For most women, the language of conversation is primarily a language of rapport. To the woman, talk is for interaction that can equate to love. Telling things is a way to show involvement, and listening is a way to show she is interested and cares.[33]

What should we do about differences in the way men and women communicate? Should women try to change to be more like men, or vice versa? Neither is the answer. It is important to simply recognize that natural differences exist. When people don't know there *are* differences in communication styles, and that they are formed in the normal course of growing up, they end up attributing communication problems to someone's bad intentions or lack of ability.

While women's and men's communication styles may be different, neither approach should be considered somehow better than the other. Instead, we should value the differences and capitalize on them for the greatest good of all. To sum up, men and women tend to communicate differently, and this is a significant factor in understanding and dealing with each other.[34]

Recognize That Men and Women Are More Alike Than They Are Different

Even though men and women are different in many ways, they are the same in many more ways. This is pictured in figure 10–1.

The Swiss psychiatrist Carl Jung recommended that people develop both the male-associated and female-associated qualities in their personalities. He believed that in this way people could achieve their full potential. Table 10–5 shows how men and women can achieve a state of androgyny in the work setting. Androgyny is the presence of desirable masculine and feminine characteristics in the same individual. Androgyny consists of assertive characteristics

FIGURE 10–1   Men and Women Are More Alike Than They Are Different

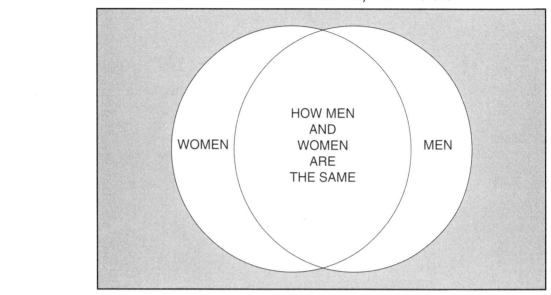

TABLE 10–5   Androgyny—Gender Role Transcendence[35]

To Achieve Full Potential in the Work Setting, Both Men and Women Need to:
1. Be willing to take risks.
2. Accept and express feelings as a valuable part of themselves.
3. Be open and direct in dealing with people.
4. Develop an identity that is not defined totally by work.
5. State personal needs clearly and without apology.
6. Learn how to fail at a task without feeling like a failure as a person.
7. Focus on tasks as well as relationships.
8. Accept imperfections that are a part of humanity.
9. Build support systems and share competencies with others.
10. Be patient and considerate when handling problems.
11. Don't turn anger and blame inward.
12. Share personal experiences with others.
13. Avoid self-limiting behaviors such as allowing oneself to be interrupted, or laughing after making serious statements.
14. Listen to people without feeling responsible for solving their problems.

such as independence and competitiveness as well as integrative characteristics such as sympathy and affection. A more descriptive term for androgyny is *gender role transcendence*.

Recognize That Each Person Is a Unique Individual

Even though individuals may be representatives of their genders, no two men and no two women are exactly the same. Each person should be treated as he or she uniquely is, realizing that even this is not a permanent state, but will change according to time and circumstance. In doing this, we demonstrate a basic belief in the importance of the individual and a respect for each person's individuality.

WOMEN IN LEADERSHIP POSITIONS

The number of women in leadership positions is increasing in America's workplace. Today, 44 percent of the Fortune 1000 service and industrial corporations have women on their boards, up from 13 percent ten years ago, and this trend is accelerating.[36] Historically, women in high leadership positions have come from nonprofit organizations, educational institutions, and public office; increasingly, they come from the business world.[37]

The Center for Creative Leadership has identified six *success factors* for women in high leadership positions:

- *Help from above.* Women in high levels of leadership have typically received the support of male mentors.

- *A "superior" track record.* Held to high standards, executive-level women have usually managed effectively and have developed an excellent record of performance.

- *A passion for success.* Senior-level women have been determined to succeed. They worked hard, seized responsibility, and achieved their objectives.

- *Outstanding "people skills."* Successful women executives typically utilize participative leadership, employee empowerment, and open communication to foster trust and high levels of morale among subordinates.

- *Career courage.* Successful women leaders have demonstrated courage to take risks, such as taking on huge responsibilities.

- *Toughness.* Senior-level women are seen as tenacious, demanding, and willing to make difficult decisions.[38]

Several factors can sidetrack women in the workplace. The "glass ceiling" is a catchphrase for the impediments women face as they seek top leadership positions. Sidetracking mechanisms include:

- *Lack of encouragement.* Women are often ignored in the grooming of executives for senior-level jobs. Men are more often moved around and cross-trained within the company to learn about different aspects of the business.[39]

- *Lack of opportunity followed by disillusionment.* In a national poll of middle-management women, 71 percent reported not having the same chances for promotion to top executive jobs as their male counterparts.[40]

- *The grass is greener outside.* One reason for the high numbers of women-owned companies is the perceived lack of opportunity in their current organizations.[41] A study of five hundred women entrepreneurs found that most of them were between thirty-five and forty-five. Thus, women leaders in the prime years for high-level positions in the corporation are engaged elsewhere.[42]

- *Closed corporate culture.* Many women who enter the executive suite do so by modeling established behavior patterns and management customs. Those who do not find that the alternative is to leave the organization.[43]

- *Women's ghettos and the feminization of jobs on the corporate staff.* Some women accept or are shunted into staff jobs that are difficult to exchange for line jobs, where salaries and responsibilities are usually greater. Many of these staff jobs are devoid of responsibility for finance and operations, two important disciplines for senior leaders to master.[44]

Men and women become sidetracked for many of the same reasons. Women, however, are typically forced into a narrower range of acceptable behavior than their male colleagues, making it more difficult to meet standards for senior leadership positions. Personal factors leading to female derailment include:

- *Inability to adapt.* This may be due partly to lack of guidance and feedback from helpful leaders.

- *Overly ambitious.* Pressure for the trappings of success, as well as ambition for womankind, can lead to the derailment of women's careers.

- *Performance problems.* Some women are promoted beyond their professional capabilities and interests.

- *Lack of independence.* Women are often encouraged to be dependent, both in their upbringing and in their professional development.

■ *Discomfort due to gender perceptions and biases.* Issues and concerns over sexuality, including sexual harassment, may limit a woman's success.[45]

Forces are in motion that make the promotion of women in the workplace more likely. These driving forces for change include:

■ Greater numbers of women in the work force, accelerating the evolution of attitudes.

■ Women attending the same colleges, joining the same clubs, and rising through the same ranks as their male colleagues. With assimilation into social and business networks formerly dominated by men, women lose less to "old boy" networks.

■ Government policies and guidelines that support women-owned businesses.

■ Increasing willingness of men to share in domestic and child-rearing tasks, giving women more time and energy for career activities.[46]

MANAGING MIXED GROUPS

For leaders who manage men and women working together, the following guidelines are suggested.

■ Accept the premise that a man and woman can work together without having an affair.

■ Make business decisions based on competence rather than gender.

■ Recognize that romantic relationships can exist that are not counter-productive.

■ Let employees know that you expect discreet, responsible behavior.

■ Avoid the temptation to protect employees from themselves.

■ Focus on possibilities rather than problems, and seek to guide rather than control.[47]

Managing diversity and achieving inclusivity require the capacity to put oneself in another person's shoes. Tolerance is an important aspect of this process. The following questionnaire provides an evaluation of your level of tolerance.

APPLICATION: TOLERANCE SCALE [48]

Directions

For each of the following questions, circle the answer that best describes you.

1. When someone does something you disapprove of, you:
   a. break off the relationship.
   b. tell how you feel, but keep in touch.
   c. tell yourself it matters little and behave as you always have.

2. You find it difficult to forgive a friend who has seriously hurt you.
   a. Yes
   b. No
   c. You forgive, but you do not forget.

3. Your view is that:
   a. censorship is essential to preserve moral standards.
   b. some censorship is necessary to protect young children.
   c. censorship is wrong.

4. Most of your friends:
   a. are very similar to you.
   b. are very different from you and from each other.
   c. are like you in some respects, but different in others.

5. The noise of children playing distracts you while you are trying to concentrate and complete a difficult task. You would:
   a. be glad the children are having a good time.
   b. make the children stop playing.
   c. be annoyed, but would allow the children to continue playing.

6. If you are visiting a foreign land and find conditions less hygienic then you are used to, you would:
   a. adapt easily.
   b. laugh at your own discomfort.
   c. leave the country as soon as possible.

7. Which quality in a mate is most important to you?
   a. Independent thinking
   b. Sociability
   c. Personal compatibility

8. Which virtue is most important to you?
   a. Kindness
   b. Objectivity
   c. Obedience

9. If a person you dislike experiences good fortune, you would:
   a. be upset.
   b. not really mind.
   c. be glad.

10. When it comes to beliefs, you:
    a. do all you can to make others see things the same way you do.
    b. actively advance your point of view, but stop short of argument.
    c. keep your feelings to yourself.

11. A friend is quite depressed. To you, things seem fine, but the friend complains bitterly. You would:
    a. listen sympathetically.
    b. tell the friend to straighten up.
    c. take the friend out to forget the problem.

12. Would you hire a person who has had emotional problems?
    a. No
    b. Yes, provided there is evidence of complete recovery.
    c. Yes, if the person is suitable for the work.

13. Do you agree with the statement, "What is right and wrong depends upon time, place, and circumstances"?
    a. Strongly agree
    b. Agree to a point
    c. Strongly disagree

14. When you disagree with someone else, you:
    a. lose your temper and argue.
    b. argue, but keep your cool.
    c. avoid arguing.

15. Do you read material that supports views different from your own?
    a. Never
    b. Sometimes
    c. Often

16. Which statement about crime and society do you agree with most?
    a. Certain and severe punishment reduces crime.
    b. A good society reduces crime.
    c. Punishment should fit the crime.

17. When it comes to society and rules, you think:
    a. rules are necessary.
    b. rules are desirable.
    c. rules should be avoided.

18. If you are religious, do you believe:
    a. your religion is the best one?
    b. all religions have something to offer?
    c. nonbelievers are evil?

19. If you are not religious, do you think:
    a. only uninformed people are religious?
    b. religion is a dangerous and evil force?
    c. religion can do good for some people?

20. You react to old people with:
    a. patience.
    b. annoyance.
    c. sometimes a, sometimes b.

21. The women's liberation movement is:
    a. run by extremists.
    b. an important social movement.
    c. a mistake.

22. Would you marry someone of a different race?
    a. Yes
    b. No
    c. Probably not

23. If someone in your family were homosexual, you would:
    a. view this as a problem and try to change the person to a heterosexual orientation.
    b. accept the person as a homosexual with no change in feelings or treatment.
    c. avoid or reject the person unless homosexuality is changed.

24. When young people question rules and authority, you usually:
    a. feel uncomfortable.
    b. approve.
    c. feel angry.

25. Which statement about marriage do you agree with most?
    a. Marriage should be avoided at all cost.
    b. Marriage is sacred and should be preserved at all cost.
    c. Marriage is good for some people and bad for others.

26. You react to little children with:
    a. patience.
    b. annoyance.
    c. sometimes a, sometimes b.

27. If you stay in a household run differently from yours (cleanliness, manners, meals, and other customs), you:
    a. adapt readily.
    b. quickly become uncomfortable and irritated.
    c. adjust for a while, but not for long.

28. Other people's personal habits annoy you:
    a. often.
    b. not at all.
    c. only if extreme.

29. Which statement do you agree with most?
    a. We should avoid judging others because no one can fully understand the motives of another person.
    b. People are responsible for their actions and have to accept the consequences.
    c. Both motives and actions are important when considering questions of right and wrong.

Scoring

Circle your answer for each question. Total the scores and insert this number on the Tolerance Scale.

1. a. 4	b. 2	c. 0	16. a. 4	b. 0	c. 2
2. a. 4	b. 0	c. 2	17. a. 2	b. 4	c. 0
3. a. 4	b. 0	c. 4	18. a. 4	b. 0	c. 4
4. a. 4	b. 0	c. 2	19. a. 4	b. 4	c. 0
5. a. 0	b. 4	c. 2	20. a. 0	b. 4	c. 2
6. a. 0	b. 0	c. 4	21. a. 4	b. 0	c. 4
7. a. 0	b. 2	c. 4	22. a. 0	b. 4	c. 2
8. a. 0	b. 2	c. 4	23. a. 2	b. 0	c. 4
9. a. 4	b. 0	c. 0	24. a. 2	b. 0	c. 4
10. a. 4	b. 2	c. 0	25. a. 4	b. 4	c. 0
11. a. 0	b. 4	c. 2	26. a. 0	b. 4	c. 2
12. a. 4	b. 2	c. 0	27. a. 0	b. 4	c. 2
13. a. 0	b. 2	c. 4	28. a. 4	b. 0	c. 2
14. a. 4	b. 2	c. 0	29. a. 0	b. 4	c. 2
15. a. 4	b. 2	c. 0			

What is your score on the Tolerance Scale? How does this affect your relations with others? Read the analysis on the following page.

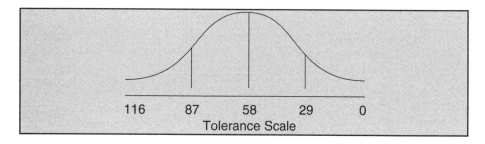

29 or below If your score is 29 or below, you are a very tolerant person, so that dealing with diversity comes easily to you. You are exceedingly aware of other people's problems and difficulties, and you have a capacity for accepting them even when their views are unlike your own. Other people may have a tendency to abuse this quality in your nature because they feel they have nothing to fear from recriminations. Even as you know this, you are tolerant and do not become extremely angry with them. Be aware, your openness to alternative points of view and your tolerance of divergent customs may upset family members, friends, and work associates who are less open-minded than you are.

30–58 You are a tolerant person, and people recognize you as such. In general, dealing with diversity presents few problems for you. If your score is above 44, however, you are probably tolerant and broad-minded in some areas only, such as attitudes toward children and older people, and you may have less tolerant ideas in other areas, such as male-female social roles and religious customs.

59–87 You are not as tolerant as most people, and if your score is 73 or higher, you are basically intolerant of people, ideas, and customs different from your own. As long as you work and live with people who are similar to you, this will have little influence on your communication and relationships. If, however, people of different views enter your arena, your intolerance may result in interpersonal conflict. Increasing diversity in society and the workplace may be difficult for you to accept.

88 or above This score indicates that you have low tolerance of diversity. The only people you are likely to respect are those with beliefs similar to your own. Being so closed to divergent views, you tend to be the preserving and conservative agent of your social group and society. Dealing with diversity involves major adjustments that you may be unwilling to make.

REFERENCES

1. John W. Gardner, "Reinventing the Community," address to the Carnegie Council on Adolescent Development, Washington, D.C.: December 11, 1992.

2. Juanita Brown, "Corporation as Community," *New Directions*, (Sandwich, Mass., 1993).

3. R. Ossolinski, "Celebration: Workplace Diversity," *Public Management* (April 92): 18–21.

4. Ossolinski, "Celebration," 18–21.

5. U.S. Bureau of Census, *Statistical Abstract of the U.S.—1989* and *Statistical Abstract of the U.S.—1994* (Washington, DC: U.S. Department of Commerce).

6. Robert B. Reich, "Metamorphis of the American Worker," *Business Month* (November 1990): 58–61, 64–66.

7. Jay A. Conger "The Brave New World of Leadership Training," *Organizational Dynamics* (Winter 1993): 46–58.

8. Lennie Copeland, "Learning to Manage a Multicultural Workforce," *Training* (May 1988): 48–49, 51, 55–56.

9. Copeland, "Learning to Manage a Multicultural Workforce."

10. Copeland, "Learning to Manage a Multicultural Workforce."

11. Copeland, "Learning to Manage a Multicultural Workforce."

12. Edwin J. Nichols, "Understanding the Philosophical Orientation of Different Cultural Groups," Address at Northern Kentucky University, 1993.

13. Copeland, "Learning to Manage a Multicultural Workforce."

14. Copeland, "Learning to Manage a Multicultural Workforce."

15. Barbara Jerich, "Four by Four," *Training and Development*, ed. Cathy Petrini (February 1989): 16.

16. Ann Morrison, *The New Leaders: Guidelines on Leadership Diversity in America*, (San Francisco: Jossey Bass Publisher, 1992), 292.

17. David Shadovitz, "Apple Computer Inc.", *Human Resources Executive*, June, 1992.

18. Ray Benedict, "Managing Differences: Critical Skills for Supervision," *Great American Insurance Companies*, 1993.

19. Keith Davis and John W. Newstrom, 8th. ed. *Human Behavior at Work* (New York: McGraw-Hill, 1989), 290–301; and Robert N. Lussier, *Human Relations in Organizations*, (Homewood, Illinois: Irwin, 1990): Chapter 12.

20. *A Class Divided*, video, PBS, 1320 Braddock Place, Alexandria, Va. 22314, and *Valuing Diversity*, video, Copeland Griggs Productions, 411 15th Ave., San Francisco, Ca. 94118.

21. Copeland, "Learning to Manage a Multicultural Workforce."

22. Conger, "The Brave New World of Leadership Training," 20.

23. Marian Wright Edelman, *The Meaning of Our Success: A Letter to My Children & Yours*, (Boston: Beacon Press, 1992).

24. U.S. Bureau of Census, *Statistical Abstract of the U.S.—1989* and *Statistical Abstract of the U.S.—1994*.

25. U.S. Bureau of Census, *Statistical Abstract of the U.S.—1989* and *Statistical Abstract of the U.S.—1994*.

26. Carolyn Lainhart, Northern Kentucky University, 1983.

27. Anne Roiphe, "Confessions of a Female Chauvinist," *New York Magazine* (1972).

28. Deborah Tannen, *You Just Don't Understand*, Ballantine Books, (New York, 1990), 216–221.

29. Tannen, *You Just Don't Understand*, 216–221.

30. Tannen, *You Just Don't Understand*, 216–221; and Rodney W. Napier and Matti K. Gershenfeld, *Groups: Theory and Experience*, 5th ed. (Boston: Houghton-Mifflin Co., 1993), 23.

31. Tannen, *You Just Don't Understand*, 216–221, and Napier and Gershenfeld, *Groups: Theory and Experience*, 23, 127.

32. Tannen, *You Just Don't Understand*, 216–221, and Napier and Gershenfeld, *Groups: Theory and Experience*, 23, 127.

33. Tannen, *You Just Don't Understand*, 216–221, and Napier and Gershenfeld, *Groups: Theory and Experience*, 23, 127.

34. Tannen, *You Just Don't Understand*, 216–221, and Napier and Gershenfeld, *Groups: Theory and Experience*, 23, 127.

35. Alice G. Sargent, *Beyond Sex Roles* (St. Paul: West Publishing Co., 1985).

36. Joseph F. Coates, Jennifer Jarratt, and John B. Mahaffie, *Future Work: Seven Critical Forces Reshaping Work and the Work Force in North America* (San Francisco: Jossey-Bass, 1990), 61; Cindy Skrzycki, "Board Room Doors Open Wider for Women," *The Washington Post*, December 3, 1987; and Cathy Trost, "Labor Letter," *The Wall Street Journal* (January 22, 1985): 1.

37. Coates, Jarratt, and Mahaffie, *Future Work*, 61; and Skrzycki, "Board Room Doors Open Wider For Women," and Anne B. Fisher, "The Ruling Class," *Savvy* (September, 1987): 36–37.

38. Coates, Jarratt, and Mahaffie, *Future Work*, 61; and Ann M. Morrison, Randall P. White, Ellen Van Velsor, *Leadership, Breaking the Glass Ceiling* (Reading, Mass.: Addison-Wesley, 1987), 10.

39. Margaret Price, "Women Reaching the Top," *Industry Week*, (May 16, 1987): 39.

40. Marilyn Loden, "Disillusion at the Corporate Top," *New York Times*, (February 9, 1986), F2.

41. Coates, Jarratt, and Mahaffie, *Future Work*, 61; and William Dunn, "USA Women Mind Their Own Business," *USA Today*.

42. Lois Therrien, Teresa Carson, Joan. O. Hamilton, and Jim Hurlock, "What Do Women Want? A Company They Can Call Their Own," *Business Week* (December 22, 1986): 60– 61.

43. Loden, *New York Times*.

44. "Why Women Exec's Stop Before the Top," *US News and World Report* (December 29, 1986): 72.

45. Coates, Jarratt, and Mahaffie, *Future Work*, 62; Ann M. Morrison, Randall P. White, Ellen Van Velsor, and The Center for Creative Leadership, "Women with Promise: Who Succeeds, Who Fails?" *Working Women* (June 1987): 79; and Glenn Collins, "Men vs. Women at the Office," *The New York Times* (January 30, 1987).

46. Coates, Jarratt, and Mahaffie, *Future Work*, 62.

47. David R. Eyler and Andrea P. Baridon, "Managing Sexual Attraction in the Workplace," *Business Quarterly* (Winter 1992): 19–21, 23–24.

48. Maria Heiselman, Naomi Miller, and Bob Schlorman, Northern Kentucky University, 1982.

PART 4

The Empowerment of People

11

Group Dynamics

Organizations years hence will bear little resemblance to the typical company, circa 1950. Traditional departments will serve as guardians of standards, as centers for training and assignment of specialists. They won't be where the work gets done: that will happen largely in task focused teams.

Peter Drucker

Community is experienced in two ways: as "a group of people" and as a "way of being." The first type of community is formed by bringing people together in place and time. The second is created when barriers between people are let down. Under such conditions, people become bonded, sensing that they can rely on and trust each other. When people experience a feeling of community, their potential for achievement becomes enormous.[1]

Adding to the richness of community is the fact that there are so many of them. They exist side by side, such as when an individual belongs to both a home community and a work community, and they exist one on another. Like Chinese boxes, a community can be enclosed within a larger community—family into tribe, tribe into state—or, in the world of work, department into division, division into organization.[2]

Author Carl Moore views community as the means by which individuals can live and work together to bring the greatest good for the greatest number of people. Communities enable people to protect themselves, acquire resources, and provide moral and social values that give dignity to existence. Members of a community share a common purpose and core values that define and sustain the group.[3]

Important forces that influence the creation and maintenance of community are **group dynamics**, member maturity, and leadership practices. This chapter features:

■ the sociology of groups;

■ the nature and characteristics of effective groups;

■ the role of the individual in building community; and

■ principles and practices for leading a high-performance group.

SOCIOLOGY OF GROUPS

Group life and mutual cooperation are necessary for the survival and evolution of humankind. In the primate species, group life is required for protection from predators and for social learning. Although a solitary bear, elk, or bird can survive on its own, a solitary primate usually cannot. Only through community have human beings come to dominate the world.[4]

A case can be made for the idea that group life and mutual cooperation have been programmed into the human species as it presently exists:

> Humans are social animals. In fact, a tendency toward community may be inherited as part of the human being's genetic makeup. This is because those hominids who lived together, sharing food and cooperating in defense, would probably survive longer and, therefore, produce more offspring than those who lived solitary lives. Solitary individuals would be likely to fall prey to other animals, or to lie sick and wounded, without care from others. More individuals with a social makeup would

thus survive, generation after generation, until eventually they replaced those who tended to be solitary. Also, humans seem to require the wide-open spaces much less than they do close physical contact with their own kind. Even in the sparsely populated Kalahari Desert, where empty land is available as far as the eye can see, Bushmen huddle together in tightly packed camps that are among the most congested places on earth.[5]

Sociologists Max Weber, Emile Durkheim, and George Simmel emphasize the importance of *community* as a means of understanding the human condition.[6] Whether preliterate or postindustrial, people have always used groups to satisfy important needs.

- For childbearing and intimacy, we use marriage and family.

- For our interest in the supernatural, we create religious sects and institutions.

- For social order and organization, we form governments.

- For education, we establish schools.

- For protection, we raise armies.

- For economic needs, we form work groups and organizations.[7]

Two changes that have marked modern society are the evolution away from family and clan, and the migration away from the village to the city. To avoid isolation and loneliness, individuals seek communities that satisfy important needs for human contact. Acting as their ancestors before them, people strive to build community because they don't want to end up naked and alone.[8]

THE IMPORTANCE OF COMMUNITY

The benefits of community apply in all areas of life and at all ages from youth to adulthood. Examples include the family in its various forms; work groups in business, industry, and government; community groups such as churches and neighborhoods; and social groups such as sport teams, hobby clubs, and professional associations. Whether one is talking about the school board, a Boy Scout troop, or a business enterprise, the experience of community is important.

For a modern example of community, no better case exists than Alcoholics Anonymous, the "Fellowship of AA." Founded in 1935 in Akron, Ohio, today there are thousands of AA groups in every town and city in America. Through the AA *community*, millions of people have received help and have found dignity in their lives. There are no dues, budgets, buildings, or elaborate organization; there is just purpose and community.[9]

Groups are like individuals in that their life spans can be different—as short as a moment and as long as years. The length of time a group exists is not the measure of its value, any more than the longevity of a simple human life is the measure of its importance. The true mark and meaning of individuals and groups transcend time. We can all remember individuals and groups that have influenced us in ways that were intrinsically good, regardless of duration. Also, the size of the group does not add or subtract from the value of the experience. The spirit and accomplishments of community are important to achieve between partners, within work groups, and in society as a whole.

THE VALUE OF WORK GROUPS

Work groups are important because they satisfy economic and social needs.

Economic Needs

Economic needs are met through the specialization and collaboration of labor. Imagine a hospital operating team, a construction crew building a home, or a professional sports team. Former Minnesota Vikings quarterback Fran Tarkenton describes the importance of collaboration:

> When a football team huddles before a play, the quarterback conveys a decision that either he or the coach on the sidelines has made. There is never much time for discussion. However, many of the Vikings' best plays have been the result of input by other team members. For example, outside receivers have often told me that they could run a specific pattern against the defense, and we have adjusted to run those plays. I would guess that 50 percent of my touchdowns have come about by receivers suggesting pass patterns. I have always tried to create an environment in which the other players felt comfortable making suggestions and offering feedback that would result in better decisions.
>
> The athletic field is one of the worst places for group decision making because of the extreme limits on time. Yet even there, the value of increasing the input and participation of all of the players is invaluable. People function best when they participate in those decisions that affect them. When leaders gain the involvement of those who must carry out those decisions, they take their organizations to a higher level of effectiveness.[10]

In *The Wisdom of Teams*, Jon Katzenbach and Douglas Smith of McKinsey & Company cite examples of American businesses capitalizing on the team concept:

> When Motorola took aim at its Japanese competition and produced the world's smallest, lightest, highest-quality cellular phone, its secret weapon was a team-based approach. Ford adopted the same strategy when it developed the Taurus—and Ford became the most profitable automobile company in the United States.

The team approach has been especially valuable for the many companies attempting to transform themselves into high-performance organizations that consistently beat the competition. Though they may use terms such as "customer driven," "total quality," or "continuous improvement" to describe their path to excellence, it is a team approach that promotes the behavior and attitudes necessary for superior performance.[11]

Social Needs

Group relationships satisfy social needs for belonging. Scott Peck explains that the members of a group who have achieved genuine community take pleasure—even delight—in knowing they have done something together, that they have collectively discovered something of great value, that they are "onto something" as a family. There is nothing competitive about the spirit of true community. To the contrary, a group possessed by a spirit of internal competitiveness—member against member—is, by definition, not a community. Competitiveness breeds exclusivity; genuine community is inclusive, meeting a basic need for belonging.[12]

The work group also provides a means for recognition and an audience for self-expression:

> People become ego-involved in decisions in which they have had an influence. These decisions become their decisions, and they develop expectancies to the effect that when the decisions are successfully implemented, they experience feelings of confidence and self-esteem. Because of this, they work to implement the decision, even though no extrinsic rewards are involved.[13]

HIGH-PERFORMANCE GROUPS

Every so often, someone captures an important concept and expresses it in such a way that it penetrates and takes root in the society. This was the case with Douglas McGregor and his book *The Human Side of Enterprise*, first published in 1960 and re-released in 1985. Like a lighthouse, it stands over the sea of literature on management and organization. This book, and his famous "Theory Y" speech delivered at MIT's Alfred P. Sloan School of Management in 1957, changed the entire concept of organizational life for the second half of the twentieth century.[14]

McGregor married the ideas of social psychologist Kurt Lewin to the theories of Abraham Maslow. To these, he added his own perspective drawn from his experiences as a professor and practicing manager. The essence of McGregor's message is that people react not to an objective world, but to a world fashioned from their own perceptions and assumptions about what the world is like. Not content to merely describe alternative theories, McGregor went on to identify strategies and practices that could be used to create enlightened workplaces.[15]

McGregor emphasized the human potential for growth, elevated the importance of the individual in the enterprise, and articulated an approach to leadership that undergirds all forms of community building. McGregor's prescriptions for effective leadership are as follows:

- Active involvement by all concerned; the practice of "inclusion" versus "exclusion," based on democratic ideals.

- Resolution of conflict between individual needs and community goals through effective interpersonal relationships between leaders and subordinates.

- Influence that relies not on traditional techniques of coercion, evasion, compromise, and bargaining, but on openness, honesty, and working through differences.

- A conception of humanity that is optimistic versus pessimistic, and that argues for humanistic treatment of people as valuable and valuing, as opposed to objects for manipulation and control.

- A transcending concern for human dignity, worth, and growth, captured best by the phrase "respect for the individual."

- A belief that human growth and goodness are innate, but that they can be thwarted by a dysfunctional environment, and that one's full potential can best be achieved in a healthy climate characterized by trust, respect, and authentic relationships.

- The importance of free individuals to have courage to act and accept responsibility for consequences.[16]

A practical application of McGregor's ideas is seen in the following exercise. A group can evaluate itself and improve both team spirit and team effectiveness based on the results. By reinforcing strengths and addressing deficiencies, people can take steps to build and sustain true community. When this is done, together everyone can accomplish more.

The Russian writer Leo Tolstoy once said, "All happy families resemble one another, and every unhappy family is unhappy in its own way." The same can be said for groups. Rather than a single thread, there is a tapestry of qualities that characterize all effective groups. Fully functioning communities and excellent teams possess twelve key characteristics.

APPLICATION: CHARACTERISTICS OF AN EFFECTIVE GROUP[17]

Directions

Consider each of the following characteristics. Evaluate your group as it is operating now (1 is the lowest rating; 10 is the highest).

1. *Clear mission:* The task or objective of the group is well understood and accepted by all.

1	2	3	4	5	6	7	8	9	10

Discussion: Have you ever been a member of a group that didn't know what it was supposed to do? If you have, you know firsthand the importance of having a clear sense of purpose that everyone understands and is committed to achieving. The number-one task facing a group is agreement on direction.

2. *Informal atmosphere:* The atmosphere is informal, comfortable, and relaxed. It is a working atmosphere, in which everyone is involved and interested. There are no signs of boredom.

1	2	3	4	5	6	7	8	9	10

Discussion: Have you ever been a member of a group that was too formal or too reserved, so that people did not feel free to be themselves and be spontaneous in their ideas and actions? If so, you know the twin casualties were personal comfort and true creativity.

3. *Lots of discussion:* Time is allowed for discussion in which everyone is encouraged to participate, and discussion remains pertinent to the task of the group.

1	2	3	4	5	6	7	8	9	10

Discussion: Have you ever known a group that didn't allow enough time for discussion? Some groups try to solve a problem in a minute, when what is actually needed is an hour-long meeting. On the other hand, have you ever known a group where that's all they did do was *talk*, . . . about the weather, about fashion, about sports, about everything except the work of the group? Effective groups focus on subjects that are important to the group's success—the customer, schedule, equipment, budget, policy, etc.—and talk these through thoroughly.

4. *Active listening:* Members listen to each other. People show respect for one another by listening when others are talking. Every idea is given a hearing.

1	2	3	4	5	6	7	8	9	10

Discussion: Have you ever been a member of a group or meeting where everyone was talking, but no one was listening? What was lacking was demonstration of respect as people failed to listen to each other in a non-judgmental manner. Another loss was synergy, the quality of a group to improve on the efforts of individuals working alone. In effective groups, every idea—conventional or novel—and every person, regardless of position in the group, is given a hearing.

5. *Trust/openness*: Members feel free to express ideas and feelings, both on the issues and on the group's operation. People are not afraid to suggest new and different ideas, even if fairly extreme.

1	2	3	4	5	6	7	8	9	10

Discussion: Have you ever been a member of a group or meeting where people had ideas, but they were afraid to express them? Maybe they had heard, "That's where they kill people is in there!" Not trusting the group, people close up and shut down, resorting to self-protective behavior. This is natural, but the price is a lack of shared knowledge and information, as well as a loss of goodwill.

6. *Disagreement is OK*: Disagreement is not suppressed or overridden by premature group action. Differences are carefully examined as the group seeks to understand all points of view. Conflict and differences of opinion are accepted as the price of creativity. Diversity is valued.

1	2	3	4	5	6	7	8	9	10

Discussion: You can't get fire unless you rub two sticks together; in the same way, people do not experience new learning and growth unless they rub their ideas against each other. When this is done in a tolerant and supportive atmosphere, great accomplishments can occur. With an atmosphere that tolerates disagreement, a group is enriched by having a variety of perspectives represented—operations and sales, female and male, customer and company, old seniority and new seniority, etc.

7. *Criticism is issue oriented, never personal*: Constructive criticism is given and accepted. Criticism is oriented toward solving problems and accomplishing the mission. Personal criticism is neither expressed nor felt.

1	2	3	4	5	6	7	8	9	10

Discussion: Have you ever felt personally attacked in group format? If so, you probably did one of two things—you attacked in return, or you retreated and went underground. Either of these approaches is harmful for group effectiveness, and can be avoided if members of the group attack ideas rather than people. This assumes maturity of group members to advance ideas, and then withdraw emotional attachment so they can be considered objectively and without censorship.

8. *Consensus is the norm*: Decisions are reached by consensus in which it is clear that everyone is in general agreement and willing to go along. Formal voting is kept to a minimum.

1	2	3	4	5	6	7	8	9	10

Discussion: There are times when by law or otherwise it is important for group members to vote formally. But this should be done only after thorough discussion and the airing of all ideas. It is important to obtain people's input in order to get their output or follow-through; but the best way to do this is through consensus, not voting. Consensus requires unity, not unanimity. When time is allowed and patience is exercised, the quality of decision making and the quality of follow-through is best when consensus is the norm.

9. *Effective leadership*: Informal leadership shifts from time to time, depending on circumstances. There is little evidence of a struggle for power as the group operates. The issue is not who controls, but how to get the job done.

1	2	3	4	5	6	7	8	9	10

Discussion: This reflects a different definition of leadership than General Lee on a white charger. It is a more contemporary definition that allows a group to gain the best contributions of all of its members. It reflects antiauthoritarian values and prodemocratic ideals.

10. *Clarity of assignments*: The group is informed of the action plan. When action is taken, clear assignments are made and accepted. People know what they are expected to do.

1	2	3	4	5	6	7	8	9	10

Discussion: Have you ever gone to a meeting and at the conclusion wondered, "What did we do?" Or have you ever been a member of a group where people didn't know what their roles were and how they related to others? Would you bet on that team? Probably not. Effective teamwork involves task interdependence so agreement on goals and roles is important. People have to know where they are going and what is expected of them. Otherwise, the group is like a team of horses pulling in opposite directions.

11. *Shared values and norms of behavior*: There is agreement on core values and norms of behavior that determine the rightness and wrongness of conduct in the group.

1	2	3	4	5	6	7	8	9	10

Discussion: Every family, tribe, and society has certain values that are at the root of its identity. These are core values that define the group. Core values of American society include personal freedom, social responsibility, and concern for others. Norms of behavior are less vital than core values, but they represent important customs in such areas as dress, language, etc., that help define group membership. Group excellence requires definite agreement on core values and general agreement on norms of behavior.

12. *Commitment*: People are committed to the goals of the group.

1	2	3	4	5	6	7	8	9	10

Discussion: In the final analysis, all decisions are personal. A group will not succeed unless its members are personally dedicated. Individual needs and goals must be fulfilled by the group's success.

Scoring

Add your score, then consult the following chart to find your group's effectiveness rating.

108–120 = Excellent
84–107 = Very good
49–83 = Average
25–48 = Poor
12–24 = Failing

Interpretation

Refer to the following discussion to interpret your group's score. Note that each characteristic is important, so strive to improve low ratings, regardless of the overall total.

Excellent   *This is a top-notch group regarding communication and teamwork.* The atmosphere is warm and supportive. The focus of attention and effort is on the mission. Creativity is encouraged, and success can be expected. Ask yourself, have you ever been a member of such a group—in the home? in the workplace? in the community at large? If you have, you know personally how satisfying and productive "community" can be.

Very good   *This is a strong group for morale and teamwork.* There is enthusiasm and an overall spirit of cooperation and dedication to accomplishing the mission. Conditions are very good. In a society where people are free to work and live where they want, these are the groups that attract and keep the best people, and then these people work as a team to achieve their goals.

Average   *Conditions are neither all good nor all bad regarding human factors.* Genuine effort is required to build on strengths and improve weaknesses. As it is, the group is only average. To personalize this, when in your life have you been satisfied with the condition or label "only average"? No doubt, this is not your way. So if you are a member or leader of such a group, you are probably suffering from cognitive dissonance and won't be able to stand it until conditions are in line with your ideals. You will want to begin today to achieve agreement on purpose, create an atmosphere of trust and respect, and employ democratic leadership practices.

Poor *This is a poor group environment.* Major work is needed to improve attitudes and performance. Without attention to team building, failure can be expected. Does this mean that a group that is presently *poor* can take steps to improve? Definitely. It happens all of the time. We can see case after case in which a poor-performing team one year improves group dynamics and, with no change in members, becomes a championship team the next year. Simply, they follow the twelve characteristics of an effective group—clear mission, lots of discussion, disagreement is OK, consensus is the norm, flexible leadership, clarity of assignments, individual commitment, etc.

Failing *Major change in group composition is in order.* Leaders and members may be reassigned. It is true that not everyone is meant to be married together, and not everyone is meant to be in a group together. There may be subtle psychological causes of failure to communicate that make staying together unacceptable. What is the answer? It is to separate and reorganize members so that the group doesn't lose any of its talented and dedicated individuals.

POSITIVE VERSUS NEGATIVE GROUP MEMBER ROLES

How do you develop a high-performance group? How do you build community in the workplace? Like everything in life, it goes back to the individual and what he or she chooses to do. And like most things in life, it depends upon the example and direction of leaders. Formal leaders and influential members of the group or organization must model and reinforce positive versus negative group member roles.[18]

Positive Roles

Roles that help build community and achieve group success are as follows:
   Encourager This person is friendly, diplomatic, and responsive to others in the group. The encourager makes others in the group feel good and helps them to make contributions. The encourager is a cheerleader, coach, and group advocate.
   Clarifier The clarifier restates problems and solutions, summarizes points after discussion, and introduces new or late members to the group by bringing them up to date on what has happened. The gift of the clarifier is to bring order to chaos, and replace confusion with clarity.
   Harmonizer The harmonizer agrees with the rest of the group, brings together opposite points of view, and is not aggressive toward others. The

harmonizer brings peace versus war, love versus hate, cooperation versus competition, and unity versus discord, and is, therefore, important for group success.

Idea generator The idea generator is spontaneous and creative. This person is unafraid of change and suggests ideas that others do not. Often these ideas are just what is needed to solve a problem. The idea generator is almost always a creative and unconventional thinker. Pose a problem, and they will generate ideas. Half-baked or fully baked, idea generators have ideas.

Ignition key This person provides the spark for group action, causing the group to meet, work, and follow through with ideas. The ignition key is often a practical organizer who orchestrates and facilitates the work of the group. In this sense, the ignition key plays a leadership role in group action.

Standard setter This person's high ideals and personal conduct serve as a model for group members. The standard setter is uncompromising in upholding the group's values and goals, and thus inspires group pride. The standard setter is often an expert, possessing knowledge and skills deemed important by the group.

Detail specialist This person considers the facts and implications of a problem. The detail specialist deals with small points that often have significant consequences in determining the overall success of a group project. A vigilant finisher, the detail specialist searches for errors and omissions and keeps the group on red alert. To show the importance of the detail specialist, consider Benjamin Franklin's famous words:

> For want of a nail, the shoe was lost; for want of a shoe, the horse was lost; for want of a horse, the battle was lost; for want of a battle, the war was lost; for want of a war, the cause was lost. The cause could be something of great importance—life, liberty, the pursuit of happiness—lost for want of a nail.

As a practical measure, consider your own group or community, and ask, "Who is playing positive group member roles?" Who is providing encouragement, harmony, new ideas, etc.? Take the time to let them know how important they are to the group's success, and how appreciated they are for their efforts in building community. Be specific and be personal if you want to reinforce these helpful behaviors.

Negative Roles

Roles that reduce community and lower group effectiveness are as follows:

Ego tripper This individual interrupts others, launches into long monologues, and is overly dogmatic. The ego tripper constantly demands attention and tries to manipulate the group to satisfy a need to feel important. Ask yourself, have you ever observed an ego tripper in operation? If so, you know how destructive and expensive this trip can be.

Negative artist This person rejects all ideas suggested by others, takes a negative attitude on issues, argues unnecessarily, and refuses to cooperate. The negative artist is pessimistic about everything and dampens group enthusiasm. Negativism is like other human emotions; it is contagious. A negative artist can depress people and depressed people will never accomplish great works. We shouldn't deny reality. But once we see things for what they are, we should accentuate the positive. Emphasize opportunities and possibilities, versus problems and deficiencies. By doing this, the group will be energized and focused, and with energy and focus a group can achieve its full potential.

Above it all This person withdraws from the group and its activities by being aloof, indifferent, and excessively formal, and by daydreaming, doodling, whispering to others, wandering from the subject, or talking about matters that are unrelated to the group discussion. The above-it-all person's attitude detracts from the group's progress. Instead of being above it all, members must get involved. It is only when people are involved that they understand things; only when they understand things can they be committed; and only when people are committed will true community be achieved.

Aggressor This person attacks and blames others, shows anger or irritation, and deflates the importance or position of the group and its members. When aggressors attack, others typically resort to coping techniques—either responding in kind, or avoiding encounters. Either response perpetuates the negative experience and its effects.

Jokester This person is present for fun, not work. The jokester fools around most of the time and will distract the group from its business just to get a laugh. IQ and sense of humor are correlated positively, but the humor of the "jokester" does not have a positive influence. The jokester diverts attention and reduces the potential for group effectiveness.

Avoider This person does anything to avoid controversy or confrontation. The avoider is dedicated to personal security and self-preservation. Sometimes avoidance behavior is a logical response to an environment that is perceived as hostile. Sometimes avoidance can be traced to lack of confidence or development of the individual. In either case, the avoider hinders new ideas and reduces group success.

Sniper The sniper lays low and attacks members of the group or the group as a whole at vulnerable moments. The bullets are words and actions that can destroy individual morale and group effectiveness. As with other negative group member roles, sniping is a habit or pattern of behavior that can and should be corrected.

What do you do about the individual who, intentionally or not, reduces the effectiveness of the group? Psychologist Harry Levinson describes a *nine-point plan* for dealing with abrasive behavior. These same principles apply with any individual who plays a negative versus positive group member role.[19]

1. When an individual disrupts the group, talk it over in a calm and patient way. Acknowledge the fact that the person has good intentions. Recognize the origins of negative behavior may be caused by feelings of insecurity, hunger for affection, vulnerable self-image, and eagerness for perfection.

2. Report observations uncritically. Describe what happened, especially the behavior to which people reacted. Ask how the person thought others felt when he said or did what you describe. Was this the result desired? If not, discuss how the person can act in the future to get the response he wants.

3. Point out that you recognize the person wants to be successful, and you want to help; but that in order to reach his goals, he must take others into account. Note also, that usually there will be defeats and disappointments along the way.

4. If the person's behavior becomes irritating, avoid the impulse to attack or withdraw. Instead, report how he made you feel and how others must feel when he behaves this way. Let him know that you are annoyed, but you nevertheless value him as a person.

5. Ask why the person behaves as he does. For example, why does he attack people in situations that are not combative? Explain that being part of a critical discussion is one thing, but turning discussion into an argument or struggle for power is another.

6. If the person challenges, philosophizes, defends, or tries to debate your observations, don't counterattack. Keep your eye on *his* goal. People do what they do for their own reasons. What exactly does the person want, and how can participation in the group help accomplish his goals?

7. Help the person understand that compromise is not necessarily second best, that the all-or-nothing principle usually results in disappointment, and that cooperation and good relations with others can be rewarding. Expect to repeat this process again and again. In all discussions point out the legitimate achievements of which he can be proud.

8. A person may be closed-minded. Perhaps he is thinking of defensive arguments, or is preoccupied with his own thoughts. Then he must be confronted with the fact and the cost of his negative group behavior.

9. If, despite your best efforts, the person does not respond, he needs to know in no uncertain terms that his behavior is unacceptable. Do not assume that he knows. He should be told repeatedly.

THE CHANGING NATURE OF ORGANIZATIONS

Management author Peter Drucker describes the changing nature of organizational structure and processes in American business.

When modern organizations first arose in the closing years of the nineteenth century, the only model was the military. The Prussian Army was as much a marvel of organization for the world of 1870 as Henry Ford's assembly line was for the world of 1920. In the army of 1870, each member did much the same thing, and the number of people with any knowledge was infinitesimally small. The army was organized by command-and-control, and business enterprise, as well as most other institutions, copied that model. This structure is not unlike that of the American football team.

Over the years, American industry developed a baseball style of team structure and process. Research did its work and passed it on to engineering. Engineering did its work and passed it on to manufacturing. Manufacturing did its work and passed it on to marketing. Accounting usually came in at the manufacturing phase. Personnel usually came in only when there was a people problem.

Then the Japanese reorganized their new product development into a soccer team approach. In such a team style, each function does its own work, but from the beginning they work together. They move with the task, so to speak, the way a soccer team moves with the ball. It took the Japanese at least fifteen years to learn how to do this. But once they had mastered the new concept, they cut development time by two-thirds. Where traditionally it has taken five years to bring out a new automobile model, Toyota, Nissan, and Honda now do it in eighteen months. This, as much as their quality control, has given the Japanese a strong hand in both the American and European automobile markets. As more and more organizations become information-based, they are transforming themselves into soccer teams; that is, into responsibility-based organizations in which every member must act as a responsible decision maker. All members, in other words, have to see themselves as "executives."[20]

To adjust to changing times, organizations are striving to become less bureaucratic and more entrepreneurial, less concerned with stability and more concerned with versatility, less concerned with preserving the past and more concerned with creating the future.

THE IMPACT OF ORGANIZATIONAL CHANGE ON INDIVIDUALS

It is inevitable that organizational change affects individuals. In an article entitled "Nobody is Safe," U.S. Secretary of Labor Robert Reich describes the "employment" impact on the American worker and the effect this can have on the relationship between employer and employee. "The first step was to reduce the benefits packages for lower-tier workers. The next step was to reduce layers of middle management. The third step was to reduce benefit packages across the board for all employees. The fourth step is to do much more business by contract, either with contingent workers and part-time employees, or by contracting out."[21]

An effect of this is that unless employees feel they will be valued over the long term, they may be less willing to go the extra mile, to work a little harder, to contribute. In the same way, if the employer feels this is not a long-term relationship, there may be reluctance to invest in employee development. There are companies that traditionally were very hesitant about laying off employees because they were concerned about their corporate culture. Citing economic pressures, they increasingly now let people go, sometimes with very little notice.[22]

What is happening in the American workplace is two countervailing trends. One is toward *empowerment*, in which organizations are strengthening relationships with employees. But a countertrend is the move toward restructuring, downsizing, and using *contingent workers*, where there is always a question mark hanging over the relationship as to whether it will continue in the future.[23]

Robert Schaen, a former company comptroller, speaks from the individual's perspective, giving the dilemma a human face. "The days of mammoth corporations are coming to an end. People are forced to create their own lives, their own careers, and their own successes. Some people may go kicking and screaming into the new world, but there is an important message here: 'Today you are in business for yourself.'" Schaen now runs his own children's publishing business. His conclusions apply for workers across all segments of society—teachers, accountants, nurses, etc. The day of cradle-to-grave job security is gone for most people.[24]

BUILDING COMMUNITY AS A SURVIVAL SKILL

How can organizations and individuals succeed in today's environment? There is at least one constant in all of this—the importance of *community*. Today's "communities" may be different from communities of the past—smaller in size, more diverse in composition, shorter in duration, spread over a larger geographic area—and there may be more of them occurring simultaneously. A single person may experience community at home, in the workplace, and in larger society all at the same time. But experience it we must, for community is a requisite for survival and success in modern society.

A new ethic exists in today's successful organizations. It goes beyond the notion of "a fair day's work for a fair day's pay" and aims toward community as a virtue that brings the greatest good for the greatest number. This ethic has certain characteristics, including agreement on purpose, shared values, an atmosphere of trust and respect, elimination of communication barriers, and empowerment as a mode of leadership. These are the elements found and valued in close-knit families, productive work groups, and successful communities everywhere.

Community is more than an abstract thought, more than a state of feeling, more than a state of doing. Community, like other human constructs—parenthood, citizenship, etc.—involves "being with others" on all three planes of experience. The fact that community cannot be measured with accuracy and cannot be managed with precision doesn't take away from the fact that it is real, powerful, and important. Indeed, to experience community personally is to know firsthand its positive potential.

In building community, individuals from the boardroom to the shop floor must behave like "executives" in Drucker's sense of the word. As we work with each other in a myriad of group formats—organic departments, cross-functional teams, customer partnerships, industry-wide associations, etc.—everyone must master attitudes and skills that help the group succeed. This is the salvation for both the organization and the individual.

The following are norms of behavior that individuals should use to help build community and achieve group success. These apply to all types of people and all types of groups.

Norms of Behavior to Build Community

Set community goals. The success of the group depends on members aligning their personal goals with overall group goals. Try to identify with the goals and activities of the community. **Traditionals** will be at home in the goal-setting process.

Work to make the group successful. This is a general, but very helpful, principle. The commitment to succeed is, in itself, a cohesive and productive force in the community. Remember Ben Franklin's admonition at the signing of the Declaration of Independence, "We must indeed all hang together, or, most assuredly, we shall all hang separately."

Appreciate differences. Differences will come up in the life of a group. If differences become personalized, the effectiveness of the group will usually be reduced. Members should criticize ideas, but not the person expressing them. If your own ideas are criticized, don't take it personally. Group creativity is increased when we appreciate and make maximum use of our differences.

Use tact. Remember that you are dealing not only with group tasks, but with the feelings of other people. Be tactful and you will contribute to a healthy group.

Be enthusiastic. You do not have to be excited about everything that comes up. However, you should show enthusiasm for your own ideas and show genuine interest in the ideas of others.

Be friendly. Establish an easygoing, friendly relationship with the other members of the group. If you do not already know the other people, become acquainted with them early, and try to remain friendly throughout the life of the group. Membership in a group should be satisfying. **Participatives** will be an asset here.

Be cooperative. Help develop a spirit of teamwork by being cooperative with other members of the group. In particular, be willing to compromise as long as you do not compromise your value system. Remember that a team effort is basically a cooperative activity.

A group of young boys were on a hike when they came across an abandoned section of railroad tracks. Each of the boys took turns trying to walk the rails; but inevitably, each would fall off. Then two boys saw the solution to the problem. They bet the others they could walk the entire section without falling. When the other boys agreed to the wager, each maintained a separate rail and extended his hand to the other. Side by side, balancing each other, as a team, they accomplished the task.[25]

Keep a sense of humor. This does not mean you should restrict your contributions to jokes and humorous anecdotes. It means you should keep a sense of balance about things that happen in the life of the group. Don't allow yourself to become annoyed at minor setbacks or at irritating things said in discussions. The wry sense of humor and unusual thought processes of the **individualist** can be an asset here.

Consider the rewards. Belonging to a group may involve some personal costs: You may have to deal with people you do not like, or you may find some of the discussions to be uninteresting and tedious. On the other hand, rewards are many: pleasant associations, satisfaction with the results of the group's efforts, and pride of membership in the community. Your attitude should maximize the rewards and minimize the costs.

STAGES IN THE LIFE OF A GROUP

Regardless of size or type, a group typically goes through predictable stages over the course of time. Figure 11–1 is an illustration of four stages of group life as presented by Glen Parker and R. B. Lacoursiere.

Stage I *Forming.* In the start-up stage, the group is formed, but its purpose and members' expectations are unclear. This stage incorporates all of the discomfort and apprehension found in any new social situation. It is characterized by caution and tentative steps to test the water. Individuals try to determine acceptable behavior, the nature of the group's task, and how to deal with each other to get work done. Interactions are superficial and tend to be directed toward the formal leader. Skills and knowledge as a team are undeveloped. See table 11–1.

Stage II *Storming.* The initial stage of forming is followed by a period of storming. In this stage, individuals react to what has to be done, question authority, and feel increasingly comfortable being themselves. This stage can be characterized by conflict and resistance to the group's task and structure, even as productivity begins to increase as skills and knowledge develop. Group members express concerns and frustrations, and feel fairly free to exchange ideas. Members learn to deal with differences in order to work together to meet the group's goals. A group that doesn't get through this stage successfully is marked by divisiveness and low creativity. See table 11–2.

Stage III *Norming.* The stage of storming is usually followed by a third stage in the life of a group, a period of norming. In this stage, norms of behavior are

FIGURE 11–1   Stages in the Life of a Group[26]

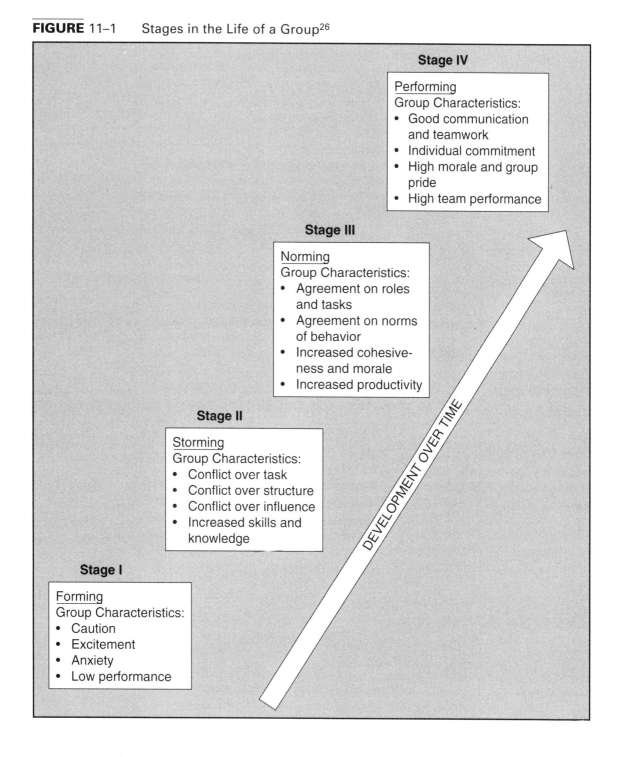

Stage IV

Performing
Group Characteristics:
• Good communication
  and teamwork
• Individual commitment
• High morale and group
  pride
• High team performance

Stage III

Norming
Group Characteristics:
• Agreement on roles
  and tasks
• Agreement on norms
  of behavior
• Increased cohesive-
  ness and morale
• Increased productivity

Stage II

Storming
Group Characteristics:
• Conflict over task
• Conflict over structure
• Conflict over influence
• Increased skills and
  knowledge

Stage I

Forming
Group Characteristics:
• Caution
• Excitement
• Anxiety
• Low performance

DEVELOPMENT OVER TIME

TABLE 11–1   Forming

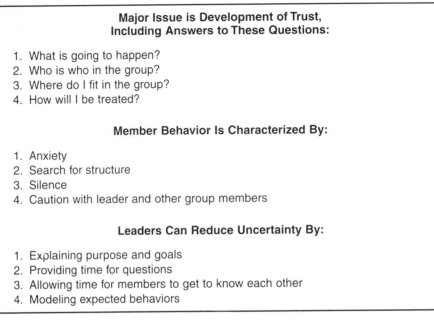

> **Major Issue is Development of Trust,**
> **Including Answers to These Questions:**
>
> 1. What is going to happen?
> 2. Who is who in the group?
> 3. Where do I fit in the group?
> 4. How will I be treated?
>
> **Member Behavior Is Characterized By:**
>
> 1. Anxiety
> 2. Search for structure
> 3. Silence
> 4. Caution with leader and other group members
>
> **Leaders Can Reduce Uncertainty By:**
>
> 1. Explaining purpose and goals
> 2. Providing time for questions
> 3. Allowing time for members to get to know each other
> 4. Modeling expected behaviors

TABLE 11–2   Storming

> **Major Issue Is Increased Conflict From:**
>
> 1. Openly dealing with problems
> 2. Increasing group interaction
> 3. Power struggles for influence
> 4. Increasing independence from leader
>
> **Member Behavior Is Characterized By:**
>
> 1. Confrontation with the leader
> 2. Polarization of team members
> 3. Testing of group tolerance
> 4. Fight or flight behavior
>
> **Leaders Can Reduce Conflict By:**
>
> 1. Hearing all points of view
> 2. Acknowledging conflict as opportunity for improvement
> 3. Adhering to core values, such as truth, trust, and respect
> 4. Maintaining democratic and humanistic ideals

developed that are considered necessary for the group to accomplish its task. These norms can be explicit or implicit. In any case, a greater degree of order begins to prevail and a sense of group cohesion develops. Members now identify with the group and develop customary ways for resolving conflict, making decisions, and completing assignments. In this stage, members typically enjoy meetings and freely exchange information. Productivity continues to increase as group skills and knowledge further develop. See table 11–3.

Stage IV *Performing.* Stage three is usually followed by a fourth stage, performing. This is the payoff stage in the life of a group. People are able to focus their energies on the task, having worked through issues of membership, purpose, structure, and roles. The group is now focused on solving problems and completing tasks. Members take initiative and their efforts emphasize results. As the group achieves significant milestones, morale goes up and people have positive feelings about each other and the accomplishments of the group. The group is no longer solely dependent upon the leader for direction and support; instead, each member takes on leadership roles as necessary. At this stage, the group shows the characteristics of an effective team. See table 11–4.

It is helpful to view each of the stages in the life of a group from two points of view. The first is *interpersonal relationships.* The group moves through predictable stages of testing and dependency (forming), tension and conflict

TABLE 11–3   Norming

Major Issue Is Development of Norms For:

1. Team member behavior
2. Decision-making processes
3. Resolving differences
4. Leadership behavior

Member Behavior Is Characterized by Shift From:

1. Power struggle to affiliation
2. Confusion to clarity
3. Personal advantage to group success
4. Detachment to involvement

Leaders Can Encourage Norm Development By:

1. Modeling listening skills
2. Fostering an atmosphere of trust
3. Teaching and facilitating consensus
4. Providing team-centered learning

TABLE 11–4   Performing

Major Issue Is Group Performance Including:

1. Using a wide range of task and process behaviors
2. Monitoring and taking pride in group accomplishments
3. Focusing on goals as well as interpersonal needs
4. Maintaining the values and norms of the group

Member Behavior Is Characterized By:

1. Interpersonal trust and mutual respect
2. Active resolution of conflict
3. Active participation
4. Personal commitment to the success of the group

Leaders Can Help the Group Succeed By:

1. Being prepared for temporary setbacks
2. Focusing on task accomplishments *and* interpersonal support
3. Providing feedback on the work of the group
4. Promoting and representing the group

(storming), building cohesion (norming), and finally, establishing functional role relationships (performing). Each of these stages focuses on problems inherent in developing relationships among group members.[27]

At the same time, the group is struggling with *accomplishing tasks*. The initial stage focuses on task definition and the exchange of information (forming). This is followed by discussion and conflict over the task (storming). Next comes a period of sharing interpretations and perspectives (norming). Finally, a stage of effective group performance is reached (performing).[28]

AVOIDING GROUPTHINK

As a group settles on norms of behavior in Stage III and into a mode of performance in Stage IV, there is a risk of falling into a pattern of groupthink. This is a well-documented pitfall in group dynamics identified by psychologist Irving Janis in *Victims of Groupthink*. Janis defined groupthink as "a mode of thinking that people engage in when they are deeply involved in a cohesive group, and when the members' striving for unanimity overrides their motivation to realistically appraise alternative courses of action."[29]

When people meet in groups they are often under strong pressure to conform to the majority view. When they don't conform, they risk being isolated or cast aside. In these situations people may make errors in judgment and conduct based on a desire to preserve group harmony and to continue to be accepted by the group and its leader.

Janis describes additional factors that, when combined with cohesiveness, can foster groupthink. These factors are a highly insulated group with restricted access to external information, and a stressful decision-making context, such as that brought on by budgetary crises, external pressure, or a history of recent setbacks. As a result of the trilogy of 1) *group cohesiveness*, 2) *isolation*, and 3) *stress*, a group can arrive at decisions that are unsuccessful and possibly even catastrophic.[30]

Janis describes eight symptoms that can give a group early warning that groupthink may be present. The following is a description of these symptoms with cases in history to illustrate their effects.[31]

Symptom 1: Illusion of Invulnerability

A feeling of power and authority is important to any decision-making group. It gives members confidence that they will be able to carry through on any decisions reached. However, if they come to believe that every decision they reach will automatically be successful, then they become prey to an *illusion of invulnerability*. Janis showed that American military leaders had this illusion in choosing not to more heavily fortify Pearl Harbor prior to the disastrous attack by the Japanese that led to U.S. entry into World War II.

Symptom 2: Belief in the Inherent Morality of the Group

People want to believe in the rightness of their actions. In the extreme, this can lead to exhortations that "God is on our side." Such claims fulfill an important function—they relieve responsibility for justifying decisions according to rational procedures. People do this as a way to protect self-esteem.

Symptom 3: Rationalization

In finalizing a decision, it is normal to downplay the drawbacks of a chosen course. The problem in a group arises when legitimate objections exist, but they are overshadowed by the perceived negative reaction to anyone voicing those objections. Key engineers in the NASA *Challenger* decision ultimately withdrew their objections to the ill-fated launch, not because of any correction in the admittedly problematic O-rings, but rather because they rationalized the risk of catastrophic launch failure as only "possible," while the risk of censure and ostracism for continuing to speak out against the launch became a virtual certainty.

Symptom 4: Stereotypes of Out-Groups

President Truman and his advisors fell victim to the temptation to falsely characterize enemy groups in 1950 with the decision to cross the 38th parallel, a line drawn by the Chinese Communists as a "line in the sand" between North and South Korea. The decision was made despite repeated warnings from Communist China that to do so would be viewed as a declaration of war by the United States upon China. How could Truman and his advisors have so seriously misinterpreted the Chinese warnings? The decision was based largely upon a false stereotype of the Chinese Communists as being weak and dominated by Russia who, it was believed, did not want war. The stereotype proved false, and the Korean "police action" became a resounding failure as the Chinese attacked with massive force.

Symptom 5: Self-Censorship

As one of the principles upon which our country was founded, the ability to express oneself without censorship has always been highly valued. It has also been considered a healthy safeguard against group coercion in our work lives. But the fact is, the most common form of censorship is that which we commit upon ourselves under the guise of group loyalty, team spirit, or adherence to *company policy*.

The decision to send a band of Cuban exiles into the Bay of Pigs by President Kennedy and his advisors has been ranked as the greatest foreign policy mistake of the Kennedy administration. The day after the Bay of Pigs, JFK said, "How could I have been so stupid?" The answer is, they wanted it to be true. Kennedy and his advisors suppressed their doubts, censoring themselves to make the operative belief seem like the truth.

Symptom 6: Direct Pressure

Pressure upon group members can surface in many forms. The net effect is the same: Group members are encouraged to keep dissident views to themselves. Janis reported that during Watergate, "Nixon time and again let everyone in the group know which policy he favored, and he did not encourage open inquiry." After several engineers had made their recommendation to postpone the *Challenger* launch, the Rogers Commission report identifies instances of group members responding with *direct pressure* on the engineers to alter their views, with statements such as "I'm appalled that they could arrive at the recommendation . . .", and "At that rate, it could be spring before the shuttle would fly."

Symptom 7: Mindguards

A bodyguard is someone charged with the protection of another person's physical well-being. In groupthink, a corollary entity may surface to protect the group from disturbing thoughts and ideas—a *mindguard*. Interestingly, such mindguards typically perform their function not within the group itself, but far from the confines of group discussion. Data, facts, and opinions that might bear directly upon the group are deliberately kept out of the group's purview. Generally this is done with a variety of justifiable intentions—the time factor, a regular member will "summarize" for the group, not pertinent, and saddest of all perhaps, "the group has already made up its mind."

Symptom 8: Illusion of Unanimity

Finally, the rationalizations, psychological pressures, and mindguards have their effect—the group coalesces around a decision. Drawbacks are downplayed and the invulnerability and morality of the final course is reinforced. Doubting group members may even feel that they have adequately put their own fears to rest. More likely, it is simply the sense of relief that the struggle has come to an end. An *illusion of unanimity* sets in.

In contrast to the destructive forces of groupthink, there are a number of techniques that can be employed to help ensure a rational survey of all available courses of action:

1. The leader of a group should assign the role of critical evaluator to each member, encouraging the group to give open airing of ideas, including objections and doubts. This practice should be reinforced by the leader's acceptance of criticism of his or her own judgments.

2. When charging a group with a task, the leader should adopt an impartial stance instead of stating personal opinions and preferences. This will encourage open discussion and impartial probing of a wide range of policy and problem-solving alternatives.

3. The group should set up outside evaluators to work on the same policy question. This can prevent the group from being insulated from important information and suggestions.

4. When the agenda calls for evaluation of decision or policy alternatives, at least one member should play devil's advocate, functioning as a lawyer in challenging the testimony of those who advocate for a position.

5. After reaching a preliminary consensus about what seems to be the best policy or decision, the group should hold a "second-chance" meeting at which every member expresses as clearly as possible all residual doubts, and rethinks the entire issue before making a final decision.[32]

GROUP EFFECTIVENESS: HOW ORDINARY PEOPLE DO EXTRAORDINARY THINGS

Individualism is a key element in the American value system. It is the wellspring of entrepreneurship and creativity. Overused though, this great strength can become a weakness if it results in neglect of cooperation and group effort.[33]

A group must gain the commitment and channel the energies of each member of the community. Group effectiveness must be developed without sacrificing individual creativity. The following are important principles and techniques in group dynamics. These will be of interest to leaders and members alike as they work together to achieve success.

Many of these ideas can be traced to the thinking of psychologist Kurt Lewin. Lewin's influence is everywhere in community building—participative leadership, the role of culture, work design, even the use of newsprint and flip charts—but never more so than in our understanding of team concepts and processes. Margaret Mead once said of Lewin, "His special understanding of American ideals of democracy led him to the clear recognition that you cannot do things to people, but only with them."[34] At the core of Lewin's teachings is the simple dictum: People want to be included versus excluded, and they want autonomy versus servitude. Therefore, they will be more committed to solutions they have helped to design than to carrying out "expert advice" or "autocratic orders."[35]

To tap the constructive power of the group, use the following principles and techniques:[36]

Manage group size. Group membership should be small enough to allow free-flowing discussion, but large enough for effective follow-through on decisions. Having too many members inhibits discussion; having too few reduces the quality of ideas generated as well as the energy and power needed to implement decisions. No fewer than four members, but no more than twelve, constitutes a good work group size; five is considered to be ideal for most purposes. A major factor to consider is practicality—who should be in the group if the group is to be successful? If less than four individuals comprise an organic group, this should be the size; if a functional work group or classification has thirteen or more members, include everyone, perhaps dividing into smaller groups. Avoid excluding people on the basis of some ideal group size.

Agree on direction. A vision for the group, including purpose and goals, is important because it provides guidelines for action, motivates group members, and helps the group conduct and evaluate activities. The group's plans should be formulated in such a way that all members can commit themselves to them. An example goal may be to identify a problem affecting the quality of work or the quality of life of the group, study causes of the problem, determine the best solution, and make recommendations for improvement, including costs and benefits.

Agree on rules. Determine the guidelines or code of conduct by which the group will function. Rules should be few, but they should be in writing. When possible, members should help develop team rules. An individual may choose not to participate because of the rules, but this is preferable to having a group without guidelines. Agreeing on rules avoids misunderstanding. Sample rules include:

- Keep an open mind; look for merit in others' ideas.
- Everyone in the group is responsible for the group's success.
- Attend meetings regularly and participate actively in group discussion.
- Criticize ideas, not people.
- Give credit to others for a job well done.
- Be friendly, cooperative, and enthusiastic in group activities.
- Have the attitude, "the only poor question is the one not asked."

Arrange a time and location for meetings. The group should meet often enough to develop team spirit and maintain momentum. The setting for group meetings should allow private and uninterrupted discussion. Meeting once a week for approximately one or two hours in a quiet conference room is usually ideal.

Allow sufficient time. Most group efforts require time. Imagine the time needed to obtain facts, analyze information, and make plans to solve a work-flow bottleneck, new product rollout, or customer relations problem. Meeting an hour or two a week over a series of weeks is usually sufficient time for a group to solve important problems.

Keep things informal. The atmosphere of the group should be informal and comfortable. People have to feel free to be themselves. If this can be accomplished, they will relate to the group and work for its success.

Help people contribute. Every member should contribute to the success of the team. Contributions may include technical knowledge, job skills, information, problem-solving ability, and group process skills. Rick Pitino, basketball coach of the University of Kentucky Wildcats, explains, "You have to make everyone know they are valuable. It just can't be your star players. Everybody has to perform if you are going to build a championship team or a successful business."[37]

Consider people's needs. Whether needs are for security, social interaction, recognition, or self-fulfillment, participation should satisfy the personal goals of each group member. Pitino states, "Every individual in an organization is motivated by something different. You must learn what makes each person act. You can't motivate an entire team to perform, unless you understand what motivates every individual."[38]

Reach out to isolates. An individual may feel unaccepted by the group and find it difficult to interact with others. If other people reach out and involve this person, team spirit and productivity usually will increase.

Provide emotional support. Support can take the form of encouraging others to express ideas, listening in order to understand, and providing help with difficult problems. The leader should set an example that will encourage group members to help one another.

Encourage communication. Every person in the group should have a voice. Although a formal leader may have ultimate responsibility to accept or reject recommendations, time and energy will be wasted if the leader exercises undue influence during discussions. No special deference to the leader should exist as the group operates. The focus of concern should be on how to get the job done, not who controls.

Give every idea a hearing. Every member of the group has a duty to listen to every other member. The person who listens to the ideas of others creates an atmosphere of respect in which others are encouraged to express themselves. Sometimes you may wish that others would be quiet and do what you want without question. You should fight this impulse, as it is inconsiderate and counterproductive in the long run.

Express ideas freely. Every member of the group should express ideas openly and share information. A common problem is fear of what others will think or say, and therefore saying nothing. Self-censure reduces the effectiveness of the team. The quality of the group's work will reflect the extent of openness of members. New, divergent, and unusual ideas should be voiced.

Build trust within the group. Conversations of the group should remain confidential. A group will fail if members do not trust each other. Gossip and stories repeated outside group meetings create serious problems. A lack of confidentiality results in distrust, reduced goodwill, and lowered overall effectiveness of the group.

Take disagreement in stride. Disagreement should be expected among group members. When it occurs, it should not be suppressed by premature peacemaking or by domination of dissenters. Carefully examine each point of conflict and consider every argument with the goal of making the best decision possible.

Don't take criticism personally. Individuals should focus on group success. An individual whose ideas are accepted should be glad for the quality of work, not for personal victory. An individual whose ideas are not accepted should not feel personal rejection, but should continue to seek the best solution for the group as a whole.

Respect informal leaders. Most groups have one or more members with leadership qualities. An informal leader can be influential in swaying group opinion and may act as spokesperson in matters of importance to the group. The formal leader who respects the contribution of informal leaders maintains morale in the group. If the formal leader shows resentment, the confidence and support of the group may be lost.

Avoid taking votes. Formal voting should be held to a minimum. The group should avoid using simple majority rule as the basis of action. Decisions should be reached only after thorough discussion. In this way, solutions represent a consensus to which all group members are in general agreement and to which all are committed.

Obtain the commitment of the whole group. Once a decision has been made, all members of the group should act as a unified whole. Effective problem solving requires divergent views when considering alternatives and convergent effort when implementing solutions. A sports team should consider many ideas when deciding which play to call, but once the course of action is determined, every individual must give total commitment if the game is to be won.

Assign responsibility for follow-through. When making a decision, members should agree on assignments and set time frames for action. Unless they do this, the principle "out of sight, out of mind" is likely to take effect, and follow-through will suffer.

Follow through on commitments. Leaders and members who fail to follow through on commitments stand a good chance of losing the respect of the group. Bonds of loyalty and trust that are so important for group cohesion will be weakened, the group will become demoralized, and overall effectiveness will be reduced. Follow-through on commitments reflects *honesty* and *dependability*. Individuals must embody these basic qualities if a group is to succeed.

Support the group. A time-tested way to increase group effectiveness is for the leader to be active in bringing the requests and the accomplishments of the group to the attention of others. Advocating for the needs and promoting the successes of the group is a proven way to build team spirit.

Build group confidence.   A group needs to feel a sense of accomplishment. When a team gets stuck, encourage it to go for an easy victory. Success, even on a small scale, will restore the winning spirit.[39]

Use competition and cooperation where appropriate.   This is an art employed by successful leaders in all areas—politics, military, business, etc. They have learned one of the best ways to develop team spirit is to rally members of the group to work with each other to combat real or imagined adversaries. Competition is encouraged against outside groups, such as competing sports teams or business organizations. At the same time, internal competition is discouraged between interdependent individuals and groups, such as line and staff, office and field, operations and maintenance, etc.

In a competitive situation, when one person reaches the goal, others will, to some degree, be unable to obtain their goals. Each person is out for himself or herself. In a cooperative situation, if one person reaches the goal, all other members are helped in reaching their goals. Whether the situation is cooperative or competitive influences a wide variety of group processes, including attitudes and willingness to work with others as well as the attractiveness, cohesiveness, and effectiveness of the group. Research shows that productivity is usually greater in cooperative than in competitive group situations, and that the quality of both the products and the group interactions are higher in cooperative groups.[40]

Conditions where people cooperate as a group in support of each other as they compete against external groups in a free and open market brings forth the greatest gain for the greatest number of people as a whole.

Follow enlightened self-interest practices.   It is true that within a group, cooperation is the best approach if the goal is to achieve the greatest good for the greatest number over a period of time. It is also true that some individuals may be tempted to put immediate self-gain above long-term group success. Given this dilemma, what is the best strategy for an individual or group to take? In an important book, *The Evolution of Cooperation*, Robert Axelrod describes a mirroring approach that helps people develop a climate of trust and respect without becoming victims of unscrupulous or immature behavior.

> In each new interaction with another person, begin or lead with overtly cooperative behavior; then respond in kind to every subsequent response. If the person cooperates, do so as well; if the person competes, do so as well. This strategy of reciprocity works when two conditions are present: First, there is an opportunity to cooperate; second, there is an anticipated opportunity for the parties to interact in the future. Because these conditions are present in most families, work groups, and other organizations, there is ample opportunity to benefit from enlightened self-interest practices. An example from the home front makes the point well: A mother tells how she gets her two boys to divide a cupcake exactly in half. "I tell them that one will do the cutting and the other will select whichever half he wants. The first child always cuts straight down the middle."[41]

Use group incentives. A key strategy for encouraging teamwork is to reward the group as a whole. If the leader receives praise, it should be shared with members of the group, since accomplishments are based on team effort. If financial rewards are gained through creative product development, efficient production, aggressive marketing, sound administrative practices, and insightful cost-saving suggestions, all members should share in the rewards. Individuals do what is reinforced. If behaving in a spirit of community is recognized positively, it will continue; if on the other hand, people receive rewards by looking out for their own interest or gain, this behavior will continue.

TEAM BUILDING—TAPPING THE CONSTRUCTIVE POWER OF THE GROUP

Douglas McGregor wrote that a strong strain of individualism is alive in all of us nurtured in the spirit of democracy. However, the complexity of the work environment and the structure of modern organizations create a situation in which it is no longer possible to comprehend or conduct the operation of the organization without some form of teamwork and team building.[42]

Writing in *The Different Drum*, Scott Peck describes the importance of self-evaluation in the team-building process.

> Community building requires self-examination from the beginning. As members become thoughtful about themselves, they also learn to become thoughtful about the group. "How are we doing?" they begin to ask with greater and greater frequency. "Are we still on target? Are we a healthy group?[43]

Peck describes self-evaluation as an ongoing activity that is characteristic of all healthy groups.

> The spirit of community once achieved is not something forever obtained. It is not something that can be bottled or preserved in aspic. It is repeatedly lost. No group can expect to be in perpetual good health. What a genuine community does do, however, is recognize its ill health when it occurs, and quickly takes appropriate action to heal itself. Indeed, the longer they exist, the more efficient healthy communities become in this recovery process. Conversely, groups that never learn to be contemplative either do not become communities in the first place or else rapidly and permanently disintegrate.[44]

New and established groups can benefit from team-building efforts. Psychologist Brendan Reddy identifies four important purposes for team building:

- Setting goals and priorities.

- Analyzing the way work is performed, including team member roles and responsibilities.

- Examining the way team processes are working, such as agenda setting, decision making, communication, and so forth.

■ Strengthening relationships among team members.[45]

In *Productive Workplaces*, Marvin Weisbord describes four conditions or requirements for effective team building:

■ *Interdependence*. The team is working on important problems in which each person has a stake. Teamwork is important for success.

■ *Leadership*. The leader wants so strongly to improve group performance that he or she will take risks and involve team members.

■ *Participation*. Team members are willing to actively participate—sharing ideas, sharing information, and making other contributions.

■ *Influence*. Each person has a chance to influence events and outcomes.[46]

In *Improving Work Groups: A Practical Manual for Team Building*, Dave Francis and Don Young describe the collective learning that is at the core of all team building. Groups must find answers to seven key questions:

1. What are we here to do? What is our purpose or goal?

2. How should we organize ourselves? Who is going to do what?

3. Who is in charge? How are decisions made?

4. Who cares about our success? Who are the stakeholders?

5. How do we work through problems? How do we resolve conflict?

6. How do we fit in with other groups? Who are our customers, suppliers, allies, and adversaries?

7. What do team members need to receive from the team?[47]

There are many approaches to team building. The most common is for members of a group to develop and grow together over the normal course of time as the team responds to challenges and successfully performs its natural functions.

Team building can be enhanced by experiential strategies and activities. Educational workshops in retreat settings are increasingly popular. This off-site format focuses on topics such as communication, teamwork, valuing diversity, characteristics of effective groups, positive versus negative group member roles, and workshops/labs to improve team performance—goal setting, values clarification, problem solving, decision making, etc.

Some organizations use outward-bound type experiences that can be quite effective at building relationships, developing group identity, and increasing team pride. These interventions are usually conducted in field settings and involve a range of activities that include "ground" or low course initiatives to build team spirit and skills, and "ropes" or high course challenges that build individual confidence and pride.

The following exercise is a process for team building that is simple, but very powerful. It is applicable to virtually any organization and any size of group. It shows the value of getting members of the community together in a supportive atmosphere free of interruptions, and taking the time to discuss basic questions affecting the life of the group. The time required varies, but usually ranges from several hours to several days.

This exercise is a variation of Kurt Lewin's famous *force field theory* for improving team performance. By looking at the group as a whole and taking steps to add to positive forces while decreasing negative forces, the group can improve overall team effectiveness.

APPLICATION: TEAM EXCELLENCE[48]

Directions

1. Individually answer the following questions.

2. Gather and display all ideas.

3. Discuss and prioritize critical points in each area.

4. Agree on actions to be taken.

5. Agree on *who* will be responsible for *what* by *when* to ensure follow-through for group effectiveness.

To operate as an effective team, we need the following:

- _____

- _____

- _____

- _____

Things we should *continue doing* are:

- _____

- _____

- _____

- _____

Things we should *start doing* are:

- ■ _____
- ■ _____
- ■ _____
- ■ _____

Things we should *stop doing* are:

- ■ _____
- ■ _____
- ■ _____
- ■ _____

We should *monitor our progress* by:

- ■ _____
- ■ _____
- ■ _____
- ■ _____

Actions to be taken, including *who* should do *what* by *when*, are as follows:

_____

_____

_____

_____

_____

_____

_____

_____

_____

DECIDING WHEN TO USE A TEAM APPROACH

There are times for the *genius stroke*, when just one person can best perform an act or accomplish a certain feat. Beethoven's music comes to mind. Also, there are times for *tapping the constructive power of the group*. Consider the following factors when deciding which approach to use.

A team approach usually works best when:

- Group acceptance is necessary for effective implementation. People tend to work harder to implement decisions they help to make.

- Knowledge and skill from more than one person is needed to make the best decision or product.

- Group members possess specific information, problem-solving expertise, and group process skills.

- There is sufficient time to meet as a group, discuss alternatives, and agree on a course of action.

- The highest quality or most effective solution is desired.[49]

An individual approach usually works best when:

- A decision involves a routine or simple task.

- Group members are already in agreement.

- Consensus or buy-in is not important.

- Immediate action is required; there is no time for discussion.

- Compliance is fairly absolute.[50]

DESIGNING TEAMS FOR SUCCESS

A team is a cooperative association that uses the contributions of each member of the group. Well-balanced teams are unlikely to be formed spontaneously. Teams can be *designed for success*.

When a group approach is appropriate, the following questionnaire can be used to construct teams for balance and diagnose existing teams for potential strengths and weaknesses. Note that the questionnaire evaluates problem-solving style, not ability.

APPLICATION: PROBLEM-SOLVING STYLES—DARWIN, EINSTEIN, SOCRATES, OR FORD—WHICH ARE YOU?[51]

Directions

There are ten sets of phrases below. Rank each set by assigning a 4 to the phrase that is most like your problem-solving style, a 3 to the one next most like your style, a 2 to the one next most like your style, and a 1 to the phrase that is least like your problem-solving style. Be sure to assign a different number to each phrase—do not make ties.

Example

_2_ Emotional	_1_ Thorough	_3_ Rational	_4_ Active
E	**R**	**T**	**A**
___ Following instincts	___ Weighing evidence	___ Developing thoughts	___ Accomplishing goals
___ Relying on feelings	___ Considering facts	___ Considering potentialities	___ Trying things out
___ Being perceptive	___ Measuring effects	___ Thinking things through	___ Taking action
___ Emotional involvement	___ Impartial investigation	___ Rational analysis	___ Practical use
___ Being aware	___ Questioning details	___ Using reason	___ Performing deeds
___ Letting intuition guide	___ Recording information	___ Summarizing truths	___ Applying solutions
___ Present-oriented	___ Evaluation-oriented	___ Future-oriented	___ Achievement-oriented
___ Open to experience	___ Reflective observation	___ Conceiving ideas	___ Applying knowledge
___ Conscious of events	___ Studying data	___ Forming theories	___ Taking risks
___ Concrete experience	___ Unbiased inquiry	___ Abstract thinking	___ Producing results

Scoring

When you have completed the questionnaire, find the total score for each column and insert in the appropriate spaces:

___ Total for   ___ Total for   ___ Total for   ___ Total for
    E column   R column   T column   A column

Record your totals for E, R, T, and A on the appropriate axes in figure 11–2, and connect these scores with straight lines to make a picture of your problem-solving style. The longest line of your four-sided figure indicates your preferred style—Darwin, Einstein, Socrates, or Henry Ford.

FIGURE 11–2   A Picture of Your Problem-Solving Style

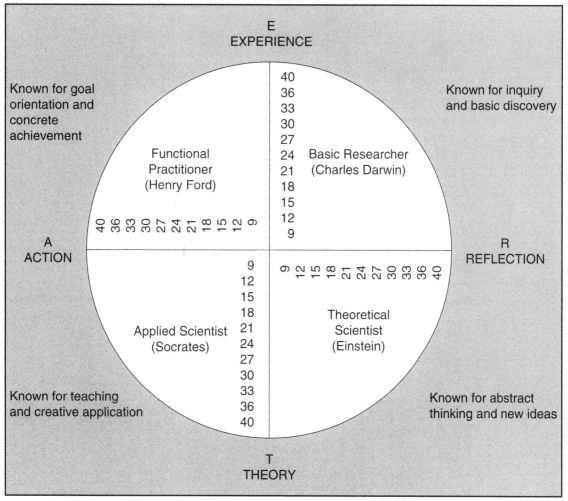

Interpretation

All problem solving involves having experience (E), reflecting on results (R), building theories (T), and taking action (A). These constitute four steps of the problem-solving cycle (see figure 11–3). The following is a description of this cycle, including the strengths and potential weaknesses of each style—Darwin, Einstein, Socrates, and Henry Ford.

Having experiences (step 1) is followed by reflecting on results (step 2). If the longest line of your four-sided figure is between E and R (see figure 11–4), your preferred style of problem-solving is like that of Charles Darwin (1809–1882), author of *On The Origin of the Species by Means of Natural Selection* and *The Descent of Man and Selection in Relation to Sex.* About himself, Darwin wrote, "My mind seems to have become a kind of machine for grinding general laws out of large collections of facts."[52]

FIGURE 11–3   The Problem-Solving Cycle

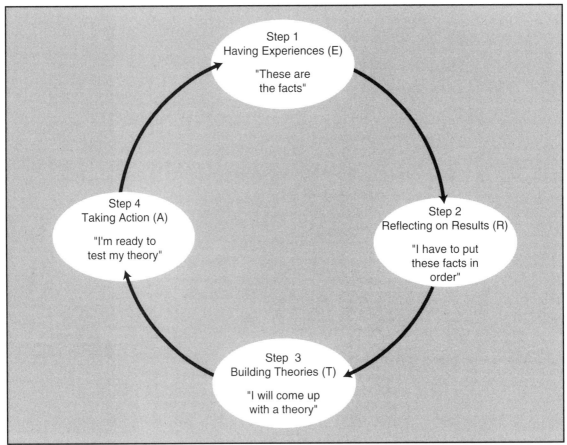

FIGURE 11–4   The Charles Darwin Problem-Solving Style

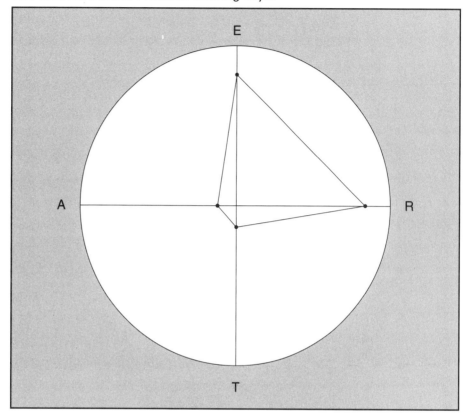

As a Darwin, your strengths are observing, recording facts, and identify-ing alternatives. Gathering data is enjoyable to you. By style, you are a basic researcher and you love the discovery process. Darwins are known in every field—social science, natural science, the arts, business, and the professions—for their thorough data collection and objective analysis. Carried to an extreme, however, the Darwin style of problem solving can lead to paralysis as each new fact becomes even more interesting than the last, resulting in indecision. It is important to look before leaping, but it is possible to look so long that one never leaps. Consider the case of Darwin himself, who had developed his theories of human evolution years before another scientist came to similar conclusions and would have received credit for these theories . . . had not Darwin at last published.

After the data are gathered, theory building takes place (step 3). At this stage, assumptions are developed and ideas are formulated. One moves from the world of experience into the world of theory, while remaining in the mode of reflecting rather than acting. If the longest line of your figure is between R and T (see figure 11–5), your preferred style of problem solving is that of the theoretical scientist—the Einstein style. Abstract conceptualization and blue-sky thinking are your forte. In his description of the world, Einstein wrote, "Physical concepts are free creations of the human mind, and are not, however it may seem, uniquely determined by the external world."

The Einstein style of problem solving is like that of the typical philosopher. Carried to an extreme, the results can be castles in the air with little practical value. This is the style of the husband whose wife says, "That's good, Albert . . . but when are you going to *do* something?"

After theories have been developed, they must be tested (step 4). If your longest line is between T and A (see figure 11–6), your preferred style is that of the applied scientist. Your strength is not in collecting and analyzing data, but

FIGURE 11–5   The Einstein Problem-Solving Style

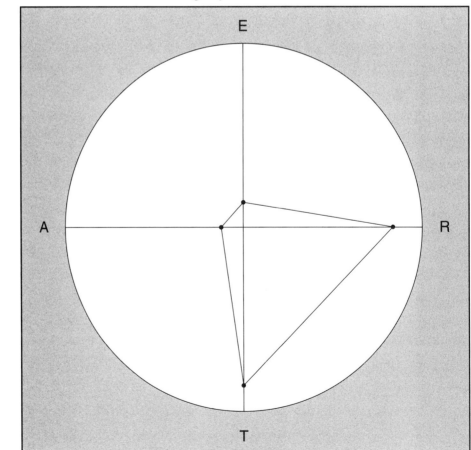

FIGURE 11–6   The Socrates Problem-Solving Style

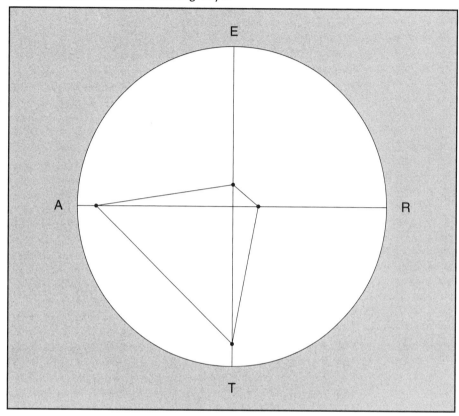

in translating ideas so they can be put into action. As such, yours is the style of the teacher Socrates (470–399 B.C.):

> Socrates wrote nothing that was published. Yet we know him as one of the greatest teachers in history, perhaps the greatest of the great men produced by Athens. His name commands admiration, honor, and reverence. Men and women were his objective; to them he had a mission. He wandered through the streets and down to the marketplace, or often he would go to the public gymnasium. Then he started business—the business of teaching. The life of Socrates was a living example of his ideas. His philosophy, as set forth by Plato, marks an epic in human thought. "He brought philosophy down from heaven to earth," wrote Cicero. For Socrates was the founder of moral philosophy. He was scoffed at for taking his examples from common life, but he did so to lead plain people to goodness, truth, and beauty.[53]

A more modern example of the Socrates problem-solving style is Thomas Alva Edison: "The only invention I can really claim as absolutely original is the phonograph," explained Edison. "I'm an awfully good sponge. I absorb ideas from every source I can and then I put them to practical use. Then I improve them until they become of some value. The ideas that I use are mostly the ideas of other people who don't develop them themselves."

Comfortable with ideas, but wanting to apply them, the applied scientist moves from a reflective to an active orientation. This person enjoys coordinating and problem-solving activities. When taken to extreme, the Socrates style of work may result in impressive, but incomplete performance. This is because these individuals dislike details. The Socrates-type person may give a beautiful speech, but fail to do thorough research.

Taking action automatically results in new experiences (step 1), so the problem-solving cycle never completely ends. In work, and in life, when one problem is solved, another arises. If your longest line is between A and C (see figure 11–7), your style of problem solving is like that of Henry Ford (1863–1947), whose strength was achieving results. Upton Sinclair described Henry Ford, the functional practitioner, as follows:

FIGURE 11–7   The Henry Ford Problem-Solving Style

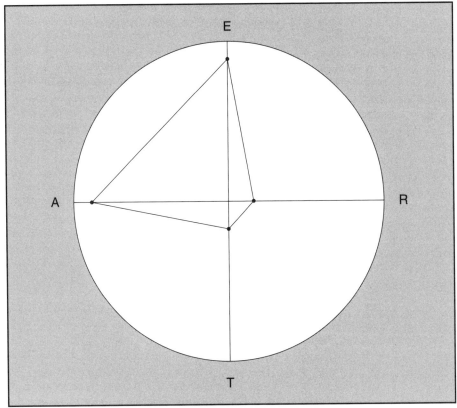

Henry Ford was now fifty-five; slender, grey-haired, with sensitive features and a quick, nervous manner. His long, thin hands were never still, but were always playing with something. He was a kind man, unassuming, not changed by his great success, the world's first billionaire. Having had less than a grammar-school education, his speech was full of the peculiarities of the plain folk of the Middle West. He had never learned to deal with theories, and when confronted with one, he would scuttle back to the facts like a rabbit to its hole. What Ford knew he had learned by experience, and if he learned more, it would be in the same manner.[54]

If the functional practitioner knows what needs to be done, the goal will usually be accomplished. This is a person of deeds and action, more than ideas and contemplation. But here, as with the other problem-solving styles, a strength may become a liability when carried to extreme. If the functional practitioner does not have sufficient facts, or fails to work from a well-conceived plan, there may be tremendous accomplishment . . . of the wrong thing.

The versatile style of problem solving is represented by figure 11–8. This individual is equally comfortable with each step of the problem-solving cycle—having

FIGURE 11–8   A Versatile Style of Problem Solving—No Dominant Preference Is Indicated

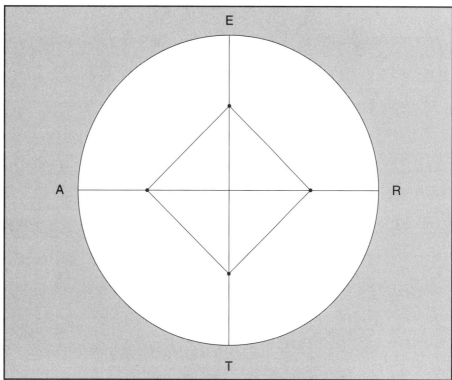

experiences, reflecting on results, building theories, and taking action. As such, this person does not have structural strengths or weaknesses resulting from style preference.

There are several important points to remember concerning styles of problem solving:

- All problem solving involves the four steps—having experiences, reflecting on results, building theories, taking action—and each step must be performed well for overall effectiveness. An independent businessperson with a Socrates style must take extra care to consider details as well as concepts, and should remember to get the facts before making decisions, even if this does not come naturally.

- It is possible to have more than one long line in a problem-solving style picture. This shows preference for more than one style of problem solving. A person may be equally comfortable as a Henry Ford and a Socrates. Such a person relates to the world in both an experiential and a theoretical sense. In either case, though, this person shows a bias for action.

- When people with different styles of problem solving live or work together, tolerance is required. A Henry Ford manager must be patient with the seeming lack of effort put forth by an Einstein employee, and a Socrates wife must try to understand her Darwin husband's preference for having experiences and reflecting on results over forming ideas and applying knowledge. An understanding and appreciation of the characteristics and needs of each type of person can go a long way toward improving relationships and increasing productivity.

- Most people have difficulty changing their styles of problem solving. This can be seen in school when a student fails or drops out. It is usually Henry Ford students who fail or drop out, not Einstein types. Often the cause is the nature of the curriculum and the style of instruction, not the ability of the student. The functional practitioner, who wants to apply knowledge and accomplish tangible results, has difficulty relating to book reading and theoretical discussion.

A community or group needs all four styles of problem solving. A balance of basic research, theoretical science, applied science, and functional practice helps to maximize individual as well as group performance. Consider the following story:

Fred was a successful research chemist when he suffered a heart attack. During his stay in the hospital, his work was performed by younger employees. Like many large organizations, Fred's company was rich in talent, and others were qualified to do his job.

When Fred recovered and returned to work, he retained his title, his office was the same, and his income was unchanged. However, he had lost a significant part of his job—his duties were now "make work" assignments, while important responsibilities and decision making were handled by others. Whereas Fred had been physically ill before, he now became depressed, and his overall health began to deteriorate. Fred had been placed on the shelf, and he knew it.

At that time, Fred's company began research and development of a new product, and the *Problem-Solving Styles* questionnaire was used to create a balanced team. On the team was a theoretical scientist, who could write formulas from wall to wall, but who few could understand. This was the Einstein. Also on the team was an applied scientist, who could understand the Einstein's ideas and who knew how to bridge the gap between thinking and doing. The team had a Socrates. The team also had a Henry Ford, who was known for his practical nature. He was a goal-oriented person with the ability to produce results. What was missing on the new-product team was a Charles Darwin, a basic scientist, who would be sure that all the facts were gathered and all the data were considered. Fred was chosen to be the team's Darwin.

Within a year, the team developed one of the company's most successful products. A year after that, Fred's wife phoned him at work. By accident, she reached his boss. She said: "Oh, Mr. Johnson, I have been wanting to talk to you for so long. I have wanted to thank you . . . for giving my Fred back to me."[55]

Fred's story shows how the needs of the individual and the needs of the community are interwoven and how both can be met by creating a balanced team incorporating all four styles of problem solving.

REFERENCES

1. M. Scott Peck, *The Different Drum* (New York: Simon and Schuster, 1987).

2. Peck, *The Different Drum*.

3. Carl M. Moore, "A Working Paper on Community," National Conference on Peacemaking and Conflict Resolution (Fairfax, VA: George Mason University, 1991).

4. Peter Farb, *Humankind* (Boston: Houghton-Mifflin, 1978), 253.

5. Farb, *Humankind*, 253.

6. Emile Durkheim, *Professional Ethics and Civic Morals*, trans. Cornelia Brookfield (New York: Routledge, 1992); Georg Simmel, *The Sociology of Georg Simmel*, trans. and ed., Kurt Wolff (Glencoe, IL: Free Press, 1950); and Max Weber, *Basic Concepts in Sociology*, trans. H. P. Secher (New York: Philosophical Library, 1962).

7. Bernard Berelson and Gary Steiner, *Human Behavior* (New York: Harcourt, Brace, and World, 1964).

8. Moore, "A Working Paper on Community."

9. Peck, *The Different Drum*, 77–78.

10. Fran Tarkenton, "The Management Huddle: Making Group Decisions Work," *Sky* (July 1979): 50.

11. Jon Katzenbach and Douglas Smith, *The Wisdom of Teams* (Boston: Harvard Business School Press, 1993).

12. Peck, *The Different Drum*, 73–74.

13. Ashley Montagu, *On Being Human* (New York: Henry Schuman, 1950), 103.

14. Warren Bennis, *Professional Trainer*—McGraw-Hill Training System, 5 (Winter 1985); and Douglas McGregor, *The Human Side of Enterprise* (New York: McGraw-Hill, 1960).

15. Edgar Schein in Douglas McGregor, *The Professional Manager* (New York: McGraw-Hill, 1967), xii.

16. Bennis, *Professional Trainer*.

17. Steve Martin, Northern Kentucky University, based on McGregor, *The Human Side of Enterprise*, 232–235.

18. William Stattler and N. Edd Miller, *Discussion and Conference* (Englewood Cliffs, NJ: Prentice-Hall, 1968), 297–301, 303–305, 309–312, 331–334; and John Hasling, *Group Discussion and Decision-Making* (New York: Thomas Crowell/Harper and Row,1975), 33–42.

19. Harry Levinson, "The Abrasive Personality at the Office," *Psychology Today* (May 1978): 78–84.

20. Peter Drucker, "The New Society of Organizations," *Harvard Business Review* (September/October, 1993): 101–102.

21. Robert B. Reich, "Nobody is Safe," *Time* (March 29, 1993): 46–47.

22. Reich, "Nobody is Safe."

23. Reich, "Nobody is Safe."

24. K. P. DeMuse and Walter W. Tornow, "Leadership and the Changing Psychological Contract Between Employers and Employee," *Issues and Observations, Center for Creative Leadership*, 13, no. 2 (1993).

25. Marvin G. Gregory, ed., *Bits and Pieces* (Fairfield, NJ: The Economics Press).

26. Based on Glen M. Parker, *Teamplayers and Teamwork* (San Francisco: Jossey-Bass, 1990); and R. B. Lacoursiere, *The Life Cycle of Groups* (New York: Human Service Press, 1980).

27. B. W. Tuckman and M. A. C. Jensen, "Stages of Small-Group Development Revisited," *Group and Organizational Studies*, 2, no. 4 (1977): 419–427.

28. Tuckman and Jensen, "Stages of Small-Group Development Revisited."

29. Irving L. Janis, "Groupthink," *Psychology Today*, 5, no. 6 (1971): 43–46, 74–76.

30. Janis, "Groupthink"; Irving L. Janis, *The Anatomy of Power* (New York: Houghton-Mifflin, 1982); and "Groupthink: The Challenger Disaster," and "Organization Dynamics: Groupthink," videos from CRM Educational Films, Del Mar, CA.

31. Janis, "Groupthink"; Janis, *The Anatomy of Power*; and "Groupthink: The Challenger Disaster"; and "Organization Dynamics: Groupthink."

32. Janis, "Groupthink"; Janis, *The Anatomy of Power*; and "Groupthink: The Challenger Disaster"; and "Organization Dynamics: Groupthink."

33. Marvin R. Weisbord, *Productive Workplaces* (San Francisco: Jossey-Bass, 1990), 296.

34. Margaret Mead, "Cultural Discontinuities and Personality Transformation," *Journal of Social Issues*, 39, no. 4 (1983): 161–177; reprinted from *JSI Supplement*, 8 (1954): 3–16.

35. Weisbord, *Productive Workplaces*.

36. Douglas McGregor, "The Human Side of Management," from *Proceedings of the Fifth Anniversary of the School of Industrial Management* (Cambridge, Mass: MIT, 1957); and Andrew J. DuBrin, *Comtemporary Applied Management* (Plano, TX: Business Publications, 1982), 90–152.

37. Michael Marin, "Win: A Master Motivator (Rick Pitino) Teaches You to Create Superstars," *Success* (April 1992).

38. Marin, "Win."

39. Katzenback and Smith, *The Wisdom of Teams.*

40. M. Deutsch, "An Experimental Study of the Effects of Cooperation and Competition Upon Group Process," *Human Relations,* 2 (1949): 129–152, 199–231.

41. Robert Axelrod, *Evolution of Cooperation* (New York: Basic Books, 1984).

42. McGregor, *The Professional Manager,* 181.

43. Peck, *The Different Drum,* 66.

44. Peck, *The Different Drum,* 66–67.

45. Brendan Reddy and Kaleel Jamison, *Team Building: Blueprints for Productivity and Satisfaction* (Alexandria, VA: NTL Institute for Applied Behavioral Science) and (San Diego: University Associates, 1988), 3.

46. Weisbord, *Productive Workplaces,* 299.

47. Dave Francis and Don Young, *Improving Work Groups: A Practical Manual for Team Building* (La Jolla, CA: University Associates, 1979).

48. Based on Kurt Lewin, *Field Theory in Social Science* (New York: Harper and Row, 1951).

49. Thomas F. Crum, *The Magic of Conflict: Turning a Life of Work into a Work of Art* (New York: Simon and Schuster/Touchstone Books, 1987), 345.

50. Crum, *The Magic of Conflict,* 345.

51. Billie Stockton, Anita Bullock, and Anne Locke, Northern Kentucky University, 1981 based on "Learning and Problem-Solving," in David A. Kolb, Irwin A. Rubin, and James M. McIntyre, *Organizational Psychology: An Experiential Approach,* 3rd (Englewood Cliffs, NJ: Prentice-Hall, 1979), 37–53.

52. Charles Darwin, *The Origin of Species* (New York: P. F. Collier and Son, 1909); and Charles Darwin, *The Decent of Man and Selection in Relation to Sex* (New York: A. L. Burt, 1874).

53. John Allen, ed., *100 Great Lives* (New York: Journal of Living Publishing Corp., 1944), 20–22, 25.

54. Upton Sinclair, *The Flivver King* (New York: Phaedra, 1969).

55. Teambuilding story from the authors' files.

CHAPTER 12

Communication
at Work

During World War II, Americans had to conserve
gasoline for the war effort. The government issued
placards to go on the dash of all vehicles, asking: "Is
this trip necessary?" If the answer was "yes," then by
all means the trip was to be taken; if the answer was
"no," people were supposed to conserve energy and
stay home. Wouldn't it be good if organizations
today had placards on the desks of all members, asking: "Is this meeting necessary?" If so, then proceed
with vigor. It is just what is needed. If not, conserve
resources, reduce waste, and stay home.

John McCollister

Increasingly, the world of work is viewed as an important place for community building. For many people whose families are dispersed, whose neighbors are not home, and for whom traditional institutions lack relevance, the workplace is the best opportunity to experience community. Yet one of the biggest problems people face at work is the failure to communicate.

This chapter discusses the communication challenges most organizations face, and presents principles and practices that help build community. Topics include:

- solving communication problems;

- managing conflict;

- effective meeting management; and

- systems for effective communication.

THE IMPORTANCE OF COMMUNICATION IN THE WORKPLACE

Many workplaces are characterized by low morale and poor performance, and often these problems can be traced to a failure to communicate. Even successful organizations must be concerned with communications. With success comes new people, new products, new procedures—in other words, the need to communicate.

When communication breaks down, tasks that should be done are left undone, and information and ideas that should be brought to the attention of others are lost or not carried out because they are not properly understood.[1] When communication improves, so does performance. That is why good **communication**—the flow of ideas upward, downward, and laterally—is so vital to success. The key to workplace effectiveness is having informed people working toward mutual objectives.

As figure 12–1 shows, the failure to communicate can lead to interesting outcomes.

CAUSES AND CONSEQUENCES OF COMMUNICATION PROBLEMS

Psychologist Gordon Lippitt discusses eight communication problems that lower morale, reduce productivity, and generally work against community in the workplace. These problems are found in all types and sizes of organizations.[2]

Problem #1: Distance

People may be too removed from each other, either physically or emotionally. Infrequent or impersonal contact can result in lack of information, misunderstanding, and reduced support.

FIGURE 12–1   What We Have Here Is a Failure to Communicate

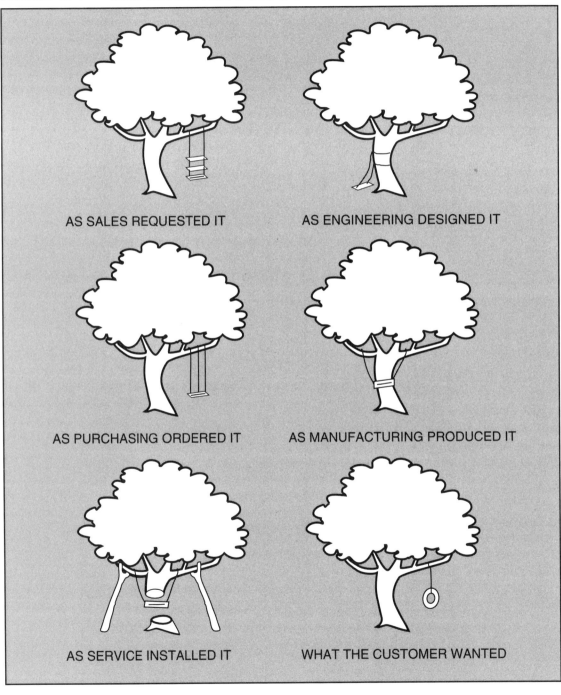

AS SALES REQUESTED IT

AS ENGINEERING DESIGNED IT

AS PURCHASING ORDERED IT

AS MANUFACTURING PRODUCED IT

AS SERVICE INSTALLED IT

WHAT THE CUSTOMER WANTED

Rx. Organizations may waste time looking for gimmicks to overcome this problem when the best solution is readily available—frequent, visible, and meaningful personal interaction. If people have access to each other, communication usually improves. Specific actions that can reduce physical and psychological "distance" include:

- Dealing with people face to face.

- Agreeing on purpose, shared values, and common goals.

- Being open and receptive.

- Involving people in decisions that affect them.

- Being less judgmental in day-to-day dealings.

- Showing courtesy—saying "hello," "please," and "thank you."

- Planning occasional social events; getting to know people as people.

- Keeping a calendar of birthdays, hire dates, etc., and recognizing people either verbally or by sending cards or notes.

Problem #2: Fear

People may find it hard to be truthful because of fear of punishment. If they have made a mistake, it may be difficult to communicate this information for fear of the reaction.

Rx. Fear can be reduced by showing appreciation for honesty, even when mistakes are made. To create a supportive work environment, follow four proven principles:

- Foster the attitude "let's fix the problem, not place the blame."

- Show confidence by revealing relevant information, and show support by listening for understanding.

- See things from the other person's view. Put yourself in his or her position.

- Recognize that people, as well as tasks, are important. One way to demonstrate this attitude is to be patient and listen more than you talk.

Problem #3: Trust

Open and free-flowing communication depends on what people believe will be done with reported information. If they think bad news will result in disciplinary action or public criticism, they will be reluctant to report bad news. If they think written reports will not be acted upon, few reports will be submitted voluntarily.

Rx. The answer is to reward people positively when they convey information, and let them know the results of their communication efforts. The best way to foster trust is to reward truth-telling.

Problem #4: Size

The size of an organization influences the communication process. Sometimes the distance between policy makers and action takers may be too great. Those who implement a policy or decision may have no role in establishing the policy and thus may feel little responsibility for its success, while those in policy-making positions may have too little experience and current information to make the best decisions.

Rx. A rule of thumb is to set a limit on the size of work units. Once an autonomous unit such as a company, division, or site exceeds 200 members, the quality of work and the quality of work life usually go down. The atmosphere is not as friendly, because people do not know each other as individuals, and loyalty decreases as well. People do not seem to care as much as they used to when the group was smaller. By decentralizing and making decisions at the lowest reasonable level, communication and community can be increased.[3]

Problem #5: Distortion

By the time people act on communication problems, frequently the facts are distorted. Problems may not have been handled while they were still simple, easy to understand, and easy to solve. When they are finally addressed, so many people have said so many things over so long a period of time that it is difficult to separate truth from fiction.

Rx. The best solution is to address communication problems as soon as they arise—before distortion occurs. Factors that can reduce distortion include clear instructions, effective listening, and open attitudes.

Problem #6: Complexes

Status and role issues can cause communication problems. When people feel they have low status, they may be overly critical of their own ideas and correspondingly reluctant to communicate information to others. They may actually feel inferior. Conversely, a person who is status conscious may feel superior and may fail to listen to people in lower status positions.

Rx. The solution for communication problems caused by status and roles is to treat all people with equal respect; seek out and listen to the ideas of everyone at all levels of the hierarchy. More than any other action, the willingness to listen demonstrates respect, opens communications, and builds community.

Problem #7: Structure

The formal structure of an organization may inhibit communication between members. A problem in many organizations is having too many layers of management. Some organizations have as many as fourteen levels in the chain of command. Besides the extra payroll costs, the inefficiencies and frustrations of a highly vertical organizational structure work against member empowerment and quick reaction in a competitive environment.

Rx. A review of the organization chart may be necessary to determine which channels are being used and which exist only on paper. Analysis of work processes and informal work relationships may give ideas for clarifying and streamlining the chain of command. In some instances, such a review can form the basis for a new and more effective organization. In general, by keeping levels of the hierarchy to a minimum, and putting resources and power at the lowest organizational level, member pride goes up, performance increases, and the overall sense of community is raised.

Problem #8: Conflict

Personality conflict sometimes creates communication breakdown. Sometimes, too, power struggles to gain control of a group or a situation can cause communication to become almost nonexistent.

Rx. The factors causing conflict should be diagnosed, areas requiring improvement identified, and action taken to solve the problem as soon as possible. Communication problems caused by conflict usually do not solve themselves. Early intervention is recommended for the benefit of the individuals involved and, in some cases, the survival of the group.

MANAGING CONFLICT

Conflicting purposes and personalities are inevitable in a pluralistic world, and they are part of the normal functioning of a healthy community. But without knowledge and skills in conflict resolution, groups, and ultimately individuals, will fail to achieve their full potential.[4] There are many strategies for managing conflict. The following points should be remembered.[5]

- Recognize that conflict is natural; indeed, nature uses conflict as an agent for change, creating beautiful beaches, canyons, and pearls.

- It is not *if* we will have conflict in life—we will. Everyone has his or her share. It is how we *handle* conflict that makes the difference.

- We can view conflict as either a problem or an opportunity. We can dwell on the negative or accentuate the positive. By choosing optimism over pessimism, we can be energized by events and focused in our efforts. With energy and focus we are better equipped to resolve conflicts and achieve our goals.

- Dealing with conflict effectively is rarely about who is right and who is wrong; it is more about what different people need and want. If everyone's "needs" are satisfied reasonably and everyone's "wants" are considered fairly, conflict can be a gift of energy that can result in a new and better condition for all.

- An important question to address is, "Do all parties want to resolve the conflict; will all sides try with goodwill to settle their differences?" If the answer is no, the best course is to agree to disagree, invite third-party resolution, and walk separate paths. Every student of history knows that war is the unacceptable alternative.

- If people want to resolve conflict, it helps to "reframe" the problem. This can be done by having each person see things from the other person's point of view. See things from the customer's standpoint, the employee's eyes, or the owner's perspective. In doing this, each party restates the problem from the other person's standpoint. This process often provides the breakthrough needed for constructive dialogue and the resolution of the problem. In their classic work *Barriers and Gateways to Communication*, Carl Rogers and Fritz Roethlisberger describe this process as **listening for understanding**:

  You can see what this would mean. Practically speaking, it means that before presenting your own point of view, it would be necessary for you to achieve the other person's frame of reference—to understand his thoughts and feelings so well that you could summarize them for him. It sounds simple, but if you try it, you will discover that it is one of the most difficult things you have ever tried to do. However, once you have been able to see the other person's point of view, your own comments will have to be drastically revised. You will also find the antagonism going out of the discussion, the differences being reduced, and those differences which remain being of a rational and understandable sort.[6]

WHERE PEOPLE WANT TO GET INFORMATION

One of the best ways to prevent communication problems is to recognize where most people prefer to get information, as opposed to where they actually receive it. Table 12–1 shows various types of communication and ranks them, both as actual and as preferred information sources.

TABLE 12–1   Where People Go for Information[7]

Actual Rank	Source	Major Source For:	Preferred Rank
1	Immediate supervisor	55.1%	1
2	Grapevine	39.8	15
3	Policy handbook and other written information	32.0	4
4	Bulletin board(s)	31.5	9
5	Small group meetings	28.1	2
6	Regular, general member publication	27.9	6
7	Annual business report	24.6	7
8	Regular, local member publication	20.2	8
9	Mass meetings	15.9	11
10	Union	13.2	13
11	Orientation program	12.5	5
12	Top executives	11.7	3
13	Audiovisual programs	10.2	12
14	Mass media	9.7	14
15	Upward communication programs	9.0	10

The *immediate supervisor* is ranked first as both a current and preferred source of information. Unfortunately, many more people would like to receive information from their supervisors than actually do (55.1 percent). This clearly indicates a need for better supervisor-subordinate communications.

It may be no surprise that the second highest actual source of information is the well-known *grapevine*. It was reported as a source by 39.8 percent, although respondents preferred it least of all, listing it as fifteenth.

Among publications, the *policy handbook* ranked third as an actual source, and fourth as a preferred source. A regular *general member publication* came in sixth, both as an actual and as a preferred source of information. People find these publications to be interesting and current sources of important news. Fewer respondents saw *local member publications* as a major source of information, ranking this as eighth. The *annual business report* was listed seventh as both an actual and preferred source (24.6 percent cited it).

Bulletin boards ranked fourth as an actual source, and ninth as a preferred source of information. However, this communication method was particularly popular with front-line personnel.

Among respondents citing the *union* as a preferred source of news, only 13.2 percent listed it as an actual source. As might be expected, the percentage of hourly employees looking to the union for information was higher.

Small group meetings were listed second as a preference, yet only fifth as an actual source of employee communications, showing the need for more staff and work group meetings. *Mass meetings* are presently not a strong source (ninth), nor are they something people prefer (listed as eleventh).

Orientation programs could be doing a better job; only 12.5 percent of respondents named them as a major current source (placing them eleventh), although they rated fifth as a preferred source of information.

Communication with top leaders was third in preference, but it was cited only twelfth as an actual source. An example of a CEO who achieves good results through communication is John Amerman of Mattel, the California-based toy company. To announce earnings results to the work force, Amerman put together a rap routine: "Supersonic motivating toys we're creating/Everybody knows that Mattel's devastating," chanted the CEO, his backup chiming in. "It brought the house down," recalls Amerman. "All of the employees came up and thanked me. It was like I hit a home run in the ninth inning of the seventh game of the World Series." Amerman credits good communications for Mattel's rebound from a loss of 113 million dollars to record earnings of 91 million dollars just four years later.

Videotape is an effective tool used by some top executives who want unfiltered communications with the troops. McDonnell Douglas puts out a quarterly video, narrated by CEO John McDonnell and mailed to employees' homes. These tapes can be brutally honest. One segment featured interviews with employees who had recently been laid off. The tapes drive home management's appreciation for the employee's right to know company news. They also help employees explain corporate decisions to their families, since family members can all watch the videos together.

Employees do not presently seem to be getting much information from traditional *audiovisual programs* (thirteenth in actual rank), and *mass media*—television, radio, and the press—are not important factors for organizational communications, coming in fourteenth, just ahead of the rather ineffective *upward communication programs* that were ranked last as a current source.

In summary, the actual and preferred rankings of "where people go for information" shows that people want accurate, timely, and complete information, and that their most preferred sources are the immediate supervisor, small group meetings, top executives, the policy handbook, orientation programs, and member newsletters.

MEETINGS: ACHIEVING HIGH-TOUCH COMMUNICATION IN A HIGH-TECH WORLD

A major cause of communication problems is ineffective meetings, as the story on the following page by Jim Lavenson shows.

How Not to Conduct a Meeting

Fifty people from all over the country arrived the night before, but it's 9:30 A.M. when the 9:00 sales meeting begins. The welcome message from the president was naturally delayed until he arrived. But waiting for the president is not only polite, it's smart; and what's a half-hour? Actually, for fifty sales people it's only twenty-five hours or three full days of selling time.

"My friends," says the president, "good morning and welcome to home base. I don't want to take any more of your valuable time, but I asked Artie if I could say a few words before you get down to work. I know it will be a fruitful and busy day for you who are, in my opinion, the most important asset this company has. Welcome. I'm sorry I can't spend time with each of you, but I've got a plane to catch." And the president leaves, smiling to the applause of the audience who gives him a standing ovation, principally because the chairs haven't arrived yet.

"Folks," says Artie the sales manager, "you've heard from our president; now let's get down to business. But to use the time until the tables and chairs arrive, I have a few housekeeping announcements. The coffee break will be at 10:30 instead of 10:00, so make a note of that on your agenda."

"I didn't get an agenda," one of the salesmen says.

"Those of you who got an agenda can share it," says Artie and continues.

"Although our president has already set the tone of this meeting, I want to add a few words before we get down to the nitty-gritty. You people represent the finest sales organization in our industry. Why? Because your company demands, and gets, selling skills and performance above and beyond the call of duty. That's why at this year's meeting, there are so many new faces."

"Artie, a question please?" comes a plea from one of the salesmen.

"Sure, Joe, fire away. But before you do, for the benefit of the new people, let me tell them who you are. Folks, Joe is our 'rep' in the Midwest who is doing one heckuva job. Really knows the market, his customers, and the product. How long have you been knocking 'em dead for the company, Joe? Four years? Five?"

"Eight months," says Joe.

"Oh, yeah, right. Now, what's the question?"

"Are we going to talk about the competition today?"

"You're worried about what the competition is doing right now?"

"What they're doing right now," says Joe.

"You tell me. What is the competition doing now?" Artie is smirking.

"What the competition is doing right now," says Joe, "is calling on our customers while we're in this meeting."[8]

Meetings are necessary to exchange information and coordinate activities. Yet the preceding example is not too unusual. It shows the need for people at all levels of responsibility to know how to plan, conduct, and participate in meetings effectively.

Have you ever attended a meeting that you considered to be a waste of time, energy, or resources? In contrast, have you ever attended a meeting that was just what was needed to tap the constructive power of the group? In order to have fewer of the first and more of the second, use the following guidelines:[9]

In general, a meeting is a good idea when:

- all members of the group should be involved in making a decision;
- there is an issue that needs to be clarified through group discussion;
- there are concerns or there is new information to share with the group as a whole;
- the group itself wants a meeting;
- there is an issue that involves people from different groups;
- there is an opportunity or problem, and it is not clear what it is or who is responsible for dealing with it.

In general, a meeting is not a good idea when:

- there is inadequate information or poor preparation;
- something could be communicated better by telephone, fax, memo, etc., or one-to-one discussion;
- the subject matter is so personal that it should not be shared in a group meeting;
- the leader's mind is made up and a decision has been made;
- the subject is trivial; and
- there is too much anger and hostility between people and they need time to calm down before they meet together as a group.

EFFECTIVE MEETING MANAGEMENT

The least productive time in many people's days is spent in meetings. Arthur Ciervo of Pennsylvania State University estimates that the average manager spends fourteen to twenty hours a week in meetings, and that half of these hours are wasted.[10] People at all levels in an organization spend endless hours in meetings that are poorly planned, ineffectively conducted, and go nowhere. The following are five ingredients for effective meeting management.[11]

1. A leader and a group committed to resolving issues—not just talking about them.

2. A meeting design that focuses on important issues and guides the group in resolving them.

3. A leader and members who have been trained in the skills needed to work together effectively.

4. A means for recording ideas and keeping track of what goes on.

5. A meeting location free of interruption from other activities.

The following principles should be remembered for conducting effective meetings.[12]

- Participants should be stimulated through a variety of activities to keep alert and tuned to the subject.

- Participants should experience a sense of progress with outcomes that show the meeting has been worthwhile.

- Participants should feel ownership and personal responsibility for the success of the group.

- Participants should feel that the group and its cause merit their personal time and effort.

- Participants should be challenged so they have to extend themselves beyond what might be called "routine."

- If a group meets on a regular basis, effort should be made to create a sense of identity and belonging, so that participants will support each other and will be committed to the group's success.

GENERATING IDEAS AND IMPROVING COMMUNICATION THROUGH BRAINSTORMING

The first real departure from strictly rational and highly controlled approaches to problem solving came nearly half a century ago when Alex Osborn introduced the concept of *brainstorming*. He discovered that by establishing a few simple rules and using a limited amount of time in a different manner, he could dramatically alter the atmosphere in a problem-solving session and, in his estimation, create more and often better ideas than might otherwise occur.[13]

Brainstorming is an effective community-building activity that generates interest and energy in group members. It gets many ideas and suggestions "out on the table" in a nonthreatening way. The goal is to be uninhibited and creative. Brainstorming sessions are relaxed, free-flowing, and nonjudgmental. The process can be tailored to the nature and goals of the group.

A typical procedure for brainstorming is as follows:

- Define the topic to be discussed. You might ask, "What are the bottlenecks and problems affecting the quality of work or the quality of life in our work group or organization?"

- Give each person paper and a pencil for making a list. Allow approximately five minutes.

- Write all problems on a note pad, wall board, or flip chart. Give each person a chance to speak. Encourage participation. Obtain responses by going around the table, allowing each person to identify a problem. Keep the process flowing. Continue until all of the ideas have been expressed. Additional problems commonly surface during this process; include these as well. This usually takes ten to fifteen minutes.

- After all of the problems are written on the board, allow a few minutes to let them "soak in"—as many as twenty to forty ideas may have surfaced. Review all points. Show respect and appreciation for all ideas.

- Put problems in priority order by determining which ones are the most serious (having the most adverse impact on the community). This ranking process is done by group discussion and consensus, and usually takes fifteen to twenty minutes.

- Narrow the list of problems to those considered to be most critical. To do this, apply the 80/20 principle (80 percent of the pain is caused by 20 percent of the problems). For example, 20 percent of twenty problems is four. The four most serious problems are probably causing 80 percent of the damage.

- Select one problem (from the 20 percent) for solving. This problem should be one that is important to solve and solvable. Selection is done by group discussion and usually takes ten to fifteen minutes to reach a consensus.

- Repeat the process using brainstorming to consider causes and solutions to the problem.

Certain rules should be followed for brainstorming to be most effective:

- *Accentuate the positive.* Negative attitudes should be minimized. They dampen enthusiasm and reduce creativity. Good-natured laughter and informality should be encouraged.

- *Quantity is the goal.* The more ideas that are generated, the greater will be the chance that a high-quality fact, suggestion, or solution will emerge.

- *Go easy on early evaluation and judgment.* Withhold criticism during initial brainstorming. This comes during the priority-ranking and 80/20 processes.

- *Freewheeling discussion is welcome.* The more spontaneous the group and the less conventional the ideas, the better. What may seem like an offbeat idea could lead other group members into practical suggestions.

Brainstorming offers many advantages in team building, problem solving, and planning activities. By design, it is very difficult for one person to dominate discussion, assume the role of expert, and inhibit participation of other members. The process encourages involvement from those who normally hold back. Also, the group is less likely to go off on a tangent and stray from the problem at hand—improved quality of work and improved quality of work life. Finally, research shows that a solution based on a combination of ideas is usually better than one derived from a single source. It is usually more correct and is supported more readily by those who must implement it.[14]

WHAT TO DO WHEN PEOPLE COMPLAIN

An important subject in communications and community building is how to handle complaints. If people think a mistake has been made, it is only natural for them to be upset, especially if the matter is important to them. When people complain, they want to be taken seriously and treated with courtesy. They also want to clear up the problem as soon as possible, so that it won't happen again. Management author Wendy Leebov recommends the following guidelines for handling complaints.[15]

- *Keep cool, calm, and collected.* A polite and friendly manner works best, even with the most irritated people. A phrase to remember is maintain grace under pressure.

- *Listen patiently without interrupting.* Don't argue or become defensive; allow the person to vent emotions.

- *Accept and acknowledge the person's point of view.* Show empathy. Consider how you would feel if you were in the other person's shoes.

- *Ask questions to fully understand the problem and to fully understand what the person wants.* Don't jump to conclusions about how the problem should be resolved.

- *Fully discuss possible solutions.* Explain clearly what can and cannot be done.

- *Reach closure.* Don't leave the person hanging. If you can't solve the problem, find someone who can. Arrange a time and method for communicating the results.

- *Genuinely thank the person for speaking up.* Explain why you are glad that he or she pointed out a shortcoming. For example, "It gives me a chance to make things right," or "It helps us improve for the future."

- *Follow through.* Do what you say you will do when you say you will do it. Keep promises.

Handling complaints is everyone's responsibility. It is a practical and tangible demonstration of respect for people. If done effectively, it can help keep small irritations from becoming major problems, and it can be an important asset in building and maintaining community.

CASE STUDIES IN EFFECTIVE COMMUNICATION

In their influential book, *In Search of Excellence: Lessons from America's Best-Run Companies*, Tom Peters and Robert Waterman report on five characteristics of effective communication systems.[16]

1. Communication systems are informal

At the 3M Company there are endless meetings, although few are scheduled. Most are characterized by people gathering together from different disciplines to discuss problems. The campus-like setting at St. Paul helps, as does the shirt-sleeves atmosphere, the no-nonsense midwestern backgrounds, and the inbred nature of the organization that helps people get to know each other over time. It adds up to the right people being in touch with one another on a regular basis.

At McDonald's, the top leadership team works together informally, setting a tone that pervades the business. At Digital, the chief executive meets regularly with a committee of twenty employees from all levels of the company. The chair sets the agenda and periodically disbands and reconstitutes the group to maintain a fresh flow of ideas, viewing the chair's role as that of a catalyst and colleague.

2. Communication intensity is extraordinary

Two companies known for effective communication in highly competitive industries are Exxon and Citibank. Observations of the senior managers in action show that the difference between their behavior and that of their competitors is dramatic. They make a presentation, and then the exchange begins. Questions are unabashed; the communication is free-flowing; everyone is involved. Nobody hesitates to address the chairman, the president, or a board member.

This contrasts sharply with the behavior of most companies. Senior people, who have sometimes worked together for twenty years or more, won't attend gatherings unless there are formal agendas. They can't seem to do anything other than watch formal presentations and then politely comment on the contents. At the extreme, people whose offices are on the same floor communicate only in writing. Such behavior contrasts vividly with Caterpillar's daily "no holds barred" meeting among the top ten, Fluor's daily "coffee klatch" among the top ten to fifteen, and McDonald's daily "informal get-together" among its top leaders.

3. Communication is given physical support

A senior scientist recently changed jobs, taking an important research assignment in another company. He walked into an executive's office several weeks after arriving, closed the door, and said, "I've got a problem. I don't understand why you don't have blackboards around here," said the scientist. "How do people talk to each other and exchange ideas without blackboards everywhere?" His point was well taken. Physical aids such as these help spur the spontaneous, informal communication that underpins regular innovation.

At the macro level there are disproportionately large numbers of "campuses" among successful companies. Examples include Deere's complex in Moline, Caterpillar's Peoria facility, the St. Paul campus of 3M, the Procter & Gamble setting in Cincinnati, Dana's Toledo center, Dow's headquarters in Midlands, Hewlett-Packard's beehive in Palo Alto, Texas Instrument's major Dallas complex, or Kodak's Kodak Park in Rochester. In most of these companies, important disciplines are gathered together in campus-like settings conducive to open communication and collaboration on ideas.

4. Forcing devices are used

These devices are aspects of communication that spawn innovation. IBM's "Fellows" program is a classic. Fellows are a manifestation of founder Tom Watson, Sr.'s desire to foster "wild ducks," people who will get outside the box and view things from a different perspective. IBM Fellows are viewed as heretics, mavericks, and geniuses. "There are fewer of us than there are corporate vice presidents," said one. Each Fellow is given a free rein for five years. The role is simple: to think.

One Fellow was on a night flight from San Jose to New York. He had just spent several million dollars buying products—essentially out of catalogs—from Silicon Valley companies. He said, "We must have six different labs at IBM working on these products. But nobody has bothered to find out what is already being made." It is amazing what one highly charged, unconventional person can do. An evaluation of the projects in which this Fellow has been involved shows that he has played a major role in no less than a half-dozen substantial IBM innovations.

5. Informal communications act as a tight control system

3M is a good example of this: "Of course, we are under control. No team can spend more than a few thousand dollars without people checking on progress; not kicking them around, but being genuinely interested in how things are going." Similar "informal controls" are found throughout successful companies. You can't spend much time at a truly great company without people asking and caring about how things are going. In less successful companies where controls are more "rigid and formal," you can spend 5 million dollars without bending the first piece of tin and no one will know—as long as you fill out the forms correctly.

The following exercise can be used to improve communications in your organization.

APPLICATION: EFFECTIVE COMMUNICATION—WHAT DO YOU RECOMMEND?

Directions

Critique your organization on five characteristics of effective communication. Describe conditions; cite examples. What suggestions would you recommend?

Communication systems are informal.

_____

_____

_____

_____

_____

_____

_____

_____

_____

Communication intensity is extraordinary.

_____

_____

_____

_____

_____

_____

_____

_____

_____

Communication is given physical support.

_____

_____

_____

_____

_____

_____

_____

_____

Forcing devices are used.

_____

_____

_____

_____

_____

_____

_____

_____

Informal communications act as a tight control system.

_____

_____

_____

_____

_____

_____

_____

_____

In summary, communication is a challenge faced by all organizations, large and small. It is important to have free-flowing and constant information about issues and events. Without communication, people may be so busy protecting their own interests that they fail to understand the needs and problems of others. In a real sense, successful communities and productive workplaces are masters of communication.

REFERENCES

1. Jesse S. Nirenberg, *Getting Through to People* (Englewood Cliffs, NJ: Prentice-Hall, Inc., 1963).

2. Gordon Lippitt, *Organizational Renewal*, 2nd ed. (Englewood Cliffs, NJ: Prentice-Hall, Inc., 1982), 99–100; and Leslie This, *The Small Meeting Planner*, 2nd ed. (Houston: Gulf Publishing Co., 1979).

3. Lucien Rhodes, "The Un-Manager," *Inc.* (August 1982): 38–39.

4. John W. Gardner, "Building Community," prepared for the Leadership Studies Program of the Independent Sector (Washington, D.C.: American Institutes for Research, 1991).

5. Robert Lussier, *Human Relations in Organizations*, 2nd ed. (Homewood, IL: Irwin, 1993), 258–269; and M. Afzalur Rahim, Jan Edward Garrett, and Gabriel F. Buntzman, "Ethics of Managing Interpersonal Conflict in Organizations," *Journal of Business Ethics*, 11 (1992): 423–432.

6. Fritz J. Roethlisberger, *Man-in-Organization* (Cambridge, Mass.: Harvard University Press, 1968); and Carl Rogers and Fritz J. Roethlisberger, "Barriers and Gateways to Communication," *Harvard Business Review* (July/August 1952): 52.

7. Selma Friedman, "Where Employees Go for Information (some surprises!)," *Administrative Management* (September, 1981): 72–73.

8. Jim Lavenson, "Meeting the Issue," *Selling Made Simple* (Sales and Marketing Management, 1973).

9. Alan Zimmerman, ed. "We've Got to Keep Meeting Like This," *Communi-Care* (Winter 1991); Karen E. Silva, *Meetings that Work* (Homewood, IL: Business One Irwin, 1994); and Lussier, *Human Relations in Organizations*.

10. Zimmerman, "We've Got to Keep Meeting Like This."

11. Zimmerman, "We've Got to Keep Meeting Like This;" Silva, *Meetings that Work*; and Lussier, *Human Relations in Organizations*.

12. Samuel B. Shapiro, "A Primer on the Workings of Committees," *Leadership* (November 1979): 23–25.

13. Alex Osborn, *Wake Up Your Mind: 101 Ways to Develop Creativeness* (New York: Scribner, 1952).

14. Donald L. Dewar, *Quality Circle Member Manual* (Red Bluff, CA: Quality Circle Institute, 1980), 3:1–3:14; and Ford Motor Company/United Auto Workers, *Guidelines for Employee Involvement Circles* (Detroit: 1984 rev.), 3:16–3:18.

15. Wendy Leebov, *Effective Complaint Handling in Health Care* (Chicago: American Hospital Publishing, Inc., 1990).

16. Thomas J. Peters and Robert H. Waterman, Jr., *In Search of Excellence: Lessons from America's Best Run Companies* (New York: Harper and Row, 1982).

CHAPTER 13

The Quality Movement

I predict that the quality movement will be hailed in the twenty-first century as the most important paradigm shift to come out of the twentieth century.

Joel Barker

Increasingly, organizations are focusing on **quality** as a virtue—quality of products and services for the benefit of customers, and quality of work life for the benefit of employees. In their efforts to achieve quality as an ideal, empowering people and building community occupy center stage.

This chapter addresses the following topics:

- the quality movement as a success story in building community;

- the role of empowerment in achieving quality;

- the democratic philosophy behind member empowerment; and

- improving performance through quality initiatives.

QUALITY AS A VIRTUE

In his poem "Mending Wall," Robert Frost attributes the following observation to his neighbor: "Good fences make good neighbors." For years many managers in American business and industry have been acting on this premise. The result has been communication barriers between employers and employees and compartmentalization into such areas as operations, maintenance, marketing, finance, purchasing, and personnel, with "walls" placed between these functional silos. These managers have forgotten or ignored the other element in Frost's equation: "Something there is that doesn't love a wall."[1]

A great deal of community in the workplace is generated by efforts to improve quality of products and services. As companies are forced to compete in an increasingly difficult global economy, they are finding that the path to quality is long and winding. On that path are many boulders and pebbles that must be cleared. It takes the strength of upper management to remove the boulders—build a new plant, create a new product, etc. And it takes the attention and effort of employees to cast away the pebbles—solve problems with products and meet customer needs. All members of the community must work together. Participative leadership is the philosophy needed to tear down walls, energize employees, and gain employee contributions. Total Quality Management (TQM), Continuous Quality Improvement (CQI), and other forms of empowerment are effective interventions to accomplish this goal.[2]

Joseph Jablonski writes in *Implementing Total Quality Management*, "This is a cooperative form of doing business that relies on the talents and capabilities of both labor and management to continually improve quality and productivity using teams."[3] Implicit in this definition are three essential ingredients: 1) participative management, 2) continuous process improvement, and 3) the use of groups. The last element makes the quality movement an interesting, contemporary application of small group processes and community building.

The philosophy behind the quality movement is that the people closest to the work usually have the experience and knowledge needed to come up with the best solutions to work-related problems. This is a philosophy of inclusion and empowerment. Ren McPherson, former president of Dana Corporation and dean of business at Stanford University, points out:

> Until we believe that the expert in any particular job is most often the person performing it, we shall forever limit the potential of that person, in terms of contribution to the organization and in terms of personal development. Consider a manufacturing setting: Within their 25-square-foot area, nobody knows more about how to operate a machine, maximize its output, improve its quality, optimize the material flow, and keep it operating efficiently than do the machine operators, material handlers, and maintenance people responsible for it. Nobody.[4]

W. EDWARDS DEMING

The influence of one person, W. Edwards Deming, has been critical in the history of the quality movement. In 1947 he was recruited by American authorities in Japan to help prepare a census, and immediately he took an interest in the restructuring of the Japanese economy. In 1950 a forty-nine-year-old Deming delivered a speech to the Japanese Union of Scientists and Engineers (JUSE) entitled "The Virtues of Quality Control as a Manufacturing Philosophy." This speech was to have a profound effect on Deming's audience. The Japanese believed in this teacher from the United States with his spartan dedication to work and Socratic teaching style, and they applied his ideas.[5]

Deming became a Japanese folk hero, and since 1951, the Deming Prize has been awarded annually in recognition of outstanding achievement in quality control. In an interview before his death in 1993, Deming said, "I think I was the only man in 1950 who believed the Japanese could invade the markets of the world, and would, within five years." They did this through a dedicated and sustained commitment to quality.[6]

The following are Deming's now famous "Fourteen Steps to Quality."

1. Innovate. Plan products with an eye to the long-range needs of the company; don't succumb to the pressures of the quarterly report.

2. Set high standards. No company can compete in the world market until its management discards old notions about acceptable levels of mistakes, defects, and inadequate training and supervision.

3. Eliminate dependence on mass inspection for quality. Use statistical controls for incoming and outgoing goods.

4. Reduce the number of suppliers.

5. Recognize that there are two sources of quality problems: faulty systems (85 percent probability) and the production worker (15 percent probability). Strive to constantly improve the system.

6. Improve job training.

7. Provide a higher level of supervision.

8. Eliminate unsuitable material. Create a team consisting of design, research, sales, purchasing, and production personnel for that express purpose.

9. Stamp out fear by encouraging open, two-way communication.

10. Abolish numerical goals and slogans.

11. Examine closely the impact of work standards. Do they help employees do a better job, or are they actually impediments to productivity?

12. Teach statistical techniques. The rudiments can be learned in a five-day intensive course.

13. Institute a vigorous training program in new skills.

14. Make maximum use of the statistical knowledge and talent in your company.[7]

The primary result of Deming's influence in Japan was that people at the production level were taught the statistical techniques of quality control, and then were delegated the task and the power to organize their work so that the quality of products could be improved. Also, Deming was able to convince top management of the necessity of personal involvement and commitment to building quality products.

In a lecture at the Hotel de Yama near Hakone, Japan, Deming produced a simple flow diagram to illustrate his concept of a quality system. That diagram, or a slight variation thereof, can be found in just about every Japanese corporation today. Essentially, Deming taught that the more quality you build into anything, the less it costs over a period of time.[8] Also, he taught the importance of designing a good system and process. To demonstrate this idea, Deming developed what he called the "Red Bead Experiment."

Ten people are picked and assigned jobs: six "willing workers," two "inspectors," one "chief inspector," and one "recorder." The objective is to show how a poorly managed system, not the workers, leads to defects and poor quality.

Deming explains that the "company" has received orders to make white beads. Unfortunately, the raw materials used in production contain a certain number of defects, or red beads.

With both the white and red beads in a plastic container, the six workers are given a paddle with fifty indentations in it and told to dip it into the container and pull it out with each indentation filled with a bead. They then take the paddle to the first inspector, who counts the red beads, or "defects." The second inspector does the same, and the chief inspector checks their tally, which the recorder then records.

Deming, playing the role of a misguided manager, acts upon the results. A worker drawing out a paddle with fifteen red beads is put on probation, while a worker with just six red beads gets a merit raise. In the next round, the worker who had six red beads now has eight, and the worker with fifteen has ten. In his "misguided manager" role, Deming thinks he understands what's happening: that the worker who got the merit raise has gotten sloppy—the raise went to his head—and the worker on probation has been frightened into performing better.

And so it continues—a cycle of reward and punishment in which management fails to understand that the defects are built into the system and that the workers have very little to do with it.

"We gave merit raises for what the system did; we put people on probation for what the system did," Deming says. "Management was chasing phantoms, rewarding and punishing good workers, creating mistrust and fear, trying to control people instead of transforming a flawed system and then managing it."[9]

Quality was Deming's message to the Japanese. They listened, they learned, and they practiced what Deming preached. And the rest, as they say, is history. Japanese corporations became profitable, well managed, and competitive.

Increasingly, American organizations—public and private, large and small—have followed the example of the successful Japanese in their efforts to improve quality. These organizations include General Electric, Motorola, Ford Motor Company, and the U.S. Army, Navy, and Air Force. By no means universally successful, most organizations have found their employees to be a valuable source of innovation and money-saving ideas. The following is a typical example:

Members of a team at Northrop Aviation were troubled because bits used to drill holes in titanium for F-5 fighter planes were breaking. The solution the group proposed: change the drilling angle, and make the bits from harder steel. This small change saved Northrop $70,000 in lost time.[10]

Experiences such as these are now commonplace as the quality movement and member empowerment have spread throughout American business, industry, and government.

WHO BENEFITS FROM EMPOWERMENT?

A story is told about a worker at a Ford plant many years ago who suggested a manufacturing improvement that saved the company hundreds of thousands of dollars. Henry Ford himself rewarded the employee and asked him when he had thought of the idea. "Years ago," the employee said. Asked by an incredulous Ford why he didn't say anything earlier, he said, "Nobody asked me."[11]

Although he admits that empowerment is not a panacea, management author Donald Dewar writes: "Every organization offering goods or services needs to involve its people in quality consciousness. Through a dedication to quality and the empowerment of people the ultimate beneficiary will be the customer."[12]

In a report for the Brookings Institution, Steve Levine and Laura D'Andrea reviewed all major studies of employee empowerment. Their findings: "If you sum it all up, employee participation has a positive impact on business success.

It is almost never negative or neutral. Moreover, studies of employee-owned companies show that stock ownership alone doesn't motivate employees to work harder, while ownership combined with participation does."[13] As an old saying goes, "The person in the boat with you never bores a hole in it."

IS EMPOWERMENT NEEDED?

For several years now, the United States has been in a competitive race against other economic powerhouses, most notably Germany and Japan. Currently the United States is using approximately 95 percent of its productive potential in the area of assets. "Assets" refers to plants, equipment, supplies, and so on. In the area of systems, U.S. companies are using approximately 85 percent of their potential. "Systems" refers to procedural questions such as how to build a bridge, fix a leak, or prepare a meal. U.S. companies are currently using only 65 percent of their potential in the area of people. "People" refers to human resources, including knowledge, attitudes, and skills. See figure 13–1.

The best way to increase performance is to make better use of our human resources—front-line employees, first-line supervisors, middle-level managers, and senior management personnel. Too many people either are sleepwalking through their days or are angry on the job. Many are present in body, but absent in heart and mind. To put it simply, the "care quotient" is low. Consequently, these people experience little job satisfaction and perform poorly. Empowerment can help tap unused human resources by increasing morale, raising commitment to the success of the organization, and improving the quality of work performed.

To diagnose the need for empowerment in a group or organization, answer the following questions:

- Do people seem uninterested in their work?
- Are absenteeism or turnover rates too high?
- Do people lack loyalty and team spirit?
- Is there a lack of trust or respect for management?
- Is there a lack of communication and teamwork among individuals and groups?
- Is there a low level of pride in the group or organization?
- Are costs too high due to waste and inefficiency?
- Does the quality of product or service need to be improved?

If the answer is "yes" to any of these questions, then empowering people can help.

FIGURE 13–1   Use of Productive Potential in America—Resource Utilization[14]

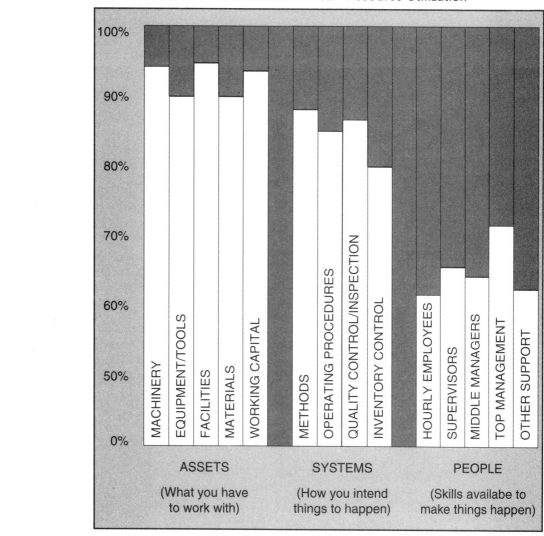

EMPOWERMENT FACILITATES CHANGE

Change is an inevitable fact of life in the workplace as new people, processes, and products come and go. Some changes are caused by forces outside the community; some originate from within. The ability to adapt to change is a key characteristic of successful groups. How do they do it? They recognize that the outcome of a change often depends on how it is introduced and who is involved. Whenever possible, people are encouraged to participate in decisions that will affect them. This tends to reduce resistance and resentment. The following, a classic study of employees in a clothing factory, illustrates the point:

> Experimenters divided employees into four groups that differed in terms of how a change in work group procedures was introduced. Group I was allowed no participation; the employees were told about the new work procedures, but were given no voice in matters. In Group II, employee representatives met and discussed the change with management. In Groups III and IV, all workers were encouraged to participate actively with management in implementing the change.
>
> The reaction of Group I was very negative. Production decreased immediately by one-third, expressions of hostility and resentment surfaced, and seventeen percent of the group quit within forty days. Group II, by allowing participation through representatives, achieved better results, but the response was not as positive as that of Groups III and IV. As a result of allowing participation by all of the workers involved, there was no hostility in Groups III and IV, and none of the employees quit. Production in these groups dropped initially, but quickly rose to a level higher than before.
>
> Encouraging broad employee participation was clearly the best method for overcoming resistance to change, a finding that has been verified by other studies.[15]

PARTICIPATIVE LEADERSHIP PRIMER

How do you tap the constructive power of people? How do you achieve both community spirit and great works? The process begins with *involving* people, which is necessary to achieve *understanding*, which is necessary to achieve *commitment*. The triggering agent that facilitates this sequence is leadership, more particularly the value system and style of behavior of those individuals with strength and influence to set direction, make policy, and decide things. These are the powerful individuals with or without title whom we call leaders. The essential character of such leaders is democratic, and their mode of behavior is best described as open, inclusive, and empowering.

Effective leaders decentralize decision making to the front-line employee. Thomas Page, vice-president of Diversified Products, reflects this approach when he writes: "I am just not smart enough to make all the right decisions by myself, so I solicit the ideas of the people around me. I try to get them involved for two reasons: One, because I value their views, and two, because I know that only they can make it work once the decision is reached. Hence, I want both their involvement and their commitment."

To develop quality products and services, and experience true community in the workplace, leaders must adopt the following philosophy:

> No matter how much factories are mechanized, as long as there are people still working there, they should be treated as human individuals. Those companies that do not give due consideration to humanity will lose their best people sooner or later. There can be no excuse for disregarding individual personality, slighting

a person's ability, regarding people as machinery, and discriminating against them. People spend much of their lifetime at their working place. It would be much more desirable to work in a pleasant place where humanity is paid due respect and where people feel their work has some real meaning. That is what quality practices aim to achieve. A mechanized factory still requires control by a workshop of people.

—Japanese Union of Scientists and Engineers (JUSE)

In recent years the Ford Motor Company has been a model for leadership, empowerment, and quality improvement. Ford is the nation's second largest industrial corporation and the second largest car and truck concern in the world, employing some 365,000 people in more than two hundred countries. In the early 1980s, when Chrysler was on the brink of collapse and was assisted by government loans, Ford was in a similar position. Had its European operations not been successful, Ford too would have had to seek government assistance. What Ford did at this crossroads in its history was to make an unprecedented strategic decision. Company management joined with the union, the UAW, to form a partnership to improve quality. The results were dramatic. Today Ford has regained its luster as a great company.[16]

Former Ford president Donald Peterson explains the company's approach:

We are working to change our style of leadership. Our goal is to adopt a "participative cooperative approach." We want to be known as a people company. Our intent is to lead rather than control and dominate. It is a fact that improved business performance begins with people—always people. And our new approach is founded on cooperation.

The changes that are taking place in Ford Motor Company today are truly revolutionary. We have committed ourselves to continuous improvement in quality, productivity, and technological development, and we are involving in this process the skills, talents, and ingenuity of all our people.

The process of changing our corporate culture requires a highly motivated work force. Today's car and truck market will accept only products that are excellent in appearance, function, and value. Firms that can't deliver on all counts will lose. We are convinced that the task before us is never-ending—the goal is continuous improvement through the efforts of our people.

The effective leader today incorporates people-oriented characteristics into his or her management style. This involves two-way communication and information sharing, and fostering greater participation of employees in decisions affecting their work. The Ford goal is to develop a well-rounded leadership approach that emphasizes a cooperative relationship with employees in accomplishing meaningful work objectives.[17]

Historically, the governance of groups has been autocratic. A few people at the top have held power and made decisions. These rulers, chiefs, and owners have passed down their orders to citizens, fighters, and workers, who have been responsible for implementing them. In the years since World War II, a democratization of Western societies and a few significant Eastern societies has occurred. This democratization has happened in the workplace as well.

Increasingly, employees have been involved in the decision-making process as management has shared the power to make important decisions.[18]

Management authors Warren Bennis and Philip Slater identify the shift toward democracy at work to be necessary for organizations to survive under conditions of chronic change. They define democracy not as permissiveness or laissez-faire management, but as a system of beliefs and common values that govern behavior. These values include:

- full and free communication, regardless of rank and power;

- a reliance on consensus, rather than on traditional forms of coercion and compromise, to manage conflict;

- the idea that influence is based on technical competence and knowledge, rather than on the vagaries of personal whim or prerogatives of power;

- an atmosphere that permits and even encourages emotional expression as well as task-oriented acts; and

- a basically human bias, one that accepts the inevitability of conflict between the organization and the individual, but that is willing to cope with and mediate this conflict on rational grounds.[19]

Some countries and companies have limited participation to the office, field, and shop floor level, while others have gone so far as to include employee representatives on the board of directors. In 1976 the West German codetermination (Mitbestimmung) law went into effect for more than eight hundred German firms. This law requires employee participation in decision making at the highest management levels.[20] In the United States, Chrysler Corporation appointed an employee representative to its board of directors in October 1979.[21] An extreme example of democracy at work is seen in the Israeli kibbutz, in which workers share ownership in the means and products of enterprise and share responsibility for all economic decisions. Examples of work systems and techniques for employee participation in the United States and abroad can be arranged along a continuum as shown in figure 13–2.

On the left part of this continuum, employees possess less power and are less involved in the decision-making process. Workers in industrial sweatshop systems exert less control over their work lives than do employees in industrial democracy systems.

This figure explains much of the popularity and success of total quality management and other empowerment efforts. It shows quality improvement teams to the right of middle—satisfying needs for member involvement, yet not so participative that owners and managers fear loss of power and ownership. William Byham, author of *Zapp!*, sees participative leadership and team efforts as the driving force behind continuous quality improvement, customer satisfaction, and business success.[23]

FIGURE 13–2   Continuum of Empowerment[22]

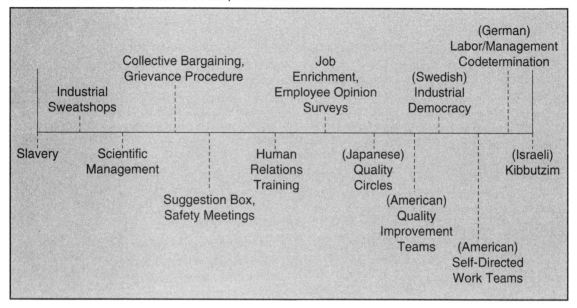

Participative leadership has been employed by many supervisors and managers to build community and achieve quality. With roots in democratic ideals, participative leadership allows the community to tap the constructive power of its members. In *Productive Workplaces,* Marvin Weisbord writes:

> The democratic process is the best procedure yet devised for promoting decision making that is a part of all social living, and at the same time safeguarding to each individual the conditions necessary for self-realization. The democratic process allows each individual to participate in making decisions that determine his or her conditions of life.[24]

PHILOSOPHICAL ROOTS OF THE QUALITY MOVEMENT

The following is a discussion of the philosophical roots of member empowerment and the quality movement.

Beginning with Taylor

In 1911 Frederick W. Taylor wrote his famous book *Principles of Scientific Management,* which was eventually translated into dozens of languages. He developed one of the first monetary incentive systems to improve the productivity of workers who were loading pig iron onto railroad cars. His principles and incentive system were soon extended to many other industries, becoming the basis for a worldwide "scientific management" movement. Peter Drucker ranks Taylor with Marx and Freud for significant impact on the modern world.[25]

Taylor is recognized today as the father of modern management and of the industrial engineering discipline. His scientific management philosophy is summarized in four basic principles:

- Develop a science for each element of an employee's work that replaces the old rule-of-thumb method.

- Scientifically select, train, teach, and develop the worker. (In the past, the employee chose the job and was self-trained.)

- Heartily cooperate with employees to ensure that all work is done in accordance with the principles of the science that have been developed.

- Divide the work and responsibility between management and employee. Managers should take over all work for which they are better fitted than the worker. (In the past, the worker took almost all of the work and the greater part of the responsibility.)[26]

Taylor has been criticized for advocating an extreme division of labor, resulting in routine, repetitive, and boring jobs on assembly lines. Considering his scientific management philosophy in the frame of reference of the early 1900s, however, it is logical and even participative in nature. He advocated a systematic approach to problem solving, cooperation between labor and management, training of employees, a fair reward system, and proper assumption of responsibility by both labor and management. These were revolutionary concepts for that time. If only slightly modified, they apply to the enlightened leadership practices of today. Taylor was the first person in history to make a scientific attempt to improve both the quality of work and the quality of life in industry.[27]

The Human Relations School

In the 1920s, Elton Mayo, Fritz Roethlisberger, and a team of researchers from Harvard University conducted a series of studies at the Hawthorne Plant of the Western Electric Company in a suburb of Chicago. These studies were to profoundly affect management theory and practice. The Hawthorne studies marked the beginning of what would later be called the "human relations school."[28]

When the Harvard team began their work, their goal was to determine how environmental conditions, such as lighting and noise levels, affected employee productivity. They soon discovered that social factors and group norms influence productivity and motivation much more than do the combined effects of physical conditions, money, discipline, and even job security. In 1939 Roethlisberger summarized these findings in his famous book *Management and the Worker.*[29]

In the 1950s and 1960s, the writings of Abraham Maslow, of "hierarchy of needs" fame, and Douglas McGregor, known for "Theory X, Theory Y," reinforced the human relations school of thought. Other behavioral scientists, including Rensis Likert (four systems of management), Chris Argyris (integrating the individual and the organization), and Frederick Herzberg (motivation hygiene theory), joined these influential figures to set the stage for many participative management experiments in the United States and abroad.[30]

Experiments in Participative Management

Some of the early pioneers in participative management included large firms, such as Texas Instruments, AT&T, General Foods, and Procter & Gamble, as well as smaller firms, such as Harwood Manufacturing and Lincoln Electric Company. These companies became famous for their innovative approaches to employee relations. Many of the participative management experiments they conducted in the 1950s and 1960s bear a close resemblance to employee empowerment and quality improvement practices of today.

Texas Instruments used "work simplification" training for line workers to help solve manufacturing problems and improve productivity. AT&T used "job enrichment" programs to increase motivation and employee output. General Foods designed a plant from the ground up around a "team concept," in which workers were classified into skill categories and could progress to the top category by learning how to do all of the jobs needed to run the plant. Procter & Gamble independently developed a concept of "group work" in the 1940s and 1950s. Many of these experiments were so successful that they are still in place today. Factors common to all successful experiments included the following:

- Management attitudes toward workers were positive; employees were viewed as important assets to the success of the company.

- Workers were given increased scope and control over job activities.

- Training in human relations, problem-solving, and decision-making skills was conducted through formal and informal means.

- Opportunities for advancement based on acquiring new skills and knowledge were provided.

- Productivity and morale increased during the period in which experiments were conducted.[31]

Quality Synthesis

As business schools and colleges expanded during the 1970s, old-line professors steeped in classical principles of management distilled from Frederick Taylor had to defend their theories against the onslaught of young "behavioral scientists" oriented toward human relations. Some time passed before both groups came to understand that there is no single best way to manage in a complex environment. Both the classicist and the behaviorist had to find that there was good in both points of view. During the 1970s and 1980s, the quality movement became the catalyst for joining these two management views. Here was one management technique that combined participative leadership practices with a problem-solving orientation, and it was being fervently employed in a real-world lab by the industrious Japanese as they outstripped competitors and set new standards of quality.[32]

The leadership philosophy behind quality improvement efforts such as TQM and CQI is both *hard*, based on scientific management, and *soft*, concerned with the human side of work. It is this balance or blend that helps to account for its general acceptance across the broad spectrum of managers today. By focusing on quality goals and using problem-solving tools and methods, quality improvement activities satisfy the needs of managers whose values lie with Frederick Taylor, the management classicists, and quantitative analysis. Such "hard-nosed" managers are drawn to the "end product" benefits of better products and services.

Likewise, by focusing on employee empowerment and personal growth, and by using group process techniques, quality improvement activities satisfy the needs of managers who trace their philosophical roots to Elton Mayo, Kurt Lewin, Abraham Maslow, Douglas McGregor, Rensis Likert, and other figures in the human relations and behavioral science school. These "soft-hearted" managers are especially pleased with the "in-process" benefits of improved morale, quality of work life, and the experience of community. See figure 13–3.

FIGURE 13–3   The Leadership Philosophy Behind Member Empowerment and the Quality Movement

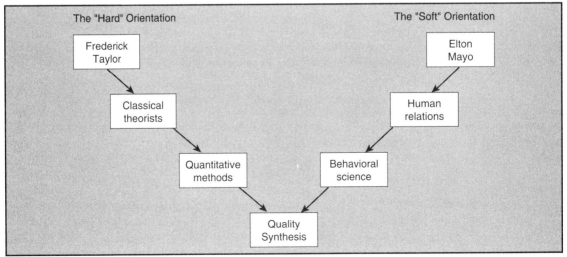

IMPROVING PERFORMANCE THROUGH QUALITY INITIATIVES

How effective is the quality movement? What results are experienced by participating organizations? A Government Accounting Office (GAO) report on American management practices shows U.S. companies are experiencing good results using quality improvement efforts to improve business performance (see the article on the following page).[33]

WHAT IS QUALITY?

The most widely accepted definition of what constitutes *quality* exists in the criteria for the Malcolm Baldrige National Quality Award. This annual award, given by the U.S. Commerce Department since 1988, recognizes U.S. companies that excel in quality achievement. To better understand ways to achieve quality, examine the concepts that serve as the basic criteria for this award.[34]

- Quality is defined by the *customer.*

- Senior leadership creates clear quality values and builds these values into the way the organization operates.

- Quality excellence derives from having well-designed and well-executed systems and processes.

- Continuous quality improvement is part of the management of all systems and processes.

- Goals are developed, as well as strategic and operational plans, to achieve quality leadership.

- Shortening the response time of all operations and processes of the organization is part of the quality-improvement effort.

- Operations and decisions of the organization are based on facts and data.

- All employees are suitably trained and involved in quality activities.

- Design quality and defect and error prevention are major elements of the quality system.

- Quality requirements are communicated to suppliers and the organization works to elevate supplier quality performance.

Implicit in the value system of the quality movement is the saying, "If you always do what you have always done, you will always get what you have always gotten." And this reflects the spirit of the childhood rhyme, "Good, better, best. Never let it rest until the good becomes better, and better becomes the best."[35]

Government Accounting Office (GAO) Report on American Management Practices

Background

Achieving high levels of quality has become an increasingly important element in competitive success. In recent years, a number of U.S. companies have found that they could not accomplish world-class quality by using traditional approaches to managing product and service quality. To enhance their competitive position, American companies have reappraised the traditional view of quality and have adopted what is known as the "total quality management" model in running their businesses.

For many years the traditional way to achieve quality was through systematic final inspection. This approach is referred to as "inspecting in quality." Intense foreign competition in general, and Japanese competition in particular, has led increasing numbers of U.S. companies to adopt total quality management practices that are prevention based. This approach is often referred to as "building in quality."

Results

- Companies that adopted quality management practices experienced an overall improvement in business performance. In nearly all cases, companies that used total quality management practices achieved better employee relations, higher productivity, greater customer satisfaction, increased market share, and improved profitability.
- Companies did not use a "cookbook" approach in implementing successful quality management systems, but common features that contributed to improved performance can be identified: Corporate attention was focused on meeting customer needs as a first priority; senior management led the way in building quality values into company operations; all employees were suitably trained, empowered, and involved in efforts to continuously improve quality and reduce costs; and systematic processes were integrated throughout the organization to foster continuous improvement.
- The diversity of companies studied showed that quality management is useful for small companies (five hundred or fewer employees) as well as large companies, and for service companies as well as manufacturers.
- Many different kinds of companies benefitted from putting quality management practices into place. However, none of these companies reaped those benefits immediately. Companies improved their performance on average in about two and one-half years. Management allowed enough time for results to be achieved rather than emphasizing short-term gains.

Specific Findings

Specific findings revealed U.S. companies can improve performance through quality efforts.

- Better employee relations were realized. Employees experienced increased job satisfaction and improved attendance; employee turnover also decreased.
- Improved quality and lower cost were attained. Companies increased the reliability and on-time delivery of their product or service and reduced errors, product lead time, and their cost of quality.
- Greater customer satisfaction was accomplished, based on the companies' survey results of their consumers' overall perceptions about a product or service, the number of complaints received, and customer retention rates.

IMPLEMENTING A QUALITY PROGRAM

Organizations may adopt quality programs for a variety of reasons. End product goals include reducing errors, saving money, increasing production, and improving customer satisfaction. In-process goals include improving communication, raising morale, and developing employee skills. The Japanese Union of Scientists and Engineers (JUSE) has found that quality programs work best when they give equal weight to business improvement and people-building goals.

The success of a quality program depends on three key elements: vision, training, and commitment. See table 13–1. Without sufficient *vision* for the program (management drive), *training* of the participants (facilitators, leaders, and team members), and *commitment* from all levels (including powerful middle managers), a program is likely to fail.

Vision. The initial thrust involves efforts of management to become familiar with the history, philosophy, concepts, and principles of the quality movement. Managers should be well read in this area and in the related areas of participative management systems and employee empowerment.

TABLE 13–1   Three Key Elements of a Successful Quality Program[36]

VISION	Management ownership; steering committee or quality council formed; creation of a vision— Mission and goals, core values, stakeholders and benefits, strategic initiatives, and critical success factors
TRAINING	Participant training—Participative leadership; quality orientation; problem-solving skills; communication and teamwork; process analysis; SQC; etc.
COMMITMENT	Organizational commitment as a sustaining force to assimilate employee empowerment and quality improvement into the company culture and day-to-day operations

After gathering background information, management should look at the goals and culture of the organization to evaluate its readiness. This may be the most difficult step in the process, because it requires an honest appraisal of the organization as a whole. An enthusiastic manager can start a quality program, but solid support from a number of managerial levels is required to keep it going.

Once the decision has been made to move ahead, it is usually best to establish a steering committee or quality council composed of line and staff managers, employee representatives, and union leaders, if there is a union. The steering committee establishes initial policies and procedures for the program and chooses a person to serve as facilitator. This step is extremely important to the success of the program.

Training. The next phase is training. A quality facilitator should be thoroughly trained before the program is begun. A number of excellent courses and professional conferences are offered in the United States and abroad by organizations such as the Association for Quality and Participation, Cincinnati, Ohio.

This period also involves selecting and training group leaders. This should take place only after careful planning by the facilitator with full discussion and approval of the steering committee. Once this point has been reached, it becomes much more difficult to scrap a quality program because a number of people have become aware of it, and expectations have been raised.

After selecting and training team leaders, management gives a general orientation to all employees within the organizational unit in which the quality initiative is to be conducted. Volunteers are requested to establish pilot quality improvement teams.

Pilot teams launch into action. Leading the teams requires constant cooperation between the facilitator and the team leaders. The "proof of the pudding" is the first presentation to the steering committee and members of management by the pilot teams. Here, team members are expected to demonstrate systematic problem-solving skills and tell how they propose to remedy specific problems. Management, in turn, is expected to listen and respond to suggestions. Figure 13–4 shows the types of training sponsored by companies involved in quality programs.

Commitment. The final phase tests the sustaining force or commitment of the organization. Is there broad management support, backed by personal involvement and budget, to keep the quality program going?

After the first round of presentations, the steering committee must decide: Should the quality program be expanded, or should it be eliminated? If the decision is made to expand, resources must be provided. More training, additional leaders, and larger budgets for team activities are usually involved.

In the commitment phase, updating and refinement of the program takes place. The culture of the organization is reevaluated, as are the employee empowerment and quality improvement goals and guidelines set by the steering committee. Facilitators receive further training, new and replacement

FIGURE 13–4   Training for Quality: What Companies Are Sponsoring[37]

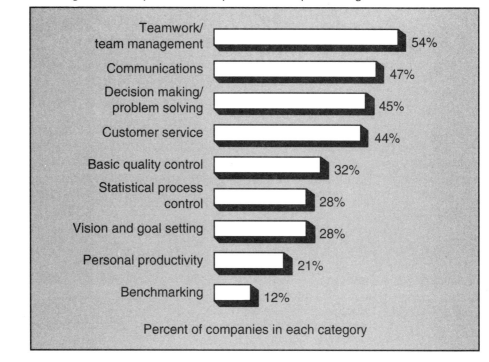

group leaders are selected and trained, and new teams may be created in remote parts of the organization. Periodic evaluation of the program is part of the sustaining process.

BENCHMARKING AS A QUALITY TOOL

An increasingly popular approach to improving quality is *benchmarking*—the practice of comparing one's own organization to others considered to be leaders and role models. John Hooper examines the myths and realities of benchmarking as an improvement strategy on the following page.

QUALITY MOVEMENT SUCCESS STORY

In the spirit of benchmarking and sharing with others, the experiences of Motorola can be instructive for any organization striving to improve quality through particpative leadership, member empowerment, and customer-focused

Benchmarking Myths and Realities

Myth: Benchmarking is getting a group of people together to visit a leading-edge company and discussing some interesting ideas.

Reality: The process is not organizational tourism. The focus is on how to learn, adapt and apply findings fast.

Myth: Benchmarking won't increase competitiveness. It is simply copying others and catching up.

Reality: Benchmarking is not mindlessly copying others. There is no single right way to do things. What works for one company may not work for another. Each company's own creative work adds value, ownership, and commitment.

Myth: Benchmarking is a management fad. It won't sustain itself over time.

Reality: Benchmarking is one of the most powerful tools for ensuring excellence and the pursuit of innovation. The changes that are produced are much greater than those that occur without it. Many leading organizations have used the method for years.

Myth: Benchmarking is too expensive. It requires a large travel budget to visit other organizations.

Reality: Benchmarking can be done through correspondence and over the phone. Site visits are appropriate in some situations. There are many highly effective methods for collecting benchmark information.

Myth: The only organizations one can learn from are Fortune 500 companies or entrepreneurial start-ups.

Reality: No organization should be considered too large or too small to benchmark. Both established and new organizations have proven their ability to innovate and implement new ideas.

Myth: Companies should confine the scope of benchmarking to similar organizations.

Reality: Good ideas are where they are found. Consider a variety of industries and organizations to discover rich ideas for dealing with customers, employees, processes, etc.

Myth: Others will give information without getting information in return.

Reality: The key feature of successful benchmarking is *sharing*. The willingness to exchange information encourages others to share. Getting and giving information helps everyone improve.[38]

business practices. Motorola is a leading provider of electronic products and services for worldwide markets. Motorola has sales of more than ten billion and more than 100,000 employees in facilities around the world. The following is their story.[39]

> A decade ago, Motorola began a journey that would shape the company's success for years to come. The issue was survival; the challenge was quality; the solution would come from our people. We didn't have a detailed map to guide us, but we set out together to achieve one very large but simple goal: to improve the way we serve our customers. During our quest, we realized that holding fast to some *old truths* about the way to do business was preventing us from achieving our best. Out of our evaluation, we generated *new truths*—insights that have helped us make some remarkable strides. The way we do business will never be the same again.

OLD TRUTH:
QUALITY IS THE QUALITY CONTROL DEPARTMENT'S RESPONSIBILITY

NEW TRUTH:
IMPROVING QUALITY IS EVERYONE'S RESPONSIBILITY

Today, quality is a daily priority and a personal obligation for every employee in our company. The pursuit of quality has become the single most important part of our culture. Unless everyone can point to his or her own personal improvements in quality, our company hasn't reached the level of commitment that is absolutely essential for success.

OLD TRUTH:
TRAINING IS COSTLY OVERHEAD

NEW TRUTH:
TRAINING DOES NOT COST

Today, all of our employees participate in a minimum of one week of training per year. Classes range from technical seminars to self-improvement workshops and foreign language courses. Employees are not only encouraged to improve their skills, but to use their new knowledge to challenge the very way they do their jobs. As a result, every person contributes to the quality effort in an individual way.

OLD TRUTH:
NEW QUALITY PROGRAMS HAVE HIGH UP-FRONT COSTS

NEW TRUTH:
THE BEST QUALITY PROGRAMS HAVE NO UP-FRONT COSTS

The average cost of poor quality in most companies is 20 percent of sales. This leaves enormous potential for savings simply by doing things better. From 1986 through 1991, our quality efforts resulted in savings of 2.2 billion dollars simply by reducing defects in the manufacturing process. This is a savings of more than 6 percent of sales—just for doing things right. We didn't sink a lot of money into our quality process in the beginning. We simply saw that we couldn't afford to do business the way it had always been done. By challenging the processes in place, we found that we had too much space for this, too much inventory for that, too many returns, and other inefficiencies that seemed harmless by themselves. But together they added up to major potential for improvements. Then we looked for simple ways to work smarter, implemented easy changes, and started saving money. This was done without costing us a cent.

OLD TRUTH:
KEEP MEASUREMENT DATA TO A MINIMUM

NEW TRUTH:
YOU CANNOT HAVE TOO MUCH RELEVANT DATA

Too often, companies operate in a vacuum—not knowing how their products and services stack up against the competition. Only with constant monitoring and continual follow-up can you get a true picture of where you stand and a clear view of where you need to go. We accomplish this by keeping records on our processes, analyzing them, learning from them, and sharing them. We use data to measure both our successes and our failures. More importantly, it helps us to manage our process improvements.

OLD TRUTH:
TO ERR IS HUMAN

NEW TRUTH:
PERFECTION—TOTAL CUSTOMER SATISFACTION—IS THE STANDARD

To achieve such an ambitious goal, we must have the dedication of every one of our employees. They must approach tasks at hand with belief in themselves and their power to do the job right. Accepting the philosophy that "to err is human" is simply a way of setting low expectations. Once that mindset is established, it is a short step toward achieving less than the best.

OLD TRUTH:
QUALITY IMPROVEMENTS ARE MADE IN SMALL CONTINUOUS STEPS

NEW TRUTH:
BOTH SMALL STEPS AND LARGE STRIDES ARE NEEDED TO IMPROVE QUALITY

The classic approach to improving products and processes is by taking one carefully considered step after another toward better quality. We've found that major improvements in quality are also very necessary and quite achievable. We encourage giant steps in improvement, along with small steps, often striving for at least 50 percent improvement in our quality or cycle time—sometimes many times that.

OLD TRUTH:
IMPROVING QUALITY TAKES TIME

NEW TRUTH:
QUALITY DOESN'T TAKE TIME—IT SAVES IT

Six Sigma™ quality and total cycle time reduction are not mutually exclusive goals. We determine the total time it takes to do something from start to finish, whether it is serving a customer or developing a new technology. By tracking data constantly, we find ways to make the process more efficient, more productive, more cost-effective, and easier to use. The end result is higher quality in less time.

OLD TRUTH:
QUALITY PROGRAMS BEST FIT PRODUCTS AND MANUFACTURING

NEW TRUTH:
QUALITY IS ALSO IMPORTANT IN ADMINISTRATION AND SERVICES

Today, service is a critical part of most businesses and the very purpose of many of them. The need for quality in this sector is just as dramatic as it is in manufacturing. We believe quality service is a matter of anticipating solutions to needs that our customers have yet to recognize themselves. This means listening closely to our customers (external and internal), asking them how we can be a better supplier and what we have to do to be worthy of their trust.

OLD TRUTH:
THOU SHALT NOT STEAL

NEW TRUTH:
THOU SHALT STEAL NONPROPRIETARY IDEAS SHAMELESSLY

Our company benchmarks the best companies. They can be competitors, or they can be in completely different businesses. We also learn from our customers and our suppliers. When your mind is open, you can learn something from practically everyone. It is a good way to keep from reinventing the wheel. For our company, benchmarking is a reciprocal process, fostering trust and mutual respect.

OLD TRUTH:
OUR COMPANY COMES FIRST—SUPPLIERS BETTER BEAT THE PRICE

NEW TRUTH:
WORLD CLASS QUALITY COMPANIES MUST BE WORLD CLASS CUSTOMERS

With 50 percent of our costs based on parts we acquire from our suppliers, we should have seen right away how critical they were to our success. If we had to do it all over again, we would have involved them from the beginning. Because our suppliers are so much smarter about all the parts they supply than we are, they can teach us. We can also teach them, and we can grow together.

THE QUALITY IMPERATIVE

In general, U.S. organizations have avoided the term "quality control circles," preferring names that de-emphasize control and underscore the empowerment of people. Popular names are *employee involvement teams* (American Electric Power), *study action teams* (Xerox), *employee participation groups* (General Motors), and *self-managing work groups* (Baptist Health Care System). In any case, the goals are the same—improve the quality of work environment and improve the quality of work performed—and the underlying principles are the same. Robert Cole, influential author and educator on the quality movement, identifies these principles as follows:

- Trust people. Assume they will work to implement organizational goals if given a chance.

- Invest in people as resources that, if cultivated, will yield positive returns. Implicit in this perspective is to aim for long-term commitment to the organization.

- Recognize accomplishments. Symbolic rewards are extremely important. Show people that they are valued.

- Decentralize decision making. Put responsibility for making decisions where the information is.

- View work as a cooperative effort, with people helping each other accomplish tasks.[40]

Implicit in these points is that people are valuable organizational resources, and that broad participation in the decision-making process is necessary for success. Is it too late, or can U.S. companies succeed in today's global economy? Before his death in 1993, Deming wrote, "Nobody's predicting anything. There is no regulation saying we must survive. We can rise from the ashes like a phoenix, but it will take a transformation in quality to do it."[41]

REFERENCES

1. Davidia M. Amsden and Robert T. Amsden, "Plan-Do-Check-Act—and then came Quality Circles," *Transactions—Sixth Annual Conference and Exhibition* (Cincinnati: International Association of Quality Circles, 1984), 26–40; and "The Mending Wall," *The Poetry of Robert Frost*, ed. Edward C. Lathem (New York: Holt, Rinehart, and Winston, 1969), 33.

2. William Lindsay, Kent Curtis, and George Manning, "A Participative Management Primer," *Journal for Quality and Participation* (June 1989): 78–84.

3. Joseph Jablonski, *Implementing Total Quality Management: An Overview* (San Diego: Pfeiffer, 1991).

4. Thomas J. Peters and Robert H. Waterman, Jr., *In Search of Excellence: Lessons from America's Best Run Companies* (New York: Harper and Row, 1982), 249–250.

5. Christopher Byron, "How Japan Does It," *Time* (March 30, 1981): 57.

6. Lloyd Dobyns, "Ed Deming Wants Big Changes and He Wants Them Fast," *Smithsonian*, 21, no. 5 (August 1990): 77; and Lloyd Dobyns, "If Japan Can Do It, Why Can't We?" *NBC News*.

7. W. Edwards Deming, *On the Management of Statistical Techniques for Quality and Productivity* (Washington, DC: Continuing Engineering Education, George Washington University, 1981) 2: 16–17.

8. Dobyns, "Ed Deming Wants Big Changes and He Wants Them Fast," 76; and Dobyns, "If Japan Can Do It, Why Can't We?"

9. Ronald Yates, "Game Plan," *Chicago Tribune Magazine* (February 16, 1992): 20; and W. Edwards Deming, "Experiment to Show Total Fault in System," *Quality, Productivity, and Competitive Position* (Cambridge: Massachusetts Institute of Technology—Center for Advanced Engineering Study, 1982), 138–146.

10. David Pauly with Joseph Contreras and William D. Marbach, "How to Do It Better," *Newsweek* (September 8, 1980): 59.

11. Schoichi Suzawa, "How the Japanese Achieve Excellence," *Training and Development Journal* (May 1985): 114.

12. Donald L. Dewar, *Quality Circles: Answers to 100 Frequently Asked Questions* (Red Bluff, CA: Quality Circle Institute, 1979), 7, 23.

13. John Hoerr, "The Payoff from Teamwork," *Business Weekly* (July 10, 1989): 60.

14. *Productivity in America* (Paoli, Pa.: Naus & Newlyn, Inc.).

15. L. Coch and J. French, Jr., "Overcoming Resistance to Change," *Human Relations*, 1, no. 4 (1948): 512–532.

16. *Ford—A Guide for Managers*, (Dearborn, MI: Ford Motor Co., May, 1984): 1; and Ernest J. Savoie, *Creating the Workforce of the Future: The Ford Focus*—statement submitted to the President's Advisory Committee on Mediation and Conciliation (Dearborn, MI: Ford Motor Co., September 16, 1986).

17. *Ford—A Guide for Managers*, (Dearborn, MI: Ford Motor Co., May, 1984): 1; and Ernest J. Savoie, *Creating the Workforce of the Future: The Ford Focus*—statement submitted to the President's Advisory Committee on Mediation and Conciliation (Dearborn, MI: Ford Motor Co., September 16, 1986).

18. Sud Ingle, *Quality Circle Master Guide: Increasing Productivity with People Power* (Englewood Cliffs, NJ: Prentice-Hall, 1982), 2–5, 7–11; and Keith Davis, "The Case for Participative Management," 6, no. 3. *Business Horizons* (Fall 1963): 55–60.

19. Philip E. Slater and Warren Bennis, "Democracy is Inevitable," *Harvard Business Review* (March/April 1964): 51–53.

20. Klaus E. Agthe, "Mitbestimmung: Report on a Social Experiment," *Business Horizons* (February 1977): 5014.

21. Robert L. Simison, "Chrysler 3-Year Pact Saves $203 Million, UAW Says; Fraser Slated for Board Seat," *The Wall Street Journal* (October 26, 1979): 3.

22. Lindsay, Curtis and Manning, "A Participative Management Primer."

23. "The Link Between Empowerment and Continuous Improvement," *Continuous Improvement IV*, no. 12 (The MGI Management Institute Newsletter of Quality Techniques: December 15, 1991); and William Byham, *Zapp! The Lightening of Empowerment* (New York: Ballantine Books, 1992).

24. Marvin R. Weisbord, *Productive Workplaces* (San Francisco: Jossey-Bass, 1990), 97.

25. Frederick W. Taylor, *Principles of Scientific Management* (New York: Harper and Brothers, 1911), 36–37; and Weisbord, *Productive Workplaces*, 27.

26. Taylor, *Principles of Scientific Management*, 27.

27. Weisbord, *Productive Workplaces*, 69.

28. Fritz Roethlisberger, *Management and the Worker* (Cambridge, Mass: Harvard University Press, 1939).

29. Roethlisberger, *Management and the Worker*.

30. Ingle, *Quality Circle Master Guide*, 170–181.

31. Ingle, *Quality Circle Master Guide*, 12; Davis, "The Case for Participative Management," 55–60.

32. Ingle, *Quality Circle Master Guide*, 12; and Davis, "The Case for Participative Management," 55–60.

33. *Management Practices: US Companies Improve Performance Through Quality Efforts* (Washington, DC: U.S. General Accounting Office, May 1991).

34. Mark Graham Brown, *Baldridge Award Winning Quality: How to Interpret the Malcolm Baldridge Award Criteria* (White Plains, NY: Quality Resources, 1991); and D. Ritter, "A Tool for Improvement Using the Baldridge Criteria," *National Productivity Review*, 12 (Spring 1993): 167–182.

35. Wendy Leebov, *The Quality Quest* (Chicago: American Hospital Publishing, 1991), 1.

36. Adapted from Jim Pfeiffer, General Dynamics, Pomona Division, "Power Adjustment for Organizational Readiness," *Transactions: 1984; Sixth Annual Conference and Exhibition* (Cincinnati: Internationational Association of Quality Circles, 1984), 44.

37. "Quality Programs and Practices," *Human Resources Issues and Trends* (Westbury, NY: Olsten Corp., 1993).

38. John Hooper, "How to Benchmark World-Class People Practices" *Human Resource Executive*, June, 1992: 38–40.

39. Motorola, *The Motorola New Truths of Quality.*

40. Cole, "Employee Involvement in Japan."

41. Dobyns, "Ed Deming Wants Big Changes and He Wants Them Fast," 80.

THE ROAD AHEAD

After the facts have been forgotten, what remains is education.

John Dewey

Completing a book is like completing a journey. So many miles have been covered and so many interesting places have been seen, it is hard to remember it all. Each chapter in *Building Community* has a central message or key concept that we see as definitely worth remembering. We hope you will adopt these as your own, pass them on to others, and use them whenever and wherever you seek to build community.

Chapter One—Vision and Community

Use the visioning process to create a vision for the community that is leader initiated, member supported, comprehensive and detailed, motivating, and, above all, worth doing.

Chapter Two—Character and Community

Understand the importance of character in the creation of community, and the importance of full-swing adherence to core values and principles.

Chapter Three—Sustaining Community

Understand the importance of psychological climate to sustain community, including the idea that sick societies make sick people and healthy climates make healthy people.

Chapter Four—Effective Human Relations

Use the Dyadic Encounter to build relationships based on trust and respect as the foundations of community.

Chapter Five—The Miracle of Dialogue

Master the art of listening and the power of the spoken word.

Chapter Six—Interpersonal Styles

Understand the unique characteristics of different types of people, and be wise, caring, and flexible to meet their needs.

Chapter Seven—Understanding People

Understand why people do what they do, especially the importance of self-concept and defense mechanisms.

Chapter Eight—Culture and Values

Understand the role of culture in the formation of values and how to handle conflict when values collide.

Chapter Nine—Social Tolerance

Understand the importance of tolerance in communications, human relationships, and building community.

Chapter Ten—Valuing Diversity

Appreciate diversity as a source of strength, and treat all people with respect and dignity.

Chapter Eleven—Group Dynamics

Understand the characteristics of effective groups and the role of positive versus negative group member roles.

Chapter Twelve—Communication at Work

Understand the causes and consequences of failure to communicate and how to achieve communication effectiveness in the workplace.

Chapter Thirteen—The Quality Movement

Adopt the democratic character and inclusive style of the participative leader to achieve quality in the workplace.

What is in store for the road ahead? Our hope is that you will apply the lessons of this book in the "spirit of the geese." We hope you will keep it handy and turn to it often.

We conclude, characteristically, with a bit of wisdom from the ages. The message is that community is not a place in itself; instead, it is a direction. This is the point Cervantes made when he wrote Don Quixote de la Mancha in 1648: "It is the road, not the inn."[1]

We end our journey with a charge to remember. In building community, it is not the location that matters: It is the purpose, the process, the spirit, and the will.

REFERENCE

1. Miguel de Cervantes, *The Adventures of Don Quixote* (New York: Macmillan, 1957).

Background Information and Teaching Suggestions

*B*uilding Community is a desk book for managers, a handbook for practitioners, and a workbook for students. It is an applied book that combines behavior theory with business practice. Each chapter teaches central concepts and skills in an important area of building community in the workplace.

The book may be used as a whole or as stand-alone parts—The Power of Vision, Interpersonal Skills Development, Valuing Human Diversity, The Empowerment of People. The subject areas are made more forceful and the impact greater by the self-evaluation questionnaires and practical exercises that are used for personal and group development.

AUDIENCE

Building Community is written for two audiences. One audience includes managers and professionals interested in building community on their own or within the context of a management or organization development program. Another audience includes students in human relations, organization behavior, and other management-related courses.

The material is appropriate for use at the four-year college and university level as well as in community colleges, proprietary schools, extension programs, and management training seminars.

CONTENT AND STYLE

The difference between most organization behavior books and *Building Community* can be compared to the difference between a lecture and a seminar. Although both are good educational vehicles, the lecture is better for conveying large amounts of information, while the seminar is better for developing skills. The good lecture is interesting and builds knowledge; the good seminar is stimulating and builds competency. *Building Community* emphasizes the interactive, seminar approach to learning.

The writing style is personal and conversational, with minimal professional jargon. True-life examples clarify points under consideration. Concepts are supported by stories and anecdotes, which are more meaningful and easy to remember than facts, figures, and lists. Each chapter includes learning activities to bridge the gap between classroom theory and on-the-job practice.

The focus of *Building Community* is self-discovery and personal development as the reader "learns by doing." The material covered is authoritative and up-to-date, reflecting current theory and practice. The level of material is appropriate for all levels of expertise (new employees and experienced managers) and all levels of education (undergraduate and graduate).

TESTING AND REVIEW PROCESS

The material in *Building Community* has been used extensively in college and university courses in this country and abroad. The information and activities have been used with hundreds of organizations in business, industry and government. Users include AT&T, American Electric Power, Bank One, Ford Motor Company, General Electric, IBM, National Institutes of Health, Shell Oil, U.S. Army, Navy and Air Force, and the World Bank.

The following are sample evaluations:

Good for student participation. My students like the exercises and learning instruments, and the fact that each chapter is a stand-alone unit that is bite-size. Their reaction: "Everyone should read this!"

> Joseph F. Ohren, Eastern Michigan University

Interesting and easy-to-use. Stories and examples help teach the topics, and applications make the material more meaningful. Ideal as a desk book for the practicing manager.

> Ray Benedict, Great American Insurance Companies

Best I've seen on the people side of work. Helps the person. Helps the company. Good for personal development as well as team building applications. Popular with people from all backgrounds.

> Charles Apple, University of Michigan

This is an excellent book on organization behavior. It puts theory into relevant, usable terminology. Methods for identifying and solving human relations problems are pinpointed. It sets the stage for understanding how people, environment, and situations interact in an organization.

> David Sprouse, AT&T

TEACHING FORMATS

Building Community is versatile and can be used in two general formats:

- seminars and training programs
- classroom education

Seminars and Training Programs

Subjects and activities should be selected to meet the objectives and needs of the participants—visioning and team building, management development, diversity training, employee empowerment, etc. Chapters can be mixed and matched for the audience and its needs. Material in each chapter is appropriate for a variety of time periods: one-half day (three to four hours); one full day (six to eight hours).

Each chapter of the book includes learning activities and questionnaires to encourage participation and personalize the subject. The book serves as "take-home" material for further reading and professional development.

Classroom Text

The book is appropriate for use as an applied text in college courses in human relations and organization behavior. The following is a sample schedule for a one-semester course:

Week	Topic	Week	Topic
1	Introduction	9	Mid-Term Exam/Report
2	Vision and Community	10	Culture and Values
3	Character and Community	11	Social Tolerance
4	Sustaining Community	12	Valuing Diversity
5	Effective Human Relations	13	Group Dynamics
6	The Miracle of Dialogue	14	Communication at Work
7	Interpersonal Styles	15	The Quality Movement
8	Understanding People	16	Final Exam/Report

When using *Building Community* as a classroom text, study quizzes can be used to evaluate content knowledge. Although quiz scores can be used to assign formal grades, students learn best when they are also asked to apply the concepts in some practical way. Examples include a term journal, research paper, small-group project, field study, and/or community-building application. Grades can be assigned on the basis of test scores and term project(s).

SUPPLEMENTAL INFORMATION AND INSTRUCTIONAL AIDS

A Resource Guide is available upon request for classroom instructors and organization development practitioners. Included for each chapter are:

- Major purpose or use of the chapter
- Chapter objectives—to focus attention
- Notes to instructor—for background information
- Notes and anecdotes—to enhance lectures
- Interactive questionnaires and exercises—for experiential learning
- Overhead transparency masters—for media support
- Discussion questions and activities—to personalize the subject
- Study quiz—to test for understanding
- Suggested books and films—for additional learning

GLOSSARY

Behavior—the way in which someone or something reacts to its environment; the manner of conducting oneself.

Building—the act, process, or art of constructing; molding, forming, creating; forming a plan or system of thought; to develop or increase.

Character—the combination of qualities that distinguish the moral or ethical structure of a person or group.

Climate—the prevailing trend of opinions and attitudes pervading a community, nation, or period.

Communications—sending, giving, or exchanging news, information, ideas, etc.

Community—being together or sharing similar interest; a group having common values, goals, or similar character.

Culture—the social structures and intellectual traits that characterize a society; the behaviors and beliefs characteristic of a particular social, ethnic, or age group.

Dialogue—communications between individuals; the exchange of information; a state of common or shared experience.

Diversity—variety; difference; being unlike in character or qualities.

Dynamics—motivating or driving forces; the pattern of growth; change and development in any system including interpersonal relationships.

Excellence—showing outstanding merit or ability; superior quality.

Group—an organized body of people with a common purpose.

Group dynamics—the interactions that influence the attitudes and behavior of people when they are grouped with others.

Human relations—the study of behavior for the purpose of improving interpersonal relationships.

Improvement—becoming better in quality; bringing to a more desirable state; taking conditions from a state of being adequate to a more satisfactory level.

Leadership—the capacity or ability to lead and guide; the establishment of a mark or new direction; social influence.

Miracle—an effect with no apparent cause; an astounding event or achievement.

Organization—a group of people gathered for some purpose or association.

Participation—taking part or having a share, as in interaction with others.

Personality—the total of the intellectual, emotional, and physical characteristics that make up the individual; the visible aspect of one's character as it impresses others.

Power—extreme force; strength of influence, as in social status.

Quality—degree or grade of excellence; a personality or character trait; an innate or acquired characteristic that determines the nature and behavior of a thing or person.

Self-concept—beliefs about one's developed and undeveloped self, including personal character, temperament, and aptitudes.

Six Sigma™—a standard of quality using statistical measures to characterize defect levels and process capabilities that achieve the 99.99966 percent conformity level.

Social—the quality of being in the company of others; friendliness in dealings; pertaining to group behavior.

Team—a number of people working together on a common task or toward a common goal.

Tolerance—willingness to allow others to believe, act, or live as they judge best; recognition of and respect for the opinions, practices, or behavior of others.

Understanding—having information and knowledge of a person or object; awareness and sensitivity to others, as in understanding problems.

Values—the abstract concepts of what is right, worthwhile, or desirable based on principles, standards, or qualities.

Vision—the way in which one sees or conceives of something; foresight; a vivid imaginative conception of events and conditions.

INDEX